# People without Rights

'The legal materials that Fede cites are sufficient support for his central message that slave law was an instrument of oppression concerned with property rights of the master, even when it appeared to recognize the legal personality of the slave .... *People Without Rights* ... is an honest and thoughtful confrontation with the evidence that has been accumulating about the actual operation of the law of slavery, and it is a tonic that we should receive.' - *Arthur Howington, Shelton State Community College, The Journal of Southern History*

First published in September 1992, the book traces the nature and development of the fundamental legal relationships among slaves, masters, and third parties. It shows how the colonial and antebellum Southern judges and legislators accommodated slavery's social relationships into the common law, and how slave law evolved in different states over time in response to social, political, economic, and intellectual developments.

The book states that the law of slavery in the US South treated slaves both as people and property. It reconciles this apparent contradiction by demonstrating that slaves were defined in the law as items of human property without any legal rights. When the lawmakers recognized slaves as people, they burdened slaves with added legal duties and disabilities. This epitomized in legal terms slavery's oppressive social relationships. The book also illustrates how cases in which the lawmakers recognized slaves as people legitimized slavery's inhumanity. References in the law to the legal humanity of people held as slaves are shown to be rhetorical devices and cruel ironies that regulated the relative rights of the slaves' owners and other free people that were embodied in people held as slaves. Thus, it is argued that it never makes sense to think of slave legal rights. This was so even when the lawmakers regulated the individual masters' rights to treat their slaves as they wished. These regulations advanced policies that the lawmakers perceived to be in the public interest within the context of a slave society.

# People Without Rights

An Interpretation of the Fundamentals of the Law of Slavery in the U.S. South

Andrew Fede

First published in 1992
by Garland Publishing, Inc.

This edition first published in 2011 by Routledge
2 Park Square, Milton Park, Abingdon, Oxon, OX14 4RN

Simultaneously published in the USA and Canada
by Routledge
270 Madison Avenue, New York, NY 10016

*Routledge is an imprint of the Taylor & Francis Group, an informa business*

© 1992 Andrew Fede

All rights reserved. No part of this book may be reprinted or reproduced or utilised in any form or by any electronic, mechanical, or other means, now known or hereafter invented, including photocopying and recording, or in any information storage or retrieval system, without permission in writing from the publishers.

**Publisher's Note**
The publisher has gone to great lengths to ensure the quality of this reprint but points out that some imperfections in the original copies may be apparent.

**Disclaimer**
The publisher has made every effort to trace copyright holders and welcomes correspondence from those they have been unable to contact.

A Library of Congress record exists under ISBN: 0815308949

ISBN 13: 978-0-415-61879-3 (hbk)
ISBN 13: 978-0-203-81558-8 (ebk)
ISBN 13: 978-0-415-66971-9 (pbk)

# PEOPLE WITHOUT RIGHTS

## An Interpretation of the Fundamentals of the Law of Slavery in the U.S. South

*by*
**Andrew Fede**

Garland Publishing, Inc.
New York & London  1992

© 1992 by Andrew Fede
All rights reserved


**Library of Congress Cataloging-in-Publication Data**

Fede, Andrew.
   People without rights : an interpretation of the fundamentals of
the law of slavery in the U.S. South / by Andrew Fede.
     p.  cm. — (Distinguished studies in American legal and
constitutional history)
    ISBN 0-8153-0894-9
     1. Slavery—Law and legislation—United States—History.
    2. Slaves—Legal status, laws, etc.—United States—History.
    3. Afro-Americans—Legal status, laws, etc.—United States—History.
    4. Slavery—United States—History. I. Title. II. Series.
KF45454.S5F42   1992
342.73'087—dc20
[347.30287]                                                        92-21666
                                                                                           CIP


*All volumes printed on acid-free, 250-year-life paper*
*Manufactured in the United States of America*

*Designed by Kathryn Semble*

To my mother, Dorothy M. Fede, and
to the memory of my father, Andrew P. Fede

# Contents

| | |
|---|---|
| Preface | ix |
| Acknowledgments | xv |
| CHAPTER 1<br>"The law as to him is only a compact between his rulers," An Interpretation | 3 |
| CHAPTER 2<br>The Legitimizing Role of Law in Slave Society | 17 |
| CHAPTER 3<br>Accommodating Slavery into the Common Law | 29 |
| CHAPTER 4<br>The Non-Legal Background to Three Trends in Antebellum Slave Law | 45 |
| CHAPTER 5<br>The Changing Scope of White Liability for Slave Killing | 61 |
| CHAPTER 6<br>The Changing Scope of White Liability for Non-Fatal Slave Abuse | 99 |
| CHAPTER 7<br>Preventing Slaves from Being a Public Nuisance: Limits on the Master's Rights to Starve and Free His Slaves | 131 |

CHAPTER 8
Slave Criminals and Protection of the Master's
Property Rights in Slaves: The Discrimination
in the Substantive Law                                                159

CHAPTER 9
Slave Criminals and Protection of the Master's
Property Rights in Slaves: What Process
Was Due?                                                              181

CHAPTER 10
The Recognition of Slave Humanity to Settle
the Rights of Whites That Were Embodied
in Slaves                                                             201

CHAPTER 11
The Impotence of Slave Humanity as an
Impediment to the Separation of Slave Families                        221

CHAPTER 12
Conclusion: The Reification of Humanity                               241

# Preface

**THE INTERPRETATION** of slavery in the United States has too often been fueled by passion and fire instead of cool reflection. Slave masters justified their "peculiar institution" with racism and paternalism, and abolitionists condemned slavery by citing examples of inhumanity and oppression. These approaches have been endorsed by various scholars who have analyzed slavery since its demise in 1865. The visceral reactions to slavery have died hard among the students of slavery, and why not? The more than two centuries of slavery still outnumber the 126 years after abolition. Thus, we live in the aftermath of slavery.

It appears, however, that the time for refighting the war between the abolitionist and the slave master world views has elapsed; the time for dispassionate analysis is overdue. The actual and the intellectual progeny of abolitionists and masters alike need to cast out the demons of the past and look at the historical evidence without preconceptions.

This approach is applied here to the law of slavery. This study does not focus on the moral, social, political, or economic aspects of slavery. Rather, it looks at the law of slavery, and only a part of that law at that—the fundamental legal relationship between slaves, masters, and third parties. To oversimplify, the question presented is why were slaves treated—at law—as both people and property. This inquiry by definition is primarily a legal one. Thus, legal materials—cases, statutes, and constitutions—hold center stage. Nevertheless, the social, political economic, and intellectual background of the law of slavery provides the necessary context for the analysis of the degree to which slave personhood was a reality in law.

The intellectual children of the slave masters should be forewarned; this book will demonstrate why slaves were treated as property at law and why all references to slaves' legal humanity constitute a cruel irony that legitimized the power of whites over slaves and that defined the relative rights of whites to slave property. Thus, it is argued that it never makes sense to think of slave "rights" in law, because slaves had no rights and were burdened with extra human legal duties. This equation epitomized the oppression of slavery—as a social relationship—in law.

Does this mean that all masters treated slaves as property without any recognition of slave humanity? Not necessarily; the point is, however, that according to law masters could think of slaves as property and treat slaves as such. Does this mean that the lawmakers anticipated that masters would take the legal invitation to dehumanize their slaves in practice? Not necessarily; but the law allowed for this possibility, and it was obviously a foreseeable consequence of the law of slavery as it was written.

This interpretation of the fundamentals of the slave's legal status is derived from the studies of slave law that were written by the abolitionist critics of slavery. This view was also expressed by Southern judges who were not abolitionists, and this is a fact that the intellectual heirs of the slave masters cannot deny. Occasionally, judges looked into the abyss and saw the reality of the legal suppression of slave humanity. They were not "abolitionist fanatics" bent on the destruction of a perceived moral evil, but were pro-slavery jurists. At other times, however, judges looked into the same abyss and chose to delude themselves into thinking that the law they made and upheld was not so bad. In fact, they often gleefully trumpeted supposed examples of the acknowledgment of slave rights and humanity in law.

This study looks at those instances of legal recognition of slaves as persons. When subjected to scrutiny, these examples are revealed—one by one—to be rhetorical devices that legitimized the inhumanity of slave law. Indeed, slaves were not hogs; therefore, the law of hogs differed from the law of slaves. By the same token, however, slaves were not legal people; therefore, the law of people differed from the law of slaves. This was the fundamental reality of slave law. This book examines why this was so and traces the origin and development of the legal relationships between masters, slaves, and third parties in the common law states of the United States South. The goal of this inquiry is to show how slavery was accommodated into the common law that was evolving in the pre Civil War South.

It should be noted at the outset that several important issues in the law of slavery are omitted from this book.[1] The first is the study of slave law in the Civil Law jurisdictions—Louisiana and South America, and the comparison of that law to the common law of slavery.[2] A second comparative approach contrasts the American slave law with the ancient, African, and Asian law of slavery.[3] The slave law of the Northern states and England, as well as the abolition of slavery there, present other salient slave law topics.[4] Other questions of note

# Preface

include the choice of law problems that arose when slave law came into conflict with the law of freedom,[5] and constitutional law issues concerning the drafting of the fugitive slave clause and the power of the United States government to regulate or prohibit slavery.[6] Another issue is the role that an understanding of the fundamentals of slavery can play in the interpretation and application of the Thirteenth Amendment to the Constitution.[7]

This study does not address any of these issues; instead, it explores the essential characteristics of the fundamental slave relations during the entire slave law era in the United States South. Colonial and antebellum legal materials are combined to trace the patterns of the development of slave law.

The approach taken herein is therefore theoretical and not exhaustive. The need for this emphasis was noted by Paul Finkelman, who cited as a "neglected" area of the law of slavery "the interaction between slave law and legal doctrine, and the theoretical underpinnings of the law of slavery."[8]

One final note: The eclectic nature of this study is intentional. Ideas are drawn from traditional doctrinal legal history, instrumentalist legal history, and the Critical Legal Studies authors. Accordingly, adherents of all of these schools of thought may find faults with this work.[9] It is hoped, nevertheless, that this study will show how all three approaches can contribute to an illumination of the essential nature of the law of slavery. The first chapter begins with a summary of the interpretation that is fully developed in the later chapters.

# NOTES

1. For recent overviews of the issues addressed by the literature, *see, e.g.*, Kermit L., Hall, ed., *The Law of American Slavery: Major Historical Interpretations* v–xv (New York, 1987); Paul Finkelman, "Exploring Southern Legal History," 64 *No. Carolina Law Review* 77, 88–97 (1985) (hereinafter cited as "Exploring"). Of course, the most valuable resource tools for cases and commentary are Helen T. Catterall, *Judicial Cases Concerning American Slavery and the Negro* (New York, reprint ed. 1968) (1926) and Jacob D. Wheeler, *A Practical Treatise on the Law of Slavery* (New York, reprint ed. 1968) (1837). For a statutory summary, with commentary, *see*, John C. Hurd, *The Law of Freedom and Bondage in the United States* (New York, reprint ed. 1968) (1862). For commentary and bibliographies of nineteenth century materials, *see*, Paul Finkelman, ed., *Slavery, Race and the American Legal*

*System, 1700–1872* (New York, 1987) (16 volumes); Paul Finkelman, *Slavery in the Courtroom: An Annotated Bibliography of American Cases* (Washington, 1985).

2. *See*, Judith Shaffer, "The Long Arm of the Law: Slave Criminals and the Supreme Court in Antebellum Louisiana," 60 *Tulane Law Review* 1247 (1986) comparing Louisiana and the common law states. A body of literature has grown comparing South American slavery with that of North America, and legal inquiry has been an important and controversial element of this topic. *Compare, e.g.*, Stanley M. Elkins, *Slavery: A Problem in American Institutional Life* 63–80 (Chicago, 3d ed. 1976); Herbert S. Klein, *Slavery in the Americas: A Comparative Study of Virginia and Cuba* 37–85 (Chicago, 1967); Frank Tannenbaum, *Slave and Citizen* 42–87 (New York, 1946); *with*, Eugene Genovese, *In Red and Black: Marxian Explorations in Southern and Afro American History* 79–92 (New York, 1971); Mark Tushnet, "The American Law of Slavery, 1810–1860: A Study in the Persistence of Legal Autonomy," 10 *L. & Soc'y Rev.* 119, 181–184 (1975) (hereinafter cited as "Tushnet 1975"); Arnold A. Sio, "Interpretations of Slavery: The Slave Status in the Americas," 7 *Comparative Studies in Society and History* 289 (1965). For a recent analysis, *see*, Alan Watson, *Slave Law in the Americas* (Athens, Ga., 1989) (hereinafter cited as "Watson 1989").

3. Orlando Patterson, *Slavery and Social Death: A Comparative Study* (Cambridge, 1982); *see, also*, Watson 1989, *supra*, Sio, *supra*.

4. *See, e.g.*, Edward J. McManus, *Black Bondage in the North* (Syracuse, 1973); Thomas D. Morris, *Free Men All: The Personal Liberty Laws of the North, 1780–1861* (Baltimore, 1972); Arthur Zilversmit, *The First Emancipation: The Abolition of Slavery in the North* (Chicago, 1967), for the Northern United States. For English Law, *see, e.g.*, David B. Davis, *The Problem of Slavery in the Age of Revolution 1770–1823* 469–501 (Ithica, 1975); 1 Hurd, *supra* at 178–193; William Wiecek, "*Somerset*: Lord Mansfield and the Legitimacy of Slavery in the Anglo American World," 42 *Chicago Law Review* 86 (1974) (hereinafter cited as "Wiecek 1974").

5. *See, e.g.*, Paul Finkelman, *An Imperfect Union: Slavery, Federalism & Comity* (Chapel Hill, 1981), and Robert M. Cover, *Justice Accused: Antislavery and the Judicial Process* (New Haven, 1975); Davis, *supra* at 102–522; 1 Hurd, *supra* at 312–393; Paul Finkelman, "The Kidnapping of John Davis and the Adoption of the Fugitive Slave Law of 1793," 56 *J. of So. Hist.* 398 (1990); *Id.*, "States' Rights, North and South in Antebellum America," in Kermit L. Hall and James W. Ely, Jr., eds., *An Uncertain Tradition: Constitutionalism and the History of the South* 125–158 (Athens, Ga., 1989); *Id.*, "The Protection of Black Rights in Seward's New York," 34 *Civil War Hist.* 211 (1988); *Id.*, "Prigg v. Pennsylvania and Northern State Courts: Antislavery Use of a Pro slavery Decision," 25 *Civil War Hist.* 5 (1979); William Wiecek, "Slavery and Abolition Before the United States Supreme Court, 1820–1860," 65 *Journal of Am. Hist.* 34 (1978); Note, "American Slavery and the Conflict of Laws," 71 *Columbia Law Review* 74 (1971); Harold Horowitz, "Choice of Law Decisions Involving Slavery: 'Interest Analysis' in the Early Nineteenth Century," 17 *U.C.L.A. Law Review* 587 (1970).

6. On the drafting of the fugitive slave clause, *see*, Paul Finkelman,

"Slavery and the Constitutional Convention: Making a Covenant With Death," in Richard Beeman, Stephen Botein, and Edward C. Carter, II, eds., *Beyond Confederation: Origins of the Constitution and American National Identity* 219 224 (Chapel Hill, 1987); William M. Wiecek, "The Witch at the Christening: Slavery and the Constitution's Origins," in Leonard W. Levy and Dennis J. Mahoney, eds., *The Framing and Ratification of the Constitution* 167 184 (New York, 1987). Other literature on these issues includes, Don Edward Fehrenbacher, *The Dred Scott Case: Its Significance in American Law and Politics* (New York, 1978); William Wiecek, *The Sources of Antislavery Constitutionalism in America, 1760–1848* (Ithaca, 1977); 1 Hurd, supra at 394 598; 2 *Id.*, at 219 790; Walter Berns, "The Constitution and the Migration of Slaves," 78 Yale L. J. 198 (1968); Robert Russell, "Constitutional Doctrines with Regard to Slavery in the Territories," 32 *J. of So. Hist.* 466 (1966); Larry Gara, "The Fugitive Slave Law: A Double Paradox," 10 *Civil War Hist.* 229 (1964); see, also, William Nelson, "The Impact of the Antislavery Movement Upon Styles of Judicial Reasoning in Nineteenth Century America," 87 *Harvard Law Review* 513 (1974).

7. A comprehensive doctrinal approach to the Thirteenth Amendment has not been written. *See, e.g.*, discussing the potentials for this theory, Andrew Koppleman, "Forced Labor: A Thirteenth Amendment Defense of Abortion," 84 *Northwestern Law Review* 480 (1990); Lea S. Vander Velde, "The Labor Vision of the Thirteenth Amendment," 138 *University of Pennsylvania Law Review* 437 (1989); G. Sidney Buchanan, "The Quest for Freedom: A Legal History of the Thirteenth Amendment," 12 *Houston Law Review* 1, 331, 357, 593, 610, 844, 871, 1070 (1974–1975); Arthur Kinoy, "The Constitutional Right of Negro Freedom," 21 *Rutgers Law Review* 387 (1967) ("Negro Freedom"); Harry H. Shapiro, "Involuntary Servitude: The Need for a More Flexible Approach," 19 *Rutgers Law Review* 65 (1964); Jacobus ten Broek, "Thirteenth Amendment to the Constitution of the United States: Consummation to Abolition and Key to the Fourteenth Amendment," 39 *California Law Review* 171 (1951). It has been argued that the Amendment, on its own creates a judicially enforceable right to freedom from slavery and its present day relics. *See, generally*, "Negro Freedom," supra. The Supreme Court has not defined slavery and its badges and indicia in a systematic fashion.

8. "Exploring," supra at 89 n. 65; see, also, A. E. K. Nash, "In re Radical Interpretations of American Law: The Relation of Law and History," 82 *Michigan Law Review* 274, 274–276 (1983) (hereinafter cited as "Radical Interpretations"), calling for a "radical" but "non Marxist" theory of slave law in response to Mark V. Tushnet, *The American Law of Slavery 1810–1860: Considerations of Humanity and Interest* (Princeton, 1981) (Tushnet).

9. *See, generally*, Robert W. Gordon and William Nelson, "An Exchange on Critical Legal Studies between Robert W. Gordon and William Nelson," 6 *Law & History Review* 139 (1988) for a debate on these approaches, *see, also*, Stephen B. Presser & Jamil S. Zainaldin, *Law and Jurisprudence in American History: Cases and Materials* 939 992 (St. Paul, 2d ed., 1989), Mark Kelman, *A Guide to Critical Legal Studies* 213 241 (Cambridge, 1987).

# Acknowledgments

THIS BOOK has its roots in a seminar paper I wrote for a course on law and social change I completed in the fall of 1980 at the S. I. Newhouse Center for Law and Justice of Rutgers University in Newark. Professor James C. N. Paul conducted that seminar and encouraged me to publish my writing. My paper resulted in two articles. One is a review essay, "Toward a Solution of the Slave Law Dilemma: A Critique of Tushnet's 'The American Law of Slavery,'" 2 *Law & Hist. Rev.* 301 (1984). Part II of that essay contains a sketch of the interpretation developed herein. The concept of reification is added to that interpretation to explain the references to slave rights and humanity in the law of slavery.

Another article, "Legitimized Violent Slave Abuse in the American South, 1619–1865: A Case Study of Law and Social Change in Six Southern States," 29 *Am. J. of Legal Hist.* 93 (1985) forms the basis for Chapters 4 to 6. That article is reprinted in *Articles on American Slavery: Law, the Constitution, and Slavery* 31 (P. Finkelman, ed. 1989). Various ideas contained in these articles are sprinkled throughout this study. In addition, parts of Chapter 10 are derived from an article "Legal Protection for Slave Buyers in the U.S. South: A Caveat Concerning *Caveat Emptor*," 31 *Am. J. of Legal Hist.* 322 (1987). That article was a revised version of a paper presented on October 24, 1986 at the annual meeting of the American Society for Legal History held in Toronto, Canada.

As with any work that has been germinating for more than ten years, I have many to thank. I begin with Professor Paul who started me on this quest and who deserves all of the credit for what is acceptable in this work and none of the blame for the bad. Also from Rutgers I thank Professor John Anthony Scott—who encouraged me to proceed and who provided a helpful critique—and Professor Arthur Kinoy.

Others who have helped me in various ways over the years include Paul Finkelman, Judith Schafer, Robert Cottrol, Raymond Diamond, Diane Maleson, and Russell Osgood. None of these parties is responsible for the defects in this work. I also thank Roberta Garey for typing my articles and various versions of this manuscript, and Lisa Fadini for proofreading initial versions.

I also thank Harold Hyman for his recommendation. Thanks also go to Martha Crubaugh for typing the final version of the book, and Daniele Cervino for proofreading.

# People Without Rights

## CHAPTER 1

# "Law as to him is only a compact between his rulers," An Interpretation

IN an 1821 Mississippi case, Judge J. G. Clarke asked: "Has the slave no rights, because he is deprived of his freedom?" The judge answered this question of fundamental importance by stating that a slave "is still a human being, and possesses all those rights, of which he is not deprived by the positive provisions of law[.]"[1] Clarke was only half correct, however; slaves were human beings, but in the law of the U.S. South, slaves—by definition—were denied all of the ordinary rights that people enjoyed. The law conceptualized this deprivation by categorizing slaves as their master's property, thereby cutting slaves off from all claims to customary human rights. Moreover, slaves were unique property because they could commit crimes against other people and property. Thus, slaves were considered persons by the criminal law. This added insult to injury because slaves were burdened with extraordinary legal duties and obligations. Consequently, the slave had a dual legal status that was consistent with and epitomized the oppression of slavery. Slaves were denied the benefits of personhood and were saddled with burdens that exceeded the obligations of "real" people.

This interpretation has roots in the antebellum studies of slave law that were published by the abolitionist critics of slavery. Harriet Beecher Stowe summarized the purposes of slave law:

> The slave-code ... of the Southern States, is designed to keep millions of human beings in the condition of chattels personal; to keep them in a condition in which the master may sell them, dispose of their time, person, and labour; in which they can do nothing, possess nothing, and acquire nothing, except for the benefit of the master; in which they are doomed in themselves and in their posterity to live without knowledge, without the power to make anything their own, to toil that another may reap. The laws of the slave-code are designed to work out this problem, consistently with the peace of the community, and the safety of that superior race which is constantly to perpetuate this outrage.

Indeed, Mrs. Stowe was not guilty of exaggeration when she defined slavery as "absolute despotism, of the most unmitigated form."[2]

The abolitionists stated that slaves were the subjects of legal despotism because they were without any legal rights. William Goodell explained this principle as follows: "Having no right to himself, to his bones, muscles, and intellect, (being all of them property of his 'owner'), [the slave] has no right to his own industry, to its wages or its products; no right to property or capability of possessing it[.]" Consequently, Goodell concluded, "Not being accounted a person, but a thing, [the slave] can have no personal rights to be protected[.]"[3] George Stroud further captured this idea when he called "the cardinal principle of slavery" the notion "that the slave is to be regarded as a thing,—is an article of property,—a chattel personal[.]"[4]

These anti-slavery, antebellum students of slavery correctly characterized the fundamentals of the slave's legal status as property. In fact, the law deprived slaves of all rights by defining them as property. This was so notwithstanding the fact that, at times, the law recognized slaves as people, for certain limited purposes. These purposes, however, did not include concern about the humanity or the rights of the slave. This book will show that all references to slave humanity and right obfuscate the real meaning of the slave law of the U.S. South. This was true even in the criminal law cases.

This point is illustrated by the opinion of Justice D. L. Wardlaw, who wrote for the South Carolina Court of Appeals in *Ex parte Boylston*.[5] In that case a male slave was charged with directing "insolent language and action" at a white woman who was not the slave's owner. It was argued on the slave's behalf that the statutory slave codes contained no such crime, and that the prosecution should therefore, be dismissed. Judge Wardlaw disagreed:

> A freeman would have a right to demand that the law should be pointed to, which provides for the punishment of the act for which he is to be tried, and to object that the erection of a new tribunal is not the creation of new offences. But a slave can invoke neither magna charta nor common law. As is well said in Kinloch v. Harvey, Harp. 514, "every endeavor to extend to him positive rights, is an attempt to reconcile inherent contradictions." In the very nature of things, he is subject to despotism. Law as to him is only a compact between his rulers, and the questions which concern him are matters agitated between them.[6]

Wardlaw also denied the relevance of any notion of slave rights: "Our inquiry here, then, is not concerning the rights of the slave, but concerning the conflict between the rights of the master and the right set up by the Court to try the slave in opposition to the master's will."[7] Thus, Wardlaw saw that any reference to "slave rights" obscured the real issue in the case—the battle of interests between slave owner and the magistrate's court that would try the slave. This was true even in a case in which the slave was prosecuted by the criminal law as a person.

Interestingly, there is a dissenting opinion, that of Justice John Belton O'Neall. O'Neall does not claim to champion slave rights; to the contrary, he joins issue with Wardlaw on the competing interests of master and magistrate:

> [N]o jurisdiction ever did exist, which is liable to more abuse than that exercised by Magistrates over slaves. Clothe them with the power to try slaves for insolence, and the result will be that passion, prejudice and ignorance will crowd abuses on this inferior jurisdiction to an extent not to be tolerated by slave owners.[8]

Consequently, O'Neall was concerned with the rights of the owner—not the slave. Accordingly, the Court expressly resolved the matters that were "agitated" between the slave's "rulers" without any reference to the rights of the slave. The case is a prototype for all cases that resolved conflicting claims of right in slave property.

Even the cases in which slaves were prosecuted for crimes implicated the diverse claims of whites to slaves. For example, in the case of *United States v. Amy*,[9] Chief Justice Roger Taney addressed the issue of whether the slave Amy was a "person" who could be prosecuted under federal criminal statute that prohibited stealing a letter from the mail. Defense counsel was John Howard; he is referred to in the report as appearing "for the owner of the defendant, Amy[.]" Howard argued that Amy was not a legal person—she was the owner's property—and thus could not be prosecuted under the general federal criminal statutes.[10]

Taney rejected this argument:

> [W]e must not lose sight of the two-fold character which belongs to the slave. He is a person, and also property. As property, the rights of the owner are entitled to the protection of the law. As a person, he is bound to obey the law, and may, like any other person, be punished if he offends against it; and he may be embraced in the provisions of the law, either by the description of property or as a person, according to the subject matter upon which congress or a state is legislating.[11]

Therefore, Taney upheld Amy's conviction and sentence to prison. This recognition of slave "personhood" was not inconsistent with the slave's legal status as property. Indeed, Taney acknowledged that the master's property rights were implicated in the case. The real rights at issue were the state's right to control slaves when the master could not, and the master's right to his slave property.

This book will show why it makes no sense to talk of slave "rights" within the common law jurisprudence, just as it is nonsense to ascribe rights to trees or other living non-human objects.[12] Indeed, Chief Justice Taney accurately characterized American slavery when he wrote, in *Scott v. Sandford*,[13] that slaves were

> regarded as beings of an inferior order, and altogether unfit to associate with the white race, either in social or political relations; and so far inferior, that they had no rights which the white man was bound to respect; and that the negro might justly and lawfully be reduced to slavery for his benefit. He was bought and sold, and treated as an ordinary article of merchandise and traffic, whenever a profit could be made by it.[14]

The pervasive reality of slave law was the legal "despotism" that lawyers, judges, and legislators legitimized and encouraged in the name of law, justice, right, and humanity. To the slave, law was "a compact between his rulers."

These fundamentals of the master and slave relationship have been analyzed by numerous students of slavery. The work of these scholars is excellent and enlightening. One question has not been satisfactorily answered, however; it is how to reconcile the legal materials that recognize slaves as people, or refer to slave rights and humanity, with the overall property orientation of slave law. Thus, it has been argued that the makers of slave law faced a dilemma and had to decide whether to treat slaves as property or people. In fact, there was no dilemma; slaves had to be treated as both people and property because they were people without rights.

## *The Slave Law Dilemma*

Kenneth Stampp, in his great history of slavery, defines the dilemma when he declares that "the slave's status as property was incompatible with his status as a person." Stampp states further, "there was no way to resolve the contradiction implicit in the very term 'human property.' Both legislators and judges frequently appeared erratic in dealing with bondsmen as both *things* and *persons*."[15] Stampp is not alone in his view of the contradictory nature of slave law.

For example, Judge A. Leon Higginbotham finds "vacillation" on the part of the Southern lawmakers on the question of whether slaves were "people" or "a species apart from white humans[.]"[16] A. E. Kier Nash, although stressing instances in which courts recognized slave rights and humanity, also cites judicial "uncertainty" as to "how much" of a given slave "was property and how much was humanity."[17] Eugene Genovese notes the illogic of the ". . . idea that chattels, as the states usually defined slaves, could have a high born nature, complete with rights inherent in man[.]"[18] Orlando Patterson calls the definition of slaves as property "a fiction found only in western societies[.]"[19] Mark Tushnet agrees that Southern slave law was internally contradictory and adds that "the social contradictions of Southern society were embedded in slave law[.]"[20] The correct analysis is, however, to the contrary. The law of slavery was true to the ghastly logic of total oppression; the law was consistent within the confines of the perceived dictates of the "despotism" of slavery. This logic, however, lies beneath the surface of apparent inconsistency.

Frank Tannenbaum argued this point in the 1940s, and thereby restated the abolitionist interpretation:

> In the absence of either religious or legal provision for the slave, it was not illogical for the planters, both in the West Indies and in the American colonies, to settle the legal issue involved by legally defining the slave as chattel.[21]

Nevertheless, Tannenbaum, like the abolitionists, does not create a jurisprudential and sociological theory to reconcile the definition of slaves as both people and property. Thus arose the pro-slavery view in the nineteenth century, and it has reappeared in the twentieth century in various forms.

The pro-slavery interpretation suggests several questions of fundamental importance: Was slave law hopelessly confused and self-contradictory because it recognized slaves as persons? Did the law reflect an ambiguity in the oppression of Southern slavery, or even an amelioration of the harshness of pure slavery? These questions were raised and answered yes in antebellum years by Southern jurists who sought to rebut the anti-slavery writers.

The pro-slavery view correctly asserted that the law of slavery did recognize slaves as people. Examples cited include the criminal law that prosecuted slaves and protected slaves from some white violence, statutes that required masters to provide slaves with food and clothing, and cases that enforced the "right" to freedom of an emancipated slave. This interpretation was established by writers such as Thomas R. R. Cobb and John Belton O'Neall, and received support in the twentieth century in the work of U. B. Phillips.[22] Nevertheless, these pro-slavery apologists fail to resolve the slave law dilemma because they do not explain why the law sometimes treated slaves as persons, but in *most* instances treated slaves as property. William Goodell summarized this point, stating that "Slaves are better protected as Property, than they are as Sentient Beings."[23] Goodell and his contemporaries had the emphasis correct, unlike their pro-slavery counterparts.

Most twentieth century writers agree with Stampp, who, like Goodell, states that, "throughout the ante-bellum South . . . legally, the slave was less a person than a thing."[24] But this type of calculus—slave = x% person + y% thing—has caused a circular and fruitless debate. Indeed, twentieth century historians and slave law specialists have relived the abolitionist and pro-slavery controversy of the antebellum years. The response to the pro-slavery writing of U. B. Phillips is presented by Tannenbaum, Herbert Klein, Stanley Elkins, and Stampp, who reassert the abolitionist interpretation. Thus, Tannenbaum states that a slave was "a chattel under the law, and in practice an animal to be bred for market."[25] He, along with Klein and Elkins, argue that the slave's "moral personality" was absent from slave law in the United States South, in contrast with Latin American slave law, which recognized the slave's personhood.[26] But because these authors follow the abolitionists, they fail to advance a theory to reconcile recognition of slave humanity, at times, with their overall interpretation. Thus, their arguments are met with a forceful critique authored by Arnold Sio. Sio's article, published in 1965, echoes the pro-slavery view, and stresses the legal recognition of humanity of the slave, but without the racist and ideological baggage of the earlier pro-slavery writers. Sio's interpretation is consistent with the view of A. E. Kier Nash, expressed in his articles published in the 1970s. Nash also argues for the salience of slave rights at law.[27] The "x" side of the equation is also highlighted by Arthur Howington, while Michael Hindus puts a greater emphasis on the "y" side.[28] It is obvious that this debate is bound to be inconclusive, subject to variations in interpretations based upon the particular evidence studied and the ideological bent of the scholar.

Professors Eugene Genovese and Mark Tushnet have interposed a Marxist analysis into the slave law debate. One might hope that a Marxist interpretation would break the deadlock between the pro-slavery and anti-slavery views. Nevertheless, the Marxist writers fail to solve the slave law dilemma; in fact, these authors, in common with bourgeois scholars, argue that contradiction was the essence of slave law. According to this interpretation, Southern United States slavery was a paternalistic institution; it was not capitalist. The South, however, was in contact with the capitalist bourgeois North, and thus the society was beset by a fundamental contradiction between recognition of slave "humanity" and the economic bourgeois "interest" embodied in slaves. These terms, however, are variations of the person/property definitions of the non-Marxist. But this view differs in that it defines slave law as "humane,"—although potentially oppressive—because it vested masters with power to regulate slaves in the name of "sentiment" and "humanity," rather than "interest" and "law," which govern in the capitalist and bourgeois courts. This interpretation also assumes that under the influence of paternalism, slave "rights" and "humanity" came to be protected in law and in reality.[29]

Consequently, this view that slave law was more harsh than the reality of everyday living reasserts the pro-slavery interpretation of Phillips. He contended that slave owners were reluctant and paternalist oppressors who did not always enforce their legal power to the limit, and even skirted the law by allowing slaves "rights" contrary to law. This "legal realism" is met by an abolitionist response to the notion that slaves had legal rights.

The abolitionists did not ignore the alleged examples of slave legal rights. These authors argued, however, that legal protection for the slave was minimal and hard to enforce; thus, they too applied a form of "legal realism"—they looked beyond statute law to actual practices. For example, although statutes allowed prosecutions of whites who abused slaves, the abolitionists urged that these protections were paltry and were impeded by procedural obstacles to prosecution. This analysis is correct as far as it goes. Nevertheless, it does not explain *why* the "protective" statutes existed. Nor does the pro-slavery realism explain why the slave owners enacted laws that they did not approve of. The Southern states were democratic, for the planters at least. They could have changed the law if they felt its strict dictates were inhumane.

To modify Nash's metaphor, then, the anti-slavery view sees the glass of slave rights being at least half-empty. The pro-slavery view sees it as half-full, and the Marxists contend that the glass is not half-empty. In contrast, Mrs. Stowe hinted correctly that the glass was empty; slaves had no legal "rights."

## *Toward a Solution of the Slave Law Dilemma*

The law of slavery causes one to lose sight of the forest while focusing on the trees. The first step to resolving the slave law dilemma is the acceptance of the pervasive importance of the definition of slaves as property. This fundamental principle of law reinforced the social, political, economic, and moral notion that slaves were not ordinary people. Southerners did come to treat slaves as property—not people:

> [S]laves *were* bartered, deeded, devised, pledged, seized, and auctioned. They were awarded as prizes in lotteries and raffles; they were wagered at gaming tables and horse races. They were, in short, property in fact as well as law.[30]

Accordingly, this definition of slaves as property must be the starting point of the analysis of slave law.

Indeed, slaves were treated as property in fact and in law. On this proposition there was no debate and no dilemma. This was true despite the fact that, at times, the law allowed for exceptions to the general rule, and treated slaves like people. The words of Sir Moses Finley—describing ancient slavery—are apt:

> As a commodity, the slave is property. . . . [S]ome sociologists and historians have persistently tried to deny the significance of that simple fact, on the ground that the slave is also a human being or that the owner's rights over a slave are often restricted by the law. All this seems to me to be futile: the fact that a slave is a human being has no relevance to the question whether or not he is also property; it merely reveals that he is a peculiar property, Aristotle's 'property with a soul.' . . . [31]

Similarly in the United States South, the law of slavery was not illogical in treating people as property for most purposes, while treating slaves like people on occasion.

This proposition was explained by Chief Justice Richmond Pearson, in an 1858 North Carolina case:

> A slave, being property, has not the legal capacity to make a contract, and is not entitled to the rights or subjected to the liabilities incident thereto. He is amenable to the criminal law, and his person (to a certain extent) and his life are protected. This, however, is not a concession to him of civil rights, but is in vindication of public justice, and for the prevention of public wrongs.[32]

Thus, Pearson acknowledged that talk of "slave rights" was grounded in delusion. When the law treated slaves as people, it did so to vindicate "public justice" and to prevent "public wrongs;" it did not thereby concede to the slave any civil rights that were inconsistent with the bondsman's property status.

To realize this, however, one must acknowledge that the logic of slave law was the logic of absolute legal oppression of one person over another. By defining slaves as property, the law stripped slaves of all legal rights. The concomitant definition of slaves as persons for other purposes was necessary and it accomplished two ends not inconsistent with this paramount aim. First, it protected the public interest and the owner's interest, and second, it burdened slaves with special legal duties and obligations that marked the complete oppression of the system. Consequently, the law created legal duties in slaves while it denied slaves' legal rights. This is the despotism of the slavery relationship expressed in legal terms.

The law legitimized this relationship, and by doing so, ignored some of the most fundamental concepts of the common law. Moreover, on the conceptual level, the courts often justified the inevitable inhumanity of slavery by referring to humanity. This cruel irony was a reification of the oppression of slavery—a concept developed in Chapter 12.

This was true even when the law limited the master's power over his slave. At times the "public justice" required that the master's power be regulated. These regulations included limitations on the master's right to kill, maim, and starve his slaves. At first blush, these appear to be prime examples of the creation of slave rights. Upon close inspection, however, they are revealed to be legal developments that legitimized the master's power over the slave, as well as regulations over that power. It must be recalled that the master's power to free his slave was also regulated. Therefore, it is apparent that these limitations failed to vest legal rights in slaves. Rather, the law vindicated the public interest when it controlled the master's right to maim, kill, starve, and free his slaves. Each of these four acts was perceived to be a potential threat to the slave holding system. The fact that slave holding was regulated in the public interest did not create personal rights in the slaves.

Consequently, the concept of the "public justice" was a complex balance of relevant interests that will be discussed in detail in the following pages. Indeed, the law recognized slaves as people when this balance of interests commanded this result, in the perception of the lawmakers. Moreover, regulations did occasionally interfere with the owner's absolute dominion over the slave, as well as the slave's economic value. Therefore, Judge Higginbotham and Barbara Kopytoff make an overstatement when they argue that the law of slavery recognized slaves as human beings only in "ways that did not interfere with the owners' dominion over them as property or their economic value to their owners."[33] Although this construct is helpful, a more complex social, political, economic, intellectual, and legal history is necessary to identify the interests that were perceived to compel the regulation of the master's power.

This book will develop this interpretation by analyzing slave law on the jurisprudential and the social levels. First is an examination of how the fundamentals of slavery were accommodated into the common law. Second, the seemingly inconsistent treatment of slaves as people and property will be reconciled with the essential aspects of the master and slave relation, along with the impact that third parties had on that relation.

After these points are established, six developments in antebellum slave law will be reconciled with the property orientation of slave law. These trends are: (1) Increased white liability for violent slave abuse, (2) Enhanced criminal procedural safeguards in slave criminal trials, (3) Judicial recognition of the slave's "right" to emancipation contrary to the nineteenth century trend against freedom for slaves, (4) The enactment of statutes that required masters to feed and clothe slaves, (5) Court decisions and statutes that limited the separation of slave families, and (6) Judicial recognition of slave "humanity" in the business law of slavery. These are the most often cited examples of the recognition of slave rights and humanity in the law of the antebellum South. Each example will be examined with reference to the interests of the "public justice" that were vindicated.

When this is accomplished, it will become clear why all of these legal developments can be reconciled with the definition of slaves as people without rights. The law continued to be a battle between the slave's rulers. Sometimes the law regulated the individual master's freedom to treat his slaves as he wished to further salient social interests that the courts and legislatures balanced against the individual master's interests. This vindication of the "public justice" was not, therefore, "a concession [to the slave] of civil rights[.]"

## *Conclusion*

A complex legal structure was necessary to accommodate the fundamentals of the master and slave relationship within the common law of the English colonies that became the United States. The law also was adapted to social change in the more than two hundred years before emancipation. Consequently, there are two issues to study: How did slave law arise, and how did it change and develop in response to social change? This analysis begins with an examination of the fundamentals of the slave's relations with others, and then the role of law in slave society.

## NOTES

1. *State v. Jones*, 1 Miss. 39, 1 Walker 88, 83–84 (1821).
2. Harriet Beecher Stowe, *The Key to Uncle Tom's Cabin* 132, 233 (New York, reprint ed. 1968) (Boston, 1853).
3. William Goodell, *The American Slave Code* 290, 291 (New York, reprint ed. 1968) (1853).
4. George M. Stroud, *A Sketch of the Laws Relating to Slavery* 11 (New York, reprint ed. 1968) (1856). [Footnote Omitted].
5. 33 S.C.L. 20, 2 Strob. 41 (1847).
6. *Ex parte Boylston, supra*, 33 S.C.L. at 21, 2 Strob. at 43. The Court cites *Kinloch v. Harvey*, 16 S.C.L. 224, Harp. 508 (1830), holding that slaves had no common law procedural rights in criminal trials.
7. *Ex parte Boylston, supra*, 33 S.C.L. at 21, 2 Strob. at 43.
8. *Id.*, 33 S.C.L. at 23, 2 Strob. at 47 (O'Neall, J., dissenting).
9. 24 F. Cas. 792 (C.C. D. Va. 1859) (No. 14,445).
10. *Id.* at 793–809.
11. *Id.* at 810.
12. Justice William O. Douglas opined that "standing" should be given to litigants "in the name of the inanimate objects about to be despoiled, defaced, or invaded by roads and bulldozers and where injury is the subject of public outrage." *See, Sierra Club v. Morton*, 405 U.S. 727, 741, 92 S. Ct. 1361, 1369, 31 L. Ed. 2d 636, 647 (1972) (Douglas, J., dissenting); *see, also*, Roderick F. Nash, *The Rights of Nature: A History of Environmental Ethics* (Madison, 1989), Christopher D. Stone, "Should the Trees Have Standing?—Toward Legal Rights for Natural Objects," 45 *So. California Law Review* 450 (1972), discussing the environmentalists' arguments in favor of vesting nature with a legal persona. Although the goals of this approach are laudable, I think it best to analyze even these difficult issues in terms of the competing interests of the individuals and groups, and not the objects themselves.
13. 60 U.S. (19 How.) 393 (1856).
14. *Id.* at 407.
15. *See*, Kenneth M. Stampp, *The Peculiar Institution: Slavery in the Antebellum South* 192–193 (New York, 1956) (emphasis in original).
16. A. Leon Higginbotham, *In the Matter of Color: Race and the American Legal Process: The Colonial Period* 7 (New York, 1978).
17. *See*, A. E. K. Nash, "A More Equitable Past? Southern Supreme Courts and the Protection of the Antebellum Negro Rights," 48 *No. Carolina Law Review* 197, 201–202 (1970) (hereinafter "Equitable Past?").
18. Eugene D. Genovese, *Roll, Jordan, Roll: The World the Slaves Made* 28 (New York, 1974) (hereinafter "Genovese").
19. *See*, Patterson, *supra* at 22.
20. *See*, Tushnet, *supra* at 217–218 and *passim*. Other writers opining to this effect include, Arthur Howington, *What Sayeth the Law: The Treatment of Slaves and Free Blacks in the State and Local Courts of Tennessee* 69–70 (New York, 1986); Terrence F. Kiely, "The Hollow Words: An Experiment

in Legal Historical Method as Applied to the Institution of Slavery," 25 *De Paul Law Review* 842, 842–859 (1976); Wilbert E. Moore, "Slave Law and the Social Structure," 26 *Journal of Southern History* 171, 191–202 (1941).

21. *See*, Tannenbaum, *supra* at 103.

22. *See*, Thomas R. R. Cobb, *An Inquiry Into the Law of Negro Slavery in the United States of America* (New York, reprint ed. 1968) (1858); John B. O'Neall, *The Negro Law of South Carolina* (Columbia, 1848) reprinted in 2 Paul Finkelman, *Statutes on Slavery: The Pamphlet Literature* (New York, 1988); William Harper, "Harper on Slavery" in *The Pro-Slavery Argument* 1–98 (New York, reprint, ed. 1968) (1852). Harriet Beecher Stowe also presents an interesting view of this interpretation, as she quotes at length from the letters of her critics. *See*, Stowe, *supra* at 124–131. For the twentieth century version of this pro-slavery interpretation of slave law, *see*, *e.g.*, Ulrich B. Phillips, *American Negro Slavery* 489–514 (Baton Rouge, reprint ed., 1966) (1918). James Oakes repeats Cobb's contention that, when the law regulated the master's treatment of his slaves it created rights in slaves. *See*, James Oakes, *Slavery and Freedom: An Interpretation of the Old South* 166 (New York, 1990) (hereinafter "Oakes—1990"), *quoting*, Cobb, *supra* at 93–94 n. 5.

23. *See*, Goodell, *supra* at 201.

24. *See*, Stampp, *supra* at 193. This view is supported by other twentieth century historians of slavery. *See*, *e.g.*, Klein, *supra* at 40–57; Elkins, *supra* at 37–63; Stampp, *supra* at 192–236; Tannenbaum, *supra* at 65–86. This interpretation is also advanced in the work of slave law specialists; *see*, *e.g.*, Michael S. Hindus, *Prison and Plantation: Crime, Justice, and Authority in Massachusetts and South Carolina, 1767–1878* (Chapel Hill, 1980); Higginbotham, *supra*; Kiely, *supra*; A. Leon Higginbotham, "Racism and the Early American Legal Process, 1619–1896," 407 *Annals* 1 (1973); Moore, *supra*.

25. Tannenbaum, *supra* at 82.

26. *See*, Klein, *supra* at 37–57; Elkins, *supra* at 37–63; Tannenbaum, *supra* at 65–86.

27. *See*, Sio, *supra* at 294–306. For Nash, *see*, "Radical Interpretations," *supra*; A. E. K. Nash, "Reason of Slavery: Understanding the Judicial Role in the Peculiar Institution," 32 *Vanderbilt Law Review* 7 (1979) (hereinafter cited as "Reason of Slavery"); A. E. K. Nash, "Fairness and Formalism in the Trials of Blacks in the State Supreme Courts of the Old South," 56 *Virginia Law Review* 64 (1970) (hereinafter cited as "Fairness"); "Equitable Past?", *supra*; A. E. K. Nash, "Negro Rights, Unionism and Greatness on the South Carolina Court of Appeals: The Extraordinary Chief Justice John Belton O'Neall," 21 *So. Carolina Law Review* 141 (1969) (hereinafter cited as "Negro Rights"); A. E. K. Nash, "The Texas Supreme Court and Trial Rights of Blacks, 1845–1860," 58 *Journal of American History* 622 (1971) (hereinafter cited as "Trial Rights"); *see*, *also*, Howington, *supra*; Arthur F. Howington, "Not in the Condition of a Horse or an Ox." *Ford v. Ford*, the Law of Testamentary Manumission, and the Tennessee Court's Recognition of Slave Humanity," 34 *Tennessee Historical Quarterly* 249 (1975) (hereinafter cited as "Howington—1975").

28. *See,* Howington, *supra* at 146–149; Hindus, *supra passim.*

29. *See,* Tushnet, *supra;* Tushnet—1975, *supra; see, also,* Mark Tushnet, "Approaches to the Study of the Law of Slavery," 25 *Civil War History* 329 (1979); Mark Tushnet, "Book Review," 45 *University of Chicago Law Review* 906 (1978); and, *see,* Genovese, *supra* at 25–70. For discussions of Tushnet's complex interpretation and the many reviews of his book, *see,* Elizabeth Fox-Genovese and Eugene Genovese, *Fruits of Merchant Capital: Slavery and Bourgeois Property in the Rise and Expansion of Capitalism* 368–387 (New York, 1983); Andrew Fede, "Toward a Solution of the Slave Law Dilemma: A Critique of Tushnet's 'The American Law of Slavery,'" 2 *Law & History Review* 301, 301–311 (1984) (hereinafter "Fede—1984"); "Radical Interpretations," *supra* at 314–343. An interpretation that is similar to that of Genovese is asserted in, Willie Lee Rose, *Slavery and Freedom* 18–36 (New York, 1982).

30. Stampp, *supra* at 201.

31. M. I. Finley, *Ancient Slavery and Modern Ideology* 73 (New York, 1980). For a similar view comparing the slave law in Virginia and Cuba, *see,* Klein, *supra* at 37–40.

32. *Howard v. Howard,* 51 N.C. 237, 238, 6 Jones 235, 236 (1858).

33. A. Leon Higginbotham and Barbara Kopytoff, "Property First, Humanity Second: The Recognition of the Slave's Human Nature in Virginia Civil Law," 50 *Ohio State Law Review* 511, 512 (1989).

## Chapter 2

# The Legitimizing Role of Law in Slave Society

SLAVERY consisted of oppressive human relations that were unknown to the common law that was brought to the New World by the English colonists. Consequently, as slavery became a social reality, the slave masters, legislators, and judges had to accommodate its fundamental elements into the body of the English common law. The earliest slave codes and court decisions were conceived and formed through this process of accommodation and development. Moreover, social, political, economic, and intellectual changes occurred throughout the slave holding era, and the lawmakers adapted slave law to the changing nonlegal reality. Therefore, the law of slavery was not static; nevertheless, it always played a legitimizing role in slave society. The law made slavery, and all of its oppressive elements, legal.

## *The Essential Elements of Slavery*

Harriet Beecher Stowe captured the essence of slavery when she called it "absolute despotism, of the most unmitigated form."[1] The most salient distinction between the master-slave relationship and other human interactions was the unlimited violence and oppression that the slave master could legitimately inflict upon his bondsman.[2] Therefore, the Africans who had been enslaved and who survived the tragic transatlantic slave passage[3] were sold to buyers who bargained for the exclusive right to "reap the fruits" of the slaves' labor, which the owners enforced by exercising their right to "uncontrolled authority" over the slave.[4] Consequently, the slaves owed their masters the duty of absolute obedience and were powerless in the face of their masters' unlimited power.[5]

Orlando Patterson's cross-cultural study of slavery through the ages identifies the fundamentals of slavery that the early colonists encountered. Patterson begins with Max Weber's view that all human relationships are "structured and defined by the relative power of the interacting persons."[6] Power forces one person to act, or refrain from acting, contrary to his own will and as a reflection of another person's will. Although power relationships are different in degree and kind, Patterson notes three "constituent elements of slavery," which in their extremes, distinguish slavery from other forms of inequity.

These three elements are: 1) the power of the master to use violence against the slave, 2) the slave's "natal alienation" (absence of "all 'rights' or claims of birth . . ."), and 3) the dishonored condition of the slave.[7] These particular incidents of slavery all flowed, either directly or indirectly, from the "despotism" that the master exercised over the slave.

Indeed, the power of the master resided in the use of force to coerce the powerless slave. Patterson identifies this element of slavery with the social level of interaction. On the cultural level, the concept of natal alienation captures the slave's isolation from the dominant community and his perpetual state of "otherness." The lack of honor relates to the level of psychology to reinforce the notion that the master is all powerful and honorable and the slave is powerless and dishonorable.[8]

## *The Role of Law in Slavery*

The essential point of Patterson's analysis is that the master and slave relationship is qualitatively different from other forms of inequality and domination. Similarly, the law had to recognize that slavery was fundamentally different from other forms of domination. To legitimize the slave's status, the law had to adapt concepts to fit the mold of the social reality of slavery.

In this respect slavery presents a difficult problem for the law; legal tools of analysis are strained by the fundamentals of slavery. The work of John Codman Hurd, published in 1858, illustrates this. Hurd correctly notes that the law usually distinguished persons and things in a fundamental way. Persons can act upon other persons and things; as such people can have legal rights and duties in reference to their actions. Things, however, can be the objects of action and can embody the relative rights of persons and the state, but things cannot have rights.[9] Slavery presents a problem because it is, by definition, the absence of legal right in persons who are slaves.

The law solved this dilemma by defining slaves as chattels. This definition cut slaves off from claims of legal right, whether by birth or against any other person. Thus, Hurd wrote that the chattel slave was without any claim of right. Hurd also held that the law could regulate "the power of the master, in view of the interests of society, without vesting the rights of a legal person in the slave."[10] Consequently, the role of law in slave society was crucial. It lent its approval to the powerlessness of the slave through the concept of chattel slavery.

Accordingly, the law served a legitimizing function in slave society; it permitted, encouraged, and, when necessary, regulated the domination of the master over the slave. Max Weber argued that in modern society the law legitimized state power and "domination." Thus, power plus authority became legitimate—or the law. Slave law had a similar effect; it legalized the "power" of the master to "dominate" the slave. Consequently, the law lent "authority" to the master's power over the slave, as well as the power of other non-related whites to control slaves as the law allowed. The white man's word was, therefore, law to the powerless slave, who had no rights that the white man was legally compelled to respect.[11]

This is a point upon which there has been much confusion. For example, James Oakes argues that when the law regulated the master's behavior toward his slaves, this created "rights" in the slave. He states that "the intrinsic ambiguity of slave law" was "the total subordination of the slave to a master who himself owed allegiance to the state[.]" This he calls the "profound dilemma" of slave law, and adds, "it was all but impossible for a liberal political culture to place limits on the masters' power without implicitly granting rights to slaves." Oakes thus concludes the law of slavery was "intrinsically subversive." Each limitation on the master's power diminished the "essence of slavery" according to Oakes.[12]

This analysis does not withstand scrutiny when the jurisprudential meaning of the term "right" is taken into account. Indeed, the notion of slave rights is an oxymoron.

## *The Fallacy of the Notion of Rights in Slaves*

The fallacy of the notion of slave rights is illustrated by the theory of W. H. Hohfeld. Hohfeld makes two essential points; the first is that "there is only one unit in the law . . . and that is a human being[.]" And second, "the only legal fact . . . is a relation between two such human beings."[13] Consequently, on this level of analysis, only people can have legal "rights." Property can have no legal rights.

The owner of property, therefore, is the possessor of rights and privileges as to other persons in reference to property. As between the owner and property, however, the property has no "right." The state does have the power, however, to regulate the owner's use of his property in the public interest; thus in this respect the owner's power over his property is not absolute.[14] This was also the case with slaves. As property, slaves were subject to their master's power, and this power was regulated not out of concern for the slave's interest, but to promote the "public interest," or the property claims of others in the slave.

M. I. Finley put the issue this way:

> Legal restrictions on the rights of a slaveowner are also a side issue: in modern sociological and juridical theories of any school, all property is understood to be a matrix of rights, rarely if ever unlimited. The precise rights that constitute the matrix vary with kinds of property and kinds of society.[15]

Finley also correctly noted that the fact that some masters refrained from treating their slaves with the cruelty that the law allowed "is interesting, even important, but it does not undermine the slave-property link conceptually."

This is because a master's decision to recognize slave privileges "was always a unilateral act on his part, never binding, always revocable."[16] Finley cites manumission as one example and indeed, the slave had no legal right, *per se*, to demand freedom. Other instances are cited by Professor Genovese. He calls these privileges "customary rights," and states:

> If the law said [slaves] had no right to property, . . . but local custom accorded them private garden plots, then woe to the master or overseer who summarily withdrew the "privilege."[17]

But, contrary to Professor Genovese, these privileges were not legal rights if the initial premise is correct, that "the law" said the slave had no such right that the courts would enforce. The question of whether the slave thought of the privilege as an entitlement and whether the master thought it best to allow the privilege was indeed a different issue—and not a legal issue.

This fundamental distinction is well illustrated by the 1845 North Carolina Supreme Court decision of *Waddill v. Martin*.[18] The case concerned a dispute between co-executors of the estate of a "wealthy planter"—James H. Martin. Martin, "who was a considerable slave holder," had for some years allowed his slaves to grow their own patches of cotton. After the harvest, Martin sold the cotton cultivated by the slaves with his main crop. Upon the sale of the cotton, Martin paid his slaves "their" share of the proceeds—less expenses. Thus, Martin's privilege was a predecessor to the sharecropping system of the post-bellum era.

The legal dispute concerned the 1836 crop. Martin's slaves proceeded to plant cotton pursuant to the custom, but their master died in July 1836. One co-executor, Waddill, paid the slaves $143.97, after the sale of the crop, for their share. The other co-executor—Martin's widow—objected.[19]

The Court upheld the payment to the slaves, in an opinion by Chief Judge Thomas Ruffin. The Court noted that Martin's practice was not harmful or in violation of the rule that prohibited slave property ownership because the Court did not hold "that negroes can hold anything against the executor[.]"[20] To the contrary, Ruffin ruled that the slave's "property" was indeed that of the master's estate, and "the master, if he will, may take it all."[21] Thus, at law, the slaves had no right to the gratuity bestowed by their master, and they had no legal basis to compel the executor to continue the privilege after 1836. Nevertheless, the master, and his executor, had the right to dispose of their property in this way. Indeed, Ruffin noted that this custom was an inducement to harmony among slaves, and by affording the slave spending money, in effect, was a credit against the expenses needed to maintain the slaves.[22]

This procedure should not, however, be confused with a legal right in the slave against the master. Roman slave law did recognize the slave's right to earn and save money in excess of his services owed to his master. This was known as the *peculium*, and Patterson notes its universality in slave societies. The common law South did not, however, acknowledge the *peculium*.[23]

The only legal right was that of the master to allocate gifts to his slaves, although legal title to the gift always remained in the master. The law did, however, limit the master's bounty when his generosity went too far. Therefore, the North Carolina Supreme Court held, in 1860, that a slave could not own a jackass,[24] and that the accumulation of $1,500 by a slave violated public policy.[25]

These cases can be reconciled with *Waddill*, but not based upon any conception of slave right. Ruffin thought that the "little" crops of Martin's slaves furthered the interests of slave control and "promote [the slave's] health, cheerfulness and contentment, and enhance his value."[26] Chief Judge Richmond Pearson wrote, however, that gifts of animals or large sums of money were "certainly calculated to make other slaves dissatisfied because they are not allowed the same degree of freedom or privilege[.]"[27] Consequently, masters who were too humane had to be restrained by the law "to promote good morals."[28]

The master was therefore all powerful in his relations with his slave. In Hohfeld's terms, the slave had no right against the master, who was privileged to treat his slaves as he wished. Nevertheless, the law interfered with the master's ownership rights when important social interests were perceived to compel regulation of the master and slave relation. When the law did so interfere, the slave remained a silent pawn in the proceedings. The law was a compact between the slave's rulers—the master and the state.

This notion of the slave as a passive object upon which the law of his oppressors operated implies that the slave's humanity was never legally relevant, unless it had an impact on the legal interests of some legal person. That person could be the slave's master, but could also include third parties or the state. This can be made clear when the law is examined against the background of the social reality out of which the law grew. Therefore, the historical and sociological assumptions about the role of law in society must be examined and made explicit.

## *The Real Interests Implicated in Slave Law Cases and Statutes: Notes on Historical and Judicial Methods*

There are two methodological points of departure between this study and the work of the earlier writers. The first is a question of legal history methods, and the second has to do with jurisprudential definition. As to the former, the complex legal structure of the law of slavery can be understood only as a process by which the courts and legislatures balanced the salient interests implicated in the issue presented. These interests included: (1) The need to foster slave control, obedience, and submissiveness; (2) The slave master class interest in perpetuating the plantation economy and preserving slave property values; (3) The slave master class need to control overseers and slave hirers, while preserving these individuals' right to discipline slaves; and (4) The master class need to control poor white violence and slave abuse, while co-opting poor whites into becoming supporters of the slave economy.[29]

The engines of legal change were the social, economic, and political changes that caused the slave owners' perceptions of the balance of these interests to shift, and their new attitudes and concerns were shared by judges and legislators who created the new legal standards. Therefore, the antebellum courts and legislatures used the civil and criminal law to protect slave property, and as an instrument of social control they asserted against poor whites, overseers, slave hirers, and between members of the master class. This latter point has not been adequately contended within the literature on slave law.

To trace the relationship between social, economic, and political conditions and the law of slavery, it is necessary to examine relevant nonlegal materials in addition to statutes, constitutions, and case law reports—what are called "law box" data by Robert Gordon.[30] This study, then is one in "external" rather than "internal" legal analysis that is generally confined to the law box.[31] Implicit in this approach, however, is an important answer to the key question concerning the relationship between law and social change: whether legal change was cause by "autonomous" forces at work inside the law box, or whether changes in law reflected changes in the society at large.

The way one defines the concept of "legal autonomy" influences how one views the relationship between law and social change. Professor Gordon posits two polar opposite definitions of this concept in terms of how the proponents of each view perceive of the contents of the law box. The first is a theory "asserting that law derives its shape almost wholly from sources within the box (*i.e.*, that it is really autonomous as well as seeming so)[.]" According to the second view, "the box is really empty, the apparent distinctiveness of its contents illusory, since they are all products of external social forces."[32] This study reveals that the law of slavery fits in toward the latter end of the continuum.

The legal and nonlaw box data examined herein support the interpretation that the formulation and reformulation of legal standards and doctrine concerning slave law took place in response to social, political, and economic changes that accompanied the development of plantation slavery. Thus, the process of legal evolution was, in essence, a reaction to nonlegal changes and was not an expression of "autonomous" legal forces.

This interpretation of legal change is akin to the "instrumentalist" model because it asserts that Southern judges and legislators viewed this law as "an instrument of social policy" that they used to encourage certain nonlegal changes and to alleviate the harmful effects of others.[33] This is not to say, however, that statutes and case law reports necessarily reflected dominant interests, or that they did so by means of a simple, unthinking reflex action.

In fact, the important institutional differences between courts and legislatures must be accounted for, along with the different natures of case and statute-law materials. Moreover, case law reports have to be interpreted with a lawyer's expertise, which accounts for the technical way lawyers and judges argue from precedents and focuses on the specific issue the litigants have brought to the courts for decision.

The most fundamental point in this regard is the need to distinguish between the holding and *dicta* in a judicial decision. Slave law scholars have not always done this sufficiently in their analysis, and this is unfortunate. Karl Llewellyn said it best when he noted that the only "law" in a judicial opinion is created when the court "speaks to the question before it[.]" As to any other question the court "says mere words, which no man needs to follow." He adds that such words are not "worthless:"

> We know them as judicial *dicta*; . . .— words dropped along the road, wayside remarks. Yet even wayside remarks shed light on the remarker. They may be very useful in the future to him, or to us. But he will not feel bound to them, as to his ex cathedra utterance.[34]

Thus, court decisions sometimes referred to slave rights, but judges at other times did not feel bound by claims to humanity or slave rights. This *dicta* tells us that references to slave humanity or right do not reconcile the cases. But an analysis of the interests cited above does reconcile apparently inconsistent *dicta*.

This is made manifest by the fact that the complex of relevant interests set forth above was explicitly balanced in many judicial opinions, and because concern about salient social change was implicit in the complex and changing structure of the legal rules and results that flowed from the case and statutory law. The evolving legal standards embodied in this law can be reconciled only in terms of how the lawmakers' perceptions of the balance of the relevant interests changed over time, thus leading to the conclusions that the balance of these interests was the motivating force behind legal change, and that the law did not change for its own "autonomous" reasons.

These methodological and theoretical assumptions represent the point of departure between this study and the work of those who have previously studied the law of Southern slavery. Accordingly, the ongoing debate continues among the schools of thought because the authors cited in chapter one draw upon and emphasize different legal materials. But more fundamentally, they confine their analysis to the law box. As a consequence, legal provisions that are not really contradictory appear irreconcilable when viewed from the internal historical perspective. The law of slavery was not inconsistent because it defined slaves as "property" while it called them persons. It is necessary, however, to interpret this changing law against the background of the relevant nonlegal history of the South. The four key components of this history are: the pattern of socioeconomic development, the white social and economic class conflicts, the rising value of slaves, and the political power of the slave-owning class.

## Conclusion

Modern historians are bound to make serious errors unless they simultaneously steep themselves in the legal and non-legal history of American slavery. This cure must be taken in equal doses; lip service to the social history of the South will not suffice. Furthermore, because legal change in the South cannot be reconciled from within the "law box," students of slave law should compare the "instrumentalist" interpretations of nineteenth century legal change and consider the parallel development of slave law and non-slave law. Thus the study of slave law is relevant to all legal historians, and lawyers in general, who want to know how our courts have formulated legal rules and doctrine of the past.[35]

The chapters that follow will build on these methodological assumptions, and will explain why it is mere obfuscation to refer to slave rights in the common law South. This will be shown first by an examination of how the fundamentals of slavery were legitimized by the law of the colonial South.

## NOTES

1. Stowe, *supra* at 233.
2. Patterson, *supra* at 1–5, 17–34.
3. *See*, generally, *e.g.*, *Id.* at 113, 119-20 for a discussion of the ways Africans who eventually reached the New World were enslaved, and *Id.* at 159–64 for a review of the patterns of transatlantic slave trade and a recent literature on this subject.
4. *See, e.g.*, *State v. Mann*, 13 N.C. 229, 31, 2 Dev. 263, 266 (1829).
5. *See, e.g.*, *Id.*; *see, also*, Patterson, *supra* at 4.
6. *Id.* at 1.
7. *Id.* at 1–101, quotation is from *Id.* at 5.
8. *Id.* at 1–14. *See, also*, Oakes—1990, *supra* at 3–39, Robert William Fogel, *Without Consent or Contract: The Rise and Fall of American Slavery* 393-406 (New York, 1989), Finley, *supra* at 73–77, Winthrop D. Jordan, *White Over Black: American Attitudes Toward the Negro, 1550–1812* 52–56 (Chapel Hill, 1968), David Brion Davis, *The Problem of Slavery in Western Culture* 30–35 (Ithaca, 1966) (Davis-1966).
9. *See*, 1 Hurd, *supra* at 18–20, 36–43.
10. *See, Id.* at 42 [footnote omitted].
11. For a general discussion of Max Weber's views of the legitimizing function of law, *see*, David Trubeck, "Max Weber on Law and the Rise of Capitalism," 1972 *Wisconsin Law Review* 720, 720–726.

12. *See*, Oakes-1990, *supra* at 159, *see also*, 1 Hurd, *supra* at 42.
13. *See*, Max Radin, "A Restatement of Hohfeld," 51 *Harvard Law Review* 1141, 1147 (1938). For a critique of Hohfeld's theory, *see*, Joseph Singer, "The Legal Rights Debate in Analytical Jurisprudence from Bentham to Hohfeld," 1982 *Wisconsin Law Review* 975.
14. *See*, Hurd, *supra* at 18–21, 36–43, *see, also*, Kenneth Vandevelde, "The New Property of the Nineteenth Century: The Development of The Modern Concept of Property," 29 *Buffalo Law Review* 325 (1980).
15. Finley, *supra* at 73.
16. *See, Id.* at 74.
17. Genovese, *supra* 15 30–31.
18. 38 N.C. (3 Ired. Eq.) 562 (1845).
19. *Id.* at 562–563.
20. *Id.* at 564.
21. *Id.* at 565; *see, also*, noting the master's ownership of "gifts" to slaves, *Carmille v. Carmille*, 27 S.C.L. 190, 198, 2 McMul. 454, 471 (1842); Moore, *supra* at 193. Also in North Carolina see, *Washington v. Emery*, 57 N.C. 42, 4 Jones Eq. 32 (1858); and *White v. Cline*, 52 N.C. 195, 7 Jones 175 (1859). *Compare*, O'Neall, *supra* at 21.
22. *Waddill v. Martin*, *supra*, 38 N.C. (3 Ired. Eq.) at 564.
23. *See*, Patterson, *supra* at 182–186; Moore, *supra* at 192–193; Goodell, *supra* at 89–90; *see, also*, Robert B. Robinson and James D. Hardy, "An *Actio de Peculio* in Ante-Bellum Alabama," 11 *Journal of Legal History* 364 (1990).
24. *See, Love v. Brindle*, 52 N.C. 584, 7 Jones 560 (1860).
25. *See, Lea v. Brown*, 58 N.C. 395, 5 Jones Eq. 380 (1860).
26. *See, Waddill v. Martin*, *supra*, 38 N.C. (3 Ired. Eq.) at 564.
27. *See, Lea v. Brown*, *supra*, 58 N.C. at 397, 5 Jones Eq. at 382.
28. *Id.*, 58 N.C. at 398, 5 Jones Eq. at 382. For statutes and cases prohibiting slave property ownership, *see*, Goodell, *supra* at 89–104; Stroud, *supra* at 29–33.
29. These interests are discussed in the texts of numerous case law opinions. *See, e.g., State v. Mann* 13 N.C. 229, 233, 2 Dev. 263, 268 (1829); and *Commonwealth v. Turner*, 26 Va. 560, 564, 5 Rand. 678, 688–90 (1827) (Brockenbrough, J., dissenting), *see, also*, Patrick S. Brady, "Slavery, Race, and the Criminal Law in Antebellum North Carolina: A Reconsideration of the Thomas Ruffin Court," 10 *North Carolina Cent. Law Journal* 248, 260 (1979) (discussing the North Carolina cases).
30. In a most helpful historiographical essay, Robert Gordon developed the law box concept as follows:

> Inside the box is "the law," whatever appears autonomous about the legal order—courts, equitable maxims, motions for summary judgment; outside lies "society," the wide realm of the nonlegal, the political, economic, religious, social . . .

Robert Gordon, "J. Willard Hurst and the Common Law Tradition in American Historiography," 10 *Law & Society Review* 9, 10 (1975).
31. Professor Gordon calls this an "external" approach to legal history because it reaches outside of the "law box" for nonlegal data, and therefore

contrasts with "internal" legal history, which confines its inquiry to the "law box." *See, Id.* at 11.

32. *See, Id.* at 10. For an "internal" approach to slave law, *see*, Watson–1989, *supra* at 1–21, 113–133.

33. *See, generally*, Morton Horwitz, *The Transformation of American Law, 1780–1860* 30 (Cambridge, 1977); J. Willard Hurst, *The Growth of American Law: The Law Makers* 1–19 (Boston, 1950); *see, also*, Hall, *supra* at 3–8 and Friedman, *supra* at 17–19 and *passim. Compare*, David J. Langum, "The Role of Intellect and Fortuity in Legal Change: An Incident from the Law of Slavery," 28 *American Journal of Legal History* 1 (1984) for a critique of this view as applied to slave law.

34. Karl N. Llewellyn, *The Bramble Bush: On Our Law and Its Study* 42 (New York, 1930). Patrick Brady also notes the need to observe these insights when reading slave law decision. *See*, Brady, *supra* at 249.

35. This paragraph is adapted from Fede-1984, *supra* at 319.

## Chapter 3

# Accommodating Slavery into the Common Law

EDMUND S. Morgan argues that the English who settled in the New World did not initially intend to establish slave colonies in the Americas. Nevertheless, as Davis and Jordan demonstrate, the 16th- and seventeenth-century English had some idea of slavery as a social reality both in antiquity and in the practices of people elsewhere in the world. Chattel slavery was not, however, part of the social heritage of the English who settled in North America after 1607.[1]

Nor was slavery a social relationship authorized by the common law of England in the early seventeenth century. The law books contained references to the ancient practices of villenage, but this legal institution was by then a relic of an earlier age. To be sure, the common law of that era would fail modern equal protection analysis. The law recognized apprenticeship, indentured servitude, and degrees of domination within the family relationships of father and child and husband and wife. But total domination and subjection to chattel slavery was unknown to the contemporary law.[2]

This point was made by Oscar and Mary Handlin, who wrote that "slavery had no meaning in law," and they meant the common law of seventeenth century England.[3] This argument is forcefully stated by John Anthony Scott:

> The law of slavery, and the philosophy that underlay that law, was the direct antithesis of the common law which white southerners, like other Americans, inherited from England. . . . Two mutually contradictory systems of law existed side by side in the antebellum South: the common law and the law of slavery.[4]

Indeed, this was the view of Lord Mansfield expressed in the *Somerset* case, that slavery was not authorized, and was in fact contrary to, the common law before the common law of slavery emerged in the colonies.[5]

Although it is subject to some debate, this interpretation is correct.

Writers such as David Konig point to Dale's Laws adopted in Virginia and earlier English statutes that impaired fundamental common law rights guaranteed to Englishmen by the common law as it had evolved by the seventeenth century.[6] But these statutory exceptions prove the rule; absent a statute to the contrary, the common law did not recognize the fundamental elements of the master and slave relation before the law of slavery developed in the English colonies.

The common law of slavery, then, had to be invented or borrowed from other peoples for use in the North American English colonies after the first blacks were introduced into Virginia in 1619. Therefore, as slavery became a social reality, the slave masters, legislators, and judges had to accommodate slavery's fundamental elements into the body of the English common law that did not authorize or legitimize slavery.

Historians have debated the issue of whether the first blacks brought to the Southern colonies were slaves from the outset, or whether slavery evolved as a social practice.[7] The limited historical evidence indicates that slavery began to develop in Maryland and Virginia between 1619 and 1660, while in Carolina, the colonists borrowed their slave practices from those already in use in Barbados. These patterns are also reflected in the law of slavery. Carolina is therefore a less interesting example because its first slave codes were adapted from the code adopted in Barbados.[8] In Virginia and Maryland, the evolution of the law followed social change in a more interesting way.

The development of early slavery and slave law is well chronicled in Maryland by Jonathan Alpert, and in Virginia by Judge Higginbotham, Winthrop Jordan, and Edmund Morgan. Moreover, William Wiecek provides a comprehensive and cogent summary of the slave law in thirteen colonies.[9] These studies will not be improved upon here. It is worth noting, nonetheless, how the fundamentals of slavery cited by Patterson were addressed in colonial Virginia.

In Virginia, slavery was accommodated with the common law until the first comprehensive slave code was enacted in 1705. Winthrop Jordan divides Virginia's early colonial history into three phases. Between 1619—when the first record of blacks exists—until 1640, Jordan states, "There simply is not enough evidence to indicate with any certainty whether Negroes were treated like white servants or not."[10] It is no surprise, therefore, that there are no significant legal decisions or statutes regarding slavery. Colonial life was still a rough frontier existence and the number of blacks—whether or not slaves—was small.

In the second period, from 1640 to 1660, Jordan finds "mounting evidence that some Negroes were in fact being treated like slaves, at least that they were being held in hereditary lifetime service."[11] Nevertheless, it was not until after 1660 that "slavery was written into statute law."[12] There were good reasons for this. Between 1640 and 1660 Virginia's black population grew six fold, while the total population did not triple:

### Table 1

**Virginia's Total and Black Population**[12]

| Year | Total Population | Black Population | % Black |
|------|------------------|------------------|---------|
| 1620 | 2,200 | 20 | .09 |
| 1640 | 10,442 | 150 | 1.4 |
| 1660 | 27,020 | 950 | 3.5 |
| 1670 | 35,309 | 2,000 | 5.6 |

With this growth in black and therefore slave population came the perceived need for the first legislation addressing the fundamentals of slavery.

The master's power to physically abuse his slave was legitimized by a 1669 statute known as "An Act about casuall [sic] killing of slaves." This Act provides:

> ... [I]f any slave resist his master ... and by the extremity of the correction should chance to die, that his death shall not be accompted Felony, but the master (or that other person appointed by the master to punish him) be acquit from molestation, since it cannot be presumed that propensed malice (which alone makes murther felony) should induce any man to destroy his own estate.[14]

This statute therefore legalized slave homicides that were apparently viewed as otherwise indictable murder under the common law of crimes.

This provision was thought to be necessary because indentured servants who resisted their masters were punished for their misdeeds by extending their time of servitude. The Assembly found that this form of punishment "cannot be inflicted on negroes" who were slaves for life. Thus, the legislators wrote that this usual means of discipline was ineffective against slaves because the "obstinancy of many slaves" could not "by other than violent meanes [sic] supress [sic]."[15] Judge Higginbotham quotes Edmund Morgan stating, "Slaves could not be made to work for fear of losing liberty, so they had to be made to fear for their lives ... in order to get an equal or greater amount of work, it was necessary to beat slaves harder than servants, so hard in fact, there was a much larger chance of killing them than had been the case with servants."[16]

Therefore, the growing numbers of lifetime slaves, the difficulty in disciplining slaves, and the advent of plantation agriculture all contributed to the adoption of this first statute dealing with the "protection" of slaves from whites. In fact, this statute represents a central tenent in slave law that later stood throughout the South. A master or overseer could not be convicted for killing a slave who, after resisting, is killed by the master because of the "extremity of correction."

It is significant to note that this legislation merely carves out a narrow exception to the general criminal law. It illustrates how the Virginia colonists viewed themselves as governed by English common law, not Biblical or civil law as some nineteenth century jurists supposed. The colonists instead passed this statute in derogation of the common law. As of 1669, however, a stranger could apparently still be indicted for the homicide of a slave. So could a master whose killing did not fit within the four corners of the statute. The legislature did not yet paint with a broad brush. Rather, the first act was aimed at a specific situation that apparently became of central importance with the growth of plantation slavery in Virginia during the latter half of the 1600s.

The power of other whites over slaves was legitimized by a statute enacted in 1680. This act prohibited slaves from bearing arms and leaving their plantations without a "certificate." Thus, it was the predecessor of the patrol laws that were adopted later. The act also provides:

> . . . [I]f any Negro lift up his hand against any Christian he shall receive thirty lashes, and if he absent himself or lie out from his master's service and resist lawful apprehension, he may be killed and this *law* shall be published every six months.[17]

In this act the legislature apparently responded to a series of growing problems in the area of slave control. A slave could no longer protect himself in self-defense. He could also now be lawfully killed while running away, not only by his master or overseer, but also by a stranger.

Once again the Assembly addressed particular problems and removed specific crimes from the ambit of the criminal law in response to the increasing need for slave discipline. This approach was continued in 1691 when the Assembly enacted "An act for supressing outlying slaves." This act provides that runaway slaves shall be arrested by the sheriff or on a justice's warrant, and if the slave should resist,

". . . it shall and may be lawfull for such person or persons to kill and destroy such negroes, mulattoes, and other slave or slaves by gunn or any otherwaise whatsoever." If the slave was killed, the act provided for compensation to the master from the public in the form of four thousand pounds of tobacco.[18] Accordingly, powerless slaves were subject to apprehension, and even killing, at the hands of the powerful whites.

The slave's "natal alienation" was confirmed by a 1662 act. That statute recited that "some doubts" had arisen whether the children fathered by "an Englishman upon a negro woman should be slave or ffree [sic][.]" The statute provided that such issue would be slaves, and that the status of slavery followed from the mother's bondage.[19] Thus, the legislators abrogated the common law rule that applied to free people. According to that axiom, the child's social standing was that of the father. In its place, the Virginians substituted the common law rule that governed domestic animals; thus the owner had the same right to the offspring of his female chattels, whether the chattels were human or non-human.[20]

This harsh principle of slave law was eventually adopted throughout the slave states, and it is significant for two reasons. First, it cut the child of a slave mother off from all claims of birth right, except the right to be held in bondage. And second, it communicated to all the legal debasement of the slaves, who were explicitly reduced to the legal level occupied by pigs and cattle.

Consequently, the command of the 1662 act also revealed the slave's dishonored condition. Another portion of the statute further marked the slave's dishonor by doubling the usual penalty for fornication when a black person was involved. The slave's lowly status was also indicated by a 1667 act. That statute stated that baptism did not free the slave. Furthermore, acts prohibiting miscegenation are examples of the slave's lack of status and honor.[21]

The dishonored and alienated condition of the slave was further enforced by the 1692 "Act for the more speedy prosecution of slaves committing Capitall [sic] Crimes." This statute established special courts and procedures for the trials of slaves accused of serious crimes. Accordingly, it deprived slaves of the usual rights that the common law afforded to people accused of crimes. Thus, the act alienated slaves from the right to accusation by a grand jury and trial by jury, and fortified the slave's alienation from the common law. These principles were continued in the South throughout the antebellum period—confirming the slave's lack of honor.[22]

Thus, Patterson's three elements of slavery were recognized in Virginia's law before 1705. Patterson omits the definition of slaves as property and racism from the constituent elements of slavery. On a cross-cultural level, Patterson is correct. Nevertheless, in the U.S. South the chattel status of slaves and the racial basis of slavery were also fundamental to the law of slavery.

## *Slaves as Property: A Constant*

The definition of slaves as property was a necessary step in the accommodation of slavery into the common law. This legitimized the master's power over the slave as well as the owner's sole right to the benefit of the slave's labor. In addition, the characterization of slaves as property presented a means of ordering the relationships between the slave, the master, and third parties. As a species of property, the slave represented the embodiment of the "bundle of rights" possessed by the master. Thus, the master's ownership rights were legitimized and easily cognizable at common law, along with the ownership rights of those who bought ordinary property.[23]

It is clear from the above, however, that the patchwork quilt of oppression constructed by the early Virginia and Maryland statutes does not begin with an act that explicitly defines the slave to be property. Thus, slavery did not begin in these colonies with "state action" embodied in a statute explicitly authorizing chattel slavery. William Wiecek makes this point; he also arrives at the conclusion that legislative acts "did in fact validate and regulate many customary elements of the legal relationship between white and black people in the colonial period."[24] As the Virginia example shows, the legislatures responded to perceived social change and legalized the requisites of the master slave relation. For example, there were contracts and deeds from the 1640s indicating that slaves were, in practice, bought and sold before the law specifically designated them as property.[25] Therefore, the law followed private practice; as slavery developed, the assembly reacted to social change and enacted the formal legal authority to legitimize the constituent elements of slavery.

After 1705, a new era dawned in Virginia as it adopted its first comprehensive slave code. This code was necessary because "by about 1700 the slave ships began spilling forth their black cargoes in greater and greater number."[26] The black population grew rapidly:

## Table 2
### Virginia's Total and Black Population[27]

| Year | Total Population | Black Population | % Black |
|------|------------------|------------------|---------|
| 1680 | 43,596 | 3,000 | 6.9 |
| 1690 | 53,046 | 9,345 | 17.6 |
| 1700 | 58,560 | 16,390 | 28.0 |
| 1710 | 78,281 | 23,118 | 29.5 |
| 1720 | 87,757 | 26,559 | 30.2 |

With this dramatic rise in the black population, and the continued growth of plantation agriculture, came the slave code.

Judge Higginbotham notes the irony of the fact that in 1705 the Virginia assembly passed an act granting a broad "panoply of legal rights" to servants while at the same time enacting the first comprehensive slave code.[28] This code, in Chapter XXIII, defined slaves to be their master's real property. It followed a 1671 Act that was directed at the problem of a minor heir's right to inherit slave property:

> 1671. Act IV. In a former act it is provided that sheep, horses, cattle should be delivered in kind to an orphan when he comes of age, to which some have desired that Negroes be added; this Assembly considering the difficulty of procuring Negroes in kind as also the value and hazard of their lives has doubted whether any sufficient men could be found who would engage themselves to deliver Negroes of equal ages if the special Negroes should die, or become by age or accident unserviceable; it is enacted, that at discretion of the courts Negroes may be appraised, sold at an outcry, or preserved in kind, as it is deemed most expedient for the preservation or advancement of the estates of orphans.[29]

This statute indicates that slave owners thought that their slaves were inheritable, but that their notions of the heirs' rights to slaves were evolving.

The 1705 code was intended to address this and other legal issues that arose as slavery was accommodated into the common law. Chapter 23 decreed that slaves were real property:

> All Negro, mulatto, and Indian slaves within this dominion shall be held to be real estate and not chattels and shall descend unto heirs and widows according to the custom of land inheritance, and be held in "fee simple." Provided that any merchant bringing slaves into this dominion shall hold slaves whilst they remain unsold as personal estate. All such slaves may be taken on execution as other chattels; slaves shall not be escheatable.

> No person selling any slave shall be obliged to have the sale recorded as upon the alienation of other real estate. Nothing in this act shall be construed to give the owner of a slave not seized of other real estate the right to vote as a freeholder.[30]

The definition of slaves as fee simple, or real estate, was significant for a number of reasons. Note, however, how this Act excluded the slaves held by slave traders from these protections. The legislators were concerned with the interests of slave owners, not slave traders or creditors, an obvious example of class bias.

This statute made it possible for slaves to be the subject of a mortgage.[31] The act also had an "estate planning" purpose. This is revealed when one considers the common law rule that prohibited the creation of estates in chattels.[32] The legal designation of slaves as realty enabled the slave master to control the rights of his heirs and others to the slave after the owner's death. Dower and courtesy rights to use slaves were also thereby created for the life of a slave owner's spouse. Thus, Robert Cottrol and Raymond Diamond correctly observe that "there are indications that the designation of slaves as real property was intended to preserve the slaves who made the land productive."[33]

Eventually, however, the colonies and states defined slaves to be chattel or personal property—not realty. This was possible because the feudal common law axioms that distinguished between chattels and real estate were being changed in the eighteenth century. For example, the courts began to recognize the creation of estates by will in valuable chattels such as stocks. Slaves were as valuable to slave owners as stocks and bonds were to industrialists. In the South, as Thomas Morris has illustrated, the courts took the lead and held that mortgages could be created in slave chattels as well as real estate.[34] Statutes also were passed protecting real estate from execution for debts, except after all of a debtor's personalty was depleted. This same protection was afforded to slaves, even after slaves were defined as personalty.[35]

Consequently, Virginia and the other common law states eventually defined slaves to be personal property, as revealed by the 1740 South Carolina code and into the nineteenth century in the Alabama Code of 1852, which states:

> The state or condition of negro or African slavery is established by law in this State, conferring on the master property in and the right to the time, labor, and services of the slave and to enforce obedience on the part of the slave to all his lawful commands.[36]

This definition of slaves fixed the fundamental relationship between the master, slave, and third parties. It stripped the slave of all claims of "human rights" while it established the legal approach to the resolution, at the common law, of claims of the master and third parties to the slave.

The designation of slaves as property therefore furthered the legal-natal alienation of the slave—to borrow Pattersons's phrase. This conception of the slave cut him off from all claims of right by birth and at common law. Thus, the slave possessed no right to own property, to be a party to a contract or a judicial proceeding, or to inherit property.[37] The master could allow the slave to tend a garden, but the slave had no *legal right* to the fruits of his labor; the master owned the slave and all right to the slave's labor.

## Slavery and Race

As noted above, Patterson does not identify racism as one of the fundamental elements of slavery. On a multi-cultural level he is correct; racism was not an essential element of slavery in, for example, ancient Greece and Rome.[38] Racism was, however, a fundamental element of the law of slavery in the U.S. South.

Southern slavery was racial slavery. To use Patterson's construct, race identified who were slaves and fixed their dishonored condition and status for all to see. Historians debate whether the notions of racism so intertwined with the nineteenth century justifications of slavery were in place in the seventeenth century, or whether these attitudes evolved as slavery developed.[39] There is no doubt, however, that beginning with a Maryland Act of 1664 and a Virginia statute of 1670, lifetime slavery was presumed for blacks.[40] Indian slavery was also recognized at law in the colonial period.[41] Nevertheless, in 1691 the Virginia legislature abolished Indian slavery and established that slavery was for blacks only.[42]

In addition, the Southern courts abrogated the common law presumption in favor of liberty when a black person sought to prove his or her rights to freedom. Only if the alleged free person appeared to be visibly black was the burden of proof put upon him to prove he was free. If a person who appeared to be white claimed unjust enslavement, the common law presumption required the proponent of bondage to bear the burden of proof. The Southern courts continued this doctrine in the nineteenth century.[43]

The most celebrated case on this issue is *Hudgins v. Wright*,[44] a Virginia decision of 1806. Various family members sought their freedom and to prevent Hudgins from taking them out of the state. Chancellor George Wythe upheld their claim to freedom and the Court of Appeals, with the primary decision by St. George Tucker, affirmed. But Tucker and Wythe disagreed on the presumption to be applied.

Wythe held that the 1776 Virginia Bill of Rights established for all persons a presumption of freedom. He relied upon the clause declaring that "all men are by nature equally free."[45] Tucker disagreed, stating:

> I do not concur with the Chancellor in his reasoning on the operation of the first clause of the Bill of Rights, which was notoriously framed with a cautious eye to this subject, and was meant to embrace the case of free citizens, or aliens only; and not by a side wind to overturn the rights of property, and give freedom to [slaves].[46]

Tucker upheld the result and the presumption of freedom as it applies to "white persons and native American Indians," but "entirely disapproved" of a presumption of freedom for blacks.[47] Because the plaintiffs traced their lineage to Indian ancestors, and because they appeared to be white or Indian, Wythe's decision could be upheld while his reasoning was disapproved.

Thus, Tucker reaffirmed the racial basis of slavery with the following example:

> Suppose three persons, a black or mulatto man or woman with a flat nose and woolly head; a copper-coloured person with long jetty black, straight hair; and one with a fair complexion, brown hair, not woolly nor inclining thereto, with a prominent Roman nose, were brought together before a Judge upon a writ Habeas Corpus, on the ground of false imprisonment and detention in slavery:. . . . How must a Judge act in such a case?[48]

Tucker wrote that absent evidence to the contrary, persons two and three should be freed. But number one had the burden to prove "his descent, in the maternal line, from a free female ancestor."[49] Such was the racial basis of slavery.

Therefore, racism and the designation of slaves as property are among the essentials of slavery; they helped in the accommodation process that occurred in the seventeenth century. These concepts established the fundamentals of oppression that formed the foundation of the slave codes and slave common law.

## The Law of Slave Crimes: The Epitome of Oppression

The criminal law of slavery in the colonial South provides the final piece in the puzzle of the accommodation process. This law, too, has been discussed elsewhere, but must be considered here as the epitome of the oppression enforced in the colonial slave codes.[50] There were several elements to this law. First, the legislatures declared certain acts to be crimes that only slaves could commit; these same actions would not result in criminal liability for a free person. For just one example, slaves could not leave their plantation without a pass from their master.[51] The law also provided for more severe punishments—including numerous capital offenses—for slaves if they were convicted of crimes that were also crimes for free people.[52]

In addition, the usual common law guarantees of criminal procedural rights were abrogated when slaves were accused of crimes. As noted above, a 1692 Virginia act established special oyer and terminer courts to swiftly hear and decide cases in which slaves were accused of crimes—including capital offenses. This oyer and terminer court system deprived slaves of the right to the protection of a grand jury indictment, a jury trial, and the right to an appeal. The courts consisted of past and present justices of the peace.[53] Thus, as Peter Hoffer states, "The oyer and terminer justices who found facts and ruled on law in slaves' cases were not their peers. The bench was composed of masters: white, free, propertied, and powerful."[54]

Slave courts were also established in Georgia, and North and South Carolina. Those courts were made up of justices of the peace and freeholders. Accordingly, slaves were denied the right to a trial by their peers, as well as the right to a grand jury indictment and an appeal.[55] In all of these courts, slave testimony contrary to whites was prohibited.[56] Fairness to the slave owner was not entirely absent from these procedures, however; a master whose slave was executed was given a right to compensation for the slave taken by the state.[57]

The law also vested whites with the right to use force to correct and discipline slaves outside of the confines of the criminal law. The colonial slave codes created patrols—a form of militia—to police slaves and ensure their obedience outside of the plantations. Patrollers were given the right to be the judge, jury, and executioner when they came upon a slave whom they thought deserved a few stripes from the ever-present whip.[58] A sub-strata of informal "trial" and punishment also existed on the plantation. This is summarized in the often quoted quip of J. D. B. DeBow, who wrote in 1853, "On our estates, we dispense with the whole machinery of public police and public courts of justice. Thus, we try, decide, and execute the sentences of thousands of cases, which in other countries would go to the courts."[59] Therefore, the white man's word was "law" to the slave, whether in the slave courts, in the patroller's whip, or in the master's prerogative.

Upon a superficial analysis, it may appear that the law, by punishing slaves for crimes, recognized slave "humanity" or "moral personality" in ways that were inconsistent with the definition of slaves as property. To the contrary, however:

> [T]he true nature of slave oppression is revealed when one realizes that not only were slaves denied all civil rights, they were also forced to adhere to legal duties beyond those demanded of legal persons. The logic of slave law is thus consistent and rational and presents no dilemma at all; it was the process of stripping slaves of their legal rights (defining them as property) and burdening them with special legal duties (calling them "people"). This is how the fundamental slave relation had to be accommodated within the common law of England, and this resolution was a constant component of the slave regime in the United States South.[60]

Consequently, the criminal law epitomizes the oppression of slavery.

## *Conclusion*

In the colonial era, the Southern legislators accommodated the fundamentals of slavery into the common law. Racism and the definition of slaves as property played parts in this process. Moreover, as William Wiecek states, the colonial statute law was "in a process of development, with legislatures usually acting in response to particular problems perceived as urgent."[61]

The provisions of the slave codes that evolved by the turn of the nineteenth century are well considered elsewhere and are not detailed here. In sum, Wiecek writes:

> . . . [T]he slave codes and session laws of the colonies break down into seven analytical categories, comprising statutes that (1) either prohibited slavery or, contrariwise, sanctioned its elementary characteristics; (2) protected such rights as slaves were accorded; (3) provided for the noncriminal policing of slaves; (4) created a criminal law of slavery, classifying the crimes that slaves might commit and specifying the procedures by which they were to be tried and punished; (5) restricted the behavior of whites in dealing with slaves and free blacks; (6) regulated manumissions; and (7) restricted the behavior of free blacks.[62]

This analysis is helpful in all respects, except Wiecek's category of "slave rights."

He attributes three legal provisions to this category. The first are statutes that allowed slaves, who alleged they were free, to bring an action in court to secure their freedom. Of course, this "right" could not be enforced directly by the slave as plaintiff; instead, a legal guardian had to be appointed to sue on the slave's behalf—as in a case involving a minor or an incompetent. Wiecek also cites statutes that required masters to provide food and clothing for their slaves. Finally, he refers to statutes that allegedly protected slaves from white violence.[63]

It is fundamentally incorrect for one to label any of these legal rules as examples of the recognition of slave rights or concern for slave humanity. Indeed, these legal developments are consistent with the principle that slaves were people without rights. The following chapters will explain why this is so by analyzing the antebellum legal materials in reference to data from outside of the "law box."

# NOTES

1. *See*, Edmund S. Morgan, *American Slavery American Freedom: The Ordeal of Colonial Virginia* 4–24 (New York, 1975); Jordan, *supra* at 48–56; Davis-1966, *supra* at 3–121, 245–247.

2. On the existence of slavery in England until the twelfth century and the demise of villeinage, *see*, 1 Federeck Pollock, Frederic William Maitland, *The History of English Law* 35, 412–432 (Boston, 2d ed. 1898); *see, also*, Jordan, *supra* at 49–51; Robert Cottrol and Raymond Diamond, "Book Review," 56 *Tulane Law Review* 1107, 1115 (1982).

3. Oscar and Mary Handlin, "Origins of the Southern Labor System," 7 *William & Mary Quarterly* 205 (3d series 1950).

4. John A. Scott, "Book Review," *Challenge* 65, 66–67 (May–June 1975).

5. For general discussions of the case of *Somerset v. Stewart*, Lofft 1, 98 Engl. Rep. 499 (K.B. 1772), *see* William M. Wiecek, *The Sources of Antislavery Constitutionalism in America, 1760–1848* 20–39 (Ithaca, 1977); David Brion Davis, *The Problem of Slavery in the Age of Revolution, 1770–1823* 471–501 (Ithica, 1975), Wiecek-1974, *supra*.

6. *See*, David Konig, "'Dale's Laws' and the Non-Common Law Origins of Criminal Justice in Virginia," 26 *American Journal of Legal History* 354 (1982), for a discussion of Konig's views and the arguments to the contrary, *see*, Thomas D. Morris, "'Villeinage . . . as it existed in England, reflects but little light on our subject:' The Problem of Southern Slave Law," 32 *American Journal of Legal History* 95, 99–100 (1988) (hereinafter cited as "Morris-1988").

7. *See*, Higginbotham, *supra* at 20–60; Jordan, *supra* at 44–98, 599–600; T. H. Breen and Stephen Innes, *"Myne Owne Ground" Race and Freedom on Virginia's Eastern Shore, 1640–1676* 19–35 (New York, 1980); Elkins, *supra* at 37–52; *see, also*, Mechal Sobel, *The World They Made Together: Black and White Values in Eighteenth Century Virginia* 11 (Princeton, 1987) (arguing that black and white culture interacted in the early days of slavery).

8. For South Carolina, *see*, Higginbotham, *supra* at 151–215 and E. Sirmans, "The Legal Status of the Slave in South Carolina, 1670–1740," 28 *Journal of Southern History* 462 (1962).

9. *See*, Jonathan L. Alpert, "The Origin of Slavery in the United States—The Maryland Precedent," 14 *American Journal of Legal History* 189 (1970); Higginbotham, *supra* at 19–60; Jordan, *supra* at 71–98; Morgan, *supra* at 295–338; Klein, *supra* at 40–57; William Wiecek, "The Statutory Law of Slavery and Race in the Thirteen Mainland Colonies of British America," 34 *William & Mary Quarterly* 258, 258–264 (1977) (hereinafter cited at "Wiecek"). For a discussion of the development of the criminal law in colonial Virginia, *see*, Philip J. Schwarz, *Twice Condemned: Slaves and the Criminal Laws of Virginia, 1705–1865* 3–34 (Baton Rouge, 1988).

10. Jordan, *supra* at 73; *see, Id.* at 74–81; Higginbotham, *supra* at 21–22.

11. Jordan, *supra* at 73; *see, Id.* at 74–81; Higginbotham, *supra* at 22–34.

12. Jordan, *supra* at 73.

13. The population figures are derived from, *United States Bureau of Census, Historical Statistics of the United States: Colonial Times to 1970* 24–37, 1168 (Washington, 1975) (hereinafter cited as *"Historical Statistics"*) and, *Id., Negro Population in the United States 1790–1915* 57 (New York, reprint ed. 1968) (1918) (hereinafter cites as *"Negro Population"*). For similar, but not identical figures, *see*, Robert McColley, "Slavery in Virginia, 1619–1660: A Reexamination" in *New Perspectives on Race and Slavery in America: Essays in Honor of Kenneth M. Stampp* 11 (Robert H. Abzug and Stephen E. Maizlish, ed., Lexington, 1986).

14. Higginbotham, *supra* at 36, *quoting*, 2 W. Hening, *Statutes at Large of Virginia* 170 (reprint ed. 1969) (1823).

15. *Id., see*, Higginbotham, *supra* at 36; Jordan, *supra* at 82.

16. Higginbotham, *supra* at 36 n. 41 *quoting*, Morgan, *supra* at 312.

17. Higginbotham, *supra* at 39. On the development of slave patrols, *see*, John Anthony Scott, "Segregation: A Fundamental Aspect of Southern Race Relations," 4 *Journal of the Early Republic* 421, 433–440 (1984) (hereinafter cited as "Segregation").

18. 3 Hening, *supra* at 86–88.

19. 2 Hening, *supra* at 170.

20. *See*, Higginbotham, *supra* at 42–44; "Morris-1988," *supra* at 108–121.

21. 2 Hening, *supra* at 260. *See*, Higginbotham, *supra* at 40–47; *see, also*, Note, "Sexual Control in the Slaveholding South: The Implementation of a Racial Caste System," 7 *Harvard Women's Law Journal* 115 (1984), Walter Wadlington, "The Loving Case: Virginia's Anti-Miscegenation Statute in Historical Perspective," 52 *Virginia Law Review* 1189 (1966).

22. 3 Hening, *supra* at 102–103; *see, also*, Schwarz, *supra* at 17, and sources cited at Note 20, *supra*.

23. *See*, Alan Watson, *Roman Slave Law* 90–101 (Baltimore, 1987); Patterson, *supra* at 20–27.
24. *See*, Wiecek, *supra* at 258.
25. Higginbotham, *supra* at 26; Jordan, *supra* at 76–77.
26. *Id.* at 82.
27. *See*, Note 20 *supra* Chapter 2.
28. *See*, Higginbotham, *supra* at 53–55.
29. *Id.* at 51.
30. *Id.* at 52 *quoting*, 3 Hening, *supra* at 333–335.
31. *See, e.g.*, on execution, Thomas D. Morris, "'Society is not marked by punctuality in the payment of debts': The Chattel Mortgages of Slaves" in *Ambivalent Legacy: A Legal History of the South* (Jackson, 1984).
32. *See, Id.* at 151.
33. *See*, R. Cottrol and R. Diamond, "Book Review," 56 *Tulane Law Review* 1107, 1110 (1982) for Virginia, and Wiecek, *supra* at 264 for South Carolina.
34. *See*, Morris, *supra* at 151.
35. *See, e.g., Walden v. Payne*, 2 Va. (2 Wash.) 1, 7 (1794) (Lyons, J.).
36. The Alabama Code of February 2, 1852, §2042, *cited in* 2 Hurd, *supra*, at 152–153; *see, also*, Wiecek, *supra* at 264; and Higginbotham, *supra* at 194 for the South Carolina Code.
37. *See, e.g.*, Stroud, *supra* at 29–53.
38. *See*, Finley, *supra* at 118.
39. *See, e.g.*, Breen and Innes, *supra* at 19–35 discussing the literature; Jordan, *supra* at 91–98; Moore, *supra* at 177–184.
40. *See*, in Virginia, 2 Hening, *supra* at 283 and in Maryland, Alpert, *supra* at 195.
41. *See*, for the South Carolina Act of 1740 and other authority, Stroud, *supra* at 1–9; Wiecek, *supra* at 263–264.
42. *See, Hudgins v. Wright*, 11 Va. (1 Hen. & M.) 133, 137–139 (1806); *see, generally*, 1 Catterall, *supra* at 60–71.
43. *See, Id.*; *see, also*, Wheeler, *supra* at 11–22 and Moore, *supra* at 187–191 citing cases and *see, Gobu v. Gobu*, 1 N.C. (1 Tay.) 164 (1802).
44. 11 Va. (1 Hen. & M.) 133 (1806). *See*, the excellent discussion of this decision in Cover, *supra* at 51–55.
45. *See, Id.* at 43 and 51–52 discussing the constitutional provision and the life and decision of Wythe, and *Id.* at 42–61 reviewing other decisions regarding similar constitutional clauses. *See, also, American Legal History: Cases and Materials* 69 (Kermit L. Hall, *et al.*, eds., New York, 1991) (discussing the intent to exclude slaves from the protection of this clause).
46. *See, Hudgins v. Wright, supra*, 11 Va. (1 Hen. & M.) at 141.
47. *Id.* at 144.
48. *Id.* at 140.
49. *Id.*
50. *See, e.g.*, Philip J. Schwarz, "Forging the Shackles: The Development of Virginia's Criminal Code for Slaves" in *Ambivalent Legacy, supra* at 125–146 reviewing Virginia law. *See, also, e.g.*, Higginbotham, *supra* at 169–198 *passim* discussing the South Carolina codes and *Id.*, at 248-263 *passim* on the Georgia codes; Wiecek, *supra* at 267–277.

51. *See, e.g., Id.* at 272.

52. *See, e.g., Id.* at 273–275. For a general discussion of slave crime, *see*, Daniel Flanigan, *The Criminal Law of Slavery and Freedom 1800–1868* 1–72 (New York, 1987).

53. *See*, 10 *American Legal Records: Criminal Proceedings in Colonial Virginia* xliv–lii (Peter Hoffer, ed., Athens, Ga. 1984).

54. *Id.* at xlix.

55. *See, generally*, on slave trial procedures, *Id.* at xliv–lii; Wiecek, *supra* at 276; *see, also, e.g.*, for North Carolina, Donna J. Spindel, *Crime and Society in North Carolina, 1663–1776* 23–24, 112–115 (Baton Rouge, 1989); Alan D. Watson, "North Carolina Slave Courts, 1715–1785," 60 *No. Carolina Historical Review* 24 (1983); for Georgia, Betty Wood, "'Until He Shall Be Dead, Dead, Dead' The Judicial Treatment of Slaves in Eighteenth Century Georgia," 71 *Georgia Historical Quarterly* 377 (1987); for Maryland, Jeffrey R. Brackett, *The Negro in Maryland: A Study in the Institution of Slavery* 117–122 (New York, reprint ed., 1969) (1889); for South Carolina, Higginbotham, *supra* at 179–181.

56. *See, e.g.*, Wiecek, *supra* at 269.

57. *See, generally, Id.* at 275; *see, also*, Marvin Kay and Lorin Cary, "'The Planters Suffer Little or Nothing': North Carolina Compensations for Executed Slaves, 1748–1772," 40 *Science and Society* 288 (1976).

58. *See, e.g.*, Wiecek, *supra* at 277.

59. *See*, Elkins, *supra* at 56.

60. Fede—1984, *supra* at 314.

61. *See*, Wiecek, *supra* at 259.

62. *Id.* [Footnote omitted].

63. *See, Id.* at 265–267.

## CHAPTER 4

# The Non-Legal Background to Three Trends in Antebellum Slave Law

**SLAVERY** continued to evolve in the antebellum South. After the American Revolution, Southern slave law also developed in three significant ways. First, whites faced increased liability—both civil and criminal—for violent slave abuse. The second trend is exhibited by the enhanced enforcement of procedural safeguards in the criminal trials of slaves. And the third is the seemingly contradictory constriction of the master's right to manumit his slaves, although some jurists resisted the last trend.[1]

These legal changes can be squared with the continued recognition of slaves as property. This reconciliation can be made only if these legal changes are examined in conjunction with the salient social, economic, political, and ideological developments of the antebellum years. As these social changes occurred, the slave owners' perceptions of their individual interest, and the interest of the "master class," became more complex and often shifted. These new attitudes were reflected in the law because judges and legislators came to share the masters' perceptions and because slave masters dominated Southern antebellum law and politics. Therefore, there are important distinctions between colonial and antebellum slave law. Regional differences also became more prominent because the slave economy became more diversified.

This chapter will sketch these non-legal developments as they relate to the legal issues to be analyzed in Chapters 5 to 9. The discussion in this Chapter is obviously only a summary; nevertheless, it provides the necessary background against which the law can be examined. The law of slavery, divorced from its context, is easily misunderstood. Indeed, all legal analysis assumes the existence of a particular non-legal reality; real people with real interests bring about all of the cases and statutes that legal historians read. The purpose of this chapter is to make explicit my assumptions about the context in which antebellum slave law developed.

## *The Pattern of Development of Plantation Slavery*

The socio-economic history of the slave states can be categorized by various stages of development. These stages highlight the types of changes that occurred, and in a given colony or state one necessarily blends into the other because of the uneven patterns of settlement and development. Finally, this approach allows one to distinguish the nature of slavery in the various states to highlight salient differences.

The largest Southern slave colonies passed through four stages of development: the frontier period, slave boom, mature plantation period, and the beginning of the decline of plantation slavery.[2] Settlement began with the frontier period—a time of great hardship—when the colonists were preoccupied with establishing a permanent settlement and with subsistence agriculture. Slaves were few in number; consequently, evidence of the development of slave law is sparse and problematic. During this time of "rough equality" neither large land holding nor complex social structures emerged.[3]

A defined law of slavery began to emerge in the slave boom, which started when a profitable combination of crop, soil, and climate was discovered, and when farmers began to grow this crop for sale. Farms tended to increase in size and the best land became increasingly concentrated in the hands of a few whites who began to emerge as the plantation elite.[4]

Nevertheless, the sharp increase in slave population and the growing size of slave holdings were the most significant changes that occurred during the slave boom, as illustrated by the following table:

## Table 3

**Approximate Percentage of Slave Population**[5]

| Virginia | South Carolina | North Carolina | Georgia |
|---|---|---|---|
| 1680   7% | 1680   17% | 1710   6% | 1740   0% |
| 1700   28 | 1700   43 | 1730   20 | 1750   19 |
| 1750   44 | 1720—1770 over 60 | 1770   35 | 1770   45 |
| 1750—1860 Between 40 & 45 | 1780—1860 Between 40 & 60 | 1780—1860 Between 25 & 34 | 1780—1860 Between 35 & 44 |

Consequently, the primary white social concern shifted from survival to slave control, and the legislators produced the first comprehensive slave codes, which tended to become more severe as slave population increased as a percentage of the population as a whole.[6]

Furthermore, the strictness of the slave codes varied from colony to colony in correlation with the rate of growth and the size of the slave population and in response to slave uprisings. The most comprehensive code was enacted in South Carolina, which was the only colony in which blacks outnumbered whites. It is understandable that "on a rice plantation in South Carolina where within a five-mile radius there were ten slaves for every white person . . . one of the major daily concerns of responsible men was the effective control of the masses of slaves."[7] The percentages also suggest one reason why, even in the nineteenth century, North Carolina, Tennessee, and Kentucky did not adopt comprehensive slave codes; the magnitude of the slave boom and the size of the slave population fell short of the other three states.

As illustrated, slave population growth steadied in all four colonies, indicating the end of he slave boom and the beginning of the mature plantation period. During this period, cash cropping took place on a relatively few large plantations that were owned by a small plantation elite who dominated the society. Both the number of plantations and the size of slave holdings increased as the number of slave holders decreased, causing growing tensions between slave owners and whites who did not own slaves. Even the slave-owing class became stratified between the elite planters and the owners of small slave holdings.[8] Therefore, white social and economic tensions began to compete with slave control as the dominant concern of the elite planter class, causing the elite to entertain the idea that white liability for slave abuse should be increased.[9]

The late eighteenth- and the early nineteenth-century settlements in Mississippi, Alabama, Missouri, Arkansas, and Texas differed in the pattern of development. Generally, the early pioneers were nonslave-owning whites. These settlers were soon replaced by slave owners who moved their slaves into the fertile agricultural areas and established plantation agriculture as the dominant activity. These states did not suffer the trauma evidenced by the slave booms of the original colonies. Instead, slave population grew steadily from the beginning. Cotton had become king, and the slave owners transplanted their mature plantation agriculture and legal system into the fertile soil of these states. But because slave owners removed the white pioneers from the best cotton lands, white class conflicts and tensions were a greater concern in these states in the early years of settlement than had been the case during the slave booms of the original colonies.[10]

Of course, differences in the scale of slavery are relevant. Among the new slave states, Mississippi and Alabama were the leaders in slave population, sizes of slave holdings, and cotton production. In comparison, Tennessee and Kentucky had smaller numbers of slaves.

The latter two states, along with the four original colonies, witnessed the decline of plantation slavery in the nineteenth century. Soil exhaustion caused some planters to move west with their slaves. Moreover, industrial slavery tended to increase toward the end of the antebellum era as slaves were employed in mines, factories, and by railroads.[11]

This changing matrix of socio-economic conditions forms the backdrop over which the patterns of legal change can be superimposed. In addition, white social class structure must be considered.

## *The Pattern of White Social and Economic Class Structure and Conflicts*

As plantation slavery developed, both white and black social and economic class structure became more complex. Whites were eventually divided into five major groups: elite slave owners, farmers with small slave holdings, yeoman farmers who owned no slaves, overseers, and poor whites.[12] Growing interclass tensions were a consequence of class stratification.

A three-way conflict arose among slave owners, poor whites, and slaves. Members of the latter two groups were often openly hostile toward each other, and masters generally shared and tolerated their slaves' antipathy toward poor whites.[13] Consequently, slave masters tried to limit slave and poor white fraternization because they feared their slaves might be "corrupted" by poor whites. Planters even came to favor using the criminal law to control excessive poor white slave abuse because poor whites were often unable to compensate owners for damage done to slave property. Similarly ambivalent feelings arose when a slave was accused of a crime against a poor white. This was especially so in rape cases if the victim was considered as the sort of immoral woman who would "associate" with blacks.

Nevertheless, the master class needed the help of poor whites in the struggle to maintain slave discipline. This was so because a well-organized "state" and urban police force did not exist in the colonial and antebellum South.[14] Thus, although poor whites became the most obvious candidates for criminal liability for violent slave abuse, poor whites always possessed rights to legally abuse and kill slaves without regard to the strict limitations of the common law of crimes. Moreover, poor white power over slaves was channeled and controlled by the laws establishing and regulating the slave patrols, which were organized bands of whites—mostly nonslave owners—who policed the South searching for slaves who were away from their plantations without passes from their masters. Therefore, both the criminal laws and the patrol laws provided the slave-owning minority with a means of physically and politically co-opting poor whites, thereby mitigating white class conflicts while promoting slave control.[15]

A second salient conflict developed between masters and overseers. As plantations grew in size, slave masters increasingly employed overseers to manage slave labor; consequently, overseers were afforded the power and authority to discipline slaves. Nevertheless, the overseer's power to correct slaves often came in conflict with the master's interest in preventing unnecessary damage to slave property and the property's "right" to self-preservation. Furthermore, because many overseers were poor whites, social class hostilities existed between overseers and masters; one planter even called overseers "a worthless set of vagabons."[16] Although masters often circumscribed their overseer's duties, they were seldom satisfied with their overseer's performance. Consequently, overseers were often fired for being either too cruel or too lenient. Economic realities also strained the master and overseer relationship. Overseers received yearly wages that ranged from $100 up to $2,000 for overseers employed on the largest plantations. Therefore, most overseers were often hard pressed to make good an owner's loss if a slave died or was injured while under an overseer's command. Accordingly, although overseers had to be granted much discretion in matters of slave discipline, masters also perceived them to be likely candidates for limited civil and criminal liability in cases of excessive slave mistreatment.[17]

As plantation slavery developed, the master class also became stratified. The most obvious conflict arose when owners hired their slaves out to slave hirers who purchased the slave's labor for a fixed fee and time period. The slave owner's interest in preserving the value of the hired salve clashed with the hirer's interest in getting as much work out of the slave as possible during the period of hire. Therefore, masters and hirers generated much civil litigation to determine liabilities if a slave was injured or killed while hired out. Hirers also became thought of as possible targets of criminal liability if the master's civil remedies proved to be inadequate.[18]

Moreover, the "master's interest" became more difficult to identify as plantation slavery developed because conflicts and tensions surfaced within the slave-owning class. According to statistics cited by U. B. Phillips, the sizes of slave holdings became less uniform as plantation slavery matured and as a select few came to own large numbers of slaves and became the elite in Southern society, a "cut above" the smaller slave owners.[19] Because these planters had so much of their wealth tied up in slaves and the slave economy, they came to believe that individual slave owner's powers to do with his slaves what he wished had to be restrained in instances when the individual's conduct posed such a threat to the slave master class interest that the class detriment outweighed the benefit that the individual master sought to obtain for himself.[20] The courts and legislatures responded to these changing perceptions of the "master class interest" when they limited the individual master's power to kill his slaves in certain cases. Similar concerns motivated restrictions on manumission.

## *The Rising Value of Slaves in the Nineteenth Century*

It was also significant that between 1800 and 1860 the value of slave property increased steadily, contributing to the perception that slaves needed added legal protection. Although slave prices did rise and fall in relation to the average price of cotton, the gap between cotton prices and slave prices widened, as illustrated by the following:

### Table 4
#### The Rising Price of Slaves[21]

| Year | Average Price of Prime Field Hands (Georgia) | Average N.Y. Price of Unpaid Cotton |
|------|----------------------------------------------|-------------------------------------|
| 1800 | $ 450 | 30¢ |
| 1809 | $ 600 | 19¢ |
| 1813 | $ 450 | 12¢ |
| 1818 | $1,000 | 29¢ |
| 1828 | $ 700 | 10¢ |
| 1840 | $ 700 | 9¢ |
| 1851 | $1,050 | 12¢ |
| 1859 | $1,650 | 11¢ |

Thus, U. B. Phillips states that between 1800 and 1860 "there was an advance of some 1,000 or 1,200 percent in the price of slaves as measured in cotton,"[22] and this advance held true when slave prices were measured against the market prices of other commodities.[23] Furthermore, in recent years, economic historians have shown that the increase in slave values was not caused by what Phillips called the salve owner's "irresistible tendency to overvalue and overcapitalize slave labor," but instead represented real increases in slave productivity and profitability.[24]

The increasing value of slaves motivated two changes in law. First, it influenced increased white liability for damaging such property. Second, it caused increased concern for slave owner property rights in slaves tried for serious crimes, especially if the slaves faced capital punishment.

In addition to this quantitative increase in slave values, a qualitative element existed in the South. As stated by Bertram Wyatt-Brown, slaves were not viewed as an ordinary commodity; "Ownership of slaves and land continued to offer a distinction and moral imprimatur beyond their monetary value."[25] Accordingly, slave owners sought to elevate their status by enhancing their slave ownership, and non-slave owners—including professionals—aspired to achieve slave owning status.[26] Consequently, any threat to slave holding, such as the existence of free blacks, was suspect. This climate also encouraged regulation of manumission.

These socio-economic patterns of change, to a large extent, enable us to square the slave crime and manumission cases with each other and with the overall definition of slaves as property. In addition, the politics and ideology of the antebellum South provide the other necessary elements for an understanding of the context of legal change.

## *Slave Owner Political Power: Relating Social and Economic Trends to Legal Change*

Historians who study Southern politics recognize that slave owners dominated Southern pre-Civil War politics.[27] In the legislative and executive branches, this domination is attributed to several factors. These include property owning and wealth requirements for suffrage and legislative district lines that favored plantation regions over frontier or back country areas. In part, as a result of these biases, slave masters also benefited from a disproportionate percentage of slave-owning legislators and an even greater overrepresentation of planters who owned twenty or more slaves. Add to this the fact that slave owners tended to elect non-slave owning legislators who were sympathetic to slave holding interests, and the influence of slave masters in the elected branches of government is not surprising.[28]

Charles Sydnor and others have identified a reform trend in the Southern states in the antebellum years, as the back country and non-slave owning whites sought more political power. Nevertheless, Wooster observes that the plantation elite retained their disproportionate legislative influence throughout the antebellum years. Moreover, he concludes, "My study has shown that the number of property holders and slave holders among Southern office holders was increasing during the 1850–1860 decade."[29] Indeed, the influence of the master class was felt and is evident in legislation relating to slavery.

Nevertheless, the social stratification that occurred in the master class as slavery matured indicates the caution one must exercise when identifying the "master class interest" and its influence in law. At times, the law can be explained as a reconciliation of conflicting currents of interest, especially when the individual master's power over this slave is regulated to further the majority's notion of the overall public good. Professor Genovese explains this point well:

> The slaveholders fell back on a kind of dual power: That which they collectively exercised as a class, even against their own individual impulses, through their effective control of state power; and that which they reserved to themselves as individuals who commanded other human beings in bondage. In general, this duality appears in all systems of class rule, for the collective judgment of the ruling class, coherently organized in the common interest, cannot be expected to coincide with the sum total of the individual interests and judgments of its members[.][30]

Genovese does continue with an argument that the master class decision to regulate the master's individual power was fundamentally contradictory. With this I disagree, because regulation of the property owner's right to harm the public welfare was the only realistic limitation on the slave master's power over his slaves; the legislation of the South did not limit the master's power to kill, starve, and free his slaves out of concern for slave humanity. Legislative limitations were a reflection of perceived public needs and were enacted in furtherance of slavery.

The idea that judicial decisions reflected these same social, economic, and political considerations requires careful analysis. Here, the notion of the relative autonomy of judge-made law must be taken into account. Nevertheless, certain factors do command our attention to the notion that slave owners benefited from sympathetic ears in the judiciary.

Most upper court judges were successful lawyers before their appointments or elections to the bench.[31] This fact raises the issue of the amount of business that Southern lawyers derived, either directly or indirectly, from slavery and slave owners. Thus, one must consider the potential that lawyers who never owned slaves nevertheless were likely to have had a stake in the slavery system.[32] Moreover, many judges were involved in politics before their judicial careers, and we have seen that the surest way to political success for a non-slave owner was identification with the master class. Finally, many influential judges were slave owners.[33] Consequently, the notion that judicial decisions "reflected" the interests of the master class is indeed inescapable. For example, Terrence Kiely concludes that "the pliable system of the common law [was molded by the courts] to fit the needs of a slave and cotton economy, thus, serving as protectors of the interests of the slave holding community."[34] To this one must add that when the master class interests conflicted with the individual freedom of a slave owner, the courts resolved this conflict in a way consistent with the judges' notions of the public good in a slave society.

Consequently, the legislators and judges changed the rules regulating slavery in response to the changing perceptions of the interests of the slave owning class that dominated, directly and/or subtly, the political and legal institutions of the South. Mark Tushnet correctly cautions against the dangers of equating the judicial and legislative processes, and thereby ignoring the "institutional" differences regarding how issues get before the legislatures and courts and how individuals in these institutions perceive their lawmaking and decisions-making roles.[35] These institutional differences are relevant, but they did not cause significant differences in the statutory law as opposed to the common law of slavery.

By saying this, I also do not wish to imply that all Southern judges resolved these conflicts the same way; nor do I assume that the individual personality and philosophy of judges was irrelevant. I do contend that no Southern case I have read can be understood as anti-slavery. Judicial views differed on many salient issues. But the courts disagreed within the confines of a pro-slavery legal system; a judge's prejudices and beliefs influenced his perception of how best to preserve the slave system.[36]

## The Pro-Slavery Ideology and Legal Change

This last point raises the issue of the relevance of the changes that occurred in the social thought of the intellectual leaders of the South. In the antebellum years, the notion that slavery was a positive good earned greater support. George Fitzhugh, Thomas R. Dew, George Frederick Holmes, Henry Hughes, and Chancellor William Harper, among others, argued that slavery was morally just and necessary. The central assumption of this theory was the racial inferiority of blacks, who could never achieve a state of equality with whites because of their supposed racial defects.[37] Fitzhugh, for example, argued that slavery was not just a positive good for the South; he opined that it was superior to industrial capitalism.[38] The unfolding of this ideology is a significant social fact in the antebellum South.[39] And, not surprisingly, this ideology found its way into the antebellum Southern law.

The positive good mentality had its greatest influence in the manumission case law of the nineteenth century. The idea of allowing masters to free the inferior blacks was too much for the positive good racist mind. Therefore, both courts and legislatures restricted the master's freedom to release his slaves from bondage, as the nineteenth century wore on.

The Stephensons illustrate how the pro-slavery ideology influenced the decisions of Justice Joseph Lumpkin, the long-time Justice of the Supreme Court of Georgia. Indeed, Lumpkin thought that slavery was a moral necessity, "since blacks were divinely condemned to eternal service and since only under the tutelage of the superior white race could the black ever achieve the highest degree of civilization."[40]

Lumpkin wrote of the slavery of blacks as a biblical injunction:

> To inculcate care and industry upon the descendants of Ham, is to preach to the idle winds. To be the "servants of servants" is the judicial curse pronounced upon their race. And this Divine decree is unreversible. It will run on parallel with time itself. And heaven and earth shall sooner pass away, than one jot or tittle of it shall abate. Under the superior race and no where else, do they attain to the highest degree of civilization; . . . [God's] ways are higher than ours; and humble submission is our best wisdom, as well as our first duty![41]

Lumpkin called upon history to justify his views:

> Our ancestors settled this State when a province, as a community of white men, professing the christian religion, and possessing an

> equality of rights and privileges. The blacks were introduced into it, as a race of Pagan slaves. The prejudice, if it can be called so, of caste, is unconquerable. It was so at the beginning. It has come down to our day. The suspicion of taint even, sinks the subject of it below the common level. It is to be credited, that parity or rank would be allowed such a race?[42]

This racism fueled Lumpkin's hostility to manumission, which grew throughout his years on the bench:

> To [the free black] there is but little prospect, but a life of poverty, of depression, of ignorance, and of decay. He lives amongst us without motive and without hope. His fancied freedom is all a delusion. All practical men must admit, that the slave who receives the care and protection of a tolerable master, is superior in comfort to the free negro. Generally, society suffers, and the negro suffers by manumission.[43]

Lumpkin felt so strongly about this point that he came to oppose even foreign manumission of slaves.[44]

Lumpkin was not alone in his views of slavery. Indeed, the positive good mentality also influenced the antebellum law of slavery.[45] Nevertheless, the Stephensons are wrong when they write that Lumpkin's ideology was inconsistent, as he did at times recognize slaves as moral agents capable of human-like thought.[46] One must look at the types of cases in which Lumpkin and his brethren were forced to recognize slave humanity, and when one does so the rationale of oppression becomes clear.

It is also worth noting that Lumpkin and the positive good judges did often differ with their less virulent colleagues on points of slave law. But this did not mean that the more "liberal" judges were antislavery. The judicial philosophy of the South was pro-slavery. Judges disagreed at times as to the best way to advance the institution through law. They did not differ, however, as to the need to uphold that institution.

Moreover, it is significant that Lumpkin freely invokes the notion of humanity to the slave in his pro-slavery opinions. To Lumpkin, the oppression of slavery was humane to the slave and was dictated by the slave's racial inferiority. Therefore, the harsh results Lumpkin reached were converted, through his ideological filter, to appear as the picture of benevolence. Chapter 12 explains further how the notion of slave humanity became a reification—a structure of thought designed to promote and to mask the oppression of slavery. Lumpkin's opinions are prime examples of how the concepts of humanity and right came to justify the total despotism of slavery by making this state of affairs seem natural, good, and necessary.

## *Conclusion*

With these tools of analysis, it is possible to examine the law that developed in the nineteenth century regarding slave abuse, slave crime, manumission, and the commercial law of slavery. We begin with the former.

## NOTES

1. Rose, *supra* at 23–25. These trends present the pro-slavery and Marxist writers with their best ammunition to challenge the abolitionists' view. For example, Thomas Cobb wrote in 1858 that the "personal security of the slave" became "*quasi* a right belonging to the slave as a person." Cobb cites nineteenth century statutes that he said did "much" to "relieve the slave" from the "absolute dominion" of the master, especially with regard to the "first great right of personal security." Cobb, *supra* at 84, 93 [footnotes omitted]. U. B. Phillips agrees, and he adds that when the statutes failed to adequately protect slaves, "the courts felt themselves free to remedy the defect." Phillips, *supra* at 509; *see, also,* "Trial Rights," *supra* at 622–627; "Fairness," *supra* at 67–78; "Equitable past?," *supra*, and "Negro Rights," *supra* at 170–172. *Compare*, Howington, *supra* at 71–97 and Flanigan, *supra* at 145–188, *with*, Tushnet, *supra* at 73–76, 90–121. For Oakes, *see*, Oakes-1990, *supra* at 155–166. Similarly, Nash finds that, in the nineteenth century, "Surprisingly . . ., procedural fairness was almost always demanded by appellate judges in the trials of blacks." *See*, "Fairness," *supra* at 79. For Nash's writings on this point, *see*, *Id*. at 79–89; "Trial Rights," *supra* at 628–629; "Negro Rights," *supra* at 166–170. Cobb, Arthur Howington, Mark Tushnet, and Daniel Flanigan also examine slave procedural "rights." *See*, Cobb, *supra* at 268–269 and *Id*. at 268–277 for Cobb's views on slave trials; *see, also,* Howington, *supra* at 98–216; *compare*, Tushnet, *supra* at 121–139, with Flanigan, *supra* at 73–144. Finally, on manumission, Nash and Howington praise the liberality and humanity some Southern courts exhibited in slave suits for freedom. Nash cites pro-manumission cases, which he ascribes to the differing commitment among judges toward slavery; implying that some favored slave rights to liberty. *See*, "Reason of Slavery," *supra* at 98–184; "Trial Rights," *supra* at 629–637; "Negro Rights," *supra* at 154–166, 172–177. Howington, referring to the Tennessee courts, cites judicial recognition of slave humanity as evidence in favor of Arnold Sio's critique of the anti-slavery view. *See*, "Howington-1975," *supra* at 262–263, *citing*, Sio, *supra*; *see*, *Id*. and Howington, *supra* at 1–70. *Compare*, Tushnet, *supra* at 188–228, *with*, Cobb, *supra* at 245–251. The reach of the pro-slavery critique is revealed by the discussions of slavery written by Lawrence Friedman and Kermit Hall in their two

excellent studies of law in American history. Friedman, in the end, adopts the anti-slavery view regarding the oppressive nature of slave law. Yet he states, "some slave rights were written into law." *See*, Lawrence M. Friedman, *A History of American Law* 225 (New York, 2d ed. 1985); *see, also, Id.* at 85–89, 218–229. Similarly, Hall emphasizes how the pro-slavery mentality, the "indwelling character of slave law," and the common law tradition "provided a mask that concealed" the judge's and slave's humanity. Nevertheless, Hall states that, at times the law protected slaves. He cautions, however, that this was done in a way that did not endanger "the master's property rights or the South's economy or system of racial control. Judges were able, as a result, to reconcile fairness for slaves (and even a degree of legal equality) with a system of perpetual racial bondage." Hall does not explain the fundamental nature of this reconciliation, however. *See*, Kermit L. Hall, *The Magic Mirror: Law in American History* 134 (New York, 1989).

2. *See, generally*, Ulrich B. Phillips, *The Slave Economy of the Old South: Selected Essays in Economic and Social History* (Baton Rouge, E. Genovese, ed. 1968) (hereinafter cited as *Slave Economy*); 1 Lewis C. Gray, *History of Agriculture in the Southern United States to 1860* 312–341, 437–462 (Washington, D.C., reprint ed., 1958) (1932).

3. *See, Slave Economy, supra* at 6, 100; 1 Samuel E. Morrison, *The Oxford History of the American People* 87 (New York, 1972); *see, also*, John Anthony Scott, *Hard Trials on My Way: Slavery and the Struggle Against It 1800–1860* 26–28 (New York, 1974); Morgan, *supra* at 70–211.

4. *See*, Morgan *supra* at 215–292; *Slave Economy, supra* at 108–114. In Virginia the "magic" crop—tobacco—did not require large slave holdings; thus, the beginnings of plantation agriculture predated the slave boom. Nevertheless, slave labor became widely employed by the end of the seventeenth century when the tobacco boom "took off." *See, e.g.*, Gray, *supra* at 213–34, 312–21. North Carolina also had some small tobacco plantations in the eighteenth century. *See, Id.* at 42–48. But the plantations and slave booms in these states were dwarfted by those in Georgia and South Carolina where rice, indigo, and finally cotton could be successfully grown. *See, Id.* at 322–29; *Slave Economy, supra* at 12–16; *see, generally*, Peter Wood, *Black Majority: Negroes in Colonial South Carolina from 1670 Through the Stono Rebellion* 2–62 (New York, 1974).

5. *See, Historical Statistics, supra* at 24–37, 1168; *Negro Statistics, supra* at 576; *compare, e.g.*, Charles Sydnor, *Slavery in Mississippi* 186–187 (Gloucestoer, Mass., repint ed. 1965) (1933) (hereinafter cited as "*Slavery in Mississippi*") regarding settlement in the Mississippi and Alabama region, *with*, Wood, *supra* at 131–166 discussing population growth in South Carolina.

6. Winthrop Jordon cites public expressions of this fear of slave revolt in Virginia and South Carolina during the slave boom years. *See*, Jordan, *supra* at 101–13. Although this fear was paramount, it was not the only social concern of the emerging elite. Thus, there was also evidence of interclass tensions between the plantation elite and poor whites. *See*, in Virginia, Bacon's Rebellion of 1675, Morrison, *supra* at 161–166, and in South Carolina tensions and rebellion involving back country white "tar heels" and the plantation elite, *Id.* at 238, Jordan, *supra* at 110 n. 17.

7. *Id.* at 103. Jordan correctly states that the influence of demographics can be overestimated. *See, Id.* at 101. For example, many early settlers in South Carolina came from Barbados and thus copied from the Barbadian slave code that they-unlike settlers of other colonies-had at hand to use as a means of coping with the growing number of slaves. *See, Id.* at 85. Nevertheless, there is an obvious relationship between the strictness of slave codes and the rate of slave population growth; Virginia, South Carolina, and Georgia all passed their most comprehensive slave codes during the colonial slave booms. Slave population growth was but one of the relevant social and economic factors that influenced the origin of slave law and its subsequent development.

8. *See*, Stampp, *supra* at 29–33; *Slave Economy, supra* at 97, 108–114; and Bertram Wyatt-Brown, *Southern Honor: Ethics and Behavior in the Old South* 376–377 (New York, 1982).

9. The concern about slave revolts was ever present in the South; it did not disappear when slave population growth steadied as evidenced by the furor that rippled throughout the South over the 1831 Nat Turner Rebellion in Virginia and Denmark Vesey's South Carolina revolt of 1822. *See*, Scott, *supra* at 72–86; Stampp, *supra* at 132–40. Rather, the courts and legislatures merely began to take other interests into account in redefining the line between legitimized violence and criminal liability. Important differences remained, however, among the four Southern colonies after they became states. South Carolina continued to have the highest percentage of slave population, joining Georgia as a cotton-producing state. *See, e.g.*, A. Meier & E. Rudwick, *From Plantation to Ghetto* 54–55 (New York, 3d ed. 1976). Masters in these states were more likely to be concerned with controlling these slaves than the masters of Virginia and North Carolina, where the plantation economies entered a decline and began a fourth stage of economic development. *See, e.g., Slave Economy, supra* at 18–20.

10. *See*, Phillips, *supra* at 171-82; Scott, *supra* at 26–34; *Slave Economy, supra* at 97. *See, also*, Oakes-1990, *supra* at 104–108.

11. Ronald L. Lewis, *Coal, Iron & Slaves: Industrial Slavery in Maryland and Virginia, 1715–1865* (Westport, Ct., 1979); Robert S. Starobin, *Industrial Slavery in the Old South* (New York, 1970).

12. *See*, Scott, *supra* at 28–34; Stampp, *supra* at 29.

13. *See, e.g.*, Stowe, *supra* at 365–80; Jordan, *supra* at 110 n. 17; Stampp, *supra* at 151, 380; Genovese, *supra* at 22–23.

14. *See, e.g.*, Stampp, *supra* at 425–29.

15. *See*, Hindus, *supra* at xix; Genovese, *supra* at 43–44; Scott, *supra* at 122–24; Stampp, *supra* at 214–15; "Segregation," *supra* at 433–440. In addition, the planter class co-opted slaves, known as drivers or foremen, who also became instrumentalities for controlling the masses of slaves. *See*, Genovese, *supra* at 365–88; Stampp, *supra* at 40–41, 151–52.

16. *See, Id.* at 40, *see also*, William C. Scarborough, *The Overseer: Plantation Management in the Old South* 102–137 (Baton Rouge, 1966).

17. *See, Id.* at 29, 93–101, *see also*, Genovese, *supra* at 12–15; Stampp, *supra* at 38–43, 82–83, 106–109, 180–185.

18. *See,* Genovese, *supra* at 390–392; Stampp, *supra* at 67–72, 84, 185, 204, 318.
19. *See, Slave Economy, supra* at 108–16.
20. *See,* Genovese, *supra* at 47.
21. This table is a condensed version of the chart compiled by Phillips. *See, Slave Economy, supra* at 127. This pattern is also exhibited on Phillips' more extensive chart covering other states. *See,* Phillips, *supra* facing Page 370; *see, also,* Elkins, *supra* at 211 n. 126 and the authorites cited therein. These increasing slave prices were attributed to the closing of legal foreign slave trade in 1808, and the beginning of the cotton boom that followed the invention of the cotton gin. *See, e.g., Slave Economy, supra* at 123–24.
22. *See, Id.* at 126.
23. *See,* Phillips, *supra* at 385–386.
24. *Compare, Slave Economy, supra* at 128, Gavin Wright, "Prosperity, Progress and American Slavery," in *Reckoning with Slavery: A Critical Study in the Quantitative History of American Negro Slavery* 302–336 (New York, 1976) (hereinafter *"Reckoning with Slavery"*), *with,* Alfred H. Conrad and John R. Meyer, "The Economics of Slavery in the Ante-Bellum South," 66 *Journal of Pol. Econ.* 95, 115-119 (1958).
25. Wyatt-Brown, *supra* at 73.
26. *See,* James Oakes, *The Ruling Race: A History of American Slaveholders* 51–67, 71–72, and 199–200 (New York, 1982).
27. For the colonial period, *see, e.g.,* Higginbotham, *supra passim*; Elkins, *supra* at 37–52; Clement Eaton, *A History of the Old South: The Emergence of a Reluctant Nation* 52–54 (New York, 3d ed. 1975). For the antebellum years, *see, e.g.,* Eugene Genovese, *The Political Economy of Slavery: Studies in the Economy and Society of the Slave South* 28 (New York, 1961); Charles Sydnor, *The Development of Southern Sectionalism 1819–1848* 52, 293 (Baton Rouge, 1966) (1948) (hereainfter "Sydnor").
28. Ralph A. Wooster, *Politicians, Planters, and Plain Folk: Courthouse and Statehouse in the Upper South, 1850–1860* 3–21, 33–42, 119–128, 163–172 (Knoxville, Tenn., 1975); Eaton, *supra* at 65–66; Sydnor, *supra* at 47–49; *Slavery in Mississippi, supra* at 247–248.
29. *See,* Wooster, *supra* at 127–129; Sydnor, *supra* at 275–293.
30. Genovese, *supra* at 46–47.
31. *See,* Wooster, *supra* at 93–96.
32. *Compare,* Horwitz, *supra* at 140–159 for a discussion of the relationship between Northern lawyers and emerging commerical and industrial intersts.
33. *See,* Wooster, *supra* at 93–96.
34. *See,* Kiely, *supra* at 894.
35. *See,* Mark Tushnet, "Book Review," 45 *University of Chiago Law Review* 906, 912–916 (1978) (criticizing Judge Higginbotham's work).
36. A. E. Keir Nash is the slave-law scholar who is most interested in the individual biographies of the antebellum Southern judges, and who stresses the importance of the degree to which judges were "antislavery" and "unionist" or "pro-slavery" and "separatist." *See, generally, Reason of Slavery, supra* at 89. I do not suggest that the individual ideas and prejudices of judges are

irrelevant, but it does not make sense to label judges as antislavery or proslavery. They all were pro-slavery.

37. *See, generally, e.g.,* Elkins, *supra* at 206–222 and the sources cited therein for a general discussion; *see, also* Robert A. Garson, "Proslavery as Political Theory: The Examples of John C. Calhoun and George Fitzhugh," 84 *So. Atlantic Quarterly* 84 (1985).

38. *See, e.g.,* George Fitzhugh, *Cannibals All! or Slaves Without Masters, passim* (Cambridge, reprint ed. 1960) (Richmond, 1857).

39. *See, e.g.,* Eugene Genovese, *The World the Slaveholders Made: Two Essays in Interpretation* 117–224 (Vintage, ed., New York, 1969).

40. *See,* Mason W. Stephenson and D. Grier Stephenson, Jr., "'To Protect and Defend': Joseph Henry Lumpkin, The Supreme Court of Georgia, and Slavery," 25 *Emory Law Journal* 579, 583 (1976).

41. *American Colonization Society v. Gartrell,* 23 Ga. 448, 464–465 (1857).

42. *Bryan v. Walton,* 14 Ga. 185, 202 (1853).

43. *Id.* at 205–206.

44. *See,* Stephenson, *supra* at 597–607.

45. *Compare, e.g.,* Cobb, *supra* at ccxii to ccxxi, comparing the overall benefits of slavery and noting evils of the system.

46. *See,* Stephenson, *supra* at 584–586.

## Chapter 5

# The Changing Scope of White Liability for Slave Killing

**The task** of studying legal and non-legal change in tandem is best begun with the changing law of legitimized violence. As noted in Chapter 3, the colonial slave codes legalized white violence against slaves, even though that violence would have resulted in criminal liability at common law. The late eighteenth century and early nineteenth century law increased the scope of white civil and criminal liability for slave abuse. Nevertheless, even this law had a legitimizing effect; it continued to decriminalize white violence that would have been criminal at common law, to the extent that the violence at issue was thought to be a "necessary" or "ordinary" incident of slavery.

This calculation of the relevant interests was consistent with the definition of slaves as property and was made without any real regard to slave humanity or rights, although it was often cloaked in the garb of such *dicta*.[1] This is made clear by the fact that slaves were never given the level of protection that the common law of crimes applied to the rights to personal safety that people enjoyed. White liability for slave abuse contracted and expanded without regard to slave rights; instead, this legal change was caused by changing perceptions of the following factors: The need to control slaves, class conflicts among whites, the value of slave property, slave master political power, and the ideology of slave owners.

In fact, the cases and statues concerning white violence directed at slaves should not be thought of as crimes against the person of the slave. Rather, these offenses are best considered as crimes against the most valuable property of the slave owner. This becomes clear when the degrees of criminality are compared over time and with reference to the class identity of the white defendant. We begin with slave homicide statutes.

## Colonial Statutes That Legitimized Slave Killings

A white person's right to legally kill a slave contracted and expanded in conjunction with the patterns of social and economic development. One legal principle remained constant, however; the master's right to kill exceeded the right of a stranger to the slave. The broadest decriminalization of slave killing occurred in the early colonial statutes adopted in South Carolina, Georgia, North Carolina, and Virginia.

As described in Chapters 3 and 4, Virginia, South Carolina, and Georgia experienced periods of rapid growth in the slave population, as a proportion of the total population, in the early colonial years. During these growth spurts, the need for slave control was obviously thought to be paramount. Accordingly, the colonial legislatures preempted the common law crime of murder—the malicious killing of another human being[2]—when a slave was the victim. This was so whether the killer was the slave's owner or was a stranger to the slave. These statutes nevertheless vested masters with a greater right to kill their slaves than mere strangers enjoyed.

For example, the South Carolina slave codes enacted from 1712 through 1740 required willful and malicious slave killers to merely pay a fine if convicted, although slave killers were also required to compensate the owner for the full monetary value of the "murdered" slave. Therefore, a master faced a lesser penalty than non-owners were required to pay. If the killer was a white servant, the 1712 code provided for a prison term of three months, with four years of service for the slave's owner to enable the owner to recover his loss. The 1740 code fixed a £700 fine for malicious killings and £350 for killings "on a sudden heat or passion, or by undue correction[.]" This code afforded masters accused of slave homicide a right to exculpate themselves on their own oath, a privilege that continued even after malicious slave killing became a felony in South Carolina. These codes also decriminalized slave killings if the slave was at large without a pass and refused to submit to the examination of any white person.[3]

A 1755 Georgia act was to the same effect. For the first offense the killer was required to pay the owner's loss. Only on a second conviction did the defendant face death and forfeiture of wealth sufficient to compensate the slave's owner. But a willful murder conviction require the oath of two witnesses.[4] These acts made it clear that the killing of a slave was not punished according to the common law. These statutes also indicate that the colonists thought that the killing of a slave might otherwise be considered murder; consequently, the legislation served to reduce slave killing to a less serious crime befitting the slave's status as property.

A statute to achieve this end was not adopted in North Carolina until 1774. That act may, in part, have been caused by the fact that slave population grew rapidly in the mid-1700s. It may also have been a response to North Carolina's Chief Justice Martin Howard's 1771 grand jury charge that offered the opinion that slave killing could be common law murder.

Howard justified this view with the common law definition of murder—the unlawful killing of "any reasonable creature, being under the King's peace."[5] Howard thought that this definition applied to slaves. He was moved to publish his views in response to a grand jury's refusal to indict a white man for the murder of a slave.[6] Howard based his opinion on calls to humanity, as well as the recognition that unnecessary violence directed at slaves could provoke slave disquiet and even a revolt. The Chief Justice explained his fears as follows:

> The number of slaves in this country is already very great and daily increasing; they are kept in the most stupid ignorance—they are incapable of doing any thing from a motive of virtue, and are retained in subjection by the principle of Fear alone. What effect time may produce from these circumstance is a question that may merit some serious consideration. I will venture to say, that nothing will so effectually preserve us from the horrors of a BELLUM SERVILE, or rebellion of slaves, as a mild, humane and gentle treatment of them.
>
> Cruelty is ever bad policy, and history will shew [sic] us, that when men are allowed to share the common rights of mankind, they will in times of difficulty adhere to their superiors or masters with fidelity and perseverance; but on the other hand, when they are degraded from every right of human nature, they will seize the first occasion to revenge all past injuries, and oppressions.
>
> If you should publish to your slaves, that their loss of liberty includes the loss of life, whenever the humour or caprice of a white man should be pleased to take it away from them—depressed as they are in spirits I question if they could bear such an addition to their burden. We should, therefore, be careful not to make them desperate, lest we ourselves should become the first sacrifices to the maxims of our own cruelty.[7]

Legislative action followed unsuccessfully in 1773, the year after this charge was published.

In 1774, however, the North Carolina General Assembly passed the following act:

An Act to prevent the willful and malicious killing of Slaves.

I. WHEREAS some Doubts have arisen with Respect to the Punishment proper to be inflicted upon such as have been guilty of wilfully and maliciously killing Slaves:

II. BE it therefore enacted by the Governor, Council, and Assembly, and by the Authority of the same, That from and after the First Day of May next, if any Person shall be guilty of wilfully and maliciously killing a Slave, so that, if he had in the same Manner killed a Freeman, he would by the Laws of the Realm be held and deemed guilty of Murder, that then and in that Case such Offender shall, upon due and legal Conviction thereof, in the Superior Court of the District where such Offence shall happen, or have been committed, suffer Twelve Months Imprisonment: And upon a second Conviction thereof, shall be adjudged guilty of Murder, and shall suffer Death, without Benefit of Clergy.

III. AND be it further enacted by the Authority aforesaid, That if the Slave so wilfully and maliciously killed, shall be the Property of another, and not of the Offender, he shall, on the first Conviction thereof, pay the owner thereof such Sum as shall be the Value of the said Slave, to be assessed by the Inferior court of the County where such Slave was killed, and shall stand committed to the Gaol of the District where such Conviction shall happen, until he shall satisfy and pay the same Sum so assessed.

IV. PROVIDED always, That this Act shall not extend to the Person killing any Slave outlawed by Virtue of any Act of Assembly in this Province, or to any Slave in the Act of Resistance to his lawful Owner or Master, or to any Slave dying under moderate Correction.[8]

The latter clause referred to a 1741 act that legitimized slave homicides that occurred "in the dispersing of any unlawful Assemblies of rebel Slaves or Conspirators" or in the apprehensions of runaway or outlawed slaves. A slave would be declared an outlaw if he ran away from his master, concealed himself, and killed a hog or cattle for sustenance. There is evidence that outlawry continued in North Carolina even into the 1850s.[9]

This statute, therefore, protected the master's prerogatives as well as the stranger's right to kill slaves when the public interest so required. Obviously, the North Carolina Assembly resolved the doubts about the question raised by Chief Justice Howard by decriminalizing common law slave murder the creating a new crime designed to protect the master's property and his right to correct his slaves, while preserving the public peace. The Virginia legislature adopted a different approach to the issue of slave murder, however.

No Virginia statute precluded common law murder indictments for malicious slave killing. Consequently, the Virginia lawmakers always recognized the possibility of slave murder as a capital crime.

The legislators did, nevertheless, modify the common law to legitimize certain necessary killings that would have been murder at common law.

It must be recalled that three key principles of law were established in the seventeenth-century Virginia statutes. First, a 1669 act exculpated all killings by masters that were caused by ordinary correction of a slave. Second, a 1680 act justified slave killings when a slave lifted up his hand in resistance to any white. Third, a 1691 statute legalized the killing of runaway slaves.[10] The 1705 slave code repeated these three postulates.[11] The codes of 1723 and 1748 added the following provisions:

> ... [W]here any slave shall happen to die, by reason of any stroke, or blow given, during his, or her correction, by his, or her owner, or by reason of any accidental blow whatsoever, given by such owner, no person concerned in such correction, or accidental homicide, shall be liable to any prosecution, or punishment for the same, unless upon examination before the county court, it shall be proved, by the oath of at least one lawful and credible witness, that such slave was killed wilfully, or maliciously, or designedly; and no person indicted for the murder of a slave, and upon trial found guilty of manslaughter only, shall incur any forfeiture, or punishment, for such offence, or misfortune.[12]

This statute thus gave masters enhanced procedural rights and decriminalized all slave killings that would have been common law manslaughter.

Indeed, the other colonial legislatures also legitimized or reduced the penalties for the crime of manslaughter—the killing of a human being in the "heat of passion"[13]—when slaves were the victims. The Virginia codes of 1723 and 1748 explicitly excused white strangers from criminal liability in cases of slave killings that would have been common law manslaughter, a result achieved by judge-made law in North Carolina.[14] Furthermore, the South Carolina and Georgia codes punished non-malicious slave killers with only a fine upon conviction.[15]

The statutes of these colonies also contained provisions that legitimized white slave killings if the victims committed offenses such as running away from their masters.[16] For example, the 1740 South Carolina code stated:

> If any slave who shall be out of the house or plantation where such slave shall live . . . or without some white person in the company with such slave, shall refuse to submit to undergo the examination of any white person, it shall be lawful for any such white person to pursue, apprehend, and moderately correct such slave; and if such slave shall assault and strike such white person, such slave may be lawfully killed.[17]

Indeed, during the colonial years, a slave's life did not have the benefit of the protection that the common law of crimes afforded "real people's" lives. Instead, slaves received an inferior level of protection befitting their status as valuable, and potentially dangerous property, in these Southern colonies. Moreover, Tennessee inherited the North Carolina approach when it became a territory in 1790 and a state in 1796.[18] Such was the law of slave homicide when the Southern colonies became states.

## *The Expansion of White Liability for Slave Killing and the Protection of the Master's Prerogatives*

After 1788 and through the 1790s, the legislators of the Southern states provided more severe punishments for slave killers, including the death penalty for malicious destruction of slave property. This trend began with a 1788 Virginia statute. That act repealed the portion of the 1748 code that is quoted above.[19] Accordingly, the special procedural benefits were taken away from slave masters accused of slave homicide, and the manslaughter exculpation was eliminated. This statute may have been influence by *Thomas Sorrell's Case*,[20] a 1786 prosecution of a hirer for slave murder.

Sorrell sought the pre-indictment review provided for by the 1748 code. It was held that that right belonged to masters only. Sorrell was then indicted, but was found not guilty of slave murder. The legislators may have seen this case as an indication that juries would be reluctant to find slave killers guilty of murder, and the crime of manslaughter was needed to protect slave property. After 1788, the legislature adopted various codes that defined first degree murder to include killings caused by willful, malicious, and excessive whipping.[21]

North Carolina followed with a 1791 act that repealed the 1774 statute:

> III. And whereas by another act of Assembly passed in the year 1774, the killing of a slave, however wanton, cruel and deliberate, is only punishable in the first instance by imprisonment and paying the value thereof to the owner; which distinction of criminality between the murder of a white person and of one who is equally an human creature, but merely of a different complexion [sic], is disgraceful to humanity and degrading in the highest degree to the laws and principles of a free, christian and enlightened country: Be it enacted by the authority aforesaid, That if any person shall hereafter be guilty of wilfully and maliciously killing a slave, such offender

shall upon the first conviction therefore be adjudged guilty of murder, and shall suffer the same punishment as if he had killed a free man; any law, usage or custom to the contrary notwithstanding. Provided always, That this act shall not extend to any person killing a slave outlawed by virtue of any act of Assembly of this state, or to any slave in the act of resistance to his lawful owner or master, or to any slave dying under moderate correction.[22]

This act thus preserved the master's right to kill, as established by the last proviso of the 1774 statute, but sought to equate malicious slave killing with murder. Ironically, in 1801, the North Carolina Conference Court held that the laudable sentiments expressed in the preamble of this act were inadmissible in the interpretation of its purposes. Therefore, this statute was held to be too vague to be enforced.[23] It was not until 1817 that the legislature passed another statute that stated, "the offense of Killing a Slave shall . . . be . . . considered homicide, and shall partake of the same degree of guilt when accompanied with the like circumstances that homicide now does at common law." The courts did not, however, give effect to the plain meaning of this act.[24]

Acts that were similar to the 1791 North Carolina law were adopted in Georgia and Tennessee in 1799. These statutes, in sum, made malicious slave killing a capital crime. They also decriminalized killings by masters in cases of slave "insurrection" or "resistance," as well as deaths that resulted from the master's "moderate correction" of the slave.[25] Therefore, these statutes had a two-fold effect; they were inculpatory acts as to strangers who killed slaves, but were exculpatory as to slave owners.

This raises, then, the difficult question of the motives for these statutes. Were the legislators concerned about slave "humanity" and thus upholding the ideals of the recent revolution? Or did the lawmakers adopt these statutes to better protect slave property from non-masters who killed slaves without cause and thereby threatened the master's interest in order and property?

The latter is the view that is supported by the evidence. This legal change cannot be understood as a spontaneous outpouring of concern for slave "humanity" because it is unclear why it would take over one hundred years for these feelings to surface. Nor is it clear why a concern for slave rights would motivate the preservation of the master's right to correct and kill his slaves. Although the Virginia, North Carolina, Tennessee, and Georgia legislators enacted these statutes before the widespread publication of case law reports that might illuminate the relevant concerns of the lawmakers, the writings of Douglas Hay provide a salient analogy.

According to Hay:

> [T]he criminal law is as much concerned with authority as it is with property. For wealth does not exist outside a social context, theft is given definition only within a set of social relations, and the connections between property, power and authority are close and crucial. The criminal law was critically important in maintaining bonds of obedience and deference, in legitimizing the status quo, in constantly recreating the structure of authority which arose from property and in turn protected its interests.[26]

Hay wrote about the new capital crimes created in eighteenth century England. He opined that these crimes, such as forgery, struck at the heart of the emerging commercial economy and were perceived by the elite as a threat to salient class interests. Similarly, wanton poor writes slave killers posed a serious threat to both the individual economic interests of slave owners as well as the master class interest in maintaining the power and authority of the slave-owning regime. Therefore, slave masters supported capital punishment for malicious slave killers, and this perception was shared by the legislators who changed the law accordingly.

Consequently, in the colonial years, the "bonds of obedience and deference" were imposed upon slaves, but as social change occurred, whites were subjected to increasing liability for damaging slave property values and challenging the "structure of authority" that arose from the slave property relationship. Nevertheless, the law always "legitimized the status quo" of the white power over slaves by legalizing as much white violence as was thought to be "necessary," although this violence would have resulted in criminal liability had the victim been white.

The analogy with Hay's thesis is natural because the criminal law of the Southern states in the Revolutionary years resembled the eighteenth century English model described by Hay. Capital punishment was widespread in the statute books, but the courts and the governors had discretion to employ concepts of mercy and justice to temper excesses and preserve the law's majesty.[27] All the while, however, the criminal law protected the power and authority of the master class.

It must be remembered that when a white stranger maliciously killed a slave, he caused a great economic loss to the owner. This was also true in cases of slave stealing. The cases and statutes enforcing punishments for the theft of slaves are discussed in detail in Chapter 10. It is worth noting here, however, that the Tennessee legislature made slave killing a capital offense in 1799, the same year that the death penalty was applied to slave stealing. In South Carolina, moreover, slave theft was declared a capital offense 67 years before the 1821 statute was passed providing the death penalty for malicious slave killers.[28] Clearly, slave stealing and wanton slave murder were perceived as serious threats to property and to the social order. Slave killing involved a more delicate balance of interests than slave stealing. This was because of the perceived need for slave control. Consequently, capital punishment was applied to slave killings with concern for the need to preserve slave discipline. The carefully limited way that slave killing was made a capital crime indicates that the increased punishment for slave killers was consistent with the definition of slaves as property.

Furthermore, the South Carolina case law verifies this hypothesis. Until 1821, the South Carolina codes punished malicious slave killers with fines. As the plantation economy matured, whites were prosecuted under these provisions.[29] By the late 1810s, however, slave owners began to think that the codes inadequately protected their slaves from poor white slave killers, and they therefore sought relief in the courts. In an 1818 civil case, the defendant shot and killed the plaintiff's slave after he saw the slave run away from the plaintiff's overseer. The appellate court upheld a money judgment that was awarded to the plaintiff, stating:

> [I]t can never be considered politic to subject a valuable species of property to the disposal of any unprincipled, unfeeling man in society; nor is it less impolitic with regard to the slaves themselves—for where there is no protection to life, there is no incitement to action.[30]

Another 1818 decision upheld a similar verdict. The court recognized that two interests conflicted in these cases: The requirement that slaves be controlled and the need to protect slaves from whites who were the "violent" and "unthinking" people of the community.[31] These two cases show that judges shared the slave owners' concern about slave killing.

Moreover, from 1806 until 1820, there were attempts to persuade the General Assembly to increase the punishment provisions of the 1740 code. H. M. Henry notes that in June 1806, a Charleston newspaper called for such legislation, referring to the fact "that the penalty for killing a negro was less than for stealing him."[32] In the fall of that year, a legislator gave notice that he intended to introduce a bill to increase the penalty for slave killing. In fact, a bill was proposed, but it was not enacted. Henry also cites two grand jury presentments that called for legislative action because the jurors believed that the existing laws intended to prevent slave murder were inadequate. Henry also quotes a trial jury verdict that recommended mercy for a convicted slave stealer; the jury reached its decision because the crime of slave killing did not carry the death penalty, while slave stealing was a capital offense.[33]

In 1820, the governor referred to the inadequate penalty for slave killing in his annual message. It was not until 1821, however, that the legislature responded. Henry suggests that a well known killing by a master of a runaway slave caused the legislature to act. The statute enacted applied the death penalty to willful, malicious, and deliberate slave killers. The statute also provided for a $500 fine and up to six month's imprisonment for those convicted of killing slaves "on a sudden heat and passion." In 1826, the court of Appeals held that this statute continued the 1740 act's abolition of common law manslaughter. Moreover, the court opined that although the 1821 act was intended to increase the punishment for the murder of slaves, it also eliminated the criminalization of killings caused by "undue correction," thereby legalizing this type of slave killing.[34]

These statutes did not afford slaves' lives equal protection as humanity. The rights of masters were preserved, but even non-owners were granted broad rights to kill slaves in order to preserve order. This will be made clear by reference to the enforcement of these statues in cases of killings of slaves by strangers.

## *Slave Killings by Strangers*

Although the statute law impaired a stranger's right to kill another person's slave in the post-Revolutionary years, Southern lawmakers were also concerned about slave control. Therefore, slaves never benefitted from the full measure of protection that the common law afforded to "real people." For example, even in the nineteenth century, masters brought civil actions in the courts seeking money damages from whites who killed their slaves. The books are replete with these cases. Accordingly, after the 1821 South Carolina act made slave killing a felony, slave masters pursued their civil remedies against slave killers.[35] These cases are noteworthy for two reasons other than their ubiquity.

The first is that the issue of the survival of the slave's "right of action" in tort against the killer was never questioned. It was an ancient rule, revived in the nineteenth century, that the common law denied a survivor the right to sue in tort one who killed a decedent. In an 1808 English case, Lord Ellenborough reaffirmed this rule, holding, "In a civil Court, the death of a human being could not be complained of as an injury[.]"[36] This decision was followed in the United States, necessitating the wrongful death acts that allowed surviving plaintiffs to sue a killer for damages, as did England's Lord Campbell's Act of 1846.[37]

The common law rule against the survival of tort actions posed no problem in the slave states for two obvious reasons. First, the "right" violated when a slave was killed was the property right of the master—not the right of the slave. Thus, the slave's death did not terminate the cause of action. A second reason is apparent from the context. The courts in England and the North favored the rule against survival as a way to limit the liability of railroads and industries. The rule was to the contrary in the South, where the courts were favorable to the "rights" at issue when a slave was killed. Here the "victim" was a slave owner, not a railroad employee or passenger.[38]

The wrongful death actions were significant for one more reason. The common law created another potential obstacle to the master's right to recover, a rule that required a felony to be prosecuted before a civil damage remedy could be recovered from the felon.[39] The Alabama courts adopted this rule in slave death suits, but this doctrine was either expressly or impliedly rejected elsewhere in the South.[40]

Obviously, in the civil cases filed by masters against slave killers, the courts sought to protect the masters' economic interests in their slaves. This interest had to compete, however, with the public need to maintain slave control and order. Accordingly, strangers had rights to apprehend and subdue runaway slaves. Nevertheless, strangers faced civil liability if they used excessive or unnecessary violence in this endeavor, and the slave died. For example, in an 1855 Mississippi case, a master—Young—sued a stranger—Thompson—who shot Young's runaway slave. The defendant sought to avoid liability by contending that the slave resisted capture. That defense was held to be insufficient by the Mississippi Supreme Court.

The court cited a statue that allowed strangers to arrest runaway slaves. If the slave resisted capture and threatened the stranger's life, he could kill the slave. Thompson failed to specify how Young's slave threatened his life; therefore the court upheld Young's demurrer and rejected Thompson's defense. In so ruling, the court considered the need to properly govern the slave population, the safety of the community, and the master's economic interest. The court also stated:

> The law is careful of the safety of the slave within his prescribed sphere. Regarded in the twofold aspect of persons and property, the same law which protects the master, guards their rights as persons.[41]

The fictional reference to slave rights is shown because, in the end, neither the slave nor his heirs received any monetary compensation in these cases. The real right that was protected was that of the owner.

Therefore, slave owners had a choice of remedy based upon the social and economic class of the white slave killer and his concurrent ability to pay the master damages.[42] Civil damages for dead slaves often exceeded $1,000. If a "gentlemen" could pay an owner for his loss the master probably thought that the punishment was adequate. Nevertheless, capital punishment was reserved as a means to deter slave killings by poor whites who were unable to pay the dead slave's owner his just due.

It is not surprising, then, that non-masters were prosecuted and convicted for slave murder and manslaughter after the American Revolution. Philip Schwarz found trial court records of "scattered trials" of slave killers in the years after the 1788 Virginia statute was passed. He does not indicate whether the killers were masters, but the appellate court records do reveal prosecutions of killings by stranger in the nineteenth century.[43]

It must be remembered, however, that the antebellum courts refused to apply common law standards of mitigation and extenuation to slave killings that were labeled "murder" and "manslaughter." The leading case, decided by the North Carolina Supreme Court in 1820, is *State v. Tackett*.[44] A nonslave-owning white, a journeyman carpenter, was indicted and convicted for murdering a slave.[45] Chief Justice John L. Taylor wrote the opinion for the court and reversed the conviction. The trial judge had instructed the jury that the common law standards of provocation and mitigation applied. The Supreme Court disagreed and held:

> It exists in the nature of things, that where slavery prevails, the relation between a white man and a slave differs from that, which subsists between free persons; and every individual in the community feels and understands, that the homicide of a slave may be extenuated by acts, which would not produce a legal provocation if done by a white person.[46]

The Supreme Court reached this holding despite the plain wording of an 1817 act, which stated that the "killing of a slave shall partake of the same degree of guilt, when accompanied with like circumstances, that homicide now does."[47] The Supreme Court held that the legislature "did not mean to declare that homicide, where a slave is killed, could be only extenuated by such provocation as would have the same effect where a white person was killed." Rather, the court read the act to merely criminalize slave manslaughter, which it stated was not a criminal act in North Carolina before 1817.[48]

Although Taylor stated that the relevant interests included "the rights respectively belonging to the slave and white man—to the just claims of humanity," he acknowledged that the "supreme law" at issue was "the safety of the citizens."[49] Accordingly, the court recognized that "neither words of reproach, insulting gestures, nor a trespass against goods or land" would extenuate a murder when a killer used a deadly weapon and both parties were white. Nevertheless, Chief Justice Taylor held:

> But it can not [sic] be laid down as a rule, that some of these provocations, if offered by a slave, well known to be turbulent and disorderly, would not extenuate the killing, if it were instantly done under the heat of passion, and without circumstances of cruelty.[50]

Moreover, the *Tackett* court stated that a slave's "temper and disposition" as well as his "usual deportment toward white persons" were relevant evidence admissible to mitigate the murder charge to manslaughter.[51] Consequently, the trial court's ruling that such evidence was admissible only if it would prove that the deceased slave was "insolent and impudent" to the white killer in particular was held to be another error of law.[52]

The implications of *Tackett* are hard to overstate. Although there were reported cases in which whites were found guilty of slave "murder" or "manslaughter," according to the *Tackett* doctrine indisputable instances of common law murder would be slave manslaughter, and flagrant examples of common law manslaughter would be justified slave killings.[53] Consequently, the fundamental implication of *Tackett* was that slaves were "protected" by the law of homicide only to the extent that was "necessary" to protect their property values from wanton white killers and to promote the power and authority of the master class—always with due regard for slave control and without any regard to slave "rights" or "humanity."

Accordingly, when reviewing the slave "murder" and "manslaughter" convictions upheld in the Southern states one must keep in mind Justice Holmes' axiom: "A word is not a crystal, transparent and unchanged; it is the skin of a living thought[.]"[54] The crimes of slave "murder" and "manslaughter" were not equated with the common law meaning of those words. This is because there is no evidence that the *Tackett* rule was rejected elsewhere; in fact, it was reaffirmed in a Kentucky case decided as late as 1860.[55]

The often quoted cases of State v. Jones,[56] Fields v. State,[57] and Chandler v. State,[58] are not to the contrary. The most discussed opinion is that of Judge J.G. Clarke in *Jones*. The defendant there was indicted and convicted upon a charge of murdering a slave. On his motion in arrest of judgment, the defendant argued that he could not be so indicted and convicted. Jones contended that the malicious killing of a slave was not common law murder, and that no Mississippi statute criminalized slave killing. In essence, Jones argued that the act for which he was convicted was perfectly legal in Mississippi in 1821. His appeal attempted to deny the court the power to make malicious slave killing a crime by means of judge-made law.[59]

Therefore, based upon the narrow issue raised in *Jones*, when the court upheld the defendant's conviction it merely held that malicious slave killing was a capital crime according to judge-made law. But the notion that malicious slave killers would be held criminally liable was not remarkable when read in its proper legal and historical context. The *Jones* case was decided in 1821, the year in which even the South Carolina legislature had concluded that it was necessary to augment the slave owners' civil remedies with the threat of capital punishment for malicious slave killers. And, after all, Pennsylvania courts had 33 years earlier upheld a common law indictment for malicious horse killing.[60]

Students of *Jones* have, nevertheless, exaggerated the import of this opinion and have been misled by the following language that the court used to answer the defendant's arguments:

> Has the slave no rights, because he is deprived of his freedom? He is still a human being, and possesses all those rights, of which he is not deprived by the positive provisions of law, but in vain shall we look for any law passed by the enlightened and philanthropic legislature of this state, giving even to the master, *much less to a stranger*, power over the life of a slave.[61]

These words, however, are merely *dictum* that must be distinguished from the holding of the court, which is that malicious slave killing was a criminal offense. The *Jones* opinion did not hold that slaves were entitled to the protection of the common law of homicide because issues of mitigation and extenuation were not raised by the defendant, and therefore were not decided by the court.

The class identity of the defendant in *Jones* is not stated by the court. From the underlined language quoted above, as well as the tone of the entire opinion, it appears that Jones was a stranger to the slave. This is a logical deduction because the pattern of settlement in the nineteenth century slave states differed from the original colonies; poor white slave owner tensions were a greater social concern as slave owners displaced the poor white pioneers who first settled these regions. Consequently, slave master concerns about poor white slave killings were likely to be expressed as legal issues during the early years of settlement in Mississippi. The *Jones* case probably was an expression of the slave master's fears of poor white slave killers who threatened slave-property values as well as the power and authority of the slave-owning class. It is worth noting that the defendants in the first reported Alabama slave homicide case were characterized as "laborers," most likely white nonslave owners.[62]

Even if Judge Clarke's opinion applied to the case of a slave master, however, the Jones court's dictum concerning slave "rights" is irreconcilable with the subsequent holding of the Mississippi Supreme Court in *Oliver v. State*.[63] In that case the court held, as a matter of judge-made law, that slave masters had a greater right to kill their slaves than the common law of crimes afforded them, and an even greater right to kill than the law of slavery vested with strangers to a slave. Thus, the *Oliver* court deprived slaves of their supposed "rights" as "human beings," although these rights had not been abrogated by "the positive provisions of law." What manner of "concern for slave rights" could wax and wane depending upon the class identity of the white killer?

Indeed, the slave's rights were irrelevant because the slave never benefitted from the full measure of protection afforded by the common law of crimes. This fact is further illustrated by *Fields v. State*, a Tennessee case of 1829, and *Chandler v. State*, a Texas case decided in 1847. Both decisions upheld manslaughter convictions of strangers to the slave by equating the slave's status with that of the ancient English villein, whose killer could be convicted of murder or manslaughter. Thus, the offense of killing a slave was found, by analogy, to exist at "common law, because it is the unlawful killing of a human being[.]"[64] The *Chandler* case, however, in citing *Fields*, impliedly recognized the *Tackett* principle. Justice Royall T. Wheeler, in *Chandler*, upheld the jury charge that vested whites with the power to suppress a slave who merely raised a hand to a white man.[65]

The *dicta* in these cases are just that, and are inconsistent with the holdings of subsequent cases. Thus, in *Neal v. Farmer*,[66] the analogy between slaves and villeins was rejected. Moreover, the thought that slaves were protected by the common law was also rebuked by Judge Eugenius A. Nisbet:

> It is theoretically every where [sic], and in Georgia experimentally true, that two races of men living together, one in the character of masters and the other in the character of slaves, cannot be governed by the same laws. Whatever rights humanity, or religion, or policy, may concede to the slave, they must, in the nature of the relation, be often different from those of the master . . . The civil rights of the master do not appertain to the slave. Of these, he can have none whatever. The rights personal, if they might be so designated, of the slave, are, some of them, essentially different from those of the master, and cannot, therefore, be the subject of a common system of laws. *They must be defined by positive enactments, which, whilst they protect*

> *the slave, guard the rights of the master.* If the Common Law be applicable to a state of slavery, it would seem to be applicable as much in one as another particular. If it protects the life of the slave, why not his liberty? and if it protects his liberty, then it breaks down, at once, the *status* of the slave. The Colonies received the Common Law, as applicable to their condition . . . as *slaveholding* communities, and as applicable to them as slaveholders. It is absurd to talk about the Common Law being applicable to an institution which it would destroy.[67]

Accordingly, the view that slave killing could be a common law crime was rejected by the court.

But the issue in *Neal v. Farmer* was not whether a criminal defendant was guilty of a crime. Rather, it was whether one who killed a slave could be held civilly liable by a master before the defendant was prosecuted criminally for the felony. In *Neal*, it was in the master's interest that it be held that slave killing was not a felony at common law, and it was so held. In *Jones, Fields*, and *Chandler*, the master's interest weighed in favor of criminal liability, and the courts so held. Thus, the notion of slave rights is irrelevant to a reconciliation of these various cases. This irrelevancy is further illustrated by the homicide cases involving slave master defendants.

It must be recalled that masters had much to fear from strangers who were too zealous in policing slaves. For example, in an 1854 South Carolina case, three white men caught a runaway slave and cruelly whipped and tortured the slave the death. One of the defendants was the owner's son. Clearly, the owner had an interest in the return of the slave, but his interest was not served by the protracted abuse that caused the slave's demise. Thus the defendants were convicted.[68] Slave owners also were concerned about whites who fraternized with slaves. People who did so were obviously held in ill repute by the master class. The greatest threat to the master's interest in slave property values, as well as the public peace, arose when fatal violence broke out between a slave and a poor white of this ilk.

A South Carolina case decided in 1834 illustrates this point. The defendant was indicted and convicted of murder under the 1821 act. The trial judge charged the jury on the issue of mitigation consistently with the holding in *Tackett*, and the Court of Appeals opinion of Justice William Harper upheld the conviction. The official case report does not recite the facts of the case, but H.M. Henry notes a published version of the facts:

> According to this account the prisoner had been in the habit of gambling with negroes, which was regarded as about the meanest thing a white man could do. The negro, who was the victim of the

murderous attack . . ., proved to be a more shrewd player and won all the stakes. This enraged the white man and [he killed the slave].

Henry adds that "the prejudice against gambling with negroes" influenced the conviction.[69] It was also likely that the defendant did not have sufficient means to repay the owner for his loss. In cases such as this the criminal law was a necessary addition to the master's civil remedies.

## *Slave Killings by Masters, Hirers, and Overseers*

Slave masters, hirers, and overseers always possessed a greater right to kill slaves under their command than mere strangers to the slave enjoyed. As noted *supra*, the seventeenth- and eighteenth-century slave codes legitimized all slave killings perpetrated while the master was correcting this slave for any offense the slave may have allegedly committed. Although the courts and legislatures of the late eighteenth and early nineteenth centuries expanded the scope of the white stranger's potential criminal liability and punishment for slave killings, they contemporaneously preserved the master's almost unlimited right to kill his slaves with impunity in cases of slave "insurrection" and "resistance," as well as deaths that resulted from the master's "moderate correction" of the slave.

The Southern legislators were more subtle than to explicitly justify malicious slave killings and killings that would have been manslaughter under the common law standards, or even the diminished standards applied by the courts to strangers who killed slaves. Instead, by using amorphous terms such as "moderate" or "necessary" correction what was "usual" was justified, and jury questions were created to give meaning to these terms in a given slave master's case. Thus, it was up to the slave master juries to decide to convict one of their own for slave killings not on the basis of common law standards but on their own standards.[70]

Nevertheless, the master's power to kill resisting slaves excused all but the most wanton killings imaginable. This is illustrated by the 1860 Mississippi case of *Oliver v. State*.[71] The court reversed the defendant slave master's manslaughter conviction for killings his own slave. It held that when a slave was in a state of "resistance," the master's power to kill the rebellious slave was unlimited.

The state's case in *Oliver* charged the defendant with murdering his own slave, John, and was based upon the testimony of Bramel, who was the defendant's overseer. Bramel stated that on the day of the killing he was working in the defendant's corn crib with John and another slave. This second slave had the job of pushing corn into a sheller with a five-foot long stick. It was stated that John was not allowed to use this stick because of his "awkwardness." Nevertheless, there was evidence that John was a very stout, strong, "violent, turbulent and rebellious slave." Bramel then left the crib and returned fifteen minutes later, finding the defendant in the crib. The case report continues:

> . . . [Bramel heard Oliver say], in a quiet and unexcited tone, 'Give up the stick;' and then in a short time he said, violently, 'Give up the stick.' By this time [Bramel] reached a point where he could see what was going on. He saw deceased and accused struggling together for the possession of the stick before described, both having hold of it. The countenance of the deceased at the time had a very vicious and savage look. Very soon the accused succeeded in wrestling the stick from the hands of the deceased, and he immediately struck deceased with the same on the head, and deceased fell and almost immediately expired. Immediately upon his falling accused struck in rapid succession two other blows at deceased, but neither of them struck him.[72]

The jury may have been more predisposed to convict this defendant because of their consideration of evidence that was originally admitted and was later excluded by the court. The prosecution impeached Bramel, its own witness, by the subsequent testimony of two witnesses who testified that, on the day of the killing, Bramel told them Oliver killed John, "and when they asked him why [Oliver] did it, [Bramel] replied, 'for nothing'—'that the negro was in the corn-crib shelling corn, and that he did not seem to work fast enough, and Oliver told him to work faster and the negro didn't do it, and Oliver took the shelling-stick from him and killed him with it."[73]

The Mississippi High Court of Errors and Appeals reversed, in an opinion written by William Harris. Harris disagreed with the trial judge's instructions to the jury. The jury was told that masters could use only "lawful instruments of correction," thus excluding "a staff or such means as are likely to kill or maim." Justice Harris struck down this limitation on the master's power over the slave because he found that John's acts constituted resistance. When a slave resisted his master, Harris opined that the only inquiry was "whether the blow inflicted on the negro slave was or [was] not necessary to overcome the resistance of the slave to the lawful authority of the master."[74] If the answer to this question was "yes," then the master's right to kill was established.

Consequently, Harris described the master's right to kill his slave in sweeping terms:

> [I]f the master, in the exercise of lawful authority, in a lawful manner, be resisted by his slave, then the master may use just such force as may be requisite to reduce his slave to obedience, even to the death of the slave, if that become [sic] necessary to preserve the master's life, or to maintain his lawful authority.[75]

It was axiomatic, however, that the master's "lawful authority" included the right to demand absolute obedience on the part of the slave.

The facts in *Oliver v. State* support this proposition. The defendant killed his slave by striking him with a stick that was five feet long and that was initially in the slave's hands. The defendant asked the deceased to hand him the stick, but the court did not examine why the defendant asked for the stick. Slave masters had the right to demand anything of their slaves. Thus, the only relevant inquiry was whether the fact that the slave refused to hand Oliver the stick constituted "resistance" that justified Oliver's act of taking the stick from the deceased and immediately killing him with a sharp blow to the head.

Therefore, the only concept of any significance was "resistance," which encompassed much more than common law self defense. Resistance was said to exist:

> If the slave throws off the authority of the master, puts himself in a hostile attitude towards him, resists his dominion and control by physical force, evincing by his acts, while in a personal conflict with the master, a design to make that resistance effectual in escaping from his dominion and authority[.][76]

Consequently, a master could be held criminally liable only if the slave he killed was completely submissive and under the master's absolute control.

Furthermore, the finding of resistance did not require proof of any threat by the slave to inflict physical harm on the master. All the slave had to do was threaten the master's authority; thereafter, the owner could legally kill his slave. In *Oliver*, for example, there is no evidence that John threatened to use the stick as a weapon against the defendant. This did not preclude Justice Harris from finding that the slave was in a state of resistance. It was enough that the slave refused to obey Oliver's command to hand over the stick. When John decided to struggle with his master for the stick, the bondsman wrote his own death warrant. At that point any question concerning Oliver's right to immediately kill John was resolved against the slave's life.

Consequently, the *Oliver* case makes it clear that a slave owner risked criminal liability for killing his own slave under two conditions. First, the slave must have expressed no challenge to the master's authority; and second, the master must then have administered "immoderate" means of punishment that caused the slave's death. One may ask, however, whether this limited restriction on the master's freedom to kill his slave is inconsistent with the definition of slaves as property and represents a small measure of legal concern for slave humanity. This question can be answered only in the negative if one carefully analyzes the available data construing the legal significance of terms such as "moderate correction." This vague phrase guaranteed that "in such instances as convictions were won, the murder had been accompanied by torture or extreme cruelty, inescapably identifiable as 'cruel and unusual' punishment."[77] Thus the paltry protection that submissive slaves received from the criminal law against their master's violence indicates that something other than concern for slave humanity had to be the moving force that shaped the terrible texture of this law.

Initially, a problem of proof arises because prosecutions of slave masters that resulted in acquittals do not appear in the appellate case reports. Nevertheless, it can be inferred that the cases in which juries did return convictions reveal the type of correction that was thought to be immoderate and that violence short of this was moderate and legitimized a slave's death. In fact, the reported slave master convictions that were appealed and have full factual descriptions prove that juries apparently legitimized all killings but those among the most brutal and extreme cases in recorded human history; these cases were examples of the most gratuitous and sadistic killings imaginable.[78] The facts of one such case, *Souther v. Commonwealth*,[79] are typical:

> The indictment contains fifteen counts, and sets forth a case of the most cruel and excessive whipping and torture. The negro was tied to a tree and whipped with switches. When Souther became fatigued with the labour of whipping, he called upon a negro man of his, and made him cob Sam with a shingle. He also made a negro woman of his help to cob him. And after cobbing and whipping, he applied fire to the body of the slave; about his back, belly and private parts. He then caused him to be washed down with hot water, in which pods of red pepper had been steeped. The negro was also tied to a log and to the bed post with ropes, which choked him, and he was kicked and stamped by Souther. This sort of punishment was continued and repeated until the negro died under its infliction. It is believed that the records of criminal jurisprudence do not contain a case of more atrocious and wicked cruelty than was presented upon the trial of Souther[.][80]

But even in this case, the jury found the defendant guilty of only second degree murder, and he was sentenced to but five years in jail.[81]

The only other two reported appellate cases of convictions with full factual descriptions, *State v. Robbins*[82] and *State v. Hoover*,[83] rival the immeasurable brutality depicted in Souther's case. The facts are set forth in the footnotes to show that this statement is not an exaggeration. While upholding the murder conviction in *Hoover*, Judge Thomas Ruffin indicated that judges, as well as juries, perceived themselves to be dealing with very different issues in cases of slave killings by masters than in instances of fatal violence perpetrated by strangers:

> If death unhappily ensue from the master's chastisement of his slave, inflicted apparently with a good intent, for reformation or example, and with no purpose to take life, or to put it in jeopardy, the law would doubtless tenderly regard every circumstance which, judging from the conduct generally of masters towards slaves, might reasonably be supposed to have hurried the party into excess.[84]

Accordingly, Judge Ruffin stated that the master's unlimited right to kill his own slaves included all but instances of punishment so "immoderate and unreasonable in the measure, the continuances, and the instruments" that it "loses all character of correction *in foro domestico*, and denotes plainly that the prisoner must have contemplated the fatal termination, which was the natural consequence of such barbarous cruelties."[85]

There is abundant evidence from various sources that only crimes of similar brutality led to convictions of masters. A few examples will have to suffice. H.M. Henry wrote of the South Carolina case of a hirer indicted for slave murder in 1852. There is no record of a conviction, but the indictment "alleges torture for a period of three months."[86] James Sellers cites an 1837 Alabama indictment of a master for slave murder. The defendant was convicted of manslaughter and sentenced to a two-month prison term and a $500 fine. The crime is reported to be of similar brutality as that of Souther's:

> I first saw the negro on Friday. He was tied with his hands over his head in a very peculiar manner and seemed to be in great pain. He begged to be untied, upon which his master struck him over the head three or four times with a large hickory stick. The boy fell . . . and while laying on the floor, Hall kicked him on the forehead once or twice. The boy's head bled profusely, but deponent does not know whether it was from the blows with the stick or the kicks he received while laying on the floor. The boy was taken out and tied to a tree. Deponent did not go out immediately, but hearing the sound of the lash, he finally did so, and after begging for the boy for some time without effect . . . Hall [the defendant] must have whipped the boy two hours without cessation[.][87]

James Oakes cites another example:

> William Pitman shocked even his family when he came home in a drunken rage one night and tied up a young slave by the neck and heels, beat the boy with a vine, and then "stomped him to death." Pitman's children testified against their father, and one newspaper editor declared that the convicted murderer had "justly incurred the penalties of the law."[88]

Finally, of note is a South Carolina case reported by Harriet Beecher Stowe, which occurred between the years of 1807 to 1810. The defendant was a ship's captain who had a slave tied up and beheaded with an axe "in the very harbour of Charleston, within a few yards of the shore, unblushingly, in the face of open day." The court sentenced the defendant to a fine of seven hundred pounds and in default of payment a seven-year prison term.[89]

Other persuasive evidence of the scope of legitimized slave killings by masters exists in the prosecutions that did not result in an indictment or conviction. The earliest case may be a trial that took place in Maryland in 1658 and 1659. The defendant was a "planter of some note" named Overzee who was tried for murdering a slave. The facts are described as follows:

> the negro was put in chains by order of his mistress for some misdemeanor; . . . he refused then to work, and pretended to be in a fit; . . . he was then whipped with a little switch, had hot lard poured down his back, and then, when he got up, was tied to a ladder. Still being stubborn, he was left tied; a cold wind arose, and he soon died.

Upon hearing this evidence, the "jury have a verdict of ignoramus, the evidence not being found sufficient to convict."[90] In a 1743 North Carolina case, a slave owner who beat and then "roasted and burned" his slave was discharged from prosecution.[91]

Cases such as these also arose in the nineteenth century. Bertram Wyatt-Brown cites three inquests that exonerated masters. In one case, the master's slave "died after a severe paddling, [and] the Mississippi slaveholder himself at once called for a coroner's jury." The jury found "that the wound at the base of [the slave] Jim's skull caused by a piece of metal was not the cause of death." An 1848 a South Carolina case involved the death of a slave who "underwent a severe lashing which so dehydrated her system that she kept drinking buckets of water. Her master importuned the neighbors to look kindly on the sad business. Her death was duly attributed to a 'cramp in the Stomack.'" Wyatt-Brown also reports on the 1849 case of James H. Sandiford, a South Carolina planter. This matter is set forth in the journal of Thomas Chaplin, a slaveholder who sat on a coroner's jury that found in favor of the master. The slave, who Chapin calls a "poor cripple," was whipped in an outhouse and was found dead having choked because of a chain around his neck. The jury found that the slave slipped into the position he was found.[92]

Two cases of slave master acquittals reported in the antebellum press, and cited by Harriet Beecher Stowe, indicate that what Southern juries called "moderate correction" was violence of a very extreme nature. In a Virginia case, a slave master and his father were found not guilty of the charge of murdering a slave who was suspected of theft. The slave died after being whipped and hung by his neck with a chain that was strung from the ceiling.[93] In a South Carolina case, a female slave owner was acquitted of murdering, or causing another slave to murder, her fifty-five-year-old female slave who had "misbehaved." The evidence showed that the slave died of multiple blows to the head. Nevertheless, the defendant was allowed to enter into evidence a written exculpatory affidavit, and the jury apparently agreed with the defense attorney who stated: "[t]ruth had been distorted in this case, and murder manufactured out of what was nothing more than ordinary domestic discipline."[94] James Sellers cites a similar case from Alabama in 1811. The defendant master was tried and found not guilty on the charge of "beating, brusing, wounding, and other cruel treatment" of his slave who fled into the woods and died of hunger and thirst.[95]

Statistical evidence derived from lower court records in Tennessee also supports the proposition that slave masters had wide latitude to kill their slaves. Arthur Howington found thirty-three murder prosecutions in the counties he studied. He concluded that, "[o]nly three of the cases involved owners of the slave victims." None of the slave owners was tried because in each case the defendant "was not to be found."[96] This is particularly startling when one notes that a majority of the other thirty cases went to trial, resulting in three convictions, twelve acquittals, and two mistrials.[97]

It could be argued that even this limited liability for slave killing that masters faced was an expression of concern for slave humanity, which was inconsistent with the definition of slaves as property. Nevertheless, this minimal criminality was indeed consistent with the definition of slaves as property without legal rights because the law intervened to protect only against outrageous examples of violent killings by masters. Consequently, only the extremes of violence exhibited by Souther, Robbins, and Hoover tipped the balance of these interests in favor of criminalization. This was so because their brutalities were perceived to be "unnecessary" for the promotion of individual instances of slave discipline and because it was thought that such extremes disrupted the orderly, everyday routine of inhumanity and oppression that was essential to community slave control and discipline.[98]

It should be further noted that these cases were products of the mature plantation period, and this was no accident. As slave society matured, the slave owners' perceptions of salient interests changed. The lawmakers responded by affording slave property a special legal status that both groups thought it deserved because it was the most valuable and dangerous form of property in the slave economy. Consequently, the freedom of the individual slave owner to treat his human property came to be restricted in various ways, but the lawmakers intervened only when the perceived threat that the master's actions posed to the slave property values of others and the community interest in slave control and order outweighed the benefits the individual would have to forego as a result of legal intervention.

Therefore, in the nineteenth century, the master's right to kill his bondsmen came to be circumscribed, but so did the master's right to free his slaves, as will be shown in Chapter 7. The latter legal change occurred as a result of changing perceptions of the value of slaves and Southerner's fears of the dangers posed by large numbers of free blacks in the plantation regions. The former change was caused by evolving perceptions of the degree of legitimized violence that was a "necessary" incident of slavery and that was consistent with the community's need to maintain slave discipline and property values. Neither legal transformation, however, was motivated by any real regard for slave "rights" or "humanity." Nor were these changes in law in any way inconsistent with the slave's non-person status.

Intra-class tensions may have also contributed to the expansion of slave master liability. As plantation slavery matured, the homogeneity of the slaveholding class broke down. Bertram Wyatt-Brown observes, "Slaveholders without much local standing . . . were more likely to get caught in the toils of criminal justice than better-placed masters, hardly surprising in the rank-conscious South."[99] He cites two cases from lower court proceedings to support this proposition. In one case, a "poor North Carolina yeoman" who castrated his slave was fined $20 and was jailed for twenty days. In the other, an inebriated slave owner and his "one-eyed drifter" brother-in-law killed a runaway slave belonging to the defendant slave owner. There is no record of a conviction of the latter two, and Wyatt-Brown notes that as to the former, the county jailkeeper refused to allow the defendant to serve his penalty.[100] This concern for social status is also revealed by the law that applied to slave killings by hirers and overseers.

The lawmakers granted slave hirers the same broad right to kill bondsmen.[101] Most slave hirers owned their own slaves, and it was apparently thought they could not face a greater scope of criminal liability for killing slaves they hired than they faced for killing their own slaves. Nevertheless, slave owners could sue to collect civil monetary damages from hirers who unreasonably killed a hired slave, therefore adequately protecting the owner's property interest while balancing the hirer's need to maintain slave control.[102]

The rule restricting the slave owner to his civil damage remedies was, however, perceived to be inadequate if the slave killer was an overseer. Overseers generally were not paid well enough to satisfy a civil judgment they might owe a slave master for a dead slave, and the social class tensions that evidenced themselves between masters and overseers were generally not present between hirers and slave owners. Consequently, the lawmakers created a third category of criminal culpability for slave killers who were overseers that was more restrictive than the law governing slave killers who were hirers or masters, but granted overseers a greater right to kill slaves than mere strangers enjoyed.[103] For example, the Alabama statutes provided that first degree murder could be found:

> If any person shall, with malice aforethought, cause the death of a slave by cruel, barbarous or inhuman whipping or beating, or by any cruel or inhuman treatment, or by the use of any instrument in its nature calculated to produce death[.][104]

The next section stated that, except in cases of self defense, an "overseer or manager" was guilty of second degree murder if he killed a slave under the same conditions, but "without intention to kill." The section defining second degree murder committed by a master went a step further and justified all killings that resulted from "the use of so much force as [was] necessary to procure obedience on the part of the slave[.]"[105] Consequently, this statute recognized the overseer's intermediate status in society and as a slave killer, as it protected the master's superior position.

These statues and court decisions show how the substantive law afforded the slave's life the most minimal level of protection. There were also procedural and systemic biases in the criminal courts, which had the effect of decriminalizing white slave killings.

## *Legitimization of Violence by Procedure*

The abolitionists argued that the apparent protection of a slave's life that the law gave by statute or court decision was in fact taken away by the rule of evidence that prevented a slave from being a witness against a white person. Indeed, this rule of evidence was adopted in every Southern state, either by custom or by statute. In addition, whites had to initiate prosecutions because slaves could not bring actions in the courts.[106]

The effect of these rules was described by George Stroud:

> A white man may, with impunity, if no other white be present, torture, maim, and even murder his slave, in the midst of any number of negroes and mulattoes.[107]

Of course, this is an overstatement, because prosecutions could be brought by outraged white citizens based upon circumstantial evidence. As illustrated by the cases discussed above, however, those cases were almost always unsuccessful. At least in part, this can be attributed to the prohibition of black testimony.

There is also statistical evidence that these procedural roadblocks had an effect on the "outputs" of the Southern courts in slave murder prosecutions. A correlation of the work of two scholars illustrates this point. Both Michael Hindus and H.M. Henry studied the lower court records of the South Carolina antebellum courts. By combining the data reported by these writers, it is possible to compare slave murder conviction rates with overall murder conviction rates.[108] First, Hindus found an overall simple conviction rate of 50.5 percent for murder cases, meaning that accused murderers who were tried were convicted in that percentage of the trials held. An analysis of Henry's data indicates that a simple conviction rate of 36.3 percent is shown in slave murder trials.[109] This simple conviction rate tells only a part of the story, however.

Hindus also found that a large percentage of murder charges did not result in trials at all because grand juries failed to indict and some prosecutions were dropped. All murder charges had a 13 percent pre-trial disposition rate. According to Henry's data, slave murder charges were disposed without trial in 32.4 percent of the cases.[110] This makes the simple conviction rate disparity even more shocking. Slave murderers were found guilty at a lower rate even after almost one third of the charges had been "weeded out" in the pre-trial stage.[111]

Hindus also used an effective conviction rate to evaluate the performance of the criminal courts. This rate establishes the percentage of charges that resulted in convictions or guilty pleas. The rate in South Carolina was 37.5 percent in all murder cases. According to Henry's data, this rate was 23 percent in slave murder cases.[112] This was after the substantive criminal law had decriminalized homicides as illustrated by this chapter.

Accordingly, it is appropriate to think of the slave killing cases as property crimes, not crimes against persons. The law—in both substance and procedure—treated slaves as non-persons. One final point makes this clear. Hindus found for theft in South Carolina the following rates: Simple conviction rate of 46 percent, pre-trial disposition rate of 32.1 percent, and effective conviction rate of 21.9 percent.[113] These rates resemble Henry's slave murder data more than the overall murder ratios.

Certainly these conviction ratios tell only part of the story. When they are read in conjunction with the substantive law, however, the minimal protection afforded the slave's life, even in the antebellum years is made clear. In short, the law always legitimized white killings of slaves without regard to the common law of crimes to further the salient interests in slave society.

## *Conclusion*

In law and in practice, Southern lawmakers and juries granted slave owners a greater right to kill their slaves than strangers. This was because when masters killed their slaves two salient interests—the individual owner's right to control his slaves as he saw fit and the master class interest in maintaining slave control and property values—conflicted in a way that they did not in cases in which strangers killed slaves. Therefore, masters and hirers had the greatest right to kill slaves with impunity; overseers were next in line, and strangers were third. Even as to strangers, however, the slave was not granted the full protections guaranteed by the common law.

The different degrees of criminal culpability among masters and non-slave owners are, moreover, consistent with the overall patterns of the criminal law enforcement in the South. For example, Donna Spindel studied the lower court records from North Carolina for the years 1663 to 1776. She found that:

> . . . there is no question that laborers, . . ., were most likely to be indicted and convicted. Conversely, grand juries returned no bills for planters in greater proportions than for laborers, and trial juries convicted planters in smaller proportions.[114]

This pattern was reflected in the law of slave homicide and was even more evident in the law of non-fatal slave abuse that is discussed in the next chapter.

The scope of white civil and criminal liability for slave killing did increase, however, when the colonial and antebellum periods are compared. The nature of this change is revealed by the table that follows:

## Table 5
### Scope of Liability for Fatal Slave Abuse[115]

| Strangers | | Masters/Hirers | | Overseers |
|---|---|---|---|---|
| *Slave Boom* | *Plantation Period* | *Slave Boom* | *Plantation Period* | *Plantation Period* |

*Manslaughter:*

| | | | | |
|---|---|---|---|---|
| Criminal—Either no liability or fine, mitigation based on slave's status | Criminal—Fine and/or jail, mitigation based on slave's status | Criminal—No Liability | Criminal—No Libaility | Criminal—Fine and/or jail term, mitigation based on slave's status |
| Civil—Slave's Value | Civil—Slave's Value | Civil—Slave's Value | Civil—Slave's Value | Civil—Slave's Value |

*Murder:*

| | | | | |
|---|---|---|---|---|
| Criminal—Slave's value and fine, second offense capital | Criminal—Capital punishment, mitigation based on slave's status | Criminal—Either no liability or fine, exculpation or "moderate correction" | Criminal—Capital punishment, exculpation if "rebellion" or "moderate correction" | Criminal—Capital punishment, mitigation based on slave's status |
| Civil—Slave's Value | Civil—Slave's Value | Civil—Slave's Value | Civil—Slave's Value | Civil—Slave's Value |

This outline reveals the complexity of the changing criminal and civil standards that were constructed by the courts and legislatures. Even if some judges and legislators of the antebellum years sought to preserve slave humanity with this law, the limits on that protection show that concerns for slave rights to personal security were not really relevant at all.

In cases involving non-slave owners, the preservation of the slave's life extended only as far as it was thought to be necessary to protect the master's interests. The boundary lines of that protection, however, were defined by other important social concerns, such as the need to keep the slave population under control. Class conflicts among whites were also considered by the lawmakers. Thus, this law of slave homicide was indeed a pact made among the slave's rulers. The shifting measure of protection adjusted the rights of the white "superiors" of the slave.

It is manifest, however, that these calculations of interest were made without any regard for "slave rights." This is so although the law constrained the master's right to unnecessarily kill or main his slaves. These boundary lines were also consistent with the fundamental definition of slaves as people without rights. This was so because the law often regulates an owner's freedom to do what he wishes with his property. This is done to accomplish broader social goals, but not out of concern for the property that is "protected." Such was also the case with slave property.

Of course, some masters may have refused to exercise their legal physical power over their slaves, just as others exceeded the bounds of the law. This point raises an issue beyond the scope of this study; it is the debate about the extent and frequency of slave whippings and mistreatment in the U.S. South. All agree that physical punishment was a part of the system of rewards and punishments that constituted the actual practices of slave owners.[116] And, as M.I. Finley wrote, "The failure of any individual slave owner to exercise all his rights over his slave-property was always a unilateral act on his part, never binding, always revocable. That is a critical fact."[117] Indeed, the law gave masters and other whites rights to abuse slaves and this decriminalized violence was a reality.

Therefore, the slave's second class status was only partially alleviated in the antebellum years. This is further illustrated by the law regarding legitimized non-fatal violence.

# NOTES

1. Too much emphasis has been placed on this *dicta; see, generally,* Andrew Fede, "Legitimized Violent Slave Abuse in the American South, 1619–1865: A Case Study of Law and Social Change in Six Southern States," 29 *American Journal of Legal History* 93, 99–101 n. 22–27 (1985) (hereinafter "Fede—1985") discussing the literature.

2. See, generally, Wayne R. LaFave and Austin W. Scott, Jr., *Handbook on Criminal Law* 528–530 (St. Paul, 1972) (hereinafter cited as "LaFave").

3. See, Higginbotham, *supra* at 189 and 195–196; Goodell, *supra* at 178–179; Stowe, *supra* at 177–188. See, also, State v. Welch, 1 S.C.L. 69, 1 Bay 172 (1791); State v. Cheatwood, 20 S.C.L. 252, 255, 2 Hill 459, 465 (1834); State v. Raines, 14 S.C.L. 215, 220, 3 McCord 533, 545–56 (1826); Howell Meadoes Henry, *The Police Control of the Slave in South Carolina* 66 (New York, reprint ed. 1968) (1914).

4. See, Higginbotham, *supra* at 253–254.

5. See, Don Higginbotham and William S. Price, Jr., "Was It Murder for a White Man to Kill a Slave? Chief Justice Martin Howard Condemns the Peculiar Institution in North Carolina," 36 *Wm. & Mary Q.* 593, 601 (1979) [Emphasis omitted] (hereinafter cited as "Was It Murder").

6. *Id.* at 595. There is apparently no record of the case Chief Justice Howard cites, except for the result. *See, Id.* Donna Spindel does cite a 1743 North Carolina case she found in the General Court Records. Matthew Hardy was charged with attacking his female slave Lucy "with stocks and staves[.]" He then allegedly tied Lucy to a ladder, set a fire, and "roasted and burned [her]." Spindel reports that the defendant was discharged. *See,* Donna J. Spindel, *Crime and Society in North Carolina, 1663–1776* 48 (Baton Rouge, 1989). This case does not directly refute Howard's views, but it appears inconsistent with even the extreme cases of violence against slaves that later resulted in criminal liability for slave masters who killed slaves. *See,* text and notes at Notes 79 to 95.

7. "Was It Murder," *supra* at 600.

8. Laws of North Carolina, 1774, Chapter XXXI, *quoted in,* Paul Finkelman, *The Law of Freedom & Bondage: A Casebook* 200 (New York, 1986) ("*Freedom & Bondage*"); *see,* "Was It Murder," *supra* at 596.

9. *See, Freedom & Bondage, supra* at 199–200, *quoting,* The Laws of North Carolina 1741, Chapter XXIV; *see, also, State v. Boon,* 1 N.C. 103, 109, Tay. 246 (1801). On outlawry, *see,* Goodell, *supra* at 181 and Stowe, *supra* at 156, 159–161.

10. *See,* Chapter 3, *supra* at notes 14 to 18.

11. *See,* 3 Hening, *supra* at 459; Higginbotham, *supra* at 55–56.

12. 6 Hening, *supra* at 111, *quoting,* the 1748 Code, Section XXIII. For the 1723 Code, Section XIX, *see,* 4 Hening, *supra* at 132.

13. *See, generally, e.g.,* LaFave, *supra* at 571–572.

14. *See, State v. Piver,* 3 N.C. 109, 2 Hay. 79 (1799); *State v. Weaver,* 3 N.C. 77, 2 Hay. 54 (1798).

15. *See,* Higginbotham, *supra* at 254; Stroud, *supra* at 24; 1 Hurd, *supra* a 306.

16. *See, e.g.,* 3 Hening, *supra* at 86 for the 1691 Virginia act that continued until 1785. *See, also,* 12 Hening, *supra* at 192; Higginbotham, *supra* at 254.

17. *Cited in* Goodell, *supra* at 306–307 [citation and emphasis omitted].

18. *See,* Caleb Perry Patterson, *The Negro in Tennessee, 1790–1865* 12 (New York, reprint ed. 1968) (1922) (hereinafter cited as "*Negro in Tennessee*").

19. *See,* 12 Hening, *supra* at 681; 1 Hurd, *supra* at 242.

20. 3 Va. 66, 1 Va. Cas. 253 (1786).

21. *See,* Stroud, *supra* at 21 n. *.

22. *Freedom & Bondage, supra* at 200–201; Goodell, *supra* at 180, Stowe, *supra* at 156.

23. *See, State v. Boon,* 1 N.C. 103, Tay. 246 (1801) (statute held ambiguous and principle of strict construction of criminal statutes applied). Judges Johnston and Taylor opined—in *dicta*—that slave murder would be a common law crime, and Hall disagreed.

24. *See, Freedom & Bondage, supra* at 201 *quoting,* Chapter XVIII of the Laws of 1817. In *State v. Reed,* 9 N.C. (2 Hawks.) 454 (1823) the Supreme Court upheld a common law indictment for slave murder. As noted *infra,* however, the North Carolina courts did not equate crimes against slaves with the dictates of the common law. *See, State v. Tackett,* 8 N.C. (1 Hawks.) 210 (1820).

25. *See, Negro in Tennessee, supra* at 37; Stroud, *supra* at 23. The Georgia constitution justified killings if the slave was in a state of "insurrection," or if "death should happen by accident in giving such moderate correction." *Id.* [citations and emphasis omitted]; *see, also,* Stowe, *supra* at 157.

26. Douglas Hay, "Property, Authority and the Criminal Law" in *Albion's Fatal Tree: Crime & Society in Eighteenth Century England* 25 (New York, 1975).

27. For Hay's views, *see, Id.* at 17–63. For discussions of Hay's approach in relation to the criminal law in America, *see,* Hindus, *supra* at 96–124 (South Carolina); Kathryn Preyer, "Crime, the Criminal Law and Reform in Post-Revolutionary Virginia," 1 *Law & History Review* 53 (1983); *see, generally,* Hall, *supra* at 30–35; Douglas Greenberg, "Crime, Law Enforcement, and Social Control in Colonial America," 26 *American Journal of Legal History* 293 (1982); Kathryn Preyer, "Penal Measures in the American Colonies: An Overview," 26 *American Journal of Legal History* 326 (1982). The nineteenth-century reforms in the criminal law came later in these states and did not effect slavery offenses. *See,* Hall, *supra* at 168–188; Friedman, *supra* at 280–294.

28. *See,* for the Tennessee statutes of 1799, *Negro in Tennessee, supra* at 37, 44–45; and, for the South Carolina law, Henry, *supra* at 108.

29. *See, State v. Smith,* 10 S.C.L. 6, 1 Nott & McC. 13 (1817); *State v. Welch,* 1 S.C.L. 69, 1 Bay 172 (1791); *State v. Gee,* 1 S.C.L. 65, 1 Bay 163 (1791). Howell Meadoes Henry notes an 1807 conviction of a master who ordered his slave to chop off the head of another slave. Henry also cites one 1815 conviction for willful killing and several for manslaughter in the lower court records he studied in nine South Carolina counties. *See,* Henry, *supra* at 66 and 73.

30. *Arthur v. Wells,* 9 S.C.L. 83, 84, 2 Mill 314, 316 (1818).

31. *Witsell v. Earnest,* 10 S.C.L. 71, 72, 1 Nott & McC. 182, 183 (1818).

32. *See,* Henry, *supra* at 67.

33. *See, Id.* at 66–68.

34. *See, Id.* at 68; Stroud, *supra* at 24–25; *State v. Raines,* 14 S.C.L. 215, 219, 3 McC. 533, 542–543 (1826). *But see, State v. Gaffney,* 24 S.C.L. 180, 181–182, Rice 431, 435–437 (1839) criticizing the *dicta* in *Raines* as to the decriminalization of killings by undue correction, and stating that such killings would fall under Section 2 of the 1821 Act.

35. *See, e.g., Jennings v. Fundeberg,* 15 S.C.L. 61, 4 McCord. 161 (1827); *Braker v. Knight,* 14 S.C.L. 32, 3 McCord. 80 (1825).

36. *Baker v. Bolton,* 1 Camp. 493, 170 Eng. Rep. 1033 (1808); *see,* Stuart Speiser, *Recovery for Wrongful Death* 2–10 (Rochester, 2d ed. 1975).

37. *See, e.g.,* Friedman, *supra* at 473–474; William L. Prosser, *Handbook of the Law of Torts* 898-903 (St. Paul, 4th ed., 1971); Speiser, *supra* at 10–13 noting that there were American cases contrary to the *Baker* rule before its widespread endorsement in the nineteenth century.

38. *See,* Friedman, *supra* at 480–481.

39. *See,* Prosser, *supra* at 898; Speiser, *supra* at 6–8.

40. *Compare, Brunson v. Martin,* 17 Ark. 270 (1856); *Newell v. Cowan,* 30 Miss. 492 (1855); *Neal v. Farmer,* 9 Ga. 555 (1851) (majority rule), *with,*

*Middleton v. Holmes*, 3 Port. 424 (Ala. 1836); *Morgan v. Rhodes*, 1 Stew. 70 (Ala. 1827); *McGrew v. Cato's Executors*, Minor 8 (Ala. 1820).

41. *See, Thompson v. Young*, 30 Miss. 17, 18 (1855); *see, also*, text and notes at Notes 30 and 31 *supra*.

42. *See*, Henry, *supra* at 74; Goodell, *supra* at 216–217.

43. *See*, Schwarz, *supra* at 24; *Commonwealth v. Cohen*, 3 Va. 182, 2 Va. Cas. 158 (1819) (conviction for second degree murder upheld); *Thomas Sorrell's Case*, 3 Va. 6, 1 Va. Cas. 253 (1786) (acquittal on charge of slave murder).

44. 8 N.C. (1 Hawks.) 210 (1820).

45. *See, Id.* at 210–214. The jury's verdict may have been influenced by the fact that there was evidence that the defendant was "guilty" of miscegenation; there were statements of "rumour and belief" that he "kept" the deceased slave's black woman. *See, Id.* at 211. Moreover, evidence was presented showing that hostility between Tackett and the deceased was caused by Tackett's relationship with this woman. *See, Id.* at 210–213.

46. *See, Id.* at 217; *compare, Id.* at 213–14.

47. *Id.* at 215.

48. *Id.* at 217.

49. *Id.* at 218.

50. *See, Id.*

51. *See, Id.* at 216–18.

52. *Id.*

53. *See*, Tushnet, *supra* at 100–102, 104.

54. *See, Towne v. Eisner*, 245 U.S. 418, 425 (1918).

55. *Commonwealth v. Lee*, 60 Ky. (3 Met.) 229 (1860). *See, also, State v. Raines*, 14 S.C.L. 215, 219–220, 3 McC. 533, 542–543 (1826) holding that the 1821 South Carolina Act did make slave murder a crime, but did not adopt the common law definition of manslaughter; a defendant could be guilty for killing on a sudden heat and passion and not for killings caused by undue correction. In South Carolina, the *Tackett* rule was applied even to free blacks, *State v. Harden*, 29 S.C.L. 63, 2 Speers 151 (1832). A Mississippi court distinguished *Tackett* in a case in which the defendant was convicted by a jury of slave manslaughter. The appellate court affirmed, despite the defendant's claim that the trial court erred when it excluded evidence that the deceased was generally "insolent and impudent to white persons." The court found that this was not error where, unlike *Tackett*, there was no evidence of provocation or previous threats and quarrels between the deceased and the defendant, and where the manner of the killing was explained. *See, Jolly v. State*, 21 Miss. 93, 13 S. & M. 223 (1849). The jury in *Jolly*, however, found the defendant guilty of manslaughter, not murder, thus raising on appeal the issue of justification and not mitigation—which was the issue in *Tackett*. Evidence of slave "insolence" and "impudence" was therefore held admissible when the mitigation issue was properly raised, but could not justify slave homicides where there was no evidence of any provocation; otherwise, almost all slave killings would be decriminalized, as was the case during the colonial years. *Compare*, "Equitable Past?," *supra* at 218–219.

56. 1 Miss. 39, 1 Walker 83 (1821).

57. 9 Tenn. (1 Yer.) 156 (1829).

58. 2 Tex. 305 (1847).
59. See, State v. Jones, 1 Miss. 39, 1 Walker 83, 83–84 (1821).
60. Respublica v. Teischer, 1 Dall. 335, 338 (Sup. Ct. Pa. 1788); see, generally, 3A C.J.S., "Animals" § 317 (1973) for the general rule.
61. State v. Jones, supra, 1 Miss. at 39, 1 Walker at 84. [emphasis added].
62. See, State v. Coleman, 5 Port. 32 (Ala. 1837).
63. 39 Miss. 526 (1860).
64. See, Fields v. State, supra, 9 Tenn. (1 Yer.) at 141–142.
65. See, Chandler v. State, supra, 2 Tex. at 307. See, also, State v. Cheatwood, 20 S.C.L. 252, 2 Hill 459 (1834) upholding a like charge after a conviction. Similarly, in State v. Boon, 1 N.C. 103, Tay. 246 (1801), two North Carolina judges opined that slave killing could be common law murder but in dicta. One judge, Hall, disagreed. After the 1817 statute equated slave homicide with the common law, the majority of Chief Justice Taylor and Justice Henderson upheld a common law indictment for slave murder. Justice Hall dissented. See, State v. Reed, 9 N.C. (2 Hawks.) 454 (1823). Neither case is clear regarding the class identity of the killer. Nevertheless, the same North Carolina Supreme Court held, in 1820, that the 1817 statute did not apply the common law of homicide in its full measure to the life of a slave, in an opinion by Chief Justice Taylor. See, State v. Tackett, 8 N.C. (1 Hawks.) 210 (1820). As discussed in the next Chapter, the master's unique power over his slave was reaffirmed in State v. Mann, 13 N.C. 229, 2 Dev. 263 (1829). Compare, "Equitable Past?", supra, at 206–219.
66. 9 Ga. 555 (1851).
67. Id. at 579–580 [emphasis in original].
68. See, State v. Motley, 41 S.C.L. 128, 7 Rich. 327 (1854); Henry, supra at 71. Civil suits filed by masters against whites who killed runaway slaves are numerous. See, e.g., Thompson v. Young, 30 Miss. 17 (1855); Jennings v. Fundeburg, 15 S.C.L. 61, 4 McC. 161 (1827); Witsell v. Earnest, 10 S.C.L. 71, 1 N. & McC. 182 (1818).
69. See, State v. Cheatwood, 20 S.C.L. 252, 2 Hill 459 (1834); Henry, supra at 70. Cf., State v. Smith, 33 S.C.L. 37, 2 Strob. 77 (1847) (conviction for murder of slave upheld, defendant, a member of a "drunken crowd" shot at a white victim and hit the slave who was killed). There are other reported convictions of strangers for slave killings, but most omit factual discussions. See, e.g., Hudson v. State, 34 Ala. 253 (1859); State v. Winningham, 44 S.C.L. 86, 10 Rich. 257 (1857); Cobia v. State, 16 Ala. 781 (1849); State v. Harden, 31 S.C.L. 213, 2 Rich. 533 (1846); State v. Gaffney, 24 S.C.L. 180, Rice 431 (1839); State v. McKee, 17 S.C.L. 297, 1 Bailey 651 (1830); State v. Wimberly, 14 S.C.L. 76, 3 McC. 190 (1825); State v. Gulden, 13 S.C.L. 206, 2 McC. 524 (1823); State v. Smith, 10 S.C.L. 6, 1 Nott & McC. 13 (1817); State v. Gee, 1 S.C.L. 65, 1 Bay. 161 (1791).
70. See, Goodell, supra at 162; Tushnet, supra at 106–108. These same result were achieved in Mississippi by judge-made law when the holding of State v. Jones—that the killing of a slave could be a crime—was extended to a slave master and overseer, in Kelly v. State, 11 Miss. 204, 3 S. & M. 518 (1844) (first degree manslaughter conviction and seven-year sentence affirmed against master and overseer who, while intoxicated, killed master's

slave as a result of mistreatment). The limits on the *Jones/Kelly* doctrine are noted immediately *infra.*

71. 39 Miss. 526 (1860).
72. *See, Id.* at 527–528.
73. *Id.* at 530.
74. *Id.* at 540 and 539.
75. *Id.* at 540.
76. *Dave v. State,* 22 Ala. 23, 33 (1853).
77. *See,* Willie Lee Rose, ed., *A Documentary History of Slavery in North America* 210 (New York, 1976) (hereinafter *"Documentary History"*).
78. *See, State v. Robbins,* 48 N.C. 253, 3 Jones 250 (1855) (murder conviction upheld); *Souther v. Commonwealth,* 48 Va. 338, 7 Gratt. 673 (1851) (second degree murder conviction upheld); *State v. Hoover,* 20 N.C. 393, 4 Dev. & Bat. 500 (1839) (murder conviction upheld). All contain detailed factual discussions. *Cf., State v. Taylor,* 13 S.C.L. 190, 2 McCord 483 (1823) (master shot tied-up slave apparently because slave stole hogs, motion to quash indictment denied).

The other reported cases of appeals from convictions of slave master do not include full factual descriptions. *See,* in Georgia: *Camp v. State,* 25 Ga. 689 (1858) (manslaughter conviction upheld); *Bailey v. State,* 26 Ga. 579 (1858), 20 Ga. 742 (1856) (manslaughter conviction upheld); *State v. Abbot,* 1 Gran. 203, R.M.C. 244 (1822) (bail denied after charge of felonious homicide, no record of conviction); in South Carolina: *State v. Bradley,* 43 S.C.L. 57, 9 Rich. 168 (1855) (conviction upheld); *State v. Posey,* 35 S.C.L. 54, 4 Strob. 103, 35 S.C.L. 74, 4 Strob. 142 (1849) (conviction upheld—defendant ordered slave to kill defendant's wife and thereafter defendant killed slave); *State v. Fleming,* 33 S.C.L. 219, 2 Strob. 464 (1848) (manslaughter conviction and fine upheld); *Rowe v. State,* 2 S.C.L. 225, 2 Bay 565 (1804) (defendant pardoned by governor after conviction for killing slave by undue correction); in Alabama: *State v. Jones,* 5 Ala. 666 (1843) (second degree murder conviction and ten-year sentence affirmed).

79. 48 Va. 338, 7 Gratt. 673 (1851).
80. *Id.* at 339, 7 Gratt. at 679.
81. One appeals court judge also apparently agreed with the jury that intent to kill, required for a first degree murder conviction, had not been shown. *Id.* at 340, 7 Gratt. at 681.
82. 48 N.C. 253, 3 Jones 250 (1855). The defendant in *Robbins* was indicated and convicted on a charge of murdering his sixty-year-old male slave who the defendant apparently believed had failed to fee a horse. *See, Id.* at 255, 3 Jones at 252. The facts of the case were reported as follows:

> The evidence was principally the testimony of three step-children of the defendant, the eldest of whom, Mary Jane, was about seventeen years old. She stated that the prisoner came home on the evening of the 20th of July last, from a tax-paying, between sun-set and dark, and after asking a question as to the weather, and receiving an answer, sat down at the door for a minute or two, seemed serious and held his head down. He then got up and went out, and was out for some time; the precise time not stated. She next heard the deceased at the wood-pile crying out, "don't kill me," and the prisoner

cursing him, and saying, "he intended to kill him." On going to the door, she saw the prisoner beating the deceased with the handle of an axe, holding the blade in both hands. He beat the deceased, she stated, two or three times around the wood-pile, from thence to the barn, and from thence to the house, still using the handle of the axe. This handle, she said, was split before the beating began, for about a finger's length from the end, and that the force used to split it further, to within a finger's length of the blade. This handle, she said, was of hickory, and about the usual size. Afterwards, she said, she saw blood on the axe-handle. The deceased then ran into the kitchen, saying to the prisoner, that he would kill him, to which he, prisoner, replied he intended to do so. The prisoner then putting down the axe at the door, went in, and striking the deceased with his fist on the side of the head, knocked him against the fire-board, from which he fell violently on the floor. From that time, she said, the negro became speechless. She heard him making groans several times in the house and out of it.

After the deceased fell, the prisoner jumped on him, and stamped him for more than ten minutes; that he stamped him upon the head, shoulders, back and sides; indeed, all over; that the prisoner then called for his wagon-whip, and with the butt of it beat the deceased a long time, to wit, for half an hour, upon the head, back and sides; that he would beat until he became exhausted, and then rest and commence again; that he then called for scalding water, and there being none, had water heated, and poured it on the head, back and sides of the deceased; that he then took salt, and putting it on the back of the deceased, whipped it into the flesh with the wagon-whip. She said that he heated water four or five times, and poured it on the deceased; that this stamping, whipping with the wagon-whip, and pouring the scalding water, continued without cessation until 9 or 10 o'clock at night. He then made the witness and her sister drag the deceased out of the house into the yard, and said "damn you, you may rest there while I rest in here," and went to bed.

The other two children, Martha, about thirteen years of age, and Pinkney, about fifteen, proved in substance the same. It was then proved that the wagon-whip was of a large size, with a butt-end of wood covered with leather.

*Id.* at 253–54, 3 Jones at 250–51.
The slave died at about one o'clock the following morning.
*Id.* at 254–55, 3 Jones at 251.
83. 20 N.C. 393, 4 Dev. & Bat. 500 (1839). The defendant was indicted and convicted on a charge of murdering his female slave as a result of mistreatment spanning a period of four months, part of which time she was pregnant. The eloquent words of Judge Ruffin highlight the cruelties perpetrated by the defendant:

[W]ithout any consideration for the sex, health, or strength of the deceased, through a period of four months, including the latter stages of pregnancy, delivery, and recent recovery therefrom, by a series of cruelties and privations in their nature unusual, and in degree excessive beyond the capacity of a stout frame to sustain, the prisoner employed himself from day to day in practicing grievous torture upon an enfeebled female, which finally wore out the energies of nature and destroyed life. He beat her with clubs, iron chains, and other deadly weapons, time after time; burnt her, inflicted stripes over and often, with scourges, which literally excoriated her whole body; forced her out to work in inclement seasons, without being duly clad; provided for her insufficient food; exacted labor beyond her strength, and wantonly beat her because she could not comply with his requisitions. These enormities, besides others too disgusting to be particularly designated, the prisoner, without his heart once relenting or softening practiced from the first of December until the latter end of the ensuing March; and he did not relax even up the last hour of his victim's existence.

*Id.* at 396, 4 Dev. & Bat. at 504.
84. *Id.* at 395, 4 Dev. 7 Bat. at 503.
85. *See, Id.* at 396, 4 Dev. 7 Bat. at 503.
86. *See,* Henry, *supra* at 70.
87. James Sellers, *Slavery in Alabama* 227 (University, Alabama, 2d ed. 1964) citing the journal of H.V. Wooten quoting the testimony of M.B. Smith.
88. Oakes, *supra* at 24.
89. *See,* Stowe, *supra* at 189–191.
90. *See,* Jeffrey R. Brackett, *The Negro in Maryland: A Study of the Institution of Slavery* 142 (New York, reprint ed. 1969) (1889); 4 Catterall, *supra* at 11–13; Alpert, *supra* at 193.
91. *See,* Spindel, *supra* at 48.
92. *See,* Wyatt-Brown, *supra* at 374–376; *see, also* Theodore Rosengarten, *Tombee: Portrait of a Cotton Planter* 456–458 (New York, 1986).
93. Stowe, *supra* at 193–198.
94. *Id.* at 177–188.
95. *See,* Sellers, *supra* at 224–225. For other examples, *see,* Goodell, *supra* at 209–224.
96. *See,* Howington, *supra* at 90–91.
97. *Id.* at 258.
98. *See, e.g.,* Genovese, *supra* at 41, where Professor Genovese cites an article written by a slave owner who calls for uniformity and consistency in slave discipline among slave owning neighbors because extremes of laxity or cruelty made successful slave management difficult.
99. *See,* Wyatt-Brown, *supra* at 376.
100. *See, Id.* at 376–377.
101. Research revealed no statute or case law report to the contrary. *Cf., State v. Mann,* 13 N.C. 299, 2 Dev. 263 (1829) (hirers equated with masters for the purposes of the criminal law of violent slave abuse).
102. The case reports of the jurisdictions studied herein contain numerous appeals in civil litigation involving masters and hirers when a hired slaved died or was killed during the period of hire, whether the hirer was involved in agricultural or non-agricultural pursuits. *See, e.g., Helton v. Caston,* 18 S.C.L. 45, 2 Bail. 95 (1831).
103. *See,* criminal cases: *Jordan v. State,* 22 Ga. 545 (1857) (voluntary manslaughter conviction upheld); *Dowling v. State,* 13 Miss. 249, 5 S. & M. 664 (1846) (second degree murder conviction and five-year sentence reversed because of admission into evidence of defendant's usual means of slave punishment); *State v. Flanigin,* 5 Ala. 477 (1843) (manslaughter conviction and ten-year prison term upheld). Slave masters also pursued their civil

remedies against overseers who killed slaves. *See, e.g., David v. Hunter*, 7 Ala. 135 (1844) (judgment for master affirmed).

The complexity of the master, overseer, and slave relationship was also evidence by appeals after convictions of slaves for directing violence against their overseers. *See, Jim v. State*, 15 Ga. 535 (1854) (slave conviction for murdering overseer affirmed, killing cannot be mitigated to manslaughter when slave killed overseer); *State v. Will*, 18 N.C. 131, 1 Dev. & Bat. 122 (1834) (slaves who killed overseers could having killing mitigated to manslaughter). *See, also, David v. State*, 22 Ala. 23 (1853) (slave's conviction for assault with intent to kill reversed because the trial court excluded testimony of the defendant's "general reputation," court also stated that slaves who killed overseers could not have killings mitigated to manslaughter).

104. *Clay's Alabama Digest* 413, *cited in* Stroud, *supra* at 25; *see, also*, State v. *Flanigin*, 5 Ala. 477 (1843).

105. *See, Id.*, The Alabama Code of 1852 deleted the last limitation. *See*, 1852 Code, *quoted in, Documentary History, supra* at 192.

106. *See, e.g.*, Goodell, *supra* at 300–308; Stowe, *supra* at 168, 177–188; Stroud, *supra* at 44–52; *see, also*, Stampp, *supra* at 222–223.

107. *See*, Stroud, *supra* at 45.

108. Hindus studied the lower court records in thirteen South Carolina counties for the antebellum era. *See*, Hindus, *supra* at 65. Henry reported on lower court records found in ten of those counties. *See*, Henry, *supra* at 70–77.

109. *See*, Hindus, *supra* at 91; Henry *supra* at 70–74, (10 counties, 33 tried and 12 convictions).

110. *See*, Hindus, *supra* at 92; Henry *supra* at 70–74, (61 defendants charged, 13 no bills, and 5 non-prosecutions in 9 counties).

111. *See*, Hindus, *supra* at 93, making this same observation in comparing the overall rates in Massachusetts and South Carolina.

112. *Id.* at 91; Henry *supra* at 70–76 (sixty-one charged, eighteen cases with no trial in nine counties).

113. *See*, Hindus, *supra* at 91–92.

114. Spindel, *supra* at 102. *See, also, Id.* at 102–104 for her analysis of conviction rates and *see*, Donna Spindel, "The Administration of Justice in North Carolina, 1720–1740," 25 *American Journal of Legal History* 141, 156 (1981).

115. This table and Table 5 in Chapter 6 oversimplify to illustrate trends. The civil standards apply to hirers only in both tables. Also, because the widespread use of overseers was characteristic of the plantation period, slave boom standards for overseers are omitted.

116. *See*, Dickson D. Bruce, Jr., *Violence and Culture in the Antebellum South* 124–125 (Austin, Texas: 1979); *see, also*, text and notes at Notes 1 to 5 to Chapter 6, *infra*.

117. Finley, *supra* at 74.

## CHAPTER 6

# The Changing Scope of White Liability for Non-Fatal Slave Abuse

**THE SOUTHERN** slave law also legitimized non-fatal white abuse of slaves. The scope of legalized violence varied over time and differed according to the class status of the white defendant—as was the case with slave homicide. Nevertheless, slave law always legitimized the master's power to whip his slaves into submission. Physical punishment was seen as an indispensable weapon in the master's arsenal of oppression:

> [T]he whip was the most common instrument of punishment—indeed, it was the emblem of the master's authority. Nearly every slaveholder used it, and few grown slaves escaped it entirely. Defenders of the institution conceded that corporal punishment was essential in certain instances.[.][1]

Historians have drawn different conclusions from the historical evidence regarding the frequency of whipping.[2] The data must be considered with the following caveat:

> The frequency with which a punishment is administered is a poor measure of its effectiveness in curbing errant behavior. Presumably, it is the *fear* of eventual punishment, not the *ex post* administration of punishment, which motivates or deters behavior. But there is no obvious correlation between the number of times an individual is punished and his fear of being punished. A slave need never have felt the lash to know the consequences of disobedience.[3]

Therefore, the terror of the whip was in its use and in the threat of its sting. Indeed, "The psychological damage to the slaves inflicted by the whip did not escape white notice."[4]

The law also vested hirers, overseers, patrollers, and strangers with differing degrees of legal power to abuse slaves. In all of these examples, however, the law of slavery replaced the common law crimes of assault, battery, and mayhem with new crimes against slave property.⁵ The law thus decriminalized violence, even when it was committed by strangers to the slave.

## *Non-Fatal Abuse by Strangers*

The scope of a stranger's liability for non-fatal slave abuse contracted and expanded in conjunction with the patterns of Southern social and economic change. For example, statutes enacted in South Carolina in 1740 and Georgia in 1770 decriminalized violent acts that would have been assaults or batteries under the common law. The South Carolina act provided:

> In case any person shall wilfully cut out the tongue, put out the eye, castrate, or cruelly scald, burn, or deprive any slave of any limb or member, or shall inflict any other cruel punishment, other than whipping, or beating with a horsewhip, cowskin, switch, or small stick, or by putting irons on, or confining or imprisoning such slave, every such person shall, for every such offense, forfeit the sum of one hundred pounds, current money.⁶

Thus, slaves were "protected" by the law only if they were willfully dismembered or disfigured, or were subjected to cruel punishment of an unusual nature.

Indeed, Goodell observed that this statute expressly authorized punishment. He stated, "the methods of 'cruel punishment' forbidden are such, and such only, as diminish the pecuniary value of the slave." He concluded that the enactment is therefore consistent with the slave's status as a chattel.⁷ He was correct because this statute replaced the common law crimes that ordinarily would have protected slaves as persons.

The colonial legislators in Virginia and North Carolina did not adopt statutes identical to the Georgia and South Carolina acts. Nevertheless, the colonial Virginia codes absolutely prohibited slaves from striking whites.⁸ It therefore follows that white strangers were immune from criminal prosecution for merely striking slaves. The colonial law of North Carolina was also probably to the same effect as the other three colonies.⁹

Nevertheless, the colonial lawmakers balanced the need for slave control with slave owner economic interests. Thus, the South Carolina and Georgia codes vested slave masters with a statutory right to receive compensation for lost slave labor and medical expenses incurred that were caused by a stranger's unlawful slave whipping.¹⁰ Moreover, the courts held strangers whose violence damaged another person's slave, or caused the owner to lose some free labor, liable to the owner for the economic losses caused by the slave mistreatment. Judges therefore applied the common law rules of civil liability concerning personal property to cases of non-fatal slave abuse.[11] There also was evidence that some slave owners supplemented their civil remedies and used self-help and violence to avenge a stranger's slave abuse.[12]

In this regard, it is worth noting that the common law afforded a master or family member a right to recover damages for lost services and other damages that were caused when the tort of a third person injured a servant or relative. Therefore, the rights of one person were embodied in the person of another, and the slave master's right to sue for lost services or other actual damages was not unique.[13] Nevertheless, the courts went one step beyond the traditional rule to better protect the master's interest and authority.[14]

In the nineteenth century, as plantation slavery matured, slave owners found that the civil remedial scheme inadequately protected their slaves. This perception was caused, in part, by emerging white social class tension, and by the increasing value of slave property and slave labor. The courts and legislatures responded to these changing perceptions of interest and augmented the master's civil damage remedies. Judges borrowed from other areas of law to protect slaves in a way that was superior to ordinary forms of personal property.

For example, an interesting series of South Carolina decisions borrowed doctrine from the law of master and apprentice and real estate law to enhance the master's civil damage remedies. The courts awarded masters damages from strangers who abused slaves, although the master did not lose the benefit of the slave's services. Thus, it was held, in 1796, that a master could recover punitive damages from a white stranger who beat a slave who was carrying out the master's orders. The court stated that the defendant's acts were an "affront" to the master's "authority," which the court strove to protect.[15] An 1837 decision allowed a master to recover damages from a patrol captain who whipped a slave, although the slave was hired out to another master at the time of the beating. The court stated that, "[s]laves are our most valuable property. For its preservation, too many guards cannot be interposed between it and violent, unprincipled men."[16]

Accordingly, in the antebellum years, the general rule evolved that a slave owner could sue a third party for damages, even if the master lost no slave labor or suffered no other monetary damages. With the exception of the Supreme Court of Arkansas, the Southern courts found this rule to be necessary to preserve the master's authority and to prevent unauthorized slave abuse. This law was concerned with punishment as well as compensation for the owner.[17]

The criminal law was also employed, in the nineteenth century, to better protect the master's authority and property rights in cases of non-fatal slave abuse caused by strangers. This law did not equate slaves with people. Instead, slaves were afforded an inferior level of protection from a stranger's non-fatal violence, which was based upon a balancing of the relevant interests of the master and society. For example, in 1811, the General Court of Virginia held that strangers to a slave could be held criminally liable for slave maiming under the general mayhem statute, although that act did not explicitly include slaves within the protected class. In 1827, the court reaffirmed this ruling, stating:

> It is for the benefit of the master, and consoling to his feelings, that a third person should be restrained under the pains and penalties of felony, from maiming and disabling his slave.[18]

Thus, the court found that the maiming of slaves by a stranger constituted excessive violence, when balanced against the master's interest and his "feelings."

The antebellum law also criminalized excessive and inhumane batteries that were committed by strangers to a slave. At the same time, however, the law legitimized all assaults and ordinary batteries. This type of violent abuse was seen as being necessary for the promotion of order in slave society. For example, in *Commonwealth v. Howard*,[19] an 1841 Virginia decision, the General Court upheld a stranger's indictment for "violently and inhumanely assaulting and beating" a slave. This holding was not based upon the common law that protected persons. Instead, it was grounded in a statute that made it a misdemeanor for one to "destroy or injure" the personal property belonging to another. Therefore, slaves were "protected" by the same statute that prohibited "inhuman" beatings of pigs and horses.[20]

The *Howard* case is of both symbolic and substantive importance. On the symbolic level, it signaled to all that the slave did not deserve the protection that the criminal law afforded to whites. The slave was protected to a lesser extent, as valuable property. On the substantive plane, this opinion confirmed that the law of assault and battery was pre-empted by the law of slavery, which criminalized the inhuman abuse of slaves in a similar manner to the way that inhumane treatment of animals was punished.

The crimes of assault and simple battery were also decriminalized in South Carolina. In the 1834 case of *State v. Maner*,[21] Judge John B. O'Neall wrote: "The criminal offence of assault and battery cannot at common law be committed on the person of a slave." He continued:

[F]or some purposes a slave is regarded as a person, yet, generally, he is a mere chattel personal, and his right of personal protection belongs to the master, who can maintain an action of trespass for the battery of his slave.

O'Neall thus concluded that a battery against a slave was a crime only if it was accompanied by "circumstances of cruelty or an attempt to kill and murder." This was because the slave was not legally within the "peace of the State. He is not a citizen, and is not in that character entitled to her protection."[22]

In *Maner*, the court nevertheless upheld an indictment and conviction of a white stranger for assault and battery with the intent to kill a slave. The defendant was on "terms of intimacy" with a slave named Phil. The defendant and Phil "got into a quarrel and a fight ensued, after which the defendant shot [Phil]."[23] Judge O'Neall based his ruling on the 1821 statute that made malicious slave killing a felony. According to O'Neall, that act brought slaves within the protection of the law. He reasoned that an attempt to commit a felony was a common law misdemeanor; therefore, the attempt to commit slave homicide was a misdemeanor after 1821, when the legislature extended the law's protection to slaves.[24]

As noted above, the 1740 South Carolina code did protect slaves from dismemberment as well as cruel and excessive punishment. White strangers were prosecuted under this provision. Moreover, an 1841 statute called for a fine or imprisonment of any person who "shall unlawfully whip or beat any slave, not under his or her charge, without sufficient provocation by word or act[.]"[25] These statutes and the *Maner* case made it clear, however, that the slave in South Carolina was denied the equal protection of the law of assault and battery.

The *Maner* decision is significant because it arose out of a pattern of slave and white "intimacy" and violence that was a growing concern of nineteenth century slave owners and lawmakers. This concern was further explored by the North Carolina Supreme Court in the 1823 case of *State v. Hale*.[26]

That decision held that a stranger could be indicted at common law for the "inhuman assault and battery" upon a slave, absent sufficient justification. This ruling is consistent with the law established in Virginia and South Carolina because the court also denied to slaves the common law's protection against assault and simple battery. Writing for the court, Chief Judge John Taylor listed a number of reasons that would have justified upholding the indictment. These included the preservation of the "public peace" and the need to avoid awakening "resentment" and "vengeance" in the hearts of slave owners whose slaves were beaten by others.[27] But most significantly, the court stated:

> These offenses are usually committed by men of dissolute habits, hanging loose upon society, who, being repelled from association with well-disposed citizens, take refuge in the company of coloured persons and slaves, whom they deprave by their example, embolden by their familiarity, and then beat, under the expectation that a slave dare not resent a blow from a white man.
>
> If such offenses may be committed with impunity, the public peace will not only be rendered extremely insecure, but the value of slave property must be much impaired, for the offenders can seldom make any reparation in damages.[28]

The court also noted that those who felt wronged by a slave had an alternative to self-help. The law provided a means to punish insolent slaves by public whipping by a justice.[29]

Chief Judge Taylor then set forth the basis for common law liability:

> The common law has often been called into efficient operation for the punishment of public cruelty inflicted upon animals for needless and wanton barbarity exercised even by masters upon their slaves, and for various violations of decency, morals and comfort. Reason and analogy seem to require that a human being, although the subject of property, should be so far protected as the public might be injured through him.
>
> For all purposes necessary to enforce the obedience of the slave, and to render him useful as property, the law secures to the master a complete authority over him, and it will not lightly interfere with the relation just established. It is a more effectual guarantee of his right of property when the slave is protected from wanton abuse from those who have no power over him; for it cannot be disputed that a slave is rendered less capable of performing his master's service when he finds himself exposed by the law to the capricious violence of every turbulent man in the community.[30]

Thus, the court did not rule by analogy to the law of humans; rather, it referred to the law that protected the public peace in instances, for example, of the public abuse of animals. Although this opinion also spoke of the "protection of slaves" and of concerns for slave "humanity,"[31] the *Hale* court did not hold that slaves deserved the full measure of protection that the common law of crimes bestowed upon people.

To the contrary, the court stated that in cases involving slaves:

> [M]any circumstances which would not constitute a legal provocation for a battery committed by one white man on another would justify it if committed on a slave, provided the battery were not excessive.[32]

Therefore, the actual holding of the court in *Hale* sustained an indictment for the same manner of "inhuman battery," absent provocation unique to the slave white relationship, that was criminalized under the Virginia statute that protected slaves, horses, and pigs. The *Hale* decision thus denied slaves the protection of the common law of crimes while it protected slave master property interests from poor white violence.

No case from the other Southern states rejected the *Hale* provocation doctrine. An 1839 Alabama statute stated that a stranger who was not on patrol and who assaulted a slave without "just cause" was criminally liable, as if he assaulted a white person.[33] No decision held, however, that the causes that would excuse slave assaults were equated with the violence that would justify attacks directed against whites.[34] In fact, the *Hale* rule was approved of and adopted in a Kentucky case that was decided as late as 1860.[35]

Therefore, in all the states studied in this book, strangers had the right to commit simple battery on a slave and escape criminal liability, although, white strangers were held criminally liable for excessive slave batteries. Nevertheless, slave masters always retained their rights to pursue civil causes of action against whites whose slave abuse caused the owner an economic loss.

## Non-Fatal Slave Abuse by Masters and Hirers

In stark contrast to the changing scope of legitimized non-fatal slave abuse perpetrated by strangers, a fixed principle of slave law granted masters the unlimited right to abuse their slaves to any extreme of brutality and wantonness as long as the slave did not lose his life or a limb. Even nineteenth-century lawmakers held that because the slave was his owner's property, "the master is entitled to the absolute dominion and control over the slave," and that the "slave owes absolute and unconditional submission to the master."[36] Consequently, masters, hirers, and overseers possessed the legal "right to chastise and punish the slave in order to enforce his obedience, and to compel him to the performance of his duties,"[37] and therefore could not be held criminally liable for common law assault or battery if they beat or shot a slave under their command.[38] In addition, the courts and legislatures placed no legal limitation upon the master's, hirer's, and overseer's right to commit slave battery to any extreme if the slave was in a state of "resistance" against the authority of these "superiors."[39]

Nevertheless, the right to chastise a submissive slave as cruelly as one wished depended upon whether the punisher was the slave's master, hirer, or overseer. In this regard, the slave master's power remained unlimited; the appellate case reports of the Southern common law states contain no case in which a master was successfully prosecuted for excessive slave punishment,[40] although the historical record exhibits many accounts of the reality of slave master brutality.[41] Therefore, William Goodell correctly states: "[T]he Slave being 'Property' can have no protection against the Master, and has no remedy or redress for injuries inflicted by him."[42] But the lawmakers of the states studied herein established this unlimited right in two different ways. Case law confirmed the master's power in Virginia and North Carolina. In the other states, statute law legitimized the master's rights.

The Virginia and North Carolina colonial statutes initially granted slave masters the unlimited right to punish their slaves. The first relevant statute, enacted in Virginia in 1669, did not do so explicitly.[43] Instead, the master's right to correct his slaves was derived from the principles of English customary and common law that permitted "superiors" to correct their "inferiors."[44] Thus, the colonists drew upon the rules of law that allowed them to discipline servants, apprentices, and children without facing criminal prosecution for simple battery;[45] they soon found, however, that this privilege was limited in ways that were inappropriate for the institution of slavery.[46]

Therefore, in 1669, the Virginians enlarged the permissible scope of legal correction to fit the master and slave relationship.[47] A statute passed in that year provided that if a slave resisted his master, "and by the extremity of the correction should chance to die," the master's killing was explicitly declared a non-criminal act.[48] Because masters could legally kill rebellious slaves, *a fortiori* no lesser punishment could result in criminal liability. Moreover, the 1723 code extended the master's right to kill her slaves if the death resulted from correction that was prompted by any offense the master thought the slave committed, whether the slave was resisting or submissive.[49] *A fortiori*, this rule also applied to all forms of non-fatal chastisement. The eighteenth-century law of North Carolina also contained this odious principle of justice.[50] The early colonial legislatures apparently perceived the need for slave control to be a pressing interest that precluded any state interference with the slave master's right to brutally terrorize and torture his own slaves.

Because the legislators of the latter years of the eighteenth century expanded the criminal liability of strangers who killed or abused slaves and masters who brutally killed their slaves, the issue arose whether a slave owner could be held criminally liable for cruel correction of his own slave who was actually submitting to his or her "rightful" punishment. Nevertheless, in the 1820's a Virginia court in *Commonwealth v. Turner*[51] and a North Carolina court in *State v. Mann*[52] reaffirmed the master's right to punish her own slaves without any limitation by judge-made or common law. Although these two courts reached the same result, they employed different legal doctrines to achieve and justify this rule.

The defendant in *Turner* was indicted for assaulting his own slave by using "certain rods, whips and sticks" to willfully and maliciously, violently, cruelly, immoderately, and excessively beat, scourge, and whip" his victim.[53] All of the judges assumed that a simple battery was legal; thus the only issue for the court was whether the excessive nature of the battery compelled them to impose criminal liability on the defendant. The General Court, with one dissent, held that the defendant could not be so indicted in Virginia in 1827.[54]

In his majority opinion, Judge William Dade acknowledged that no statute precluded the common law indictment.[55] This was so because the colonial statutes that had legitimized all non-fatal slave punishment inflicted by masters were repealed by the legislature in 1788.[56] Therefore, the door was opened for the court to uphold the indictment as a matter of judge-made law based upon the slave's common law rights to personal security. Judge Dade responded, however, by quickly closing off this reasoning, stating that the slave's supposed personal rights were of no import whatsoever. He argued that the court could sustain the indictment only by exercising its power to criminalize cruel slave battery because this type of behavior by a master "disturbed the harmony of society, was offensive to public decency, and directly tended to a breach of the peace." The judge stated further:

> The same would be the law, if a horse had been so beaten. And yet it would not be pretended, that it was in respect to the rights of the horse, or the feelings of humanity, that this interposition would take place.[57]

Accordingly, Judge Dade reasoned that if the court approved the indictment for cruel slave battery it would be creating a new common law crime *contra bonos mores*. He disclaimed the court's power to do so.[58]

Instead, Judge Dade argued that it was the legislature's role to declare a master's cruel slave battery to be a crime. Dade declared that this new crime amounted to legal change that was too swift and severe for a common law court to make. He stated that the courts could only effect "silent, and almost imperceptible changes," so that "society [could] easily conform itself to the law."[59] Judge Dade found no precedent for this prosecution; in fact, he thought it was a "new idea" whose time had not yet come.[60]

But how could Judge Dade frame the issue to avoid the slave's common law "personal rights" when only six months earlier, in *Commonwealth v. Carver*,[61] the General Court held that a slave was protected by the criminal code's mayhem provision from a stranger's violence, although the legislature did not explicitly include slaves in the protected class? Was it not also for the legislature to explicitly include slaves within the intended statutory definition of "persons?" Judge Dade did not even attempt to harmonize his reasoning in *Turner* with the *Carver* holding. But the lone *Turner* dissenter, Judge William Brockenbrough, made his thought process more explicit. His analysis is the key to understanding these two cases.

Judge Brockenbrough thought that the issue at bar in *Turner* did involve the slave's "personal rights" at common law; however, he asserted that the scope and nature of these slave "rights" was not to be defined by traditional common law notions. Rather, he argued that the extent of slave "personal rights" should be determined by balancing the interests relevant to slave mistreatment within the context of slave society.[62] Therefore, he stated that a slave is entitled to protection as a "person" by the common law "except so far as the application of it conflicted with the enjoyment of the slave as a thing."[63]

Judge Brockenbrough struck a different balance of these interests than Judge Dade. The dissenter found that if the court upheld the indictment for cruel battery, the master's interest in the "full enjoyment of the right or property" in the slave would not be interfered with, because cruel punishment was "unnecessary" for "enjoyment of the slave as a thing," and that the master's security interests, the "peace of society," and slave subordination would all be served by criminalizing the conduct of the defendant.[64] He also argued that because "our Courts and Juries are composed of men who, for the most part, are masters, I cannot conceive that any injury can accrue to the rights and interests of that class of the community."[65] Furthermore, this same desire to protect property rights motivated him to hold in *Commonwealth v. Carver*[66] that a stranger could be indicted for non-fatal slave abuse under the criminal code's mayhem provision. In that case, Brockenbrough wrote:

> It is for the benefit of the master, and consoling to his feelings, that a third person should be restrained . . ., from maiming and disabling his slave.[67]

Judge Brockenbrough struck the same balance in both *Turner* and *Carver*; he thought the "interest" of the master and the "safety" of the slave were forwarded by upholding both indictments. In *Carver* the majority agreed, and in *Turner* they disagreed with his analysis. Nevertheless, the results of *Turner* and *Carver* are consistent if one realizes that concern for slave "humanity" was irrelevant to these judges. They decided how they would extend the criminal law of persons to protect slaves based upon their conceptions of slaves as valuable property. The criminal law was perceived as a tool they could use to better protect this property, but which had to be applied very carefully and always with the best interests of the master class in mind.

The North Carolina Supreme Court reached the same result two years later in *State v. Mann*.[68] The defendant Mann hired a slave, Lydia, from her master. During this period of hire, Lydia committed "some small offense, for which the defendant undertook to chastise her[.]" Lydia "ran off" during this chastisement, "whereupon the defendant called upon her to stop, which being refused, he shot at and wounded her."[69] The defendant was indicted and convicted for assault and battery.[70] Writing for a unanimous court, Judge Thomas Ruffin reversed the conviction. He equated the hirer with a master and declared that a master could not be indicted for assault and battery upon his slave at common law.[71]

Judge Ruffin found the distinction between the resisting and submissive slave to be irrelevant. He stated that in both instances the master has "uncontrolled authority over the body" of his slave.[72] He continued:

> [T]here may be particular instances of cruelty and deliberate barbarity where, in conscience, the law might properly interfere . . . But we cannot look at the matter in that light. . . We cannot allow the right of the master to be brought into discussion in the courts of justice. The slave, to remain a slave, must be made sensible that there is no appeal from his master[.][73]

Judge Ruffin cited no legal authority for this proposition; his holding was based on the realities of the master-slave relation that made it imperative that the master have this unlimited power.

Unlike Judge Dade, Judge Ruffin was forced to explicitly discuss his conception of the foundations of the master and slave relationship in order to distinguish it from the body of common law authority that permitted "superiors" to correct their children, pupils, and apprentices without liability for simple battery, but that limited the extent of the legal battery. He based this distinction on the fact that the slave relationship, unlike the others, had as its "end . . . the profit of the master, his security and the public safety"; therefore, the judge reasoned that the slave must labor and never "reap the fruits" of his toil—which was for the master's profit alone. Judge Ruffin then stated:

> What moral considerations shall be addressed to such a being to convince him what it is impossible but that the most stupid must feel and know can never be true—that he is thus to labor upon a principle of natural duty, or for the sake of his own personal happiness, such services can only be expected from one who has no will of his own; who surrenders his will in implicit obedience to that of another. Such obedience is the consequence only of uncontrolled authority over the body. There is nothing else which can operate to produce the effect. The power of the master must be absolute to render the submission of the slave perfect.[74]

Judge Ruffin noted further:

> There have been no prosecutions of the sort. The established habits and uniform practice of the country in this respect is the best evidence of the portion of power deemed by the whole community requisite to the preservation of the master's dominion.[75]

Like Judge Brockenbrough, Judge Ruffin explicitly balanced the relevant interests. But to Ruffin, the master's "full dominion" over his slave:

> [I]s essential to the value of slaves as property, to the security of the master, and the public tranquility, greatly dependent upon their subordination; and, in fine, as most effectually securing the general protection and comfort of the slaves themselves.[76]

Judge Ruffin's perceptions of these interests formed the basis of the reasoning that caused him to reach the terrible result in *Mann*. Ruffin's concern for slave "protection" and "comfort" was, in reality, an interest of no weight.

It must be noted that Judge Ruffin's opinion had to account—in some way—for the slave's "humanity" because of the holding in *State v. Hale*[77] that a white stranger could be indicted at common law for assault and battery upon a slave. The defendant in *Mann* was indicted at common law for the same crime; therefore, Judge Dade's argument that slaves were always property was not available to Ruffin. Nevertheless, Ruffin distinguished the *Hale* precedent and reached the same result as Judge Dade and the *Turner* majority. But the only way Ruffin could achieve the end he desired was to abandon the legal fiction of concern for "slave human rights" and lay bare the balance of the "pragmatic" interests that all the courts and legislatures implicitly or explicitly balanced in determining whether to criminalize or legitimize a given form of violent slave abuse by a given white defendant.

Therefore, Judge Ruffin's references to "sentiment" and "humanity" were merely *dicta* when one reconciles the results reached by the court with its precedential context. Both *Mann* and *Turner* vindicated the master's and hirer's right to cruelly and maliciously beat and torture a slave without any limit at common law as long as the slave lost neither life nor limb. It is true that Judge Dade "deplored that an offense so odious and revolting . . . should exist to the reproach of humanity,"[78] and Judge Ruffin could not "but lament when such cases as the present are brought into judgment."[79] But these words, whether sincere or not, did not square with the results reached by both courts, which vindicated the "absolute despotism" that was at the heart of American Southern slavery. In fact, these references revealed how the concept of humanity was perverted and reified in the minds of these judges.[80] Furthermore, the legislators of Virginia and North Carolina never enacted statutes prohibiting cruel and unusual slave punishment to thereby abrogate the *Turner-Mann* doctrine. Thus, by inaction they added their votes in favor of the legal standard these opinions established.[81]

Masters in the other jurisdictions obtained the absolute right to commit slave batteries by a different legal means. The legislatures enacted statutes prohibiting "cruel or unusual" slave punishment. The Alabama act was typical:

> No cruel or unusual punishment shall be inflicted on any slave, and any master, or other person having charge of a slave, who shall be guilty of inflicting such punishment, or authorizing or permitting the same . . . [shall be subject to a fine ranging from $50 to $1,000, depending upon the severity of the punishment].[82]

The Texas statutes were more detailed than the norm. They granted masters—and those acting in the place of a master—the right "to inflict any punishment upon the slave, not affecting life or limb, and not coming within the definition of cruel treatment, or unreasonable abuse[.]" The master was established, however, as the "exclusive judge of the necessity" for moderate correction. These statutes defined unreasonable abuse as the infliction of punishment "greatly disproportionate to the nature of the offense" or beating with "unusual implements." Cruel treatment was defined as torturing, causing unusual pain and suffering, or punishment that was severe enough to injure the slave's health or "depreciate his value."[83]

Accordingly, these enactments authorized the "usual" modes of punishment. They also provided that a master could not be indicted at common law for assault or battery on his own slave, in derogation of the common law.

It was unclear, however, whether the legislators intended that these statutes do anything more than justify batteries by masters.[84] William Goodell's words are relevant:

> It could hardly be supposed that, in any civilized country, the Legislature would, by express statute, authorize the master to commit cruel outrages upon the persons of his slaves[.][85]

He also notes that the cruel and unusual punishment statues did—in a subtle way—authorize the "usual" forms of punishment:

> That which is *"usual"* is *authorized*, whatever it may be, short of maiming[,] mutilation, and murder . . . In short the current *usages* of the fraternity of slaveholders (with the exceptions specified) are proclaimed . . . to constitute *the law*.[86]

Nevertheless, even if some legislators intended to limit the master's legal right to correct his slaves, the appellate case reports of the relevant states do not contain a single case in which a master was successfully prosecuted for cruel slave punishment in violation of one of these statutes.

There are several cases in which masters were indicted for cruel and unusual punishment. Randolph Campbell reports of the Texas case of Thomas Steen. In 1847, Steen was indicted "for cruel treatment of three young slaves by denying them adequate food or clothing, exposing them to inclement weather, and whipping them with unusual severity." Steen was acquitted. The next year, however, Steen's son was indicted on similar charges. The younger Steen was convicted and fined. Nevertheless, he was not the master, and the ultimate punishment was merely a fine of $262.49.[87]

The only reported conviction for a master for cruel punishment is reported in the 1843 Alabama case of *Turnipseed v. State*.[88] The master was fined the minimum sum—fifty dollars. The Alabama Supreme Court reversed the conviction, holding that the indictment was defective. The prosecution argued that the indictment was sufficient because it followed the wording of the statute. The court disagreed, and its holding was based on its concern for the "vague" wording of the statute. The court opined that the statute "merely denounces the cruel and unusual punishment of a slave as a public offense," and "does not declare with particularity" the "elements" of this offense.[89] Consequently, the court held that the state must allege in its indictment "what punishment was inflicted and how," so that "the court might judge whether the accused should have been put upon his trial; that he may know what he is to defend against, and the jury know how to apply the evidence."[90]

The court therefore allowed the defendant the opportunity to first have his indictment reviewed by the trial judge to avoid a jury trial altogether. Even if his motion to quash the indictment was denied and he was convicted by the jury, the appellate court could review the denial of the motion to quash as well as the conviction itself.

This cure for statutory vagueness afforded trial and appellate judges the opportunity to apply a "sliding scale" of culpability for cruel or unusual punishment based upon the class identity of the white defendant, before a jury trial. This desired end may explain why the court did not find the statute "ambiguous," and apply the rule that required strict construction of ambiguous criminal statues.[91] By using this technique, the court could have "saved" the statute by reading into the words "cruel and unusual" the element of willfulness. This was the method used by the nineteenth-century Massachusetts courts to save a similarly ambiguous cruelty to animals prohibition.[92] Under that doctrine, the prosecution was not required to specify the acts of cruelty in the indictment; an allegation of cruelty was sufficient to exclude accidental injuries and lawful punishments. The Alabama legislature adopted the latter approach; it enacted a statute "overruling" the *Turnipseed* court's specificity requirement. That statute entrusted the jury with the duty to determine if there was proof of the necessary degree of cruelty.[93]

The Southern courts and legislators nevertheless recognized that the cruel and unusual punishment statutes legalized the master's right to punish his slaves. This is further illustrated by the 1859 Missouri decision in *State v. Peters*.[94] Three defendants—Lewis Peters, Mary Peters, and John Peters—were indicted for cruel slave punishment in violation of the Missouri anticruelty statutes. Lewis Peters was the slave's owner. He was discharged from prosecution and was not tried. The other two defendant were tried and convicted. The Missouri Supreme Court reversed the conviction. The court held that only masters, or those in legal control of the slave, could be punished under the act: "When slaves are cruelly used by those who do not bear to them the relation of master or *quasi*-master, such offenses stand on the same ground as when white persons cruelly use each other."[95] The import of this holding is that the white strangers should have been indicted for assault or battery, but that masters were exempt from those crimes. They could be indicted only for cruel punishment. It was left to the juries to define what punishment and treatment crossed the line from a necessary assault or battery to cruel treatment.[96]

Thus, the "cruel or unusual" punishment statutes saved the courts in these states from facing the harsh realities of slavery illustrated in the *Turner* and *Mann* decisions. Consequently, the court in *Turnipseed* could denounce the offense as "odious" while it dismissed the indictment on "autonomous" legal grounds. These statutes, therefore, confirmed the master's power to punish his slaves and lent legitimacy to this power. This would have been the case even if there were dozens of successful prosecutions of masters for cruel and unusual slave abuse. The dearth of cases permits one to conclude, however, that the master's complete immunity from punishment for batteries was vindicated by these statutes.

Slave hirers also were vested with the master's right to cruelly punish submissive slaves. When masters hired their slaves out to others, the owner's property interest in the hired slave often conflicted with the hirer's need to maintain slave discipline.[97] The nineteenth-century courts accommodated these interests by equating hirers with masters as a matter of criminal law, while allowing masters to recover monetary damages from hirers who cruelly abused slaves. In *State v. Mann*,[98] the only hirer conviction on the appeals records, explicitly extended to hirers the master's unlimited authority to punish slaves.[99] This rule must have appeared to be necessary to the Southern courts and legislatures. Most hirers were slave owners;[100] how could they be under a duty to refrain from cruelly punishing their hired slaves when they possessed unrestrained power to torture and beat their own slaves?

Moreover, Judge Ruffin recognized that the *Mann* decision did not interfere with the slave owner's right to recover damages from a hirer "for an injury permanently impairing the value of the slave."[101] In fact, the appellate case reports contain countless civil suits in which owners recovered monetary damages from hirers who injured slave property. Most hirers were slave owners who usually possessed property and wealth sufficient to pay a judgment to a fellow slave owner. The courts and legislatures, therefore, thought that the civil remedies afforded slave owners sufficient protection.

The law did limit the power of masters and hirers to dismember slaves, but only to the extent that slave murder was regulated. Mayhem was a common law crime that prohibited willful dismemberment, disablement, or disfigurement.[102] The earliest cruel and unusual punishment statutes preserved this crime, while they decriminalized assaults and batteries that did not rise to the level of extreme punishment. A fine was the only penalty for this offense.[103] Even after *Turner*, it is possible that a master could have been held culpable under Virginia's general mayhem statute. In addition, the *Mann* decision did not foreclose a common law prosecution for mayhem perpetrated on a slave's person.[104]

Moreover, the legal toleration of slave maiming apparently declined over the years. The colonial laws of South Carolina and Virginia actually required that slaves be disfigured if they committed serious offenses. By the latter years of the eighteenth century, however, most of the provisions calling for maiming were eliminated from the statute books.[105]

The Alabama constitution went so far as to require that the punishment for cases of malicious slave dismemberment be the same as in cases in which a white was the victim, with an exception "in case of the insurrection of such slave."[106] This concept of insurrection, however, was used to decriminalize all but the most heinous killings by masters. It also marked off the only possible limit on the master's power to maim his slaves, even in the nineteenth century.

In fact, there are but two reported cases in the states studied herein in which a master was prosecuted for willfully maiming his slave. One conviction was reversed in *Eskridge v. State*.[107] As the court in *Turnipseed*, the *Eskridge* court was concerned with a seemingly technical error in the indictment, which stated that the slave belonged to "Mrs. Eskridge" when the defendant was the owner.[108] Implicit in the court's reasoning was the notion that different standards would be applied depending upon the class identity of the defendant. Obviously, the most lenient approach would be reserved for slave owners and hirers.

This is revealed by the other reported case, which was decided in 1850 in Tennessee. The defendant was convicted of committing mayhem on his own slave. The slave was tied down and castrated to effect "moral reform."[109] Clearly, the subdued slave was not dismembered in the act of resistance or insurrection. This is the only successful prosecution in the appellate cases. It indicates that only the dismemberment of a submissive slave could result in criminal liability. Thus, masters and hirers could disable, maim, or kill slaves who posed any threat to the master's or hirer's authority.

The dearth of any other successful maiming prosecutions can also be explained because the court in Tennessee may have perceived the relevant interests differently than the courts in the other slave states. The percentage of slave population grew slowly in Tennessee over the years; in 1860 it amounted to only 25 percent, a lower percentage than most of the other Southern states. The absence of cases elsewhere can be explained by a different resolution of the relevant interests in these states than in Tennessee. The need for slave control may have still weighed in favor of giving the master unlimited discretion to maim his slave, in the minds of the masters and lawmakers of the other states. Nevertheless, the available data indicate that the slave was denied the protection of the common law crime of mayhem, as well as murder, if he was in a state of rebellion or insurrection against a master or hirer.

## Non-Fatal Abuse by Overseers and Patrols

Overseers, unlike masters and hirers, risked criminal liability for excessive punishment of slaves. The overseer's need to maintain slave discipline conflicted with the master's interest in preventing unnecessary damage to slave property. Consequently, slave owners did sue overseers to recover monetary compensation for damage to slaves.[110] But because of social and economic class tensions, masters and the lawmakers thought that the master's civil remedies were inadequate.[111] Therefore, in *Scott v. State*[112] the court upheld an overseer's conviction for cruel slave punishment, indicating that the "cruel and unusual" punishment statutes had two purposes. First, they justified the master's and overseer's rights to punish slaves in the usual manner. Second, because of the vague wording of these statues, the courts could read them to hold overseers to a stricter standard than masters or hirers.[113]

Thus, the court in *Scott* stated that "to exempt overseers from the penalties of the act . . . would, to a great extent, defeat the benign and salutary purposes of the law."[114] Although the court did not specify what it thought these purposes were, its holding helped protect slave property from unnecessary damage by criminalizing the cruel acts of overseers.[115] Nevertheless, the courts recognized the overseer's need to have discretionary power to correct slaves and maintain order on the plantation. Thus, the law legitimized violence directed against slaves, but in degrees depending upon the class status of the white offender.

The Southern states also legalized white violence with the patrol laws. These statutes established patrols as a form of militia to police slaves who were not on their plantations nor under the direct supervision of a responsible white person. The patrols served a necessary security function in the South in the absence of a modern urban police force.[116]

The patrol laws had their origin in the colonial legislation of Virginia, South Carolina, and Georgia. As slaves became more numerous in these colonies, the patrol laws became more and more comprehensive.[117] In the antebellum years, patrol laws existed by state statute throughout the South, and by ordinance or regulations in the cities. Generally, these laws required all white males, including slaveowners, to serve patrol duty on a rotating basis. Penalties were provided for those who failed to serve.

A key element in the patrol system was the requirement that all slaves away from their plantations exhibit a written pass or ticket from their master. The aim here was to restrict, but not eliminate, the slave's freedom of movement. The slave was merely the extension of his master's authority. Therefore, the slave could travel under his master's orders, but could not move about of his own volition.

The patrol laws legitimized white violence in the way the restrictions on slave locomotion were enforced. The patrols were charged with the duty to police all roads at night to prevent escapes by slaves and could apprehend all slaves to determine if the slaves had passes from their masters. Patrollers were vested with the authority to break up unauthorized slave gatherings and search slaves for arms and other illegal possessions. If a slave resisted arrest by a patrol, the law provided that the slave could be subdued and killed.

Most statutes stated that if a slave was caught away from his plantation without a pass, the patrol should whip the slave on the spot. Moreover, the Alabama Code of 1852 vested patrollers with the

> power to enter, in a peaceable manner, upon any plantation; to enter by force, if necessary, all negro cabins or quarters . . ., and to apprehend all slaves who may there be found, not belonging to the plantation or household, without a pass from their owner or overseer[.]

Slaves caught in violation of this statute were subject to an immediate whipping of up to thirty-nine stripes.[118]

This type of provision, according to the North Carolina Supreme Court, gave the patrollers "a judicial or *quasi-* judicial, and executive character." The court explained that the patrols were judicial because they could decide "upon each case of a slave taken up by them; whether the law has been violated by him or not, and adjudging the punishment to be inflicted."[119] The patrol's executive authority arose when it administered immediate punishment in accordance with its collective judgment.

The policy behind the patrol laws was explained by Justice Elihu Bay for the South Carolina Court of Appeals. He wrote that the patrol act

> . . . may and ought to be considered as one of the safeguards of the people of South Carolina, for the protection of their dwellings and habitations, and for the prevention of unlawful assembling of a particular class of our population, and as a security against insurrection; a danger of such a nature, that it never can or ought to be lost sight of in the southern States. It may justly be considered as a branch of our militia system; our grand national defence against foreign enemies, and for our internal tranquility at home. It is easy, therefore, to see that the summary and decisive powers ought to be vested in the hands of those who are charged with the execution of this important duty.[120]

This broad grant of authority to patrols was thus viewed as an essential supplement to the power of the master to discipline his slaves.

Consequently, the patrol system set aside the common law and vested patrollers with powers to confine and abuse slaves in excess of the powers afforded other whites who were strangers to the slave. Patrollers could beat slaves without fear of prosecution for battery under the common law. Nevertheless, there were legal limits to the patroller's authority. Here again, interclass tensions among whites surfaced:

> The nonslaveholding whites, to whom most patrol service was relegated, frequently disliked masters almost as intensely as the Negroes, and as patrollers they were in a position to vent their feelings toward both.[121]

Slave owners also felt prejudices toward the patrols. Thus Stampp notes that slaveholders and patrollers were often involved in litigation in which a master alleged that a patrol abused its power and thereby damaged the master's property or invaded the master's authority.[122]

Of course, if the unwarranted exercise of a patrol's powers caused injury or death to a slave, the master could sue the offending patrollers for trespass and recover money damages.[123] An 1839 South Carolina act provided for a five dollar fine for patrollers who abused their office in addition to the offender's liability for trespass.[124] There were also criminal prosecutions against patrols for common law riot when the patrollers acted beyond the scope of their authority.[125] In addition, there is evidence of cases in which masters were accused of physically opposing patrols.[126]

Therefore, the patrols held a problematic, but necessary position. The law authorized their right to abuse slaves when the patrollers acted within the law. Their authority was broad indeed; but patrols were not privileged to vent their hostility toward slave masters through abuse of the owner's slaves. Thus, the patrols were regulated, not out of any concern for slave right, but in the interest of the master and his property and position. This is noted by the South Carolina Court of Appeals:

> [It] would be a violation of all law [to] place the slaves of this country at the mercy of every unprincipled and unfeeling man, who may be clothed with this brief authority.
> It is the duty as well as the interest of every master to protect his slave from unnecessary punishment, and to resist the abuse of legal authority.[127]

Slaves were, however, always subject to "necessary" punishment at the hands of the patrols. This the law allowed to further slave control.

## Conclusion

The antebellum law of non-fatal slave abuse lent legitimacy to the oppression of slavery. This is because the law continued to legalize white violence that would otherwise have been criminal under the common law of crimes. This is illustrated by the following:

### Table 6
#### Scope of Liability for Non-Fatal Slave Abuse

| Strangers | | Masters/Hirers | | Overseers |
| --- | --- | --- | --- | --- |
| Slave Boom | Plantation Period | Slave Boom | Plantation Period | Plantation Period |
| *Simple Battery:* | | | | |
| Criminal—No Liablity | Criminal—No Liablity | Criminal—No Liability | Criminal—No Liablity | Criminal—No Liablity |
| Civil—No Liablity | Civil—Nominal Damages | Civil—No Liablity | Civil—No Liability | Civil—No Liability |
| *Excessive Battery:* | | | | |
| Criminal—No Liability | Criminal—Fine and/or jail, mitigation based on slave's status | Criminal—No Liability | Criminal—No Liability | Criminal—No Liability |
| Civil—Actual Damages | Civil—Actual Damages and Nominal Damages | Civil—Actual Damages | Civil—Actual Damages | Civil—Actual Damages |
| *Cruel or unusual punishment:* | | | | |
| Criminal—Either no liability or fine | Criminal—Fine and/or jail | Criminal—No Liablity | Criminal—No Liability | Criminal—Fine and/or jail |
| Civil—Actual Damages | Civil—Actual Damages and Nominal Damages | Civil—Actual Damages | Civil—Actual Damages | Civil—Actual Damages |

This law, even in the antebellum years, discriminated against slaves, and it also reflected class bias and conflict within white culture.

The South Carolina lower court records studied by Hindus and Henry show how these substantive differences were translated into practice. Hindus found a 35.3 percent effective conviction ratio in all assault cases. But based upon Henry's data, a 30.8 percent effective conviction rate was achieved in slave assault cases.[128] This rate is especially shocking when one realizes that the substantive law decriminalized simple assaults against slaves; thus, the lower conviction ratio came about after this legalization of violence. Accordingly, the slave's person was protected only to the most minimal extent.

This is further shown when one compares the ratio of murder to assault charges. Hindus found that for each murder charge there were 24.8 assault cases statewide in South Carolina. According to Henry's figures, however, in slave cases there were only 1.7 assault cases for each murder charge.[129] Consequently, the legalization of slave assaults is reflected in this data.

When examining these statistics and legal materials, we must recall that the law legitimized the masters' unlimited power to correct their slaves, as long as they took neither life nor limb.

Accordingly, the master's power over his slaves was limited only in instances that were perceived to threaten the public peace and the general welfare, a point that is further explored in the next chapter.

Nevertheless, masters who hired overseers did seek to control their employees' power over slaves. Slaveowners "often fixed the number of stripes [overseers] could inflict for each specific offense, or a maximum number whatever the offense."[130] The law reflected this ambivalence about the overseer's right to correct slaves.

There was no doubt about the master's authority, which remained almost entirely unchecked. Slave masters did not "think that they were committing a crime by whipping their slaves."[131] This attitude, on occasion, resulted in what was perceived as cruelty; indeed, as Stampp wrote, "cruelty was endemic in all slaveholding communities[.]" The problem here is that one master's cruelty might be another's prudence:

> Southerners . . . found it difficult to draw a sharp line between acts of cruelty and such measures of physical force as were an inextricable part of slavery.[132]

The law recognized this ambiguity and allowed masters wide discretion in slave correction.

Why was it not clear, however, that all whipping was inhumane? This was because the inherent cruelties of the master's domination over the slave blinded the Southerners to the inherent inhumanity of their way of life. Moreover, slaveowners saw the whip as being necessary for their own survival:

> Slaves lived in perpetual fear—fear of producing too little, fear of oversleeping, fear of the searing, bloody lash that cowed them into outward submission. But we must also look at the other side of the coin: the slaveholders, too, lived in perpetual terror of the black volcano upon which they sat. The violence they used was an exact expression of their understanding that human beings could not be kept in slavery without the constant threat of brutal punishment if they dared to resist or to rebel.[133]

Therefore, a prohibition against physical punishment may have been too much to ask of nineteenth-century Southerners.[134] Nevertheless, the master's unlimited right to whip his slaves short of death was a new innovation in the common law that arose in the United States South. The law legitimated this brutality.


# NOTES

1. Stampp, *supra* at 174; *see, also,* Oakes-1990, supra at 6.
2. For example, Fogel and Engerman argue that slave whippings were not too frequent, only "an average of 0.7 whippings per hand per year." *See,* Robert W. Fogel and Stanley L. Engerman, *Time on the Cross: The Economics of American Negro Slavery* 145 (Boston, 1974). These data are taken from the records of the Louisiana plantation of Bennet Barrow. Gutman and Sutch contend, however, that the actual frequency on Barrow's plantation was 1.19 whippings per hand per year. *See,* Herbert G. Gutman and Richard Sutch, "Sambo Makes Good, or Were Slaves Imbued with the Protestant Work Ethic?," (hereinafter "Sambo Makes Good") in *Reckoning with Slavery, supra* at 63. In any case, even using the Fogel and Engerman average, among Barrow's 160 to 140 slaves:

> A slave ... was whipped every 4.56 days. Three slaves were whipped every two weeks. Among them ... (37.5 percent) were females. A male was whipped once a week, and a female once every twelve days.

Herbert G. Gutman, *Slavery and the Numbers Game: A Critique of "Time on the Cross"* 19 (Urbana, 1975).

Thus, whippings were a part of the regular weekly routine.
3. "Sambo Makes Good" in *Reckoning with Slavery, supra* at 58.
4. Genovese, *supra* at 66, *see, also,* Oakes-1990, *supra* at 19–21.
5. Goodell, *supra* at 162. Common law mayhem consisted of the violent

deprivation of another person's use of his limbs, resulting in disfigurement or disablement. *See, generally,* LaFave, *supra* at 614—617. Battery is defined as contact resulting in an injury, or offensive touching; while assault occurs without touching and is defined as the intentional frightening of another person. *See, Id.* at 602–603.

6. Goodell, *supra* at 159–160 [emphasis omitted]. The Georgia act with similar language is quoted in Higginbotham, *supra* at 255.

7. *See, e.g.*, Goodell, *supra* at 160.

8. *See,* Higginbotham, *supra* at 55.

9. Although there were no cases concerning colonial North Carolina criminal law, *see, Tate v. O'Neal,* 8 N.C. (1 Hawks) 418 (1821) for civil authority. The first reported conviction for assault and battery on a slave is from the 1820's. *See, infra,* Notes 26–31 and accompanying text.

10. *See, e.g.*, Higginbotham, *supra* at 195, 255; Goodell, *supra* at 202.

11. *See, e.g., Tate v. O'Neal,* 8 N.C. (1 Hawks) 418 (1821); *Belmore v. Caldwell,* 5 Ky. (2 Bibb) 76 (1810); *Cornfute v. Dale,* 1 H. & J. 4 (Md. 1800); *see, also, Mangham v. Reed,* 11 Ga. 137 (1852).

12. *See, Hoomes v. Kuhn,* 8 Va. (4 Call.) 274 (1792) (Hoome's slave was severely whipped by Kuhn; in a subsequent fight with Hoomes, Kuhn was "much worsted," and was also held liable by the court to Hoomes for £17 in damages for whipping the slave).

13. *See,* for the common law requirement of actual lost services in a master's suit, Prosser, *supra* at 929 and 873–897; *Magee v. Holland,* 27 N.J.L. 86 (Sup. Ct. 1858).

14. It was also a tort for one to interfere with a master's contract with his servant. Of course, there was no contract between the master and the slave. The courts did, however, protect the master's right to obtain his slave's services. For example, in a Texas case, the court allowed a master to recover the value of a slave from the defendants whose "interference" with the slave's attempt to drive plaintiff's oxen led the slave to flee from the defendants' assault, fearing for his life. *See, Hedgepett v. Robertson,* 18 Tex. 858 (1857).

15. *White v. Chambers,* 2 S.C.L. 29, 30, 2 Bay 70, 75 (1796).

16. *Tennent v. Dendy,* 23 S.C.L. 35, 36, Dud. 83, 86 (1837).

17. *Compare, e.g., West v. Forrest,* 22 Mo. 344 (1856); *Garey v. Johnson,* 10 F. Cas. 1 (D.C. Cir. 1814) (No. 5,240) and an 1816 Kentucky statute cited by Stroud, *supra* at 39 (right to recover without actual damages), *with, Hervy v. Armstrong,* 15 Ark. 162 (1854); *Voss v. Howard,* 28 F. Cas. 1301 (D.C. Cir. 1805) (No. 17,013) (actual damages required).

18. *Commonwealth v. Carver,* 26 Va. 553, 555, 5 Rand 660, 665 (1827), *see, also, Commonwealth v. Chapple,* 3 Va. 50, 1 Va. Cas. 184 (1811).

19. 38 Va. 738, 11 Leigh 631 (1841).

20. The statute of 1822–1823, Ch. 34 is *cited* in *Commonwealth v. Israel,* 31 Va. 1074, 4 Leigh 675 (1833) (horse was injured). *See, also, Commonwealth v. Percavil,* 31 Va. 1078, 4 Leigh 868 (1834) (statute applied to pigs); *cf., Brown v. May,* 15 Va. 114, 1 Munf. 288 (1810) (judgment for $150 upheld—beating plaintiff's slave without owner's authority).

21. 20 S.C.L. 249, 2 Hill 453 (1834).

22. *See, Id.* at 249, 2 Hill at 454.

23. *Id.* at 249, 2 Hill at 453.
24. *See, Id.* at 250, 2 Hill at 455–456.
25. *See, Hadden v. Leiberschultz,* 45 S.C.L. 172, 11 Rich. 505 (1857) (conviction under 1839 patrol law for exceeding authority reversed); *State v. Harlan,* 39 S.C.L. 139, 5 Rich. 470 (1852) (conviction under 1841 act prohibiting strangers from whipping slaves if without authority or provocation upheld, defendant appears to be a nonslave holder); *State v. Boozer,* 36 S.C.L. 11, 5 Strob. 21 (1850) (conviction of patrol for unlawful slave whipping upheld, master tried to prevent whipping); *Caldwell v. Langford,* 26 S.C.L. 119, 1 McMul. 275 (1841) (patroller's conviction under 1839 act upheld for whipping beyond authority); *State v. Wilson,* 25 S.C.L. 66, 1 Chev. 163 (1840) (conviction under 1740 code prohibiting cruel punishment upheld, fine of £100); *State v. James,* 2 S.C.L. 86, 2 Bay 215 (1799) (conviction under 1740 code's anticruelty provision reversed).
26. 9 N.C. (2 Hawks) 582 (1823).
27. *Id.* at 584.
28. *Id.* at 585. These concerns about poor white/slave fraternization and violence also reconcile the North Carolina cases in which slaves had convictions for murdering poor whites reversed on appeal. The North Carolina Supreme Court held that slaves were entitled to have homicides mitigated from murder to manslaughter based upon the slave's unique subservient status, not traditional common law standards. *See, State v. Caesar,* 31 N.C. (9 Ired.) 39 (1849); *State v. Jarrott,* 23 N.C. 51, 1 Ired.. 76 (1840). *Contra, John v. State,* 16 Ga. 200, 203 (1854) where Judge Joseph Lumpkin stated that in no case in which a slave kills a white should the law mitigate murder to manslaughter. *See,* text and notes at Chapter 8, Notes 32 to 88, *infra.*
29. *See, State v. Hale, supra,* 9 N.C. at 585.
30. *See, Id.* at 585–586.
31. *See, Id.* at 583.
32. *See, Id.* at 586; *see, also, Id.* at 586–87 (Hall, J.) ("I think it would be highly improper that every assault and battery upon a slave should be considered an indictable offence[.]")
33. *See,* 2 Hurd, *supra* at 152.
34. *See, Carpenter v. State,* 23 Ala. 84 (1853) (conviction upheld); *Bradley v. State,* 18 Miss. 241, 10 S. & M. 618 (1848) (conviction reversed); *see, also, Wheat v. Croom,* 7 Ala. 349 (1845) (trespass for assault and battery upon slave, master's damages not limited to actual damages, jury may award "vindictive damages" to compensate owner for slave's "suffering").
35. *Commonwealth v. Lee,* 60 Ky. (3 Met.) 229, 231 (1860); *cf., Nix v. State,* 13 Tex. 575 (1855) (no provocation shown—violent and cruel battery).
36. *See, Dave v. State,* 22 Ala. 23, 33 (1853); *see, also, generally, Tillman v. Chadwick,* 37 Ala. 317, 318 (1861); *Oliver v. State,* 39 Miss. 526, 540 (1860); *State v. Mann,* 13 N.C. 229, 31, 2 Dev. 263, 266 (1829).
37. *Dave v. State,* 22 Ala. at 33; *see, State v. Mann,* 13 N.C. at 231, 2 Dev. at 266.
38. "Assault and battery are two separate common-law misdemeanors ... Battery requires ... injury or touching. Assault, on the other hand, needs no physical contact" (emphasis omitted). *See,* LaFave, *supra* at 603. Although

it is more correct to distinguish between these two crimes, the fact that the master was free from liability for battery against his slave subsumes justification for assault. Therefore, I will refer to justified batteries or assault and battery interchangeably. *See, Commonwealth v. Booth*, 3 Va. 283, 2 Va. Cas. 394 (1824).

39. *See, Commonwealth v. Turner*, 26 Va. 560, 5 Rand. 678 (1827); *State v. Mann, supra*, 13 N.C. at 231, 2 Dev. at 266.

40. I am aware of one case in Louisiana in which a master's conviction for cruel punishment of his slave was affirmed by the appeals court. *See, State v. Morris*, 4 La. Ann. 177 (1849). Because this study concentrates on common law jurisdictions and the relationship between common law and statute law, I have not analyzed this case in the materials that follow because Louisiana is a civil law jurisdiction. In the District of Columbia, the courts held that a master could be indicted for cruel or inhuman slave punishment, but only if the inhumanity was inflicted in a public place. Accordingly, the crime was not against the slave; rather, it arose out of the creation of "an annoyance or nuisance to citizens, whose pleasure or business carry them near the scene of the infliction[.]" *See, Hickerson v. United States*, 30 F. Cas. 1087, 1088 (D.C. Cir. 1856) (No. 18,301). *Compare, United States v. Lloyd*, 26 F. Cas. 987 (D.C. Cir. 1834) (No. 15,618) ($100 fine on conviction of master upheld, indictment for cruel beating and public exposure of same), *with, United States v. Bockett*, 24 F. Ca. 1241 (D.C. Cir. 1823) (No. 14,651) (no limit to beatings in private as long as neither life nor limb taken, master found not guilty).

41. *See, e.g.*, Stampp, *supra* at 111, 171-91; Scott, *supra* at 55.

42. Goodell, *supra* at 122.

43. 2 Hening, *supra* at 270.

44. *See, Commonwealth v. Turner*, 26 Va. at 564, 5 Rand. at 688 (Brockenbrough, J., dissenting). *See, also*, Higginbotham, *supra* at 163 citing the Fundamental Constitution of Carolina written in 1669:

> Every Freeman of Carolina shall have absolute power and authority over Negro slaves, of what opinion or Religion soever.

Even in eighteenth-century Georgia, while slavery was illegal, Salzburgian settlers who did not know how to treat rebellious or runaway slaves quickly learned that it was the custom to beat their slaves for such infractions. *See, Id.* at 223.

45. *See, e.g., Commonwealth v. Turner*, 26 Va. at 564, 5 Rand. at 688-89 (Brockenbrough, J., dissenting); *State v. Weaver*, 3 N.C. 77, 2 Tay. 54 (1798).

46. *E.g.*, a parent can correct her child without risk of indictment for assault and battery, but the correction must not be excessive or cruel. *See, generally, Annot.*, 89 A.L.R. 2d 396 (1963 & Supp. 1984); *Annot.*, 37 A.L.R. 704 (1925); *State v. Mann*, 13 N.C. at 231, 2 Dev. at 265-66.

47. White indentured servants were punished by extending their time of service, but by 1669 blacks were held as slaves for life in Virginia. Therefore, the legislature found, in enacting the 1669 Act, that this usual means of punishing servants was ineffective against slaves because the "obstinacy" of

"many" slaves could not "by other than violent means suppress." *See*, Higginbotham, *supra* at 36; 2 Hening, *supra* at 270.

48. *See, Id.*

49. *See,* 4 Hening, *supra* at 132.

50. A 1774 act provided a one-year prison terms, and payment of full value of the slave to the master, for the first instance of malicious killing of a slave. Upon the second such conviction, the killer faced death and forfeiture of the value of the slave killed to the master. *See, State v. Boon,* 1 N.C. 103, 108–09, Tay. 246 (1801). This statute impliedly recognized the master's right to kill the slave without punishment, and *a fortiori* the right to punish with impunity.

51. 26 Va. 560, 5 Rand. 678 (1827).

52. 13 N.C. 229, 2 Dev. 263 (1829).

53. *Commonwealth v. Turner,* 26 Va. at 560, 5 Rand. at 678.

54. In Virginia in 1827 the General Court was the court of last resort in criminal matters. *See, e.g., Brief Sketch of the Courts of This Commonwealth,* 3 Va. 101, 102 (1826). *Preface,* 2 Va. Cas. 99 (1826). Ten judges sat for the November 1827 term. One judge dissented from the *Turner* holding. The case went to the General Court from the Superior Court before trial. The Superior Court could so adjourn questions to the General Court with the consent of the defendant. *See, Id.*

55. *See, Commonwealth v. Turner,* 26 Va. at 563, 5 Rand. at 685.

56. *See, Id.*

57. *See, Id.* at 561, 5 Rand. at 680.

58. *See, Commonwealth v. Turner,* 26 Va. at 561, 5 Rand. at 679. Courts in the United States and England declared certain acts to be crimes, although no statute criminalized the behavior. These are common law crimes; acts that the courts declare are immoral, or that tend to disturb the peace, and are therefore punishable as crimes *contra bonos mores. See, generally,* LaFave, *supra* at 57—69. Judge Dade cited two cases as precedent for his rejection of the power to declare common law crimes *contra bonos mores. See, Anderson v. Commonwealth,* 26 Va. 518, 5 Rand. 627 (1826) (indictment at common law for "enticing" away from her mother a child over the age of sixteen for the purpose of "prostituting and carnally knowing her" could not be maintained *contra bonos mores* when statute prohibits the same acts against children under the age of sixteen); *Commonwealth v. Isaacs,* 26 Va. 523, 5 Rand. 634 (1826) (man and woman living together as man and wife without being married had to be indicted for violation of a statute prohibiting fornication, they could not be indicted for a common law offense of fornication in public on the facts presented). In Anderson, Judge Dade wrote for the court and reserved opinion as to the application of the doctrine of common law crimes as a general matter. He stated:

> [I]f something peculiar in our situation had given rise to a class of cases contra bonos mores, as in regard to our slaves, which could not have existed in England, we might be justified in applying the rule in the absence of all precedent.

*Anderson v. Commonwealth,* 26 Va. at 519, 5 Rand. at 631–32.

59. *See, Commonwealth v. Turner*, 26 Va. at 561, 563, 5 Rand. at 680, 686.
60. *See, Id.* at 563, 5 Rand. at 685.
61. 26 Va. 553, 5 Rand. 660 (1827).
62. After he framed the issue in this way, Judge Brockenbrough found the authority to sustain the indictment from the common law principle that allowed a "superior" to correct his "inferior." He stated that such a right was not without limit:

> [W]hilst the common law protected all persons in the just exercise of any authority or power conferred on them by law; yet, for the abuse of that authority, or an excess in the exercise of it, they were liable to be prosecuted as delinquents.

*Commonwealth v. Turner*, 26 Va. at 564, 5 Rand. at 690.
63. *See, Id.* at 564, 5 Rand. at 688–89.
64. *See, Id.* at 564, 5 Rand. at 688–90.
65. *Id.* at 564, 5 Rand. at 690.
66. 26 Va. 553, 5 Rand. 660 (1827).
67. *Id.* at 555, 5 Rand. at 665.
68. 13 N.C. 229, 2 Dev. 263 (1829).
69. *See, Id.*
70. Although Mann was indicted for "assault and battery," the trial judge, like the judges in *Turner*, assumed that the hirer's ordinary battery was perfectly legal. He therefore charged the jury that they could find the defendant guilty only "if they believed the punishment inflicted by the defendant was cruel and unwarrantable, and disproportionate to the offence committed by the slave[.]" *See, Id.*
71. *See, Id.* at 230, 2 Dev. at 265. Judge Ruffin recognized that he could have found the indictment insufficient for failing to state that the defendant was a hirer, thereby acknowledging that "different justifications" applied depending upon whether the defendant was a master, hirer, or stranger to the abused slave, as the court did in *Commonwealth v. Booth*, 3 Va. 283, 2 Va. Cas. 394 (1824). *See, Id.* However, this would leave for another day a determination of the master's and hirer's power over their slaves. Judge Ruffin apparently wanted to avoid any uncertainty.
72. *State v. Mann*, 13 N.C. at 231, 2 Dev. at 266.
73. *Id.* at 232, 2 Dev. at 267.
74. *Id.* at 231, 2 Dev. at 266.
75. *Id.* at 230–231, 2 Dev. at 265.
76. *Id.* at 233, 2 Dev. at 268.
77. 9 N.C. (2 Hawks) 528 (1823).
78. *See, Commonwealth v. Turner*, 26 Va. at 563, 5 Rand. at 686.
79. *See, State v. Mann*, 13 N.C. at 229, 2 Dev. at 264.
80. Nevertheless, after devoting almost a dozen pages of analysis to the *Mann* decision, Mark Tushnet stated that Judge Ruffin's opinion was an example of judicial recognition of slave humanity." Tushnet reached this conclusion because the judge did not write in terms of the "market relations" that existed between the master and hirer. *See*, Tushnet, *supra* at 54—65. What Tushnet failed to recognize, however, was that Ruffin could not ground

his analysis on these "market relations," or the property-oriented analysis of Dade, because of the "autonomous" constraints of legal precedent that Dade did not have to distinguish. For a discussion of Tushnet's views on this point, see, Fede-1985, supra at Note 277, and Fede–1984, supra at 308–311.

81. This was despite the pleas, whether sincere or not, of Judges Ruffin and Dade who called for such legislation. See, State v. Mann, 13 N.C. at 233, 2 Dev. at 268; Commonwealth v. Turner, 26 Va. at 563, 5 Rand. at 686.

82. Cited in Turnipseed v. State, 6 Ala. 664, 665 (1843); see, Goodell, supra at 165; Sellers, supra at 224. The first cruel and unusual punishment statute was enacted in South Carolina in 1740. See, text and note at Note 6 supra. That act was replaced in 1858 by a statute that prohibited cruel and unusual punishment by masters or those with control over a slave, subject, however, to the following proviso:

> [N]othing herein contained shall be so construed as to prevent the owner . . . from inflicting on such slave such punishment as may be necessary for the good government of the same.

Cited in 2 Hurd, supra at 100.

A Georgia act of 1770 was similar to the 1740 South Carolina statute cited above. See, Higginbotham, supra at 255. An act of 1817 provided punishment of slave owners "who shall cruelly treat such slave . . . by unnecessary or excessive whipping[.]" Cited in Goodell, supra at 130; see, Higginbotham, supra at 255. For the Mississippi act, see, Goodell, supra at 163—65. And for the Missouri act, see, State v. Peters, 28 Mo. 241, 241–242 (1859).

83. See, Randolph B. Campbell, The Peculiar Institution in Texas, 1821–1865 144–145 (Baton Rouge, 1989).

84. It is interesting to again note that the legislatures in North Carolina and Virginia never did pass statutes prohibiting cruel or unusual punishment after the Turner and Mann decisions became law. This fact lends support to the notion that legislatures perceived these statutes as a justification for the master's batteries upon his slaves and nothing more. Because the courts achieved this end in these two states, there was no need for legislation. In fact, if such legislation was passed after these decisions, it would then appear that the legislators really intended the act to protect slaves and that it should be used against masters. Since the legislatures of Virginia and North Carolina did not pass cruel and unusual punishment acts, it is logical to infer that they did not want to leave any such impression; they did not want to see masters brought before the courts on charges of cruel or unusual punishment.

85. Goodell, supra at 157 (emphasis omitted).
86. Id. at 162.
87. See, Campbell, supra at 149–150.
88. 6 Ala. 664 (1843).
89. See, Id. at 664–667. The "void for vagueness" doctrine is based on modern due process doctrine. It enables courts to declare vaguely worded criminal statutes unconstitutional. See, generally, LaFave, supra 83–89. In the nineteenth century, the courts dealt with the same concerns by requiring that indictments cure the ambiguity, as the court did in Turnipseed. See, also,

31 *C.J.* "Indictments and Informations" § 260 (1923), 42 *C.J.S.* "Indictments and Informations" § 139(a) (1944).
  90. *Turnipseed v. State*, 6 Ala. at 667.
  91. *See, generally,* LaFave, *supra* at 72–74.
  92. *See, Commonwealth v. Magoon*, 172 Mass. 214, 51 N.E. 1082 (1898); *Commonwealth v. McClellan*, 101 Mass. (5 Browne) 34 (1869); *Commonwealth v. Lufkin*, 89 Mass. (7 Allen) 579 (1863).
  93. The Alabama Code of 1852 § 3298, *quoted in, Documentary History, supra* at 192.
  94. 28 Mo. 241 (1859).
  95. *Id.* at 242.
  96. *See, Scott v. State*, 31 Miss. 473 (1856).
  97. *See,* Stampp, *supra* at 84, 185, 318.
  98. 13 N.C. 229, 2 Dev. 263 (1829).
  99. *Id.,* 13 N.C. at 230, 2 Dev. at 265.
  100. *See,* Stampp, *supra* at 70–71.
  101. *See, State v. Mann, supra,* 13 N.C. at 230, 2 Dev. at 264.
  102. *See,* LaFave, *supra* at 614–617.
  103. *See,* text and notes at Note 6 *supra.*
  104. *See, Commonwealth v. Turner, supra,* 26 Va. at 563, 5 Rand. at 685.
  105. Between 1723 and 1769, the Virginia slave codes provided for "dismemberment" of runaway slaves. *See,* 4 Hening, *supra* at 132. The South Carolina code of 1712 also required that slaves who repeatedly ran away be maimed. *See,* Higginbotham, *supra* at 177–78. A 1769 Virginia act prohibited dismemberment. The legislature found this activity to be "contrary to the principles of humanity." But the legislature determined that this form of punishment continued to be "humane" punishment if a black man raped a white woman, until 1805, when this penalty was eliminated *See,* Jordan, *supra* at 473; 8 Hening, *supra* at 358.
  106. *See, Eskridge v. State*, 25 Ala. 30, 33 (1854), *citing* Article VI, Title Slaves, § 3.
  107. 25 Ala. 30 (1854).
  108. *Id.* at 31, 34–35.
  109. *Wherley v. State*, 30 Tenn. 119, 11 Hum. 171 (1850).
  110. *See, e.g., Walker v. Walker*, 26 Ala. 262 (1855); *Gillian v. Senter*, 9 Ala. 395 (1846); *Davis v. Hunter*, 7 Ala. 135 (1844); *see, also, Martin v. Everett*, 11 Ala. 375 (1847).
  111. The overseers' lack of wealth helps to explain cases such as *McCoy v. McKowen*, 26 Miss. 487 (1853), in which a slave owner attempted to hold a slave hirer liable when it would have been much easier to obtain a judgment against the hirer's overseer who administered the fatal beating of the slave. The court reversed the judgment for the plaintiff, holding there was insufficient evidence that the hirer defendant had knowledge of the overseer's acts. *See, also, Jones v. Glass*, 35 N.C. (13 Ired..) 305 (1853) (master held liable for overseer's negligence).
  112. 31 Miss. 473 (1856).
  113. This is the teaching of *Turnipseed v. State.* The sliding scale was inferred from the *Turnipseed* court's requirement that the indictment for cruel or

unusual punishment identify whether the defendant was master or overseer of the slave and describe the punishment inflicted upon the slave. The prosecution in *Scott* followed this procedure so the courts could be adequately informed of the proper standard of conduct to apply to the defendant. *See, Scott v. State,* 31 Miss. at 476–77.

114. *See, Id.* at 479.

115. The statute prohibited "cruel or unusual" slave punishment by "any master or other person entitled to the service of any slave[.]" *See, Id.* at 475. The defendant argued on appeal from his conviction that the indictment, which referred to him as an "overseer," did not sufficiently follow the wording of the statute. *See, Id.* at 473–74. The court rejected this argument, recognizing that it implied that the legislature intended to exclude overseers from criminal liability. *See, Id.* at 479.

116. *See, e.g.,* "Segregation," *supra* at 433–440.

117. On the colonial acts, *see, e.g.,* Higginbotham, *supra* at 259–262, Wood, *supra* at 272–276.

118. The foregoing summary is derived from "Segregation," *supra* at 434–441; Scott, *supra* at 122–124; Stampp, *supra* at 214–215, *Slavery in Mississippi, supra* at 77–79; John H. Franklin, *The Militant South 1800–1861* 72–76 (Cambridge, 1956); Henry, *supra* at 28–52, *Negro in Tennessee, supra* at 38–41. On patrols in the cities, *see,* Richard C. Wade, *Slavery in the Cities: The South 1820–1860* 80–82, 98–102 (New York, 1964). *See, also,* The Alabama Code of 1852 §§ 992–993, *quoted in Documentary History, supra* at 180.

119. *State v. Hailey,* 28 N.C. 21, 22, 6 Ired.. 11, 12 (1845).

120. *Gist v. Cole,* 11 S.C.L. 183, 186, 2 N. & McCord. 456, 463 (1820).

121. Stampp, *supra* at 215.

122. *Id.*

123. Civil actions by masters to recover damages caused by physical abuse to slaves include, *Tomlinson v. Darnall,* 39 Tenn. (2 Head) 538 (1859) ($15 verdict reversed and remanded for new trial); *Dargan v. Mayor,* 31 Ala. 469 (1858) (action against city, slave killed by city guard, held city not responsible); *Hervy v. Armstrong,* 15 Ark. 162 (1854) (master cannot recover against patrol without special damages); *Brooks v. Ashburn,* 9 Ga. 197 (1851) (slave killed by patrol); *Walker v. Brown,* 31 Tenn. (11 Hum.) 179 (1850) ($40 verdict upheld); *Tennent v. Dendy,* 23 S.C.L. 35, Dud. 83 (1837) (verdict for master who had hired out slaves, no special damages required for illegal whipping action); *Tate v. O'Neal,* 8 N.C. (1 Hawks) 418 (1821) (action for excessive whipping, jury verdict affirmed for defendant); *Hogg v. Keller,* 11 S.C.L. 46, 2 N. & McCord 113 (1819) (verdict for defendant reversed—illegal whipping); *Richardson v. Saltar,* 4 N.C. (Term) 505 (1817) (verdict for defendant reversed—illegal whipping). Masters also sued when the patrols confiscated property—such as guns or animals—in the possession of slaves. *See, e.g., Rice v. Parham,* 23 S.C.L. 156, Dud. 373 (1838) (guns); *Clarke v. Blake,* 14 S.C.L. 72, 3 McCord 179 (1825) (horses); *Porteous v. Hazel,* 16 S.C.L. 147, Harp. 332 (1824) (gun). Other related actions include *Spruill v. The North Carolina Mutual Life Insurance Co.,* 46 N.C. 127 1 Jones 126 (1853) (action on insurance policy taken on slave who was killed by patrol—held, not excluded from coverage); *Bosworth v. Brand,* 31 Ky. (1 Dana) 377 (1833) (action by owner

of slave when slave was killed by patrol while on defendant's plantation held no right of action).

124. *See, e.g., Hadden v. Leibeschultz,* 45 S.C.L. 172, 11 Rich. 505 (1857) (conviction under 1839 patrol law for exceeding authority reversed); *Caldwell v. Langford,* 26 S.C.L. 119, 121, 1 McMul. 275, 279 (1841) (patroller's conviction for whipping upheld). *See, also, State v. Boozer,* 36 S.C.L. 11, 5 Strob, 21 (1850) (conviction of patrol for unlawful whipping, master tried to prevent whipping).

125. *See, e.g., State v. Atkinson,* 51 N.C. 77, 6 Jones 65 (1858); *State v. Cole,* 13 S.C.L. 46, 2 McCord 117 (1822).

126. *See, State v. Hailey,* 28 N.C. 21, 6 Ired.. 11 (1845); *Bell v. Graham,* 10 S.C.L. 112, 1 N. & McCord. 278 (1818); Henry, *supra* at 41–42.

127. *See, Hogg v. Keller, supra,* 11 S.C.L. at 46, 2 N. & McCord. at 114.

128. *See,* Hindus, *supra* at 91; Henry, *supra* at 75–77 (in 10 counties, 104 defendants charged, 28 convicted, and 4 guilty pleas).

129. *See,* Hindus, *supra* at 65 (7,018 assault cases and 283 murder cases); Henry, *supra* at 70–77 (104 assault cases and 61 murder cases).

130. Stampp, *supra* at 175.

131. Genovese, *supra* at 64.

132. Stampp, *supra* at 185.

133. Scott, *supra* at 53.

134. Genovese, *supra* at 64.

## CHAPTER 7

# Preventing Slaves from Being a Public Nuisance: Limits of the Master's Right to Starve and to Free His Slaves

**THE COMMON** law of the nineteenth century recognized that property rights were subject to legal limitations. Owners were obligated to adequately maintain their property so that it did not become a threat to the health, safety, and welfare of society. Property that did so injure the public good was known as a public nuisance in the common law. One who maintained his property as a public nuisance was liable in tort for damages caused by his property. A property owner was also subject to prosecution under the common law of crimes for creating a public nuisance.[1]

These general principles were applied to vest slave owners with a duty to maintain their slaves in ways to avoid the creation of a public nuisance. These regulations of the master's property rights were not inconsistent with the idea that the slaves in question remained property; nor were rights created in the property that was subject to regulation.

These legal principles were inherent in two related limitations on the master's freedom. In one example, the law required masters to adequately feed and clothe their slaves. The second trend was the increasing limitation on the master's right to free his slaves. Both of these legal developments manifest the exercise of community control over the slave owner's property rights.

The adequate food and clothing requirements, when considered in isolation, might appear to be motivated by legislative concern for the slave's right to support. These statutes must be read in their social context, however, and in relation to the acts that first regulated and eventually prohibited manumission. When this is done, the common thread that runs through these aspects of slave law will be illustrated.

## The Slave as a Public Nuisance: The Master's Duty of Maintenance

The fear of the slave as a potential public nuisance motivated both the adequate food and clothing statues and the acts that regulated manumission. The purposes of the former statues, and their relationship to limits on manumission, are illustrated by a Maryland act of 1752. That statute recited the evil it was intended to ameliorate: the tendency of masters to use their slaves while profits could be made, and then turn the slaves "adrift to burden the community or perish through want, to the great scandal of Christian society[.]" Thus, the legislature limited and regulated manumission. It also required masters to provide some of their slaves with adequate food and clothing. The statute fixed a fine for masters who neglected "to provide for old or disabled slaves" or allowed "them to leave their homes, or wander about begging, becoming nuisances to the public[.]"[2] Obviously, the law could not allow famishing slaves to become public nuisances.

Similarly, the 1722 and 1740 South Carolina Codes and the Georgia Code of 1755 required masters, hirers, or overseers to provide "sufficient clothing, covering or food" for slaves under their charge. Violators faced fines if convicted, and the 1852 Alabama code contained a similar provision.[3] These statutes compelled masters to provide for their slaves so the slaves would not provide for themselves by theft, all legal means of property acquisition being taboo to slaves.

This purpose is further revealed by a North Carolina act of 1753. That statute allowed persons who suffered damages caused by thieving slaves to sue the slave owner for damages, if the slaves were not "sufficiently fed and clothed[.]"[4] An 1815 Georgia statute exhibited a concern that masters were abandoning infirm or elderly slaves. It allowed those who rendered relief to these slaves the right to sue the owner for damages. A Georgia act passed two years later provided punishments to masters who withheld "proper" food and sustenance from their slaves.[5]

These statutes were consistent with the notion that slaves were property and possessed no rights. The legislators, in fact, implicitly recognized and legitimated the slave's own lack of property rights and dependence on his master for support. If the master failed to properly maintain his property, theft and disorder could result. For example, in *Richardson v. Dukes*,[6] a slave was shot and killed by the defendant while the slave was stealing potatoes. The plaintiff-owner was granted a civil judgment that was affirmed on appeal. Slave theft could not be entirely pre-empted, but perhaps it could be minimized if the slave had no pressing need to steal. Only the master could alleviate that cause of slave theft by adequately providing for his slaves.

There are two reported cases enforcing these statues. One 1849 case from South Carolina is *State v. Bowen*.[7] In this often-cited case, a slave owner was prosecuted for failing to provide adequate food and clothing for his slaves. The master was charged with violating Section 38 of the 1740 Code. This section stated that if the owner or person in charge of a slave "shall deny, neglect, or refuse to allow" his slaves "sufficient clothing, covering, or food," any other person may bring an action on behalf of the slaves "to the next neighboring justice" in the parish where the slave lives. The justice could make orders as he saw fit "for the relief of such slaves" if he found the complaint true, and could fine the owner a maximum of £20. The owner was allowed the privilege to exculpate himself on his own oath "where positive proof is not given of the offense[.]"[8] William Goodell wrote that this provision rendered the statute nugatory because slaves could not testify to offer the "positive proof" needed to overcome a master's oath.[9] No doubt this would have been true in many instances, but the defendant Bowen was nevertheless prosecuted.

Indeed, Bowen was convicted by the lower court, and he appealed this decision. His conviction was not reversed because no appeal was given the defendant from the magistrate's decision. Therefore, the Court of Appeals could have dismissed the appeal without any further opinion, as Justice Edward Frost noted for the majority.[10] The concurring Justice D.L. Wardlaw so wrote in a two-sentence opinion.[11] But the majority felt the need to justify the result by addressing the defendant's arguments.

On appeal the defendant questioned the weight of the evidence, Justice Frost found that, although contradictory, it was sufficient to constitute "positive proof" to overcome the defendant's oath. The defendant also argued that the magistrate erred in concluding that the statute required that meat must be given to slaves. The appeals court held that this error was harmless because the defendant's overseer testified that insufficient corn meal and clothing were provided.[12] The court also rejected the defendant's argument that the statute was unconstitutional. Judge Frost wrote:

> The law is salutary, even more by the opprobium which follows a conviction, than by the penalties for its violation. Public opinion derives force from its sanction; and the rapaciousness of the owner is checked by the fear of its active interference. Instances do sometimes, though rarely, occur in which it is necessary to interfere in behalf of the slave against the avarice of his master. In such cases the law should interpose its authority. It is due to public sentiment, and is necessary to protect property from the depradation of famishing slaves.[13]

Thus, in the end the court justified the statute as protection for the public from the nuisance of "famishing slaves."

The only other case reporting a prosecution alleging inadequate care, food, and clothing is an 1862 Alabama decision that reversed a slave master's conviction.[14] Moreover, there is no record of a common law prosecution of a master for maintaining his slaves as a public nuisance. But in *Britain v. State*,[15] a Tennessee master was indicted and convicted of "lewdness." The defendant was accused of failing to clothe his female slave so as to keep from "the view and observation of the good people" the slave's "organs of generation." The defendant was fined $25 for so clothing his slave. The concern here was not for the slave's humanity, but the "rules of public decency," which the court thought were offended by the display perpetrated by the defendant. George Stroud correctly characterized this case, stating, "it rested entirely on the ground that the *feelings of the community* were outraged by such exposure of the slave by her master's neglect. The injury or wrong to the slave is not hinted at; and it is quite certain that the law would not interfere in her behalf, no matter what extent humanity in her was affected." Stroud then stated the real basis for this class of cases and statutes:

> The principle of the decision is just the same as would be invoked against the owner of a horse who should turn out the animal to die on the commons while suffering from any loathsome disease,—the glanders or the like. The owner would be punishable, not because the *animal* deserved better treatment, but because the community interests or its taste would be offended.[16]

Thus, the law regulated the slave owner as it did the horse owner. It was considered impolitic to leave slaves to fend for themselves because of the master's neglect.

It also appears that the dearth of cases under these statutes indicates that the abolitionists who reviewed these acts correctly concluded that they were of little practical effect.[17] This is not to say that masters regularly starved their slaves; actual slave nutrition is an issue that is hotly debated by historians and is beyond the scope of this study.[18] It is clear, however, that these acts were a means of legitimization of the master's power over the slave.

These laws sought to further peace in the community when the master failed to provide for his slaves, who, in common with other domestic chattels, had no "right" to provide for themselves. A similar concern was expressed regarding the master's right to free his chattels from bondage.

## Statutes Regulating the Manumission of Slaves: The Threat to Public Safety

At the same time that the law expanded the scope of liability for slave abuse, the master's right to free his slaves became increasingly circumscribed. These two currents of legal change are not inconsistent. Both limited the individual owner's right to use his property to further salient social ends. The law seems contradictory only if the irrelevant concept of "slave rights" is considered.

Indeed, slaves in the United States South had no legal right to manumission. In fact, the frequency of manumission was very low when the United States South is compared to other slave societies. This is the finding reached by Orlando Patterson. He also concludes that the promise of manumission was not therefore a meaningful inducement to slave discipline in the South.[19]

Patterson's study indicates that manumission was a not a frequent occurrence in the United States South, based on a cross-cultural level of analysis. Indeed, the nineteenth-century law reflects an increasing hostility to the very idea of manumission, despite the clear intent of the slave owner to free his slaves. Freedmen posed a psychological and ideological threat so great to the white antebellum South that the law responded by encroaching on the owner's right to free his chattel from the shackles of bondage.

The common law allowed chattel owners, and thus slave owners, the right to dispose of their chattels as they wished, as long as the owner did not create a public nuisance or thereby injure any other person's rights. George Stroud begins his study of the restraints on emancipation by acknowledging that, "From a just consideration of the rights of *property*, it would seem . . . plain that the master might, at his pleasure, relinquish his dominion over the slave." He found the law to be to the contrary, however:

> Having degraded a rational and immortal being into a *chattel*,—a thing of bargain and sale,—it has been discovered that certain incidents result from this degradation which it concerns the welfare of the community vigorously to exact and preserve.[20]

Consequently, the Southern states, beginning with a Virginia act of 1691, adopted various statutes that limited the master's right to free his slaves.

Jacob Wheeler explained the justification for the statutes that regulated manumission:

> When it considered that slaves are a peculiar species of property, it will not excite surprise that laws are necessary for their regulation, and to protect society from even the benevolence of slave owners, in throwing among the community a great number of stupid, ignorant, and vicious persons, to disturb its peace, and to endanger its permanency.
>
> The right of society to regulate and control the ownership of this kind of property may be justified on the same grounds as some other species of property. No one can doubt the right of individuals to acquire, possess, and sell gun powder. But if the possessor chooses to take it to his house or store, in a city or populous town, the public become interested, and will restrain him within reasonable and proper limits. In New York, Philadelphia, Baltimore, and other populous places, this property, as an article of commerce, is regulated (as to the quantity to be kept in the city,) by the public laws. And the constitutionality of those laws cannot be doubted. So of slaves. The owner may keep as many as he pleases, but if he emancipates them, and turns them loose upon society, they have a right to protect themselves against his improvidence, or even his benevolence and generosity. They have a right to declare the act illegal or to restrain it within such bounds as shall secure their safety.[21]

In short, the lawmakers perceived the need to limit the master's "benevolence," when the needs of society came into conflict with "generosity."

The legislative limitations on manumission are cogently quoted and analyzed by George Stroud. He notes that these acts furthered several policy goals. The first was the need to prevent the master from freeing old or infirm slaves to rid himself of the obligations of ownership and place that burden on the public. Statutes therefore required the master to post a bond to maintain slaves of this type, whether the slave was emancipated by deed during the master's life or by will. Regulations of this nature were adopted in the statutes of Kentucky, Missouri, Maryland, Arkansas, and Delaware.[22]

Statutes also protected the rights of creditors and the widow of a deceased master. Therefore, creditors could override a manumission if the master was insolvent. And where a widow was entitled to a one-third share of the slave owner's estate, statutes disallowed the manumission of slaves to the extent necessary to satisfy the one-third share.[23] The legislators were also concerned about fraudulent manumission claims. Under the common law, courts held that no formal requirements existed for the establishment of manumission, and oral statements were found to be sufficient proof of a master's intent to free his slaves. The legislators of the late eighteenth and early nineteenth century enacted statutes that created requirements that manumission be by a written deed or will, and deeds of manumission were to be recorded to memorialize the master's intent. The master was required to meet the statutory formalities; otherwise, the slave could not enjoy his freedom.[24]

Stroud states that in the Southern states, these were the least restrictive limits that were initially placed on the master's freedom to emancipate his slave by a deed duly executed and filed or a will. Nevertheless, a progressively more stringent regime was adopted in the courts and legislatures.

Anti-manumission acts fell into three categories. North Carolina, South Carolina, Georgia, Alabama, and Mississippi prohibited in-state manumissions except by a special act of the legislature, or a court ruling, based upon proof of the slave's meritorious service. The next class of acts prohibited all in-state manumission and required the removal of slaves who were freed. Even this limitation was found insufficient in the late antebellum years in some Southern states. Thus, the South Carolina legislature, in 1841, passed an act that prohibited all in-state and out-of-state manumissions. In the 1850s, legislators in Georgia, Alabama, Mississippi, and Arkansas followed suit and outlawed all manumissions. In Virginia and Tennessee, the law changed over the years. Both states enacted early prohibitions of manumission, except in cases of meritorious service by the slave. Virginia abrogated this limitation in 1782, and Tennessee did so in 1801. Nevertheless, the law in both states, Texas, Florida, Maryland, Kentucky, and North Carolina evolved to the no in-state manumission position by 1860.[25] Consequently, the trend toward increased regulation of manumission is clear.

In these states, the anti-emancipation statues obviously furthered several policy goals in addition to those cited above. The first goal was to limit the number of free blacks. Arthur Howington has studied the lower court records in Tennessee and finds that the various changes in the manumission statutes did influence the number of legally manumitted slaves. He also shows how the fears caused among slave owners by the Nat Turner rebellion contributed to the legislative hostility toward emancipation.[26]

Economics posed a second policy concern. The value of slaves increased in the nineteenth century after the legal African slave trade was stopped. According to Orlando Patterson, the high replacement costs of slaves, coupled with a limited external supply of new slaves, correlated with the low manumission rate.[27] This low rate, in turn, correlates with legislative hostility to a further reduction in the supply of slaves caused by widespread manumission.

Finally, hostility to manumission accorded with the pro-slavery ideology that developed in the nineteenth century. Judges and legislators found freed slaves to be an ideological threat, and eventually came to oppose manumission out of the state as well as in the state. This trend is illustrated in the case law interpreting the manumission statutes and was made a statutory mandate in several states on the eve of the War of the Rebellion.

## *Interpreting the Master's Will: The Manumission Cases*

The various issues raised in the Southern manumission cases have received very thorough discussions in the works of A.E.K. Nash, Arthur Howington, and Mark Tushnet. Nash reviews the case law of several key states and finds that some judges and courts, in Georgia for one example, were anti-manumission and pro-slavery, while others in states such as Tennessee were pro-manumission and even "libertarian." Howington, studying Tennessee, writes that Nash went too far in calling even that state's decisions libertarian. But he concludes that the courts did address a concern, at least in part, for slave's "rights" in the Tennessee manumission cases, opining that this "was completely compatible with and supportive of the peculiar institution." Tushnet applies the manumission cases to make further arguments, but does agree that these cases reveal the judge's pro-slavery or anti-slavery biases.[28]

Four points must be recognized at the outset, however. The first is that, legally, the slave had no "right" to manumission. That right was created in other slave societies by allowing the slave to use his *peculium* to purchase his freedom.[29] The slaves in the United States South had no right to a peculium, which was property in which the slave had some legally enforceable rights. Therefore, the slave's "right" to manumission was based solely on the master's will and intent. The master could grant or deny freedom as he elected—the "right" was his, not that of the slave.

This was the principle behind the rule that was applied to cases in which a slave sought to enforce his master's promise to free the slave if the slave performed an agreed consideration. The courts refused to enforce this type of agreement between the master and the slave because the master's promises could not constitute a legally enforceable contract. This jurisprudence was explained in an 1857 Arkansas opinion:

> If the master contract . . . that the slave shall be emancipated upon his paying to his master a sum of money, or rendering him some stipulated amount of labor, although the slave may pay the money, . . . or perform the labor, yet he cannot compel his master to execute

the contract, because both the money and the labor of the slave belong to the master and could constitute no legal consideration for the contract.[30]

An 1860 Missouri case held that this rule flowed from the nature of manumission, which was recognized as "a mere gratuity, under our laws[.]" Apparent hardship on the part of the slave who performed his contract was not an equity "of which the law can take cognizance . . ., however strongly it might appeal . . . to conscience or the moral sense."[31] Therefore, it is clear that the master's right to free his slaves was the right regulated by the manumission statutes.

Second, even the most liberal manumission laws balanced the master's rights against the rights of creditors and heirs, as well as society in general. For example, in Maryland, if the master's estate was not sufficient to satisfy his just debts, or if the slave was too old or too young to support himself, the owner's slave could not go free.[32] The master's intent to free his slaves was thus limited by the vested rights of creditors. These calculations of interest varied over time and in different states; but throughout, there was no recognition of the right of the slave to be free.

The third point is that the decisions freeing slaves were not in any real sense libertarian. No court in the South exercised the legal discretion to liberate a slave without some indicia of the master's intent to free the slave, either expressed or implied. Judges enforced the master's will in the manumission cases. They were thus antilibertarian as they tacitly legitimized the slave's lack of any right to liberty independent of the master's will. The only legally enforceable basis for freedom was the whim of the owner; another example of the slave owner's all-powerful and despotic position in relation to the rightless and powerless slave.

Fourth, one must realize that in most slave societies a pro-manumission viewpoint was consistent with a pro-slavery mind. Howington states this, but does not explain why this proposition is so. Orlando Patterson points out how the potential reward of manumission was considered a key component of many of the slavery systems in the world's history. In the United States South, however, an ideology developed that deviated from this norm, and that ideology regarded manumission as an anti-slavery act. Some dissented from this view. For example, the South Carolina jurist John Belton O'Neall tried to stem the tide against manumission in his state. O'Neall failed, however, and the anti-manumission forces prevailed, as they did in most Southern states.[33]

The latter issue is an interesting one of perception, but the key proposition for our purposes is that even in the pro-manumission states, including Tennessee, it is incorrect to think of the manumission cases as involving slave "rights" in any real sense. Nor were these pro-manumission decisions libertarian or anti-slavery in effect or purpose.

This analysis of the real interests involved in the manumission cases was set forth by T.R.R. Cobb, the pro-slavery treatise writer. On this issue, unlike the others referred to herein, Cobb was correct when he argued that the courts should apply a form of "legal realism" to the emancipation case. He stated that judges should not approach manumission with a presumption for or against liberty. Rather, he contended that:

> The true principle of hermeneutics is, that the court should incline neither the one way or the other, but should inquire, first, what is the intention of the testator? and, second, has he used sufficient words to carry out his intention? If, in either of these particulars, the bequest is insufficient, it must fail, unless in the latter case the facts make out such a case as, under the general rules of law, will authorize the court to supply words[.][34]

The same analysis applied to *inter vivos* transactions. It is also supplemented by consideration of the master's intent as compared to public policy limits contained in the anti-manumission statutes. Nowhere does any "right" of the slave arise in this analysis.

Therefore the real issues in the manumission cases were: 1) What did the master's intend, and 2) does that intent contravene a statutory public policy prohibition? In making this calculation of public versus private interests, the courts did consider the claims of creditors and heirs of the owner, but not the slave's interest.

This was so because it was accepted throughout the South that the slave had no right to sue or be a party to a non-criminal legal proceeding. Wheeler explains this rule as follows: "It would be an idle form and ceremony to make a slave a party to a suit, by the instrumentality of which he could recover nothing; or if a recovery could be had, the instant it was recovered it would belong to the master."[35] The one exception Wheeler cites is a suit for freedom. The reasons for this were twofold. First, the real dispute in a manumission case was between the slaves' "rulers"—the purported "liberator" and the state or the individuals who challenged the emancipator's expressed intention. Thus arose the second reason; the courts could hear this type of dispute *because* it did not implicate slave rights in any real sense.

With this framework of analysis in mind, it is not surprising to note—as do Nash and Howington—that many courts expressed an interest in affording slaves a "fair hearing" in manumission cases, and no right to any hearing in other types of civil cases. The manumission hearing was "fair" because at issue was the battle between the private interests of the master, other private interests, and public policy. But just how "fair" were the courts? That is the issue that the scholarship of Nash, Howington, and to a degree Tushnet, addresses. That ground will not be recovered in detail here because once the issues are framed in the proper context, the manumission case law is a rather simple subject to understand.

## *Two Trends in the Manumission Cases: Social Interests Versus the Master's Intent*

Two overall trends exist in the antebellum manumission case law. First, some courts were more willing to effectuate the master's apparent attempt to free his slaves, despite an ambiguous deed, will, or ambiguous acts allegedly proclaiming emancipation, despite the claims of heirs and creditors, and despite the applicable anti-manumission statutes. And second, hostility toward manumission is increasingly exhibited in the case law during the nineteenth century. This legal change occurred as the pro-slavery ideology grew. This mind set depicted any manumission as a threat to the slave society of the antebellum South. As this ideology took hold, it came to find itself expressed in the opinions of the most pro-slavery judges.

As to the first characteristic, Professors Nash and Tushnet show how the law in Georgia was less "liberal" than that of Tennessee.[36] Before exploring these differences, three key points must be kept in mind, lest our enthusiasm for the Tennessee courts becomes over-emphasized. The first point is that even in Tennessee, the black slave faced a presumption of slavery that derived from his black skin, a presumption that inclined toward freedom if the alleged slave appeared to be white or was an Indian.[37] In *Vaughan v. Phebe*[38] the Tennessee Supreme Court noted the effect of this presumption in a case brought by one "who is unfortunate enough to have a wooly head and a colored skin:"

> Contrary to the general rule, he who is charged with having trespassed upon his person, pleads an affirmative plea [of the slavery of the plaintiff], and yet need not prove it. He says, in justification of his trespass, that the plaintiff is a slave, and yet, on that plaintiff is devolved the *onus probandi* to show himself a freeman.[39]

The court went on to allow the alleged slave to prove his ancestry by hearsay evidence of the reputed family history, an ancient hearsay exception recognized by the common law.[40]

The second point is that even in "liberal" Tennessee, the slave could not bring a manumission claim to the court in a direct action. Rather, the slave's claims had to be brought by use of the "next friend" procedure. Consequently, a white person had to take up the slave's cause. In *Doran v. Brazelton*[41] the Tennessee Supreme Court explained this rule as follows: "A slave can have no status in court except by next friend . . . [Slaves] are property, and have no rights except such as are extended to them by some law."[42]

The third *caveat* to be kept in mind is that the slave claiming an alleged emancipation was thus a surrogate for the real party plaintiff, the deceased master. When the courts gave the slave a "fair" hearing in the manumission case, they were primarily allowing a hearing on evidence of the deceased master's intent. It is thus unremarkable that the courts were willing to air out the issues in manumission case, while closing their doors to slaves in other civil cases, where the master and slave did not have an identical interest. Nevertheless, it is clear that the Tennessee decisions are less hostile toward emancipation than those of Georgia and other states.

Nash, Tushnet, and Howington correctly isolate a series of issues that show how the emancipation decisions varied. The first issue was whether the slave could sue for damages caused by wrongful detention in slavery after winning an emancipation claim. The courts were divided; Maryland and Virginia disallowed any claims for damages, and some decisions held that the claims had to be asserted with the claim for manumission. Others held that the slave could split the cause of action; thus, after wining freedom the slave could file a second suit for damages.[43] This result is not surprising conceptually, however, because in the first action, the real issues do not involve the slave at all. After the court finds the slave to be a free person, that person becomes a cognizable legal entity who can then sue for damages.

Many of the decisions centered upon ambiguous expressions of the master's intent to manumit, and attempts by owners to circumvent the anti-emancipation laws. Three key issues were the send/free, free/send ambiguity, the use of the *cy pres* doctrine to effectuate apparent intent, and the creation of *quasi*-emancipation before slaves are to be set free.

The first arose in a state that prohibited in-state manumission. If the master's will directed his executor to send his slaves to Illinois to free them, most courts found this bequest to be acceptable, as it did not defeat the in-state anti-manumission statute's policy.[44] In

Georgia, however, the pro-slavery ideology of Justice Joseph Lumpkin came to oppose even this bequest, as the statute and case law became more restrictive of manumission claims. In short, any emancipation of slaves, even if it occurred in Canada, was perceived as a threat to the slaveholding regime.

Justice Lumpkin expressed his views in this regard in *Sanders v. Ward*.[45] The case presented a send/free will. Justice Lumpkin and the majority chose not to reverse an 1830 case that upheld such wills. Nevertheless, Lumpkin stated his equal opposition to foreign and domestic emancipation, fearing "the colonization of our Negroes upon our northwestern frontier. They facilitate the escape of our fugitive slaves. In case of civil war, they would become an element of strength to the enemy[.]"[46] Justice Lumpkin called on the legislature to remedy the situation, and in 1859 it did prohibit all postmortem manumission.[47]

The free and send wills provided a second, more serious, concern. If the will directed the executor to free the master's slaves and then send them to Illinois, this was held by some courts to defeat the anti-emancipation policy, but others upheld even this claim.[48] Mark Tushnet likens the close analysis of the free/send wills to legal formalism, which will result in encouraging clear will drafting.[49] But legal formalism can have a substantive purpose and effect, as Duncan Kennedy has shown.[50] To Justice Lumpkin, the free and send will violated the in-state manumission prohibition because the slave was not competent to take title to himself, and thus title vested in the executors in trust for the beneficiaries, upon the testator's death. Consequently, Lumpkin was concerned about creating a kind of *quasi*-freedom in the slaves until they were sent. This was a substantive difference in Lumpkin's mind, as he obviously objected to giving the slave any form of *quasi*-freedom.

The "*quasi*-freedom" cases follow a similar pattern. *Quasi*-freedom was said to result when a will directed an executor to hold the master's slaves in a free or *quasi*-unfree status for a fixed term or until sufficient money was raised to send the slaves out of state. Again, there was disunity among the judges; some courts were entirely hostile to *quasi*-freedom, and some found it to be permissible. Others made a fine distinction between the wills providing that the slaves were to be freed before the contingency occurred or after, with a similar formalism as was applied to the free/send wills.[51]

The focus in these cases, however, was not on the slave but the master's intent along with the wording and policies expressed in the various statutes. A similar concern arose in two related types of cases. In the first, the master's will called for slaves to be freed in the state if allowed, and it came to be disallowed. In the second situation, the will required the removal of the slaves to a state that no longer allowed free black migration. Some courts applied the doctrine of *cy pres* to effectuate the testator's overall intent to free his slaves.

This rule of construction allows the court to create a way of carrying out the testator's intent when it is impossible or illegal to enforce the document exactly as written. Thus, in the first example cited above, the courts ordered the removal of the slaves to another state, and in the second, the court could change the destination to one that allowed free black migration.[52] Other states, including Georgia, would not use the doctrine of *cy pres*, and would strike the bequest.[53] These differing results also reflect the dissimilar judicial views held toward emancipation.

Another telling issue arose in the slave choice cases. These cases allowed the slave to decide if he wished to be freed or held in bondage, or permitted the slave to select a new master after the testator's death. Some decisions enforced these clauses and others did not.[54] Nevertheless, the real issue was not the slave's choice, but the master's intent to allow the slave the choice. Courts that enforced the slave choice wills did not create a legal right in the slave to choose, but enforced the master's right to give the slave that choice. It was a choice by gratuity—not right. Similarly, the anti-slave choice decisions rebuked masters for giving slaves this gratuity, based upon the most virulent racism and pro-slavery arguments of the late antebellum years. But, as noted before, the courts and legislators often found it necessary to clamp down on masters who were too severe and too lenient in their relations with bondsmen. Thus, the two trends regarding manumission become clear. The majority of states became hostile to all attempts at manumission, and this hostility grew in the nineteenth century, despite the writings of a few dissenters. The efforts of John B. O'Neall, the South Carolina judge, are interesting in this respect. For years, O'Neall argued that manumission was not inherently dangerous to slavery. Indeed, O'Neall believed that masters should have had the freedom to reward "good" slaves with freedom as a means of furthering slave obedience.[55]

Unfortunately, the South Carolina legislators disagreed with O'Neall. In 1800 they adopted an act that required five freeholders to approve of the character of slaves who were to be emancipated, and a written deed was necessary to confirm a slave's freedom. In 1820, a statute prohibited emancipation except by an act of the legislature. That act did not, however, mention expressly whether it applied to emancipation by will.[56]

Judge O'Neall read this omission in favor of freedom. Thus, he upheld a free/send will that created a form of *quasi*-freedom until the slaves were freed. That decision, in the 1835 case of *Fraizer v. Fraizer*[57] was followed by another anti-manumission act.

That statute, passed in 1841, consisted of four sections. It voided all emancipations intended to be effectuated by removal of the slave from South Carolina. Second, the act voided trusts created to fund removal and liberation. Third, it voided attempts to create trusts to support in-state "nominal servitude." Finally, the statute declared illegal all gifts to slaves through trusts to be held for the benefit of slaves.[58]

In the 1842 decision in *Carmille v. Carmille*,[59] Judge O'Neall enforced two deed that created a trust that was intended to fund a state of *quasi*-freedom for the master's slaves. Those deeds were in apparent conflict with the 1841 anti-manumission act. That statute was obviously intended to "overrule" *Fraizer*, and to avoid the deeds that in 1841 were on appeal in the *Carmille* case. Nevertheless, O'Neall argued in favor of emancipation as a matter of policy:

> If it was so that a man dared not make provision to make more comfortable faithful slaves, hard indeed would be the condition of slavery. For then no motive could be held out for good conduct; and the good and the bad would stand alike. Such has never been the rule applied to our slaves, and such I hope it never will be.[60]

O'Neall's worse fears came to be reality, however. Later court decisions held that the 1841 anti-manumission act was intended to prevent all in-state and out-of-state manumissions. The prevailing doctrine was thus in harmony with the views of Lumpkin.[61]

In the 1854 opinion in *Morton v. Thompson*,[62] Chancellor G.W. Dargan criticized the *Carmille* and *Frazier* interpretations of the 1820 and 1841 statues. Dargan, like Lumpkin, wrote:

> A free African population is a curse to any country, . . . and the evil is exactly proportionate to the number of such population. This race, however conducive they may be in a state of slavery, to the advance of civilization, (by the results of their valuable labors) in a state of freedom, and in the midst of a civilized community, are a dead weight to the progress of improvement.

He argued that free blacks generally became "drones and lazaroni— consumers, without being producers," and opined that they were "governed mainly by the instincts of animal nature[.]" Dargan also contended that, as a result, free blacks became "pilferers and maurauders," and corrupted slaves.[63] Therefore, the trend against manumission was too strong for O'Neall to defeat. In the end, the virulent racism of Lumpkin and his followers caused the South to strike an atypical course in master and slave relations when compared with other societies.

## *The Effect of Differing Attitudes When the Master's Intent to Free His Slaves was Problematic*

Interesting issues of proof and policy arose in cases that could not be resolved by resort to relatively clear expressions of the master's intent to free his slaves. One example occurred in the Virginia case of *Maria v. Surbaugh*.[64] The testator willed his slave, Mary, to his son with the proviso that Mary be freed when she reached the age of 31. It was held that Mary's four children, born after the testator's death but before Mary reached 31, were slaves. This rule was adopted elsewhere, with the exception of Tennessee, in the case of *Harris v. Clarissa*.[65] Therefore, the rule of property law that the owner of the beast is entitled to the offspring applied to Mary and people in her position, unless the master's intent was expressed to the contrary.

There were differences of opinion on this issue. Justice Nathan Green, for example, dissented from the holding in *Harris v. Clarissa*. Justice Green's dissent is worthy of emphasis because both Nash and Howington place so much weight on some *dicta* in one of Green's later opinions. The holding of that case, *Ford v. Ford*,[66] is thoroughly analyzed by Howington, and the following *dicta* are emphasized in the title and in two places in the text:

> A slave is not in the condition of a horse or an ox . . . he is made in the image of the Creator. He has mental capacities, and an immortal principle in his nature, that constitute him equal to his owner that for the accidental position in which fortune has placed him . . . the laws under which he is held as a slave have not and cannot extinguish his high-born nature nor deprive him of many rights which are inherent in man.[67]

These words certainly express laudable sentiments. Do they—as Howington suggests—represent "a singularly libertarian view of slavery which emphatically underscored the humanity of the slave[?]"[68] Or do they, like the celebrated *dicta* in *State v. Jones*, tell us little about the judge because the real issue in *Ford* was whether the testator intended to revoke a will granting freedom to his slaves?

The latter seems more likely. When the element of the master's intent was removed from the equation in *Harris v. Clarissa*, Judge Green, alike with the majority of his Southern counterparts, proved he was no libertarian, although he later accepted the *Harris* rule. His support of the vindication of the master's intent in *Ford* and in other cases is completely consistent with the notion of slaves as people without rights, as was the entire Southern manumission jurisprudence.

It must be clearly noted, however, that even the *Harris v. Clarissa* holding is not an "anti-slavery" ruling. That opinion was written by Justice John Catron, who later served on the United States Supreme Court. Catron's opinion in the *Dred Scott* case shows that he was not against slavery, as he opined consistently with the majority's holding against Scott and against the constitutionality of the Missouri Compromise.[69]

Moreover, the *Harris* doctrine is in harmony with the rule applied by most Southern states to a related problem. This situation arose when a master willed his slaves for a term of years, or for the life of a life tenant, with the remainder to go to another at the end of the relevant period. If the slave gave birth to a child during the term in question, most Southern courts held that the remainderman was entitled to the increase of the slave. It was recognized that this rule was contrary to the doctrine that applied to the offspring of animals, but the slavery rule was consistent with holdings that a gratuitous bailee had no right to the issue of the bailed chattel. The tenant for a term, or for life, can be equated with the gratuitous bailee.[70]

Similarly, in the *Harris* situation, title to the issue of the slave would not be in the estate of the life tenant after her death. By emancipating the slave, the master has impliedly disclaimed all interest in the remainder, as well as any issue of the slave. Thus, there was support for the *Harris* rule in property law.

And furthermore, the child's condition was to follow that of the mother. After the testator's death and before the contingency occurs, the mother was held as a bound servant for a term of years, and thus was not a slave. So the child, born during this period was bound for the mother's term. If the mother died before her term expired, the child's service should be measured by the same term that would have been binding if the mother lived. Similar arguments were made in *State v. Anderson*,[71] a New Jersey case from 1790 that foreshadowed the *Harris* rule in the Garden State.

Both courts in *Harris* and *Anderson* refer to the presumption in favor of liberty as further support for their rulings. But in both states, the most basic tenet of that presumption was then resolved against the black slave, who had to prove his freedom, contrary to the presumption of freedom of the common law.[72] Nevertheless, the *Harris/Maria* debate highlights the disagreements that exist in the Southern emancipation law.

Another indication of the diversity of opinion regarding the advisability of manumission is revealed by the doctrine of implied manumission. Helen Tunnicliff Catterall cites the 1821 Maryland case of *Hall v. Mullin*[73] as a unique decision adopting this rationale; in fact, she called the *Hall* case a "decided novelty."⁷⁴ Under that decision, a master who devised property to a slave could be held to have intended to free the slave as well as to bestow the property on the freed slave. The reasoning behind this approach to the testator's intent was that the master must have intended to free his slave; otherwise, there would be no meaning to the devise of property to the slave.

This last point, however, illustrates why the *Hall* doctrine was a novelty; it collided with the fundamental principle of slave law that denied slaves the right to own or inherit property. Indeed, because of that rule, the *Hall* approach was rejected by the other courts that were confronted with similarly ambiguous wills. One example is the 1801 North Carolina case of *Cunningham's Heirs v. Executors of Cunningham*.⁷⁵ The testator's will stated that portions of his lands should be rented out and that three of his slaves should work the land for the benefit of the slave, Rachel, and her family. The master also left another tract of land to Rachel and her children. Moreover, he expressly stated that, "I will and desire that Rachel and her children should be set free immediately after my decease."⁷⁶

The North Carolina Conference Court of Judges Hall, Taylor, Johnson, and Macy found that the devise of property was void. Judge Taylor wrote that the testator's will clearly expressed his intent to devise property to his slave. The will was invalid, however, because

> it is indispensable to the validity of every devise, that there be a devisee appointed who is competent to take. Slaves have not that competence; for a civil incapacity results from the nature and condition of slavery. And it would be a solecism, that the law should sanction or permit the acquisition of property by those from whom it afterwards withholds that protection without which property is useless.⁷⁷

The Court distinguished the condition of the villein, who could inherit property. The slave's status differed because the slave could not inherit or own property. This result was particularly harsh because the testator clearly stated his intent to free Rachel and her children.

Nevertheless, the rule established in the *Cunningham* case was followed throughout the South.⁷⁸ The lone exception was the 1792 decision of *Guardian of Sally v. Beaty*.⁷⁹ In that case, a slave of the defendant worked "in town" with her master's permission. She paid him her stipulated wage; but "by her industry" she had "acquired a considerable sum" of additional money. With those funds she purchased another slave—Sally—and gave her freedom. The defendant then claimed Sally as his property. Chief Judge John Rutledge charged the jury that the slave could earn wages of her own, and purchase and then free Sally. The jury found for the plaintiff, and granted Sally her freedom.

That decision was questioned by Justice O'Neall in an 1842 opinion.[80] It was overruled, moreover, in the 1846 decision in *Gist v. Toohey*.[81] On a similar fact pattern, the Court held that the hired slave could not acquire property rights in money earned in addition to the agreed wage between master and slave. The slave who purchased his children in that case was held to have bought them for his master. The slave had no property right to his surplus earnings.

Indeed, the *Hall* case was singular in the jurisprudence of the South. It can be explained, in part, by the unusual facts presented by the case. Catterall's summary of that case sets forth this unique situation:

> Henry L. Hall, by his will, in 1817, had bequeathed "to Dolly Mullin one hundred and forty-one acres of land" and "two young negroes, one called Joan and the other Aaron." After bequeathing other negroes by name to other persons, he bequeathed "all the remainder part of my negroes free." He had supposed that Dolly was already free, for he had sold her in 1810 to her father, Basil, who a month later had executed a deed of manumission to her. Hall also supposed Basil to be free and therefore capable of contracting; for his owner, Benjamin Hall (Henry's father) had in his will (executed in 1803) declared: "I hereby manumit and set free from the time of my decease, my carpenter, called old Basil." But Basil was more than forty-five years old when Benjamin Hall died, and no slave could be set free in Maryland when above that age. Therefore Basil, being a slave, could not buy his daughter Dolly; nor could he emancipate her. The Maryland Court of Appeals held that the will of Henry L. Hall set Dolly free "by implication; . . . it was the intention of the testator that none of his slaves should remain slaves after his death, other than those he named and bequeathed as slaves; . . . without the aid of the residuary clause she would have a right to freedom, under those parts of the will by which property was given to her; her freedom by implication is indispensably necessary to give efficacy to those clauses of the will." (Johnson, J.) "The testator imagined Dolly was free; she was not free, but a slave, at the time the will was made, and being a slave, the will operated to give her freedom, and the lands devised to her." (Chase, C.J.)[82]

The ruling in *Hall* can be attributed, at least in part, to the master's mistaken belief that Basil was legally freed. It also may reflect a judicial attitude more favorable to emancipation than was accepted elsewhere in the South.

The doctrine of implied manumission was also applied to cases in which there was evidence that a master treated his slave as if the slave was free. As explained by Cobb:

Sometimes the courts presume a deed of manumission when the owner permits the slave, for a number of years, to do acts inconsistent with a state of slavery. It is a question generally submitted to the jury, but upon which the courts, in different States, vary their rulings.[83]

The different decisions of the courts can be attributed to diverse judicial attitudes toward emancipation. The courts in Maryland, South Carolina, Missouri, North Carolina, New York, and New Jersey adopted this rule, if the apparent term of freedom exceed twenty years.[84] The principle established in these cases came in conflict, however, with statutory provisions that prohibited masters to allow their slaves to act as if free, as well as the statutes that established formal writing requirements for a valid emancipation. Obviously, the implied emancipation rule could not exist in a state that prohibited all in-state manumissions, or required legislative or judicial approval of emancipations.[85] Therefore, this doctrine fell into disfavor in the anti-manumission climate of the antebellum years.

The decline of implied manumission, along with the prohibition on in-state and even out-of-state manumission, show how the master's freedom to manumit his slaves was confined in the nineteenth century. This trend is also illustrated by the decisions that increasingly refused to apply the doctrine of comity to uphold claims of blacks to property or freedom, when those claims were based upon Northern law.

## *The Decline of Comity and the Master's Intent*

Paul Finkelman shows how this legal change came about as Southern courts became more reluctant to grant rights to former slaves who were removed to a free state by the master and emancipated pursuant to the free state's laws. In the early antebellum years, the Southern courts did allow a slave freed in this way to enforce her right to liberty and to inherit the master's property out of respect—or comity—expressed toward the free state's laws.

Finkelman states that as the antebellum years went on, the southern courts began to revoke their gestures of comity. Although this process was not complete by the beginning of the Civil War, it represents a trend that is consistent with the increasing hostility to manumission exhibited in the antebellum law.[86]

Professor Finkelman rightly identifies the Mississippi case of *Mitchell v. Wells*[87] as the apex of the expressed judicial hostility toward comity in the South. The majority opinion of Justice William Harris held that a female ex-slave could not claim her inheritance under her father's will. Her father was her master and was a Mississippi resident. He freed her before his death by bringing her to Ohio. Later she returned to Mississippi to claim her legacy. Justice Harris wrote an often quoted opinion with the following pro-slavery sentiments:

> The State of Ohio, forgetful of her constitutional obligations to the whole race, and afflicted with a negro-mania, which inclines her to descend, rather than elevate herself to the scale of humanity, chooses to take to her embrace, as citizens, the neglected race, who by common consent of the States united, were regarded, at the formation of our government, as an inferior caste, incapable of the blessings of free government, and occupying, in the order of nature, an intermediate state between the irrational animal and the white man.[88]

Thus, Harris made no pretense about any relevance of slave rights.

Neither did the dissenter, Justice Alexander Handy, however. He expressed the same strong opposition to any emancipation, as a personal matter. Nevertheless, he advocated retention of the comity principle to maintain the Union as he understood it.[89] But Finkelman shows that Handy was no moderate, and quotes Handy's opinion that, rather than violate the "spirit and principles" of the Union, it might be better for the South to dissolve "the compact[.]"[90]

Therefore, support for comity was not inconsistent with slavery or even secession, in Justice Handy's mind. The salience of *Mitchell v. Wells* is that it shows how black rights were irrelevant to the Justices who argued about comity. The real issues were the testator's intent, which was clear, and whether public policy prevented the enforcement of that intent. Handy's position was consistent with the notion that slaves had no rights. But the Harris approach reflected the power of the pro-slavery ideology that made any black freedom an anathema.

The latter view was not held by all Southern judges. John B. O'Neall, of course, was one prime example. In the 1860 decision in *Willis v. Jolliffe*,[91] O'Neall—then Chief Justice—and Justice Job Johnstone retained the principle of comity in a case similar to *Mitchell v. Wells*. They so decided, however, over the strong dissent of Justice F.W. Wardlaw.[92]

The master in the *Willis* case brought his slaves to Ohio and freed them, but died before he could return to South Carolina. Chief Justice O'Neall allowed the slaves to receive property devised by the master. In so ruling, however, O'Neall indicated that he continued to be concerned about upholding the master's will to free his slaves:

> It is true Mr. Willis did not change his own domicil [sic] . . . He intended to return [to South Carolina], . . . but his act and intention

both concurred in placing his slaves, who before were mere chattels personal, in a country where they assumed the character of free persons. This was making Ohio their domicil [sic], and they are now in the full enjoyment of freedom which cannot be disturbed . . . [T]hey . . . were free from the moment when, by the consent of their master, they were placed upon the soil of Ohio to be free. I have no idea that the soil of Ohio per se confers freedom. It is the act of the master which has that effect.[93]

Consequently, Chief Justice O'Neall continued his strong preference for the master's intent in the *Willis* case.

The key point, however, is that O'Neall was not an advocate of the liberation of slaves unless the master intended to free his slaves. This is further shown by O'Neall's opinion in *Guillemette v. Harper*,[94] a case O'Neall referred to after the passage quoted above. It will be recalled that in that case a master brought his slaves to Ireland, and executed a will and codicil indicating his intent to free his slaves. O'Neall questioned the status of Patrick, one of the slaves, under these facts:

According to Somerset v. Steward, (Loft, 1,) he became thereby free. That case carries the law further than I should willingly acknowledge, it is true. But if the master carries a slave to Great Britain to set him free, or while there assents in any way to his freedom, there can be no objection to the validity of the freedom acquired. For if the law of the place does not prohibit emancipation, no one can object to the dissolution of the tie of slavery. It is true, if a master carried his slave to Great Britain, or elsewhere, where slavery does not exist, and against his will, his slave is allowed to go as free, I have no doubt he may reclaim him—or if the slave returns to a country where slavery is recognized, he ipso facto is remitted to his original condition.[95]

Therefore, even one of the most "liberal" of Southern judges based his defense of comity upon his respect for the master's intent, when the master's wishes did not pose a threat to the interests of slave society, as O'Neall perceived those interests. It is also clear, however, that O'Neall's view was on the wane in the nineteenth century.

## *Conclusion*

The nineteenth century manumission statutes and cases were not "libertarian" in any meaningful sense. To the contrary, they were examples of the every-increasing regulation of the master's right to free his slaves. That right was limited because of "changing perceptions of the value of slaves and the growing fears of the dangers that large numbers of free blacks posed to the orderly oppression of plantation slavery."[96] Other policy considerations caused the antebellum lawmakers to regulate the master's right to starve, maim, and kill his slaves. These trends seem inconsistent only if the irrelevance of slave rights or humanity is ignored.

Southern lawmakers and judges disagreed, however, on the question of

> ... how far the law should restrict the master's intention to manumit. Thus, the courts of Georgia were generally more restrictive than those of Tennessee. The issue in these cases, however, was not concern for slave freedom, but effectuation of the master's intent, whatever it may be, against the claims of society in general, heirs, executors, or third parties. Although some judges may have talked about "slave rights" while allowing manumission, even the most "liberal" judges were merely upholding the master's power to do what he wished with his slaves—even after the master's death. But as judicial perceptions of interest changed, the courts more often tended to regulate the master's will when they thought public policy or statute law so required.[97]

Thus, the courts and legislatures increasingly limited the master's right to manumit his slaves by will if the slaves were to stay in the master's state, and in some states, even if the master intended his slaves to leave his home state after his death. This legal trend occurred without any concern for the slave's right to be free.

In fact and in law, the slave had no such right to be free. He could be freed only if the master chose to bestow liberty, and if the state chose not to veto the master's benevolence. Accordingly, the law of manumission is another example of slave law being a compact between the slaves' rulers. The law was concerned with the interests of whites, which were embodied in the slave; the slave had no independent right to freedom.

# NOTES

1. *See,* 3 William Blackstone, *Commentaries on the Laws of England* *216–222 (1768) as to nuisance, and *211 regarding an owner's liability in trespass for damage done by loose cattle. *See, also,* Prosser, *supra* at 583–591.

2. *See,* Brackett, *supra* at 107–108, 148–149.

3. See, *generally*, Stampp, *supra* at 192; 2 Hurd, *supra* at 152–153; Henry, *supra* at 66; Wiecek, *supra* at 265–266.
4. *See*, Goodell, *supra* at 136.
5. *Id.* at 136–137.
6. 15 S.C.L. 49, 4 McCord. 156 (1827).
7. 34 S.C.L. 299, 3 Strob. 573 (1849).
8. *See*, Stroud, *supra* at 17; Goodell, *supra* at 137–8.
9. *Id.* at 140; *see, also*, Stampp, *supra* at 217–218, and Stroud, *supra* at 17.
10. *See, State v. Bowen, supra*, 34 S.C.L. at 299, 3 Strob. at 574.
11. *See, Id.*, 34 S.C.L. at 300, 3 Strob. at 574 (Wardlaw, J., concurring).
12. *See, Id.*, 34 S.C.L. at 299–300, 3 Strob. at 573–575.
13. *Id.*, 34 S.C.L. at 300, 3 Strob. at 575.
14. *Cheek v. State*, 38 Ala. 227 (1862). The Cheek case does not establish any significant doctrine in relation to the master's duty to feed and clothe his slaves. The defendant was indicted for failing to provide his slaves with adequate food and clothing, and failing to provide for them in sickness and old age, in violation of § 3297 of the 1852 Code. *See, Id.* at 228–230. The evidence at trial was presented by defendant's overseer. He testified that the defendant's slaves were given only one quarter pound of bacon a day, and none on Sunday. He also stated that by the summer of 1859, all meat on the plantation was consumed. *Id.* at 229. He gave his opinion, further, that this was insufficient food for plantation slaves, and the appeals court sustained the admission of this opinion. *See, Id.* at 229, 235.

Nevertheless, the defendant's conviction was reversed. This was because the trial court excluded evidence that in December 1858, the defendant had 33 hogs slaughtered for plantation use. *See, Id.* at 229, 236. The appellate court found that this evidence was relevant to the issue of the amount of meat that was available for the defendant's slaves. *See, Id.* at 236. The court also sustained the sufficiency of the indictment. *See, Id.* at 230–235.
15. 22 Tenn. 192, 3 Hum. 203 (1842).
16. Stroud, *supra* at 124. [Emphasis in original.]
17. *Compare*, Stowe, *supra* at 171–176; Goodell, *supra* at 135–149; Stroud, *supra* at 16–20, *with*, "Equitable Past?," *supra* at 229, "Negro Rights," *supra* at 172, Tushnet—1975, *supra* at 127 n. 32.
18. *Compare*, Fogel and Engerman, *supra* at 109–126, *with*, Richard Sutch, "The Care and Feeding of Slave," in *Reckoning with Slavery, supra* at 231–301; *see, also*, Fogel, *supra* at 132–153.
19. *See*, Patterson, *supra* at 273, 284–285.
20. *See*, Stroud, *supra* at 96; *see, also*, Wheeler, *supra* at 386–388.
21. Wheeler, *supra* at 387–388; *see, also*, Cobb, *supra* at 279.
22. *See*, Stroud, *supra* at 98–101; Cobb, *supra* at 282; Brackett, *supra* at 148–174; Wheeler, *supra* at 387.
23. *See*, Cobb, *supra* at 281–282, 294, 298–301; Stroud, *supra* at 96.
24. *See*, Cobb, *supra* at 279, 286–290; *See, also*, under the common law, *State v. M'Donald*, 1 N.J.L. 332 (Sup. Ct. 1795); *State v. Frees*, 1 N.J.L. 259 (Sup. Ct. 1794); *State v. Prall*, 1 N.J.L., 4 (Sup. Ct. 1790); and under the 1798 statute, *State v. Emmons*, 2 N.J.L. 5 (Sup. Ct. 1806).

25. *See, generally,* Stroud, *supra* at 96–97; Sellers, *supra* at 236–241; *Slavery in Mississippi, supra* at 203–238; Henry, *supra* at 168–176; "Negro Rights," *supra* at 154–166. The statutes that barred out-of-state manumission were the 1841 South Carolina Act, *Id.*, 2 Catterall, *supra* at 268; the 1859 Georgia Act, 2 Hurd, *supra* at 109; the 1857 Mississippi statute, *Mitchell v. Wells*, 37 Miss. 235, 255–256 (1859), *Slavery in Mississippi, supra* at 216–217; the Alabama Act of 1860, Sellers, *supra* at 237, and the 1859 Arkansas Act, *Phebe v. Quillin*, 21 Ark. 490 (1860). *See, generally,* for Virginia, Stroud, *supra* at 99 and *Freedom and Bondage, supra* at 108–115; for Tennessee, Howington, *supra* at 32–39, 2 Catterall, *supra* at 480; for Maryland, Brackett, *supra* at 171; for Kentucky, *Smith v. Adam*, 57 Ky. (18 B. Mon.) 685 (1857), 1 Catterall, *supra* at 276; for Florida, *Bryan v. Dennis*, 4 Fla. 445 (1852); 3 Catterall, *supra* at 107 n. 5, *quoting* the 1838 Constitution that stated, "The General Assembly shall have no power to pass laws for the emancipation of slaves."; for North Carolina, 2 Catterall, *supra* at 4–5; for Texas, 5 *Id.* at 269–270.

26. *See,* Howington, *supra* at 34–70; *see, also,* Sellers, *supra* at 236–237, 364–368; Sl*avery in Mississippi, supra* at 203; Henry, *supra* at 170–171.

27. *See,* Patterson, *supra* at 284.

28. For Nash, *see*, "Reason of Slavery," *supra* at 93–184; "Trial Rights," *supra* at 629–637; "Negro Rights," *supra* at 154–166, 172–177; *see, also,* "Radical Interpretations," *supra* at 296–314. For Howington, *see*, Howington, *supra* at 26–27. For Tushnet, *see*, Tushnet, *supra* at 188–228. *See, also,* Linda O. Smiddy, "Judicial Nullification of State Statutes Restricting the Emancipation of Slaves: A Southern Court's Call for Reform," 42 *South Carolina Law Review* 589 (1991) for an analysis of the South Carolina cases that is almost identical to that employed by Nash in "Negro Rights," *supra*, but without citing one Nash article, and, David J. Grindle, "Manumission: The Weak Link in Georgia's Law of Slavery," 41 *Mercer Law Review* 701 (1991).

29. *See,* Patterson, *supra* at 182–186, 270; Watson, *supra* at 90–101; Cobb, *supra* at 240.

30. *Jackson v. Bob*, 18 Ark. 399, 413 (1857) [citations omitted].

31. *See, Redmond v. Murray*, 30 Mo. 570, 575 (1860). *See, also,* Cobb, *supra* at 241–242; *Gist v. Toohey*, 31 S.C.L. 169, 2 Rich. 424 (1846) *Stevenson v. Singleton*, 28 Va. 33, 1 Leigh 72 (1820) and cases cited in note thereto; *Sawney v. Carter*, 27 Va. 652, 6 Rand. 173 (1828); *Richard v. Van Meter*, 20 F. Cas. 682 (D.C. Cir. 1827) (No. 11,763); *Cooke v. Cooke*, 13 Ky. (3 Litt.) 238 (1823) *Brown v. Wingard*, 4 F. Cas. 438 (D.C. Cir. 1822) (No. 2,034), *cf. Sarah v. Taylor*, 21 F. Cas. 431 (D.C. Cir. 1822) (No. 12,399) (enforced contract in which owner sold slave for 9 years, to be freed thereafter); *Blackman v. Gordon*, 19 S.C. Eq. 19, 2 Rich. Eq. 43 (1845) (anti-emancipation act could be retroactively applied as to slave not freed).

32. *See,* Brackett, *supra* at 158–161; *Wilson v. Barnett*, 9 G. & J. 158 (Md. 1837); *Anderson v. Bailey*, 8 G. & J. 32 (Md. 1836); *Hamilton v. Cragg*, 6 H. & J. 16 (Md. 1823).

33. *See,* Patterson, *supra* at 209–239; "Negro Rights," *supra* at 154–166, 172–177, 179–187 for O'Neall's views.

34. *See,* Cobb, *supra* at 298 [footnotes omitted]. For a similar approach, *see, Phebe v. Quillin,* 21 Ark. 490 (1860).
35. *Wheeler, supra* at 197; *see,* Cobb, *supra* at 247.
36. *See,* "Reason of Slavery," *supra* at 98–184; Tushnet, *supra* at 188-228.
37. *See,* Cobb, *supra* at 65–67; Wheeler, *supra* at 392–408.
38. 8 Tenn. (1 Mart & Yer.) 1 (1827).
39. *Id.* at 20.
40. *See, e.g.,* Charles McCormick, *McCormick on Evidence* 901–903 (St. Paul, 3d ed. 1984), 4 Catterall, *supra* at 3–5.
41. 32 Tenn. (2 Swan) 105 (1852).
42. *Id.* at 110, *quoted in* Howington, *supra* at 16; *see, also, Susan v. Wells,* 5 S.C.L. 6, 3 Brev. 11 (1811).
43. For Maryland, *see, e.g., State, Use of Clements v. Van Lear,* 5 Md. 91 (1853); Brackett, *supra* at 162; for Virginia, *see, Paul v. Mingo,* 31 Va. 899, 4 Leigh 163 (1833). For the Tennessee and Texas cases, *see, Moore's Adm'r v. Minerva,* 17 Tex. 20 (1856); *Matilda v. Crenshaw,* 12 Tenn. (4 Yer.) 249 (1833); and for the "majority" rule, *see,* "Reason of Slavery," *supra* at 102–103.
44. *See, e.g., Sanders v. Ward,* 25 Ga. 109 (1858); *Jordan v. Bradley,* 1 Ga. 443 (1830).
45. 25 Ga. 109 (1858).
46. *Id.* at 124.
47. *See,* "Reason of Slavery," *supra* at 118.
48. *See, Drane v. Beall,* 21 Ga. 21 (1857) and cases *cited in* "Reason of Slavery," *supra* at 111–113 n. 345–346, 200–202 n. 670–671; Tushnet, *supra,* 196–202.
49. *See,* Tushnet, *supra* at 196–198.
50. D. Kennedy, "Form and Substance in Private Law Adjudication," 89 *Harvard Law Review* 1685 (1976).
51. *See, e.g.,* for the anti-*quasi* freedom approach; *Cox v. Harris,* 17 Md. 23 (1861); *Knight v. Hardemann,* 17 Ga. 253 (1855) and *Bivens v. Crawford,* 26 Ga. 225 (1858). For the more favorable view, *see, e.g.,* Tushnet, *supra* at 203–5.
52. *See, e.g., Hogg v. Capehart,* 58 N.C. (5 Jones) 71 (1853) (court selects place for manumission).
53. *See, e.g., Hunter v. Bass,* 18 Ga. 127 (1855) (court would not substitute new destination when selected states prohibited free black migration).
54. *Compare, e.g., Beaupied v. Jennings,* 28 Mo. 254 (1859); *Redding v. Findley,* 57 N.C. (4 Jones Eq.) 216 (1858) (allows choice), *with, Curry v. Curry,* 30 Ga. 253 (1860), overruling *Cleland v. Waters,* 19 Ga. 35 (1855), 16 Ga. 496 (1854) (no choice).
55. *See,* "Negro Rights," *supra* and O'Neall, *supra* at 10–12 for O'Neall's views on manumission as expressed in his judicial opinions and his pamphlet on slave law.
56. *See,* 2 Catterall, *supra* at 267–268; Henry, *supra* at 168–171.
57. 11 S.C. Eq. 149, 2 Hill Eq. 304 (1835).
58. *See,* "Negro Rights," *supra* at 164; *Jolliffe v. Fanning,* 44 S.C.L. 61, 62–63, 10 Rich. L. 186, 190 (1856); *Morton v. Thompson,* 27 S.C. Eq. 146, 148–149, 6 Rich. Eq. 370, 375–376 (1854).

59. 27 S.C.L. 190, 2 McMul. 454 (1842).
60. *Id.*, at 197, 2 McMul. at 470.
61. *See, Escheator v. Dangerfield,* 29 S.C. Eq. 33, 8 Rich. Eq. 95 (1856); *Morton v. Thompson,* 27 S.C. Eq. 146, 6 Rich. Eq. 370 (1854); *Johnson v. Clarkson,* 24 S.C. Eq. 125, 3 Rich. Eq. 305 (1851); *Swinton v. Egleston,* 24 S.C. Eq. 83, 3 Rich. Eq. 201 (1851); *Vinyard v. Passalaigue,* 33 S.C.L. 249, 2 Strob. 536 (1848); *Blackman v. Gordon,* 19 S.c. Eq. 19, 2 Rich Eq. 43 (1845); *cf., Broughton v. Telfer,* 24 S.C. Eq. 178, 3 Rich. Eq. 431 (1851) (pre-1841 emancipation upheld under *Carmille,* but ex-slave seized under 1800 act and returned to servitude).
62. 23 S.C. Eq. 146, 6 Rich. Eq. 370 (1854).
63. *Id.* at 147, 6 Rich. Eq. at 372.
64. 23 Va. (2 Rand.) 228 (1824).
65. 14 Tenn. (6 Yer.) 153 (1834). For the majority of cases favoring the decision in *Maria, see,* Cobb, *supra* at 72–77, 283; "Reason of Slavery," *supra* at 156 n. 515–519. A Maryland statute enacted the majority presumption, *see,* Brackett, *supra* at 154–155, while a Virginia act was to the contrary. *See, Freedom & Bondage, supra* at 115. Kentucky adopted the *Maria* presumption, but it was held overridden by the master's strong anti-slavery views expressed in the wills considered in *Charles v. French,* 29 Ky. (6 J.J. Marsh.) 331 (1831) and *Hudgens v. Spencer,* 34 Ky. (4 Dana) 589 (1836); *see,* 1 Catterall, *supra* at 278–279.
66. 26 Tenn. (7 Hum.) 92 (846).
67. *Id.,* 26 Tenn. (7 Hum.) at 95–96.
68. Howington—1975, *supra* at 258.
69. *Scott v. Sandford,* 60 U.S. (19 How.) 393 (1856) (Catron., J., concurring).
70. For the majority rule applied to life tenancies and tenancies for a term, *see, generally,* Wheeler, *supra* 23–28; *see, also, e.g., Williamson v. Daniel,* 25 U.S. (12 Wheat.) 568, 6 L. Ed. 731 (1827); *Lee v. Sprague,* 14 Mo. 476 (1851); *Wilks v. Green,* 14 Ala. 437 (1848); *Miller v. McClelland,* 23 Ky. (7 T.B. Mon.) 231 (1828). For the Delaware and Maryland rule, *see, generally,* 4 Catterall, *supra* at 5, 214; Brackett, *supra* at 144–146 n. 1. The general rule as to bailees of animals, and the rule for gratuitous bailees is set forth in 3A *C.J.S.* "Animals" § 9(a) and (b) (1973).
71. 1 N.J.L. 36 (Sup. Ct. 1790). The majority rule that the slave was to be considered a slave for life during the term of years was less logical. For a Delaware decision rejecting the majority rule, *see, Elliot v. Twilley,* 5 Del. (5 Harr.) 192 (1849) (overruling *Ben v. Wootten,* 1 Del. (1 Harr.) 77 (1833), which adopted the majority rule, with dissent).
72. *See, Stoutenborough v. Haviland,* 15 N.J.L. 266 (Sup. Ct. 1836) (stating that the presumption should not be followed); *State v. Lyon,* 1 N.J.L. 403, 415 (Sup. Ct. 1789) (following presumption against blacks); and *Vaughan v. Phebe,* 7–8 Tenn. (Mart. & Yer.) 389, 400 (1827).
73. 5 H. & J. 190 (Md. 1821).
74. *See,* 4 Catterall, *supra* at 6; *see, also,* Cobb, *supra* at 311.
75. 1 N.C. (Cam. & Nor.) 353, 1 N.C. (Tay.) 209 (1801), *quoted in,* Wheeler, *supra* at 191–193.
76. *Id.* at 192.

77. *Id.* at 192–193.
78. *See, e.g.,* Cobb, *supra* at 237–238; Stroud, *supra* at 32–33.
79. 1 S.C.L. 104, 1 Bay. 260 (1792).
80. *Carmille v. Carmille's Administrator,* 27 S.C.L. 190, 198, 2 McMul. 454, 471 (1842) ("That case goes further than I desire to go; but it is ample authority to prove, that by the law of this State a slave might acquire personal property[.]").
81. 31 S.C.L. 169, 2 Rich. 424 (1846).
82. 4 Catterall, *supra* at 6–7 [footnotes omitted]. It is clear that the judicial discussions about this doctrine were *dicta*. In *Guillemette v. Harper,* 38 S.C.L. 75, 4 Rich. 186 (1850) Judge O'Neall, also in *dicta*, implies that a devise to a slave, coupled with an expressed intent to free the slave, will be persuasive to show intent to manumit. As in *Hall*, however, the devise of property did not stand alone as the basis for the slave's claim to freedom. Later South Carolina cases holding that bequests to slaves were void include, *Mallett v. Smith,* 27 S.C. Eq. 5, 6 Rich. Eq. 12 (1853); *Thorne v. Fordham,* 24 S.C. Eq. 91, 4 Rich. Eq. 222 (1852); *Swinton v. Egleston,* 24 S.C. Eq. 83, 3 Rich. Eq. 201 (1851).
83. Cobb, *supra* at 295 [footnote omitted].
84. *See, Lewis v. Hart,* 33 Mo. 535 (1863); *Henderson v. Jason,* 9 Gill 483 (Md. 1851); *Stringer v. Burcham,* 34 N.C., 12 Ired. 41 (1851); *Anderson v. Garrett,* 9 Gill 120 (Md. 1850); *State v. Hill,* 29 S.C.L. 62, 2 Speers 150 (1843); *Miller v. Reigne,* 20 S.C.L. 323, 2 Hill 592 (1835); *Burke v. Jim,* 6 G. & J. 136 (Md. 1834); *Wells v. Lane,* 9 Johns. 144 (N.Y. 1812); *State v. M'Donald,* 1 N.J.L. 332 (Sup. Ct. 1795).
85. *See, State v. Nat,* 48 N.C. 147, 13 Ired. 154 (1851); *Vinyard v. Passalaigue,* 33 S.C.L. 249, 2 Strob. 536 (1858); Cobb, *supra* at 109, 287–290.
86. See, Finkelman, *supra* at 2–6, 181–235, 285–298, and the criticism by Nash, in "Radical Interpretations," *supra* at 282–314.
87. 37 Miss. 235 (1859).
88. *Id.* at 263 [emphasis in original].
89. *Id.* at 279–283 (Handy, J., dissenting).
90. *Id.* at 286.
91. 32 S.C. Eq. 167, 11 Rich. Eq. 447 (1860).
92. *See, Id.,* 32 S.C. Eq. at 193–196, 11 Rich. Eq. at 517–527 for Wardlaw's dissent. Johnston concurred in the result.
93. *Id.* at 192, 11 Rich. Eq. at 514.
94. 38 S.C.L. 75, 4 Rich. 186 (1850).
95. *Id.* at 77, 4 Rich at 190.
96. Fede—1984, *supra* at 316. [footnote omitted].
97. *Id.* [footnote omitted].

# CHAPTER 8

# Slave Criminals and Protection of the Master's Property Rights in Slaves: The Discrimination in the Substantive Law

**THE CRIMINAL** law of slavery is another misunderstood area of slave law. That law, as pointed out in Chapter 3, did recognize the slave as a person, to a degree, when legal punishment was inflicted through the courts upon slaves who committed "crimes." In a sense, then the law recognized the slave as "humanity." But only the most superficial analysis of the law of slave criminality reveals any inconsistency in the notion that slaves were property that could be punished by the criminal law.

Moreover, the criminal law of slavery underwent two parallel changes in the nineteenth century. One tide of change increased the trial rights that slaves possessed when charged with felonies and expanded the slave's "right" to self-defense. This might appear to be a form of "sympathy" for the slave, but the lawmakers had other motives. Indeed, at the same time, the number of capital crimes that slaves could commit was increasing. These capital crimes were thought to be necessary to protect the peace in society; but they also threatened to injure the economic interests of individual slave owners whose slaves were unjustly accused. Emerging class conflicts also manifested themselves, and masters sought to protect their slaves from the violence and unjust accusations of other slave masters and poor whites.

Consequently, the increased concern for "fairness" in slave trials should be seen as a rebalancing of the need to protect the individual master's investment in his slave weighted against the social need for slave control. This legal change is thus similar to that which occurred in regard to white violence directed at slaves.

One fundamental concept must be pointed out at the outset. The master was the "real party at interest" in slave criminal law cases. Those proceedings were *in rem*; the state sought relief against a chattel. The owner of the chattel was the "legal person" whose rights the state sought to limit in the slave criminal cases. This fundamental concept can be made clear by first examining the nature of the slave's substantive criminal liability. The next Chapter reviews the procedures in slave trials.

## *The Slave As Criminal: The Purposes of the Criminal Law in Slave Society*

Slave misdeeds were punished on two levels—the private action of individuals and the state action of the courts. The master was the dispenser of justice on his plantation. He could legally punish slaves for minor and major transgressions, within the broad limits defined in Chapters 5 and 6. Similarly, overseers were given wide discretion to punish slaves in the master's stead; nevertheless, the law was more eager to limit the overseer's power to protect the master's interest.

The overseer's role is described in the Alabama case of *Gillian v. Senter*.[1] The plaintiff was a master who sued his overseer for damages caused by the defendant's violent beating of the plaintiff's slave while the plaintiff was out of the state. The slave was accused of stealing from one of the plaintiff's neighbors. The accuser stated that he would not bring the matter to the criminal courts if the overseer corrected the slave. Thus, the overseer beat the slave.

The plaintiff alleged that the overseer did not have the authority to whip the slave for the offense of stealing, as this was a crime punishable at law. Chief Justice Henry W. Collier disagreed. He held that the overseer, like the master, is "of necessity invested with the authority to inflict reasonable punishment for the breach of police regulations." He added:

> If the master intrust the management of his slaves to a third person, it is the duty of the latter, not only to see that he is faithful in the performance of the labour assigned him, but to exercise such a restraint as will prevent him, as far as may be, from an indulgence in open immoralities. Neither drunkenness, profanity, or theft should be looked on with toleration; for a connivance at either of these, tends but to subvert a proper subordination and discipline, and in the end to worse consequences. As, then, it is the duty of the overseer to cause the observance of good order upon the plantation, it is scarcely necessary to add more, to prove that he is authorized to punish slaves placed under his supervision for offences against good morals. It cannot, we think be important to inquire whether the offense is criminally punished by the law; for we can conceive of no warrant for thus limiting the power of the overseer. Such a limitation, we are sure, has not its foundation in policy. The good morals and quiet

of the State are not concerned in the prosecution of every slave who may commit a larceny. So far as it concerns the public, it is quite as well, perhaps better, that his punishment should be admeasured by a domestic tribunal. Certainly this mode of procedure would be preferable for the master, as it would relieve him both from anxiety and the necessity of expending money.[2]

The Court did allow for civil liability if the overseer inflicted "immoderate punishment," thus revealing the inherent conflict between the master and overseer.

Nevertheless, the Court recognized and legitimized the "domestic tribunal." And when the master disciplined his own slaves, there was even less of a reason to heighten anxiety and expenses by taking a case to the courts.

Slave crimes at law, however, were a necessary adjunct to the "domestic tribunal." As Patterson explains, "No slave society took the position that the slave, being a thing, could not be held responsible for his actions." Indeed, Patterson adds that "the slave usually paid more heavily for his crimes when the victim was a free man."[3] This was true in the colonial South. The early codes discriminated against slaves both procedurally and substantively.

The substantive criminal law punished slaves more severely for the crimes that slaves could commit in common with whites. And moreover, slaves were subject to legal punishments for acts that were not crimes for whites. Furthermore, the colonial codes created slave courts to try slaves. These courts deprived slaves of the most basic common law criminal trial rights. The slave was denied the right to an indictment by a grand jury, a trial by jury, and an appeal. The details of the colonial codes have been discussed elsewhere, and need only be outlined here.[4]

What is of fundamental importance is the simple question, why did the law not treat the slave like property that could not be criminally liable? The answer lies just below the surface of the various colonial codes. Slaves were, biologically, people who could commit crimes against third parties. When a master's slave injured a third party's right, somebody had to be held criminally responsible. There were only two alternatives—the master and the slave. The former was unacceptable under all theories of common law jurisprudence. The slave had to be the candidate for criminality.

Patterson correctly notes this as follows:

> Although in theory the slave had no will beyond that of his master, in no slave society was the master held responsible for [the slave's] criminal action . . . unless, of course, he ordered the crimes.[5]

Thus, it was considered unfair to hold the master criminally liable for all of his slave's acts. The law had to recognize the fact, however, that slaves could commit crimes that endangered the public peace and implicated the purposes of the criminal law. Slaves also rebelled and committed other breaches of the etiquette of slavery oppression. Slaves, moreover, violently attacked persons and committed property crimes that impaired the rights of third parties in society.

This conflict of interests and concepts was easily solved by the criminal law of slavery. The law recognized the slave as the master's human chattel, but the slave was not the master. Thus, the master was not criminally liable for his slave's acts. It is fundamental to the criminal law that the two elements of criminal liability are the guilty act and *mens rea*, or a guilty state of mind. If the law held the master criminally liable for the slave's acts, the master's responsibility would extend to the acts and state of mind of a third person. This alternative violated concepts that were too fundamental in the common law.[6]

Consequently, slave criminal liability was the only alternative; he *had* to be held liable to further the goals of the criminal law. These aims are generally known as retribution, reform and prevention.[7] The law allowed the offended party retribution through the formal punishment of the slave. This minimized self-help by the victim, and restored the all-important honor of the person whose interests were violated by the slave.

Slave punishment also could be counted on to help reform the slave, where corporal punishment was called for. Although capital punishment could not further reform, it could aid in the prevention aims as would a "good" whipping of the miscreant slave.

Therefore, society acted against criminal slaves. But this did not create any inconsistency with the definition of slaves as property. Slave criminal jurisdiction was, in fact, the functional equivalent of two common law procedures—forfeiture and the abatement of a public nuisance.

As to the latter, note, as stated in Chapter 7, that the master could not maintain his slaves as a public nuisance. When slaves went about the countryside committing crimes they did become a public nuisance. The common law recognized the right of the state to destroy animals that created a nuisance, to protect the public. Individuals also had a right to abate a public nuisance.[8] But before masters went around shooting each others' slaves, cooler heads prevailed and placed the slave courts into the picture to punish slave crimes against society.

The other common law concept related to slave crime is the *in rem* forfeiture proceeding. The analogy begins with the common law rule that an object that caused the accidental death of another was forfeited to the Crown as a deodand. That term is derived from the Latin phrase *Deo dandum*, meaning a thing to be given to God.

Forfeiture eventually lost its religious connotations and became a source of revenue for the Crown. The proceedings were justified as punishment of the owner, who was in effect absolutely liable to the extent of the value of the chattel taken. A similar concept was a part of Roman law. An aggrieved party could bring a noxal action against the slave's owner. The owner's liability was limited to the surrender of the slave.[9]

Although the noxal action and the law of deodands did not become a part of the common law in the United States, various *in rem* statutory forfeiture provisions have authorized civil proceedings against a chattel.[10] Of course, the real party at interest in a forfeiture case is the owner; he is the person whose rights are subject to forfeiture. As explained by our Supreme Court, judicial jurisdiction over a thing, which is the basis of *in rem* jurisdiction, "is a customary eliptical way of referring to jurisdiction over the interests of persons in a thing."[11] Similarly, the slave criminal cases can be viewed as forfeiture proceedings against the "deodand" that caused harm. The real party was the slave owner, who was compensated by the state when his slave property was "returned to God," through capital punishment.

With the relevant interests thus in focus, it is not surprising that the courts came to be more concerned about slave trial rights in the nineteenth century. By analogy, in *One 1958 Plymouth Sedan v. Pennsylvania*,[12] Justice Arthur Goldberg wrote for the Supreme Court that the exclusionary rule established in criminal cases in *Mapp v. Ohio*[13] and *Weeks v. United States*[14] applies to civil forfeiture proceedings. The Court was not concerned about the rights of the 1958 Plymouth. Rather, the Court recognized the real rights at stake—the rights of the vehicle owner. Similar notions were present in the antebellum law that increasingly protected slave criminal rights.

Consequently, any appearance of concern for slave rights in criminal trials must be looked at critically. This is made clear by an analysis of how the substantive criminal law of the antebellum years denied slaves equal rights when the slave's behavior was measured against the requirements of law.

## *Discrimination in the Law of Crimes in the Penalties and Offenses Applied to Slaves*

The substantive law discriminated against slaves in two ways. George Stroud presents a detailed study of how the colonial criminal law regarding slaves changed in the nineteenth century.[15] The law continued to treat slaves unequally. Stroud explains this discrimination:

Parts of this system apply to the slave exclusively, and for every infraction a large retribution is demanded; while, with respect to offences for which whites as well as slaves are amenable, punishments of much greater severity are inflicted upon the latter than upon the former.[16]

The first type of discrimination involved laws found to be necessary for keeping peace in slave society, and keeping the slave in his "place."

Stroud includes in the first category the "pass laws." These acts ordered that slaves be whipped if the slaves were found off their plantation without a pass from their master, and if the slave was not in the company of a white person. Also relevant in this respect was the provision adopted in several states that gave all whites the right to force slaves to submit to an examination and correction—to police the pass law. Whites were also privileged to whip and possibly kill slaves who resisted this on-the-spot interrogation and punishment.

Various laws also empowered masters to whip slaves who came upon their plantations, if the slave was not on lawful business. Similarly, laws prohibited groups of slaves from congregating, and subjected them to the lash.[17]

Stroud cites a South Carolina law that prohibited slaves from taking away or letting loose any boat or canoe from its landing. For a first offense, 39 lashes were provided, and until 1833, a second offense resulted in the removal of one of the slave's ears.[18] Slaves also could not keep guns or ammunition, or any other weapon. Unlawful assemblies were prohibited, and the patrols were empowered to discipline slave congregations.[19]

Slaves could not possess articles for sale and commerce, and were not allowed to barter or sell items of value without their master's consent. Various other provisions of law prevented slaves from providing for themselves—the slave was to be totally dependent upon the master. Thus, slaves could not be taught to read.[20] This prohibition also perpetuated the slave's inferior status and perceived as promoting the safety of the community.

Runaway slaves were a severe problem. The laws provided for the arrest of runaways, and any slave harboring a runaway was subject to punishment. Stroud also quotes an 1824 Mississippi statute. It orders a jailer who is entrusted with a runaway to interrogate the slave to obtain the slave's owner's name. Apparently, some slaves were reluctant to do so; thus, if the slave gave a false name, the law required the jailer to "without delay" give the slave "twenty-five lashes, well laid on," and interrogate the slave, for six months if needed to get the truth.[21] The obvious concern here was to return the slave to the master's service, which the slave so disdained that he preferred a jail.

That concern also explains why physical punishment was employed against slaves rather than imprisonment. The lawmakers did not wish to deprive slave owners of the right to the time and effort of the slave. Therefore, with the exceptions of Arkansas and Maryland, the lawmakers reserved physical punishment for the minor crimes of the slave, although the colonial barbarity of torture and legal abuse was lessened in the antebellum years.[22]

The South Carolina Court of Appeals also approved of the "common law" crime of "insolence" of a slave with a 1847 decision discussed in Chapter 1.[23] In *Ex Parte Boylston*,[24] a male slave was charged with directing "insolent language and action" at a female victim. The slave contended that he was not accused of a crime as defined by the slave code. Therefore, he challenged the jurisdiction of the magistrate's court to inflict punishment. The Court of Appeals, with Judge O'Neall dissenting, disagreed.

The key point was that the slave was not charged with any offense explicitly defined by the slave code. Nevertheless, the majority found the authority to create this slave crime implied in the entire regulatory scheme regarding patrols, passes, and runaways. These acts, the court concludes, "contemplate throughout the subordination of the servile class to every free white person, and enforce the stern policy which the relation of master and slave necessarily requires."[25] The court adds:

> Any conduct of a slave inconsistent with due subordination contravenes the purpose of these Acts, and if not liable to punishment has either been overlooked by the legislator, or been thought, from some consideration of expediency, unfit for his notice. That language and deportment of a slave towards a white person, which is inconsistent with the relation between them, and which we denominate insolence, cannot, however, be supposed to have been overlooked, when the relation was fully recognized and rights given to the white which such language and deportment contradict.[26]

Thus, the court creates the crime as a matter of "the common law of this State."[27]

The dissent of Judge O'Neall questioned the jurisdiciton of the magistrate's court to try the slave for insolence. He thought it best to leave the punishment of this offense to the domestic tribunal. He says:

> I presume that the Legislature have always acted on the belief . . . that *any* white person receiving insolence from a slave, could lawfully correct it, without any appeal to the form of law.[28]

Indeed, the white person "wronged" could do as O'Neall suggested, but could also seek vindication of his honor through the courts. Thus is revealed the first type of discrimination against slaves, the unique "slave crimes" that only slaves could commit.

Stroud points to a second area of discrimination, the unequal punishment of slaves for crimes that could be committed in common with whites. This was a serious form of discrimination because it resulted in the exposure of the slave to more capital crimes than whites faced. This pattern of inequality is well depicted by Stroud. For Virginia, he lists sixty-six crimes that carried the death penalty for slaves. Whites could be executed for one of the sixty-six offenses—first degree murder. Similarly, in Mississippi, Stroud lists twelve capital offenses for whites and slaves, but thirty-eight additional offenses that were capital for slaves only. Stroud analyzes the statutes of the other Southern states and finds a similar proliferation of capital crimes for slaves, as opposed to whites.[29]

Howington and Flanigan state further that the number of slave capital offenses tended to grow in the antebellum years, in most Southern states.[30] Howington's study is especially helpful because he examines the laws of Tennessee, a state in which the courts and legislatures increasingly provided for fairness in slave criminal cases between 1819 and 1858. Slaves were protected on the one hand, but at the same time were increasingly exposed to capital punishment. Between 1819 and 1860, the number of capital crimes grew to fourteen, while whites faced the death penalty for two offenses. A similar pattern is exhibited in the other Southern states. Consequently, more and more crimes came to implicate the ultimate punishment. It should be noted that this trend also paralleled the limitations on manumission; freedom was not a reward available to provoke good behavior on the part of the slave, so death was substituted as an inducement.

At the same time that capital punishment was on the increase, the lawmakers had to be concerned about protecting the rights of the owner. The colonial codes called for whipping and other physical abuse of slaves, reserving capital punishment for the most severe crimes. The Tennessee legislature, however, added crimes such as burning boats and endangering the safe running of the railroads to the list of slave capital offenses in 1858 and 1860.[31] Therefore, as the list of capital offenses grew, lawmakers increased the procedural and substantive safeguards that protected the life and labor of the valuable slave. Nevertheless, the law continued to discriminate against slaves, as seen in the law regarding self-defense and mitigation applied to violent confrontations between whites and blacks.

## Discrimination in the Standards of Extenuation and Mitigation of Slave Crimes

In a more subtle way, the slave was subjected to enhanced criminality by the law of mitigation and extenuation that applied to homicide and mayhem committed by slaves. Both offenses required an inquiry into the state of mind of the perpetrator to determine the nature of the crime committed in the common law of crimes. Self-defense was also recognized as an extenuating circumstance. It was a complete defense or an excuse under appropriate circumstances.

When slaves and free blacks were charged with these serious offenses, the courts could have applied the usual common law standards for mitigation and extenuation, if the courts believed that slaves were people entitled to humane treatment under the law. Indeed, the Illinois Supreme Court so held in 1854 in *Campbell v. The People*,[32] when it reversed a free black's murder conviction. The defendant requested that the jury be instructed that it was to consider the defendant's case "as if he were a white man, for the law is the same, there being no distinction in its principles in respect to color." The instruction was not given, a ruling with which the Supreme Court disagreed. The court stated that the principle of equality asserted by the defendant "is undoubtedly exceedingly plain and altogether undeniable," but that "it was still the right of the prisoner to have the law, plain as it was, declared to the jury by the court."[33] The courts of the South did not agree with this plain principle, however.

Instead, slaves, and even free blacks, were denied the defenses of mitigation and extenuation, except to the extent it was considered in harmony with the oppression of slavery. The courts looked at slave criminal prosecutions with the same interests in mind as implicated in *State v. Tackett*.[34] That North Carolina case, discussed in Chapter 5, held that different standards of mitigation and extenuation applied to determine the criminal liability of whites when slaves were the victims of crimes. Thus, the degree of legitimized white violence was expanded. Similarly, when slaves were accused of crimes, the defenses of the common law were restricted to expand the slave's criminal liability arising out of violent confrontations with whites. The oppression of this law is further revealed by the fact that this discrimination was applied to cases involving free blacks as well as slaves. And, as in the cases of white abuse of slaves, the class identity of the white victim was a deciding factor in the definition of the slave's "rights" of extenuation and self-defense.

This legal discrimination was adopted in the case law of the two allegedly more "liberal" slave states—Tennessee and North Carolina.

For example, the *Tackett* principle was applied in the 1842 Tennessee case of *Jacob v. State*.[35] Jacob was charged with the murder of his master and was convicted. On appeal, the defendant sought to mitigate the offense to manslaughter. The court held that manslaughter did not exist because the legitimate violence of the master in correcting his slave could not be a legal provocation.

The opinion of Justice William Turley affirmed the master's "perfect" right to secure the obedience of the slave, "and the [master's] power to inflict any punishment, not affecting life or limb" if it was intended to enforce this obedience. If in the exercise of this prerogative "with or without cause" the slave resists and kills the master, it is murder, according to Turley, "because the law cannot recognize the violence of the master as a legitimate cause of provocation."[36] Accordingly, the conviction was affirmed. A similar result was reached in an 1850 Tennessee case. And in an 1854 Arkansas opinion, the court applied the same rule to a stranger who attempted to subdue a slave resisting his master, when the slave killed the white stranger.[37]

Thus, a slave accused of killing his master could have his charge reduced to manslaughter only if the master went beyond the bounds of legal punishment, as defined by the cases discussed in Chapter 5. The law differed, however, when overseers and strangers were the victims of slave violence. These cases pitted the master's interest in preventing unwarranted attacks on his slaves against the state's interest in slave control. Arthur Howington discusses statistics from the Tennessee cases that reveal this tension.

Howington compared cases in which slaves were accused of killing whites who were the slave's master and other cases in which the victims of slave violence were whites who were not masters. He found in the trial courts the following:

|  | *Master Is Victim* | *Others Are Victim* |
| --- | --- | --- |
| Murder Trials | 7 | 22 |
| Convictions | 6 | 8 |
| Attempted Murder Trials | 1 | 26 |
| Convictions | 0 | 4 |

And as to appeals, Howington found that two of two cases were affirmed when masters were victims, and one of five was affirmed when non-masters were killed by slaves.[38] Although these raw data are bound to be suspect in themselves, they do confirm the currents of argument seen in the reported case.

The key issues were addressed in the often-cited case of *State v. Will*.[39] That North Carolina opinion of 1834 competes with *State v.*

*Jones*[40] as the most misunderstood case in the Southern case law. In part, this may be caused by the fact that the *Will* case is not even mentioned in the anti-slavery treatises of Stroud and Goodell.[41] Accordingly, the pro-slavery writers have each taken their turn praising the opinion of Justice William Gaston in *Will*.[42]

Patrick Brady has shown, however, that *Will* is a case that does not merit the honors it has received.[43] The holding applied the oppressive *Tackett* principle to a case of homicide in which the slave killed his overseer.

The defendant had stabbed and killed his overseer and was indicted for murder. The incident arose because of a dispute between Will and Allen, a slave foreman, over the "ownership" of a hoe. Will claimed that the hoe was his because he helved it on his own time, and Allen directed another slave to use the hoe. The foreman advised the overseer of this dispute. The decedent then obtained his gun and rode on horseback six hundred yards to where the defendant was working.

Gun in hand, the overseer ordered Will to come down from packing cotton and approach him. This Will did; "the prisoner took off his hat in a humble manner and came down[.]" The deceased then spoke some unknown words to Will. Thereafter, Will "made off," and was between ten and fifteen steps from the deceased when the deceased shot Will in the back. Will continued to flee, and the overseer pursued him. Within six or eight minutes, the overseer overtook Will. In a scuffle Will stabbed the overseer, who by then was not armed. The slave then fled. The overseer died that evening because of blood loss.

On that same day, Will surrendered himself to his master. The next day Will was arrested, and when he was told of the death "exclaimed, '*Is it possible!*' and appeared so much affected that he came near falling, and was obliged to be supported."[44]

After hearing the evidence, the jury entered a special verdict, in effect finding the facts and leaving it to the court to decide if the case was one of murder or manslaughter. The trial judge found the facts to constitute murder.[45] The Supreme Court reversed and held the case to be one of manslaughter.

Because the case came on appeal on a special verdict, the appeal presented an issue of law.[46] Gaston stated the issue as follows: "[T]he inquiry . . . is whether upon the facts found the law adjudges that the killing was committed with malice aforethought."[47] Gaston found that the homicide would have been manslaughter had the two parties been white, and Brady cites cases to support this finding.[48] Thus, the issue was whether the slave's status was relevant to cause a different result.

The court held the slave's status was indeed relevant. The court acknowledged the master's and overseer's right to punish a slave short of taking life or limb and their absolute power to reduce a rebellious slave to submission and be free of any liability for murder of mayhem.[49] The key finding here was that the defendant slave was not in a state of resistance when he was shot by the overseer.[50] Thus, the shooting by the deceased was not justified. Gaston held:

> [I]f the passions of the slave be excited into unlawful violence by the inhumanity of his master, [hirer, or overseer], is it a *conclusion of law* that such passion must spring from diabolical malice?[51]

Gaston found that such a rule would be too "repugnant" for "the law of a civilized people and of a Christian land." He added:

> The prisoner is a human being, degraded indeed by slavery, but yet having "organs, dimensions, senses, affections, passions," like our own. The unfortunate man slain was for the time, indeed, his master, yet this dominion was not like that of a sovereign who can do no wrong.[52]

Gaston's finding was that the overseer did overstep his bounds, and that the defendant's acts were not done with malice. Thus, the killing was manslaughter.

It is clear, nevertheless, that Gaston did not hold that the evaluation of the slave's response to the overseer's power was limited by the usual standards of common law mitigation. Indeed, Gaston acknowledged that his ruling was consistent with the principles expressed in earlier cases creating a double standard in criminal cases regarding slaves.[53]

This double standard was reaffirmed in cases decided in North Carolina and Tennessee. In *State v. Jarrott*,[54] Justice Gaston, in 1840, held that when a slave kills a stranger, special standards of mitigation apply which take into account "the difference of condition between the white man and the slave, as recognized by our legal institutions[.]"[55] Thus, the *Tackett* principle applied even if the white was not a master or overseer.

Justice Gaston explained this ruling as follows:

> The degrees of homicide are indeed to be ascertained by common law principles; but the principles themselves are necessarily, in their application, accommodated to the actual conditions of human beings in our society.[56]

Therefore, Gaston held that the slave faced with an excessive battery had no right to resist a stranger. Instead, Gaston wrote, "It is [the slave's] duty to submit, or flee, or seek the protection of his master[.]"[57] Accordingly, the slave's offense in killing his assailant cannot be self-defense, it can only be murder or manslaughter, according to the differing standards of mitigation based upon the slave's status.

Justice Gaston held that the special rules of mitigation were required because of "the *vast* difference which exists, under our institutions, between the social condition of the white man and of the slave; in consequence of which difference what might be felt by one as the grossest degradation is considered by the other as but a slight injury."[58] Gaston did indicate distaste for the white decedent, who was playing cards with slaves in the early morning hours when the dispute erupted. Even a white man of this low standing, however, could demand the obedience of a slave:

> It may be that the white man who debases himself by a familiar association with a slave, and, in the course of that association, is guilty of acts of meanness [sic] like that attributed, whether justly or unjustly, to the unfortunate deceased, has no claims to personal respect equal to those of the slave; but the distinction of castes yet remains, and with it remain all the passions, infirmities, and habits which grow out of this distinction.[59]

Consequently, the courts allowed slaves some legal means to defend their valuable lives against the wanton violence of debased whites, but this "right" was strictly limited based upon the perceived dictates of the institution of slavery.

A similar result was reached in the 1850 Tennessee case of *Nelson v. State*.[60] Justice Nathan Green, another alleged liberal, held that equal standard of mitigation did not apply to offenses committed by slaves, when the white victim is not the master. Green wrote that consistent with "the influence of enlightened reason," indignities that would "excite the passions of a white man, would not have a like effect, upon a slave." He ascribed this variance to "the different habits of feeling, and modes of thought of the two races." Indeed, Green argued that equality in this law between the slave and the white

> . . . would be a perversion of the principles of the common law by sticking to its letter. It would disregard entirely the character and condition of this portion of our population; and would be as repugnant to reason, as it would be mischievous in practice.[61]

Thus, Green shows his true colors; he was not about to let "formalist" concern for common law precedent get in the way of the realities of the necessary oppression of slavery.

These principles of oppression were reaffirmed in the 1849 North Carolina case of *State v. Caesar*.[62] That case arose out of an unprovoked attack by two drunken white strangers on two slaves. The court held that an excessive battery by a white stranger that is wantonly inflicted on a slave can mitigate a homicide committed by the slave. The court also extended this rule to a slave who killed a stranger who was attacking another slave. This holding was consistent with the common law rule that allowed for the mitigation of homicide when it was provoked by an attack on another person.[63]

Once again, however, the holding did not apply the common law to slaves without alteration. The issue was whether the battery that provoked the homicide was excessive. The trial judge instructed the jury that the battery was ordinary and that an ordinary battery would not mitigate the killing to manslaughter. The Supreme Court agreed with the latter statement, but was divided on the issue of excessiveness. Judge Richmond Pearson found that the battery was not ordinary and voted for a reversal. He noted that the whites in question were "two drunken ruffians," and that the reversal was consistent with the need "to protect slave property from wanton outrages, while, at the same time, due subordination is preserved."[64]

Chief Justice Ruffin dissented. He would have affirmed the conviction because he thought the battery was ordinary. Thus, the deciding vote was cast by Judge Frederic Nash.

Nash's opinion is interesting because he hints at a fundamental disagreement with the line of cases that deprived slaves of the common law's protection from ordinary batteries. He observed that he was bound by cases such as *Tackett, Hale, Jarrott*, and *Will*, but found that those cases were not dispositive of the issue in *Caesar*. In the end, however, he stated that it was his "duty to conform" to these cases, and he agreed with Pearson that only an excessive battery could mitigate the homicide.[65]

The logic of these cases was extended to an assault on a free black by a white in the 1850 North Carolina case of *State v. Jowers*.[66] In that case, Pearson reversed the white defendant's conviction because the trial judge instructed the jury that insolence by a free black could not excuse a batter committed by a white. Pearson found the free black's status to be analogous to that of a slave; thus, free blacks were not entitled to the equal protection of the common law.[67]

Howington summarizes this law, stating that the Courts did deprive slaves of the equal protection of the rules of law regarding mitigation. The Courts left local juries with the responsibility to decide

> when punishment short of danger to life or limb was improper chastisement and when a white man so exceeded the bounds of propriety that the law would not demand the slave's life for committing homicide. This position severely limited the slave's right to defend himself against personal violence if the violence took the form of punishment.[68]

Indeed, the North Carolina courts denied free blacks the equal protection of the common law of mitigation.

As oppressive as this law was, it was not sufficient to satisfy Chief Justice Lumpkin of Georgia and the Georgia Supreme Court. In *Jim v. State*,[69] an 1854 decision, the Court held that when a slave killed his overseer, the homicide could not be mitigated to manslaughter. Justice Ebenezer Starnes wrote for the court that the slave's duty was to obey his master and overseer; this was a command of "[p]olicy and humanity[.]"[70] Although the law protected the slave form immoderate chastisement, the slave was required to submit to the excesses of his superior. The court would make no allowances for "human infirmity—that is, of man's evil passions[.]"[71] To afford this defense of provocation to a slave

> would be to make him the judge, (and to suffer him to act upon his judgment), as to the reasonableness or unreasonableness of the extent and degree of that patriarchal discipline which the master is permitted to exercise—would be to place him continually in a state of insubordination, and to encourage servile insurrection and bloodshed.[72]

Therefore, in the name of "humanity" Starnes denied to the slave the right to mitigation based upon human emotions, in cases involving the master and overseer.

In *John v. State*,[73] another 1854 case, Lumpkin extended the no manslaughter rule to a case in which a slave killed a white who was not the slave's master or overseer. Lumpkin wrote that manslaughter

> ... cannot exist under our law, as between a slave and a free white person, where the former is the slayer. That every such killing is murder, or justifiable homicide. It is supposed, that where a slave is under an absolute and inexorable necessity, to take the life of a white man to save his own, who has no right to punish him or control him in any manner whatever, that such killing will be excusable. And it may be so. For myself, I have formed no very definite opinion upon this subject. But a stern and unbending necessity forbids that any such allowance should be made for the infirmity of temper or passion on the part of a slave, as to reduce or mitigate his crime from murder to manslaughter.[74]

Stephenson and Stephenson note that

> ... the legislature had provided in the slave penal code for the crime of manslaughter committed by a slave against a white man, but Lumpkin made no mention of this code section. The feared consequences of an opposite result—loss of white control over the slave—apparently led Lumpkin to reach the result he did. In fact, from the portion of the opinion quoted above, Lumpkin questioned whether a slave could even commit justifiable homicide.[75]

In fact, this extreme view was rejected by the writers of the 1861 Georgia code. The code included slave manslaughter and justifiable homicide, but with different standards than those that applied to whites.[76]

It is clear, however, that even the more "liberal" scheme of mitigation and extenuation expanded the scope of slave criminal liability. It did so by converting cases of ordinary manslaughter into murder when the slave was the perpetrator. Moreover, this law strictly limited the slave's "right" to self-defense.

As explained by Cobb:

> Subordination on the part of the slave is absolutely necessary, not only to the existence of the institution, but to the peace of the community. The policy of the law, therefore, requires that the slave should look to his master and the courts to avenge his wrongs. The rule, therefore, that justifies the freeman in repelling force by force, applies not to the slave.
>
> If, however, the life or limb of the slave is endangered, he may use sufficient force to protect and defend himself, even if in so doing he kills the aggressor.[77]

The slave's "right" to self-defense was limited, however:

> ... But as a certain amount of force is legally exercised over the slave, to justify his resistance by force it must appear that such resistance was necessary to protect his right to self-preservation, either as to life or limb. But even this must be received with some qualification, for if the slave was originally the wrongdoer, and resisting lawful authority, he cannot afterwards justify a homicide, by showing a reasonable sense of imminent danger to his own life.[78]

Therefore, the slave could not defend himself if he in any way, by his own insolence, started in motion the wheels of violence that lead to a threat to his life.

Indeed, the slave's privilege of self-defense was limited by statutes that originated in the colonial days. The Virginia act of 1669 established the master's right to kill rebellious slaves, thereby eliminating slave self-defense in a case of resistance to correction. The 1680 statute went further and prevented a slave from "lift[ing] up his hand against any Christian[.]"[79] This provision criminalized all slave self-defense. Similar acts were adopted in the other Southern colonies.[80]

Nevertheless, as slave society matured, the limited notion of slave self-defense was adopted. The 1680 Virginia act was amended in 1792 to include an exception, "in those cases where it shall appear . . . that such negro . . . was wantonly assaulted and lifted his or her hand in . . . self-defense."[81] As interclass tensions arose in white society, the right of poor whites to wantonly kill and injure slaves was narrowed, and slaves were allowed a slight privilege of self-defense.

These class conflicts are illustrated in an 1818 Virginia trial level case discussed by Philip Schwarz. A slave named Jacob was found not guilty of the charge of stabbing to death a white man. Schwarz states that the "exact nature of the incident is unknown," but he speculates that the killing arose out of a "brawl precipitated by rowdy white men." The victim and the witnesses who testified against Jacob were poor whites who did not own slaves.[82] This class was restrained by the criminal law to prevent unnecessary slave killings as slavery developed in the nineteenth century. The limited privilege of slave self-defense furthered the master class interest in protecting the master's economic interest in his slave from poor white violence.

The limited nature of this privilege is illustrated by the case of *Dave v. State*.[83] This Alabama case of 1853 arose out of the indictment of a slave belonging to Mrs. Underwood, who was hired to Frank Morgan. The slave was charged with an assault with the intent to kill Cunningham, Morgan's overseer.

The slave, Dave, was confronted by Cunningham, who asked why Dave disobeyed his orders and had not fed the horses and mules. Dave replied that he was following Morgan's orders to kill a dog that had run mad. Cunningham did not accept this slight, and began to whip Dave, who drew a knife and stabbed Cunningham after the overseer ordered another slave to wield an axe.[84]

The trial court charged the jury that the slave put himself in the wrong by disobeying Cunningham, who had the right to demand obedience and to use as much force as was necessary to make the slave submit. If the slave believed his life was endangered by Cunningham's order regarding the axe, the subsequent attack would be without intent to kill. But it is clear that the slave's privilege of self-defense did not extend to this attack because the slave had no right to question even the wanton exercise of the overseer's white power, and even if that exercise of power was contrary to the master's orders.[85]

The opinion of Justice Lymon Gibbons approved of this principle of law. The court held that the slave's privilege of self-defense arose only if the slave was not a wrongdoer. Thus, the challenge of Cunningham's authority, even under color of "right" was wrongful.[86]

In theory, a limited self-defense "right" existed, but self-defense is not strictly speaking a right at all—instead, it is best thought of as an excuse creating a privilege to act in response to another's illegal act. As seen from Chapter 5, however, it was legal for a master to intentionally kill a slave in resistance; therefore, the only privilege of slave self-defense arose if the master wantonly and for no reason attacked or brutally punished a submissive slave, with a clear intent to take the slave's life or limb.

Similarly, even when strangers and overseers were involved in altercations with a slave, only an entirely unprovoked attack could fall outside of the category cited by Cobb. If the white's violence was occasioned by any insolence, then the slave could hope only to mitigate the offense; he could not claim a defense of extenuation. The need for slave subordination was so great that the slave's privilege of self-defense was of the most limited nature.

It made sense, however, to afford the slave this limited privilege of self-defense. Otherwise, slaves would be subject to wanton attacks that were unnecessary to the overall discipline of the slave. This wanton violence would have damaged the public peace, as well as the master's interest in his valuable property, just as slave stealing would wantonly result in a deprivation of the master's property and would disrupt the peace of the state. Slaves also had to have some privilege to carry out their master's orders unmolested.

It is hard to imagine many cases that would vindicate the slave's privilege of self-defense. This is because the law of slavery deprived the slave of the common law defense of self-protection except in those cases in which self-defense was consistent with the slave's servile status. Goodell summed up the oppressive effects of this law: "If the negro be a chattel, he must needs be restrained from straying; he must be held subject, like other domestic animals, to the superior race holding dominion of him."[87] Thus, the slave was subject to abuse at the hands of whites of all social classes. Again quoting Goodell:

> Yet the existence of such laws renders more than probable, and even certain, the common prevalence of the worst outrages that could be imagined. The best laws cannot fully protect the weaker portion of a community against the stronger. The weak must be left utterly defenseless when all protecting laws are only repealed. But the climax is reached when, *by express statute*, each member of the weaker class is placed under the absolute control of *any one* of the dominant class; when resistance is forbidden on penalty of stripes and cropping by the public authorities, with the liability of being "lawfully killed" by the assailant! If civil government were designed for human demoralization and torture, it is not easy to see how its ends could be more effectually reached.[88]

## Conclusion

The criminal law of slavery discriminated against slaves. The common law was set aside by the courts and the legislatures, thereby expanding the scope of slave criminality. It has to be recalled, however, that slaves were valuable property to their owners. Consequently, procedural safeguards of some kind were appropriate when slaves were accused of one of the many serious crimes depicted in this chapter.

## NOTES

1. 9 Ala. 395 (1846).
2. *Id.* at 397.
3. *See*, Patterson, *supra* at 196.
4. *See*, Chapter 3 Notes 50 to 56, *supra*.
5. *See*, Patterson, *supra* at 196.
6. *See*, Paul H. Robinson, "A Brief History of Distinctions in Criminal Culpability," 31 Hastings L. J. 815, 821–822 (1980).
7. See, LaFave and Scott, *supra* at 9, 21–25.
8. *See, e.g., Lawton v. Steele*, 152 U.S. 133, 14 S. Ct. 499, 38 L. Ed. 385 (1894); *Manhattan Manufacturing and Fertilizing Co. v. Van Keuren*, 23 N.J. Eq. 251, 255 (Ch. 1872).
9. *See, e.g., Calero-Toledo v. Pearson Yacht Leasing Co.*, 416 U.S. 663, 680–683, 94 S. Ct. 2080, 2090–2092, 40 L. Ed. 2d 452, 466–468 (1974) and authorities cited for deodands. For the noxal action, *See*, Watson, *supra* at 67–69.
10. *See, Calero-Toledo, supra*.
11. *Shaffer v. Heitner*, 433 U.S. 186, 207, 97 S. Ct. 2569, 2581, 53 L. Ed. 2d 684, 699 (1977) [citation omitted].
12. 380 U.S. 693, 85 S. Ct. 1246, 14 L. Ed. 2d 170 (1965).
13. 367 U.S. 643, 81 S. Ct. 1684, 6 L. Ed. 2d 1181 (1961).
14. 232 U.S. 383, 34 S. Ct. 341, 58 L. Ed. 652 (1914).
15. *See*, Stroud, *supra* at 69–88.
16. *Id.* at 70 [emphasis omitted].
17. *See, Id.*, at 70–71; Goodell, *supra* at 225–231.
18. Stroud, *supra* at 71.
19. *See, Id.* at 71–72.
20. *See, Id.* at 71–73; Goodell, *supra* at 319–325.
21. *See*, Stroud, *supra* at 73–74.
22. *See*, Flanigan, *supra* at 21–23.
23. *See*, Chapter 1, Notes 5 to 8.
24. 33 S.C.L. 20, 2 Strob. 41 (1847).

25. *Id.*, 33 S.C.L. at 21, 2 Strob. at 43.
26. *Id.*, 33 S.C.L. at 21, 2 Strob. at 43–44.
27. *Id.*, 33 S.C.L. at 21, 2 Strob. at 45, *quoting* a decision of O'Neall, J.
28. *Id.*, 33 S.C.L. at 22, 2 Strob. at 47 [emphasis added].
29. *See*, Stroud, *supra* at 74–88.
30. *See*, Flanigan, *supra* at 17–21; Howington, *supra* at 140–158.
31. *See, Id.* at 158.
32. 16 Ill. 17 (1854).
33. *Id.* at 20.
34. 8 N.C. (1 Hawks.) 210 (1820).
35. 22 Tenn. (3 Hum.) 493 (1842).
36. *See, Id.* at 521.
37. *See, Moses v. State*, 30 Tenn. (11 Hum.) 166 (1850); *State v. Austin*, 14 Ark. 555, 566–567 (1854).
38. *See*, Howington, *supra* at 82–83, 231, 268. The convictions in the non-master category include murder and manslaughter.
39. 18 N.C. 131, 1 Dev. & Bat. 121 (1834).
40. 1 Miss. 39, 1 Walker 83 (1821).
41. *See*, Brady, *supra* at 251 n. 28.
42. *See, Id.* at 253–254, and citations therein, *see, also*, Oakes—1990, *supra* at 159–166 for a more recent example.
43. *See*, Brady, *supra*.
44. *See, State v. Will, supra*, 18 N.C. at 131–133, 1 Dev. & Bat. at 121–123 for the facts as found by the jury.
45. *See, Id.* at 134, 1 Dev. & Bat. at 124.
46. In a special verdict the trial judge usually instructs the jury to provide written findings of fact in response to specific written questions or instructions. *See, generally, United States v. Spock*, 416 F. 2d 165, 180–183 (1st Cir. 1969); *United States v. Ogull*, 149 F. Supp. 272, 276 (S.D. N.Y. 1957); "Verdict" *Black's Law Dictionary* 1399 (5th ed. 1979).
47. *State v. Will, supra*, 18 N.C. at 171, 1 Dev. & Bat. 163.
48. *Id.* at 172, 1 Dev. & Bat. 165; Brady, *supra* at 251 n. 25.
49. *See, State v. Will, supra* 18 N.C. at 173, 1 Dev. & Bat. at 165–166.
50. *See, Id.* at 174, 1 Dev. & Bat. at 166.
51. *Id.* at 178–179, 1 Dev. & Bat. at 171 [emphasis in original].
52. *Id.* at 179, 1 Dev. & Bat. at 171–172.
53. *See*, Brady, *supra* at 252–253.
54. 23 N.C. 51, 1 Ired. 76 (1840).
55. *Id.* at 56, 1 Ired. at 82–83.
56. *Id.* at 56; 1 Ired. 82.
57. *Id.* at 58; 1 Ired. at 86.
58. *Id.* at 56; 1 Ired. at 82 [emphasis in original].
59. *Id.* at 56; 1 Ired. at 83.
60. 29 Tenn. (10 Hum.) 518 (1850).
61. *Id.* at 529. Accordingly, Green agreed with the North Carolina rule that only an excessive battery by a stranger can be a crime against a slave. He also opined that the slave had a duty to submit to reasonable punishment, and if the slave resists and kills his chastiser, the slave will commit murder.

## Slave Criminals and Protection

If the punishment is "unreasonable and excessive," the killing could be manslaughter. But Green did not attempt to specify the dividing lines between these categories of violence; he left that calculation for juries to decide on the circumstances of each case. *Id.*

62. 31 N.C. (9 Ired.) 391 (1849).
63. *See, Id.* at 400 for a discussion of this rule; *see, also, Brady, supra* at 256 n. 61.
64. *See, State v. Caesar, supra* at 405–406.
65. *See, Id.* at 410–411. For Ruffin's dissent, *see, Id.* at 412–428. For discussions of this decision, *compare,* Tushnet, *supra* at 115–120, *with, Brady, supra* at 256–257.
66. 33 N.C. (11 Ired.) 555 (1850).
67. *See, Id.* at 556–557. *See, also, State v. Davis*, 52 N.C. 70, 7 Jones 52 (1859), where the court viewed a free black's battery on a white constable through the lens of the inferior position of the black to any white person, not based upon the usual common law standards.
68. *See,* Howington, *supra* at 81–82.
69. 15 Ga. 535 (1854).
70. *Id.* at 542.
71. *Id.* at 543.
72. *Id.* at 544.
73. 16 Ga. 200 (1854).
74. *Id.* at 203.
75. Stephenson, *supra* at 595 [footnotes omitted]. The authors cite Ga. Stat. Ch. 34 § 83, at 617–618 (Cobb 1859).
76. *See, Id.* at 595 n. 69, *citing,* Ga. Code §§ 4221–4222, 4227 at 810–821 and § 4710–4712 at 919 (1861).
77. Cobb, *supra* at 94 [footnote omitted].
78. *Id.* at 274 [footnote omitted].
79. *See,* Chapter 3, *supra* n. 14 and n. 17.
80. *See,* Stroud, *supra* at 67–69; Goodell, *supra* at 305–307.
81. *Id.* at 306.
82. *See,* Schwarz, *supra* at 240–241.
83. 22 Ala. 23 (1853).
84. *Id.* at 24–25.
85. *Id.* at 26–27.
86. *Id.* at 34–35; *see, also, State v. Abram*, 10 Ala. 928 (1847).
87. *See,* Goodell, *supra* at 307 [emphasis omitted].
88. *Id.* at 307–308 [emphasis in original].

## CHAPTER 9

# Slave Criminals and Protection of the Master's Property Rights in Slaves: What Process Was Due?

**THE CASES** and statutes concerning the procedures in slave criminal trials exhibit a heightened concern for "fairness" in procedure in the nineteenth century. Slaves were given new "rights" to appeals, jury trials, and the right to counsel—at the master's expense—in the antebellum years.[1] This pattern of legal change ameliorated the excesses of the colonial codes that denied slaves the most basic procedural protections in criminal trials.[2]

The key interpretative issue is: Why did the slave trial procedures that held sway in the colonial years fall into disfavor after the American Revolution? It must be recalled that, at the same time, the number of capital offenses that slaves could commit grew. Therefore, the development of safeguards in slave trials can only be explained in connection with the changes in the substantive law. The heightened procedural rights were thus intended to protect the real party whose private interests were at stake in slave trials, the slave owner, when those rights collided with the public interest in controlling and punishing criminal slaves. Even if the slave was accused of killing his master, the owner's heirs had an interest in a just verdict. Consequently, as the list of slave capital offenses grew, lawmakers also increased the procedural safeguards that protected the life of the valuable slave chattel.

Although the law did allow masters the right to compensation when slaves were punished, one must recall that throughout the antebellum period, the real price of slaves grew. At the same time, the external supply of fresh bodies was cut off. Thus, it is logical that masters and lawmakers came to believe that the State owed slave owners greater procedural safeguards—"due process," if you will—before the slave master was deprived of rights in such valuable property.

This reality is recognized by the various authors who have studied this area of law, yet they reject the element of pecuniary interest as the means of explaining these trends in antebellum law.[3] For example, Professor Nash argues that the antebellum Southern appellate courts protected black rights better than the post-reconstruction Southern courts.[4] Assuming for the sake of argument that this is in fact true, could not the major distinction be the removal from the equation of the master's pecuniary interest in slave trials? This is obviously a distinguishing factor, along with the master's social status that was, in fact, usually behind the slave who was accused of the crime. After the Civil War, the black defendant was on his own. During the slavery times the courts were concerned about the master's interest in slave trials when slaves faced punishments that would deprive the owner of slave labor. Although criminal and noxious slaves had to be punished by society, the master's property interest was entitled to legal protection.

This then raises the key questions: (1) What protections did the law allow slaves?, and (2) Was the level of protection consistent with the notion that slaves were people or just valuable property? The answer to the second question is that slaves were treated as property, as revealed by the varied level of protection slaves enjoyed.

## *Three Models of Due Process for Slave Owners*

There were three patterns of criminal procedure regarding the trial of slaves for capital offenses. The procedures in South Carolina, Virginia, and Louisiana continued the informal proceedings of the colonial codes into the nineteenth century. Slaves were denied the right to a grand jury, a petit jury, and an appeal—until 1833 in South Carolina. Of course, Louisiana was not a common law state, but South Carolina and Virginia were; nevertheless, slaves were denied the most basic criminal rights in these states.[5] There was some amelioration in the antebellum years, but the model of an informal means of justice prevailed. Slaves were tried by justice of the peace courts, not by juries and grand juries. Michael Hindus has studied South Carolina lower court records and finds that slaves endured much higher conviction rates than whites. This fact indicates the injustice of this form of "justice."[6] Indeed, Hindus concludes that this model of justice had a purpose, "but its primary purpose was not be to just."[7] Rather the system was obviously intended to foster social control over slaves, at the cost of the usual procedures afforded criminal defendants.

Arthur Howington finds a similar pattern in his study of the slave court records in Tennessee. He calls these courts examples of the crime control model of criminal justice, because these courts "were designed to foster control of the slave population, to facilitate 'speedy verdicts and certain punishment' for slave criminals."[8] Like Hindus, Howington closely examines the records of the slave courts. He, too, finds a high conviction rate and informal procedures.[9] Thus, Howington concludes that, "The outcome of the slave court trial was a near certainty,"[10] and the accused slave was likely to feel the lash. But with the increase in the value of slaves and the number of capital offenses, some lawmakers obviously felt that more formal and elaborate procedures were needed.

The second model of procedure allowed slaves a trial by a *petit* jury, but not a grand jury, in capital cases. Georgia, Mississippi, Arkansas, Alabama, and Maryland had systems along these lines in the nineteenth century. The most protective states were Kentucky, Tennessee, and North Carolina, which in the nineteenth century afforded slaves grand juries, *petit* juries, and the right to appeal.[11] Thus, there was diversity on the key procedural provisions as they applied to capital offenses. As to non-capital offenses, however, the informal justice of the peace system prevailed throughout the nineteenth century, except in Tennessee, which eliminated the slave courts in 1854.[12]

Therefore, where the slave's life was not at stake, it was generally agreed that slaves should be denied the three most basic rights—the grand jury, trial by jury, and an appeal. Only in capital cases, when the master's interest weighed in on the slave's side of the scales of justice, did the states diverge. That divergence indicates that reasonable minds differed on how much protection was enough for the life of a slave. But the key point is that slaves were not given the same rights that people had; they were given procedural protections thought to be appropriate to protect the owner's interest in his accused chattel.

## *Protection of the Master's Rights in Slave Trials: What Process Was Due?*

When one carefully analyzes the antebellum case law in slave felony trials, it soon becomes obvious that everyone knew that, usually, the real party at interest was the master. Of course, this was not the case when the slave was accused of killing the master. But even in that case, the heirs of the owner had an interest to protect—to prevent a slave from becoming a scapegoat while the real killer escaped. Thus arises the public interest in slave trials. The procedures had to be fair so that the truth could emerge, and so that guilty parties would not use slaves as a shield against the law.

The real nature of the interests at stake in slave trials is well illustrated by the 1859 case of *United States v. Amy*.[13] That case is discussed in Chapter 1. It will be recalled that Amy—a Virginia slave—was charged with stealing a letter from the United States' mails, a federal offense. Amy faced a prison term of two to ten years upon a conviction. As noted in Chapter 1, her owner's lawyer argued that Amy was not a "person" for the purposes of the general federal criminal statute. Chief Justice Taney, on Virginia Circuit Court duty, disagreed.

Of interest here was the second major argument made by John Howard, Amy's owner's counsel. Howard argued that the application of the statute to Amy violated the owner Hairston's rights under the takings clause and this right to due process of law, as guaranteed by the Fifth Amendment to the United States Constitution. Howard contended that the imprisonment of Amy would be unconstitutional, because it

> deprives the master of the labor and services of his slave during the term of imprisonment, and thus takes "private property for public use without just compensation"; for the slave is punished for the public benefit, as a warning and example to offenders. On this account, in Virginia, a slave who is hung or transported is paid for by the state according to his value . . . This slave may well be tried, and, if guilty, properly punished under the state laws, for larceny of the letter and its contents; and that is the course with her which ought to be pursued, and to which her owner, Mr. Hairston, would interpose no objection. She ought to be whipped, and sent about her business, and not carried beyond the jurisdiction of Virginia, to Washington, there to sleep or sicken in imprisonment, from two to ten years in the total loss of her services to her master during that time, and then to be turned loose among persons perhaps but too ready to facilitate her escape to the North.[14]

Howard explained his Fifth Amendment claim further, as follows:

> If the federal government punish slaves as persons, it must remember that they are property also, and, as such, must be protected and paid for when seized and used for the public good. The several states undoubtedly have the right to say that the owner shall lose his title to the services of his slave, if the slave commit an offence against the law; and some of the states have virtually done this, by prescribing the penalties of death or transportation for slaves, in certain cases, without providing compensation to the owner. This has been done as a part of their municipal polity and police in respect to slaves,

upon the idea that, by tying the self-interest of the master the more closely to the common weal, greater diligence would be encouraged on his part, alike by coercion and kind treatment, to keep his slaves in due subordination and goodly courses. Therefore, in some states, the master gets only half or two thirds of the value of the slave who is hung for crime, in others, nothing; of which the frequent consequence is that no sooner is a capital crime committed by the slave, than he is run off to another state, and sold, and public justice thwarted,—a condition of things avoided in Virginia, Maryland, and other states by paying the full value of the slave. Now the several states may do this, or they may take slave property, or property of any other kind, for public use, without just compensation. They may even annihilate all property in slaves by general emancipation, because they have absolute sovereignty and jurisdiction over the subject of slaves and slave property, and there is nothing in the constitution of the United States which forbids it, for the limitation in question applies not to the states, but to the federal government.[15]

Howard concluded that the Fifth Amendment applied to the federal government, and not the states; therefore, the United States government could not "take" slaves for a term of years without paying just compensation. Howard, of course, quoted Taney's *Dred Scott* opinion in support of his contentions.

Taney was not persuaded, however. He ruled:

It is true that no compensation is provided for the master for the loss of service during the period of imprisonment. But the clause in the 5th amendment of the constitution which declares that private property shall not be taken for public use without just compensation cannot, upon any fair interpretation, apply to the case of a slave who is punished in his own person for an offense committed by him, although the punishment may incidentally affect the property of another to whom he belongs. The clause obviously applied in cases where private property is taken to be used as property for the benefit of the government, and not to cases where crimes are punished by law. And if, in one of those contingencies which sometimes arise in time of war, a slave be pressed by the proper authority into the public service, in order to be employed as a laborer or teamster, or in any other manner, this clause of the constitution undoubtedly makes it the duty of congress to compensate the master for the loss he sustains. In such cases, and in all other cases where the slave is taken and used as property for the benefit of the government, the government acts directly and exclusively upon the master's right of property, without any reference to the personal rights or personal duties of the slave towards the government. It deals with him as property only, and not as a person, and, as it takes property to be used for the public emolument, it must pay for it.

Taney thus distinguished takings of slave labor for the use of the labor and takings intended to further the public peace:

> But punishment for crime stands upon very different principles. A person, whether free or slave, is not taken for public use when he is punished for an offence against the law. The public, in such cases, acts in self-defence to preserve its own existence, and protect its members in their rights of person and rights of property; and the loss which the master sustains in his property is incidental, and necessarily arises from its twofold character, since the slave, as a person, may commit offences which society has a right to punish for its own safety, although the punishment may render the property of the master of little or no value. But this hazard is unavoidably and inseparably associated with this description of property, and it can furnish no reason why a slave, like any other person, should not be punished by the United States for offences against its laws, passed within the scope of its delegated authority.[16]

Thus, the master was not entitled to compensation when society passed laws to protect itself from the crimes of slaves. This was a necessary regulation of the police power in light of the dangerous nature of the slave.

Amy's case illustrates, however, the irrelevance of Amy's "rights" to the real issues. Taney was concerned with society's need to impose a duty upon Amy, but he balanced this need against the right of the owner—not the slave. Consequently, the real party at interest was the master. This point is further illustrated by the 1859 Maryland decision of *Negro Ann Hammond v. State*.[17]

The defendant in that case was a slave who was indicted as a person under the general criminal code that prohibited obtaining goods under false pretences. The Maryland Court of Appeals held that the slave could be held accountable under the statute. The opinion by Justice William Tuck states:

> Hardship upon the master may be assumed in any case where his slave is taken under the law for punishment, for the benefit of society; but if compensation is not provided, it does not become the courts to avert the consequences of such *casus omissus*, by arresting punishment if jurisdiction be conferred.[18]

Thus, the court felt free to harm the master's property interest, in light of the legislative mandate. Indeed, the court cited Taney's decision in Amy's case to support this result. Because the Maryland Constitution did not contain the same anti-takings provision, the slave owner's property rights were less secure. This result also may have been occasioned because of an 1858 statute, which stated that slaves were not to be jailed; rather, slaves were subjected to up to forty lashes or sale out of the state. In the latter event the owner was compensated for the slave transported.[19]

The cases of *Amy* and *Hammond* are significant for their frank exposition of the rights at stake in slave trials. The idea that the slave merely represented the master's interests is further revealed in the Southern antebellum case law generated in slave felony trials, and especially in cases concerning the competency of a master to testify in favor, or against his slave.

## *The Master's Right to Testify for His Accused Slave*

It was well settled by the turn of the nineteenth century that the common law excluded the testimony of parties to a civil lawsuit, as well as persons having a direct pecuniary or proprietary interest in the outcome of the case. This disqualification was also applied to criminal cases.[20] It was not abolished in the United States until after the Civil War. Thus, the issue arose in the South whether the master could testify when his slave was on trial.[21]

*State v. Jim*[22] is a leading case on this point. Decided in 1856, the North Carolina Supreme Court held that the master could testify on behalf of his slave. The opinion, written by Justice Richmond Pearson, notes the history of the interest disqualification and the defects of the rule. He also cites the statutory repeal of the rule in England.[23] He then concludes that the rule "ought not to be extended to new cases, but be confined to cases where it has already been applied, and where the principle on which it is founded exactly fits the case."[24]

Pearson refused to apply the rule to the master. He wrote:

> Is there nothing in the difference between a trial where property is involved, and a trial where human life is at stake, to make a distinction in the application of this rule, so far as it related to a witness called in behalf of the prisoner? The idea, when a prisoner calls a witness to prove his innocence, who, it may be, is the only person on earth to whom a fact is known that will save his life, that he must be repulsed by the cold announcement, "he is our master—he has an interest in saving your life, and at all events he is liable for the costs of this prosecution, and, therefore, has a pecuniary interest which makes him incompetent, so he cannot be heard in your behalf," shocks all the best feelings of our nature, and extorts the exclamation, "This ought not to be a rule of evidence!"

> Frail as human nature may be, dollars and cents should not be weighed in the balance with life. It cannot be presumed that the "almighty dollar" is so controlling in its influence, as to overcome all other considerations. Our investigation satisfies us that the rule of exclusion, because of pecuniary interest, has not been applied to a case like the present, and we are clearly of the opinion, that the principle of the rule is not applicable.[25]

Based upon Pearson's dislike for the rule, his finding that no case required the application of the rule would seem dispositive. Pearson also cited a North Carolina Supreme Court holding that the rule did not apply to capital cases. But that case was not a slave case. Thus, the Court did not see itself bound by that decision when a slave was on trial.[26]

That was the case obviously because the real issue in a slave trial was the taking of the master's property in the guise of a slave trial. This Pearson acknowledged as follows:

> The testimony of the master cannot be excluded without manifest inconsistency. The slave is put on trial as a *human being*; entitled to have his guilt or innocence passed on by a jury. Is it not inconsistent, in the progress of the trial, to treat him as property, like chattel— a horse, in the value of which the owner has a pecuniary interest which makes him incompetent as a witness? And as respects the master, is it not enough, that in the exercise of the right of eminent domain, his property should be forfeited to the public without compensation, and he should be made liable for the costs? Must insult be super-added by saying to him, "you have a pecuniary interest, and, therefore, cannot be trusted; so, we must also take from you the poor privilege of being heard in behalf of your slave, and of having our credit passed upon by the jury?
>
> So much upon the principle of the rule; let us now look to analogy. A father has an interest in the services of his child until he arrives at the age of twenty-one; it is a pecuniary interest which the law protects by giving an action *"per quod servitum amisit,"* (indeed it is the gravamen of the action for seduction,) but the father is a competent witness in behalf of his child; so a master has a pecuniary interest in the service of his apprentice, indeed he has a property in him, qualified, it is true, for he cannot assign it, but he can maintain an action for harboring him or otherwise depriving him of his services; yet, a master is a competent witness in behalf of an apprentice who is on trial for an offence which may subject him to imprisonment, transportation or death, in either of which events the master will suffer pecuniary loss. Where, then, is the principle or the analogy which makes the master of a slave incompetent? What is to be the limit of the rule? Is one who has a negro hired for a year, incompetent to five testimony in his behalf, because, by a conviction, he will lose his services?[27]

Therefore, the Court ruled by analogy to the non-slave law cited above. In doing so, Pearson "distinguished" the *dictum* of Ruffin in *State v. Charity*, decided in 1830, which went the other way on this issue.[28]

Indeed, the courts of Tennessee, Arkansas, Alabama, and Mississippi had, between 1839 and 1854, rejected the interest disqualification, and a Georgia statute was to the same effect.[29] The Courts did write about concern for slave "humanity" in these cases. The Courts also questioned the policy behind this evidence rule, and noted by analogy, that the rule did not apply to master and apprentice and other similar cases. But the master and slave relation was fundamentally different *because* the master had such a large interest in the life of the slave.

It was therefore convenient for the courts to expound on their concern for the "hardships" of this exclusionary rule, which it was held will "illy comport with that humanity which should be extended" to slaves.[30] Pearson gave the game away, however, when he acknowledged that the master stood against the state in these cases, and he was entitled to "due process" before the state took his property, in an exercise of eminent domain. Indeed, it would "illy comport" with the master's interest if he could not testify for his slave. When the master decided to do so, he would usually be defending his slave from accusations by third persons. Thus, the slave's interest paralleled the master—to the slave's good fortune.

## *The Master's Right to be a Witness Against His Slave*

Nevertheless, the criminal law allowed the master to be the slave's accuser, as well as her defender. Thus, the master could be a witness against her slave, and could testify about confessions she obtained from the slave. A strong argument against admitting these confessions was made by Cobb. He stated that the slave

> is bound, and habituated to obey every command and wish of the [master]. He has no will to refuse obedience, even when it involves his life. The master is his protector, his counsel, his confidant. He cannot, if he will, seek the advice and direction of legal counsel.[31]

Thus, Cobb wrote that master and slave communications should be privileged as are attorney and client communications. Cobb also questioned the truthfulness of a slave's confession to a master:

> Moreover, experience shows, that the slave is always ready to mould his answers so as to please the master, and that no confidence can be placed in the truth of his statements.[32]

Cobb's view was identical to that of Chief Justice Leonard Henderson of North Carolina, as expressed in his opinion in *State v. Charity*.[33]

The Cobb/Henderson rule was not adopted by the majority of any court. Instead, the courts allowed the master to testify as to confessions he legally extracted from the slave.[34] As noted in *Sam v. State*,[35] an 1857 Mississippi decision authored by Justice Alexander Handy, it would be difficult to convict slaves if the master could not testify as to confessions:

> And the consequence of this would be, that a disposition would be created to punish slaves, otherwise than according to the rules and restraints of the law, which should operate, both in its protection and in its punishments, upon [slaves], as well as upon the white man.[36]

Accordingly, Handy encouraged masters to bring their cases to the courts when the master decided that the "domestic tribunal" was not sufficient. Also evident is Handy's concern about extra-legal violence and mob rule.

## The Admissibility of Slave Confessions

This concern is also evident in the cases putting limits on slave confessions made to masters and third parties. As to the latter, the courts were concerned about non-slave owners using force to obtain unreliable confessions from slaves, to the master's detriment. Therefore, slave confessions obtained through violence, fear, or promise of favor were ruled inadmissible. In so holding, the courts applied the antebellum common law rule.[37]

The master's fear that third party abuse of slaves would create false confessions of guilt is acknowledged by Flanigan. He notes that, in the antebellum South, a modern urban police force was not present. Therefore, "the maintenance of law and order depended upon the active participation of the citizenry."[38] He adds:

> Not only did the law encourage individuals to apprehend and sometimes administer punishment to slaves guilty of minor offenses, ... but the absence of peace officers meant that the only effective law enforcement might necessarily be entirely private in nature. Thus it was extremely important that the slaves be protected against the impositions of overzealous citizen interrogators.[39]

A prime example of this concern is expressed in the 1856 Mississippi case of *Jordan v. State*.[40]

The defendant slave was indicted for murdering another slave. The defendant confessed after being physically abused by two whites who were not the slave's owner. The court applied the common law rule to hold that the confession was inadmissible. The court reasoned:

> The power which restrains the State, equally restrains her citizens in this respect. To hold otherwise would not unfrequently [sic] expose the accused to the excited passions or fury of that class of population who in all countries are the subjects upon whom the criminal jurisprudence of the government can be most beneficially employed.[41]

Obviously, the court sought to protect the master's property interest from being indirectly interfered with by poor whites who would abuse slaves to exert false confessions.

There is also a concern about the public interest and the purposes of the criminal law expressed by the slave confession cases. If a slave were convicted and executed based upon an unreliable or forced confession, then the guilty party could go free. Consequently, slaves could be used by criminals to shield themselves from criminal liability, as slaves could not testify against whites in the courts of law, and this could happen in a case in which a master was killed as well as stranger.

These concerns are expressed in the 1858 North Carolina case of *State v. George*.[42] Three slaves were indicted for murdering their master. Justice Pearson wrote:

> The evidence disclosed a horrid murder, committed under circumstances well calculated to excite and alarm the people of the neighborhood. It was the duty of every good citizen to do his utmost in order to find out the perpetrators of the crime, but care should have been taken not to exceed the limits allowed by the rules of law. The prisoner may be guilty, but, to justify a conviction, his guilt must be proved according to law.[43]

The court held that the defendants' confessions "were extracted by means calculated to excite the fear of present death in the firmest mind."[44]

Pearson described these circumstances in a dramatic fashion:

> The prisoners were in irons; a large crowd has assembled and became much excited; one strikes Gauzy in the face and threatens to kill him "if he don't tell all about it"; another says to George, "Tell about it; *they* will hang you if you don't," and there they stood—an infuriated crowd![45]

Therefore, Pearson held that the confessions were inadmissible because they were influenced by the slaves' fear of danger and were motivated to appease the crowd.

The court's ruling was not based upon concern for "formality." Rather, there was a fear in the court of mob rule and the need to search for the truth:

> A confession extorted in this way may, or may not, be true. But there is no guaranty of its truth, and by the rules of evidence it is inadmissible.
> This case furnishes an apt illustration of the wisdom of the rule. If such evidence was received, crowds would always assemble when there was a charge of the commission of a horrid crime, in order to extort a confession.[46]

Obviously, Justice Pearson may have thought that an extorted confession might let a guilty party go free, at the expense of the heirs of the deceased master. For even when a slave was accused of killing his master, the heirs' interest in the slave weighed on the side of the public need to arrive at the truth—even in slave trials.

Mob rule is illustrated in two cases cited by Flanigan. In *Grayson v. Commonwealth*,[47] a defendant slave was hanged by a mob. Thereafter, the true perpetrator confessed. And in *Polk & Wilson Co. v. Francher*,[48] a master sued a mob for damages, alleging that his slave was wrongfully lynched. Both cases illustrate how fair procedures protected the slave master's property interest.

Confessions allegedly made to masters raised similar concerns. A master who induced a slave to confess by force or favor could not legally take the slave's life in the domestic tribunal, if the slave was not in rebellion. This is clear from Chapter 5, although the master could beat the slave into submission. Similarly, the master could not extort a questionable confession, and then have the state execute the slave based upon that unreliable confession. The state's interest in getting at the truth was quite relevant here; otherwise, a master could commit a crime and use his slave as a scapegoat. For example, *State v. Posey*[49] is an 1849 South Carolina case in which the master, Posey, employed a slave to kill the master's wife. Posey then killed his slave. He was convicted as an accessory to his wife's killing, and for murdering his slave. Similarly, he could not use the courts to kill the slave, with the aid of a coerced confession.

## *Other Procedural Rights in Slave Trials*

There were various other procedural "rights" enforced in slave trials. Indictments were read strictly and technically, in states that afforded slaves grand jury protections.[50] This should not be surprising in nineteenth century jurisprudence. Civil complaints were, after all, read with an eye to formalism,[51] and a slave felony trial was the functional equivalent of a civil forfeiture proceeding. The slave also had a "right" to avoid double jeopardy. Repeated trials for the same offense were barred with little comment by Georgia and South Carolina decisions that were the only two cases to address this issue.[52] The concept behind double jeopardy is similar to the notion of *res judicata*, which applied in civil trials. A master whose runaway horse caused damage could be sued for damages by the injured party. If the master won, he could use *res judicata* to bar a second trial. Similarly, the master who won the *in rem* proceeding involving an alleged criminal slave did not have to again defend the same slave on the same charge.

Flanigan notes that Alabama and North Carolina required slaveholder juries in slave criminal trials.[53] In *State v. Jim*,[54] Chief Justice Taylor expressed clearly the reason for this provision of law. In doing so, he indicates the concern for the master's interest that runs through the criminal cases involving slaves:

> . . . A twofold consideration dictated the policy of this law . . . It was intended to surround the life of the slave with additional safeguards, and more effectually to protect the property of the owner, by infusing into the trial the temperate and impartial feeling which would probably exist in persons owning the same sort of property. That the master would have assurance of an equitable trial by persons who had property constantly exposed to similar accusations, and who would not wantonly sacrifice the life of a slave, but yield it only to a sense of justice . . .[55]

Indeed, the nineteenth century law furthered these ends, and protected the public from all who would use the slave as a shield to a criminal from justice.

In this regard, the slave's "right" to counsel can be read in its proper context. Nash says, "it appears that the right to counsel may have been better secured to indigent blacks during the antebellum era than in any later period prior to *Gideon v. Wainwright*."[56] Indeed, the Southern states required masters to supply counsel or provided slaves with a lawyer in felony cases. When a master thought his slave was wrongly accused, he could hire high-priced and quality defense lawyers. These statutes, "protected" the slave when the master did not do so. In fact, Flanigan points out that the Southern statutes and constitutions gave the slave a greater right to counsel than whites enjoyed.[57]

Flanigan does question the quality of representation a slave would receive from court appointed counsel, when the master sided against the slave.[58] Nevertheless, he states:

> In general . . . slaves appointed appeared to have had conscientious counsel, inadequately prepared at times, but often willing to plead for the slave even after conviction.[59]

Consequently, Flanigan concludes that the Southern states "recognized that despite slaves' 'equality' in criminal trials, their status as chattels necessitated further protection."[60] In fact, the slave's "right" to counsel is fully consistent with the slave's degraded condition as a chattel without rights.

This is because the slave had no "right" to represent himself. Free people have this right in a criminal case.[61] But the slave had to be recognized in the courts through his attorney because the slave had no legal identity other than as property, and being property, the slave had no legal means to pay a lawyer. Accordingly, the state had to intervene to provide counsel; otherwise slave trials would not serve the truth-finding aim of the criminal law. To insure that guilty parties were caught and punished, the law required the slave to have *some* defense, even when his master was an accuser or refused to hire a lawyer. This was to protect the public, and not the slave. Thus, the right to counsel is a confirmation of the slave's lack of right at law.

This point is further illustrated by the discriminatory rules of evidence that developed regarding slave testimony. Flanigan summarizes this law, "No state permitted slaves to testify against whites, but every state allowed slaves to testify against their fellow bondsman."[62] Cobb explained this rule:

> That this universal exclusion of a negro from testifying may, in many supposable cases, operate harshly and to defeat justice . . . is an undeniable fact; and yet it is equally true, that the indiscriminate admission and giving credit to negro testimony would not only in many cases, defeat justice, but would be productive of innumerable evils in the relation of master and slave.[63]

Cobb wrote that the root of the rule lies in recognition of the "general idea" that blacks are "mendacious." Cobb found this to be "a fact too well established to require the production of proof, either from history, travels, or craniology."[64] Therefore, slaves could not call fellow slaves as witnesses to contradict white testimony, nor could the accused confront and rebut his white accusers.

Slaves were also denied the common law marital privilege. This privilege prevented the husband or wife of a criminal defendant from being called to testify against the accused spouse. Slaves were denied this privilege because slave marriages were given no legal status. According to Flanigan, Georgia was the only Southern state that allowed slaves the marital privilege.[65]

These cases show that even in felony cases, the slave was not treated as the equal of a white person.

## Collective Liability and Slave Rebellion

The public interest in preventing slave rebellions weighed heavily even in the nineteenth century. Despite the heightened procedural rights granted slaves in ordinary cases, extraordinary fears of rebellion caused the legislators to suspend the usual due process when the spectre of rebellion swept across the South.

This was the case even in the "liberal" state of Tennessee. In 1858, the legislature provided for summary "justice" when "five credible persons" certified in writing to a circuit court judge that slaves were involved in "an insurrectionary movement[.]" The judge was to immediately proceed with a trial, and call a special session if necessary. The alleged offenders were to be indicted by a grand jury and tried by a twelve-person petit jury while the fear of insurrection was in the minds of the community.[66]

Howington states that this statute was enacted in the aftermath of the panic of 1856 and the outbreak of mob "justice" that followed. He quotes Charles B. Dew for the notion that this provision was intended to prevent a reoccurrence of vigilante action in the future. Nevertheless, the statute was oppressive as it, in effect, legitimized summary execution "by providing for the rapid channeling of white hysteria into the regular court system."[67] Indeed, in 1831, the legislature had decided that slaves accused of rebellion or insurrection should be denied appeals.[68] Thus, the level of process due in slave trials varied based upon the balance between the master's interest and the public's interest. In an ordinary murder, the public concern was of lesser import than in a case of suspected rebellion. In the latter case, the need for swift justice was acknowledged in the law. Obviously, there was no real concern for "slave rights" evident here.

Flanigan cites an Alabama anti-rebellion statute that was even more oppressive than that of Tennessee. The statute provided for a summary trial by a written affidavit signed by the prosecutor alleging an insurrection. The trial was to be completed within fifteen days of the offense. The slave had no right to appeal and was to be executed immediately.[69] Indeed, the history of Southern justice, even in the antebellum years, is marred by lynch mob "justice."[70] The Alabama statute goes one step further; it places the lynch mob within the protection of the law, as long as the most minimal procedures were followed in the heat of local fear and hysteria. This fear was not merely a characteristic of the rough colonial days. It continued even into the days just before the Civil War.

The procedures in slave rebellion cases approach the idea of collective justice employed in Roman slave law under the doctrine of the *senatus consultum silaninum*. Pursuant to this horrible principle, when a master is murdered by one of his slaves, "all the slaves who lived under the same roof are to be subjected to torture and then condemned to death."[71]

Alan Watson quotes Gaius Cassius, who justified this doctrine:

> Our ancestors distrusted their slaves even when they were born on their estates or in their own home and experienced the kindness of their masters. But now our households are international . . . You can restrain this scum only through fear. But, it is said, even innocent people will die . . . Every great example contains some evil, but individual wrongs are weighed against the public good.[72]

Similarly in the United States South, when an insurrection was suspected, the normal means of searching for the truth were found to be too cumbersome to serve the public's perceived need to "restrain this scum . . . through fear." Therefore, if collective justice had to be extracted to quell a rebellion so be it; the slaves had no independent claim of right to prevent "individual wrongs" compelled by "the public good."

## *Conclusion*

Professor A.E. Keir Nash in one of his studies of the antebellum appeals court decisions, states of the years 1830 to 1860:

> It might be reasonable to suspect that in an era of mounting sectional hostility [a concern for fair procedures] would not have extended to the trials of black defendants[. . .] Surprisingly, however, procedural fairness was almost always demanded by appellate judges in the trials of blacks.[73]

To the contrary, however, it is not surprising that in the slave felony cases he studies, the appeals courts were concerned about fairness in the trial of valuable slave property.

Relying on Nash's studies, Edward Ayers states:

> Slaveholders . . . exercised two kinds of power through the law. By adhering to a highly formalistic system of justice for serious slave criminals, slaveholders helped legitimize their *class* rule, at least in their own eyes; by preserving their personal control over day-to-day life on the plantation, slaveholders prevented the law from insulating slaves from the master's will.[74]

The "fair" procedures also protected the master's slave from an unjust punishment, and furthered the societal interest in finding and punishing the truly guilty parties in criminal cases. Consequently, when the slave criminal procedure cases are read in their context, they are not surprising; indeed, they are consistent with the salient social and economic interests. Although the courts often spoke of treating slaves as human beings, the lawmakers never applied the common law in its full rigor to the law of slave criminal procedure. Rather, the law varied the level of protection based upon the seriousness of the crime and the punishment, in furtherance of interests that did not include the right of the chattel on trial. Consequently, in cases of suspected rebellion, the public interest outweighed the property interests of the owners, more so than in an ordinary crime. The slave's rights and personhood were thus revealed to be irrelevant to these various calculations of interest. Indeed, these cases further confirmed the perversion of the notion of humanity in slave law.

This perversion is also illustrated by the business law of slavery. Perhaps, it reached its apex in the law that legitimized the division of slave families. These two topics are considered in the following two chapters.

# NOTES

1. See, Flanigan, *supra* at 1–144; Daniel Flanigan, "Criminal Procedure in Slave Trials in the Antebellum South," 40 *Journal of Southern History* 537 (1974); "Trial Rights," *supra* at 628–629; "Fairness," *supra* at 72–389; "Negro Rights," *supra* at 166–177; Howington, *supra* at 98–216; Tushnet, *supra* at 82–84, 121–139; Mark Tushnet, "Approaches to the Study of the Law of Slavery," 25 *Civil War History* 329, 331–335 (1979).

2. *Compare*, Hindus, *supra* at 131–132; Flanigan, *supra* at 564; Higginbotham, *supra* at 179–186, 257–258, *with*, *Ibid.* at 57, 185, 254, 257.

3. *See*, "Fairness," *supra* at 82; "Negro Rights," *supra* at 170; Tushnet, *supra* at 122. *Compare*, Schwarz, *supra* at 47, 51 and Fede—1984, *supra* at

317–318 for my comments to this effect, published before Schwarz and not cited therein.

4. *See*, "Fairness," *supra* at 64–65.

5. *See, generally*, Stroud, *supra* at 91–93. For Virginia, *see*, Schwarz, *supra* at 38–58; for South Carolina, *see*, Henry, *supra* at 58–65; and for Louisiana, *see*, Schafer, *supra*.

6. *See*, Hindus, *supra* at 129–161.

7. *See*, *Id.* at 161.

8. *See*, Howington, *supra* at 116–117.

9. *See*, *Id.* at 116–140.

10. *Id.* at 123.

11. *See*, Stroud, *supra* at 89–91.

12. *See*, *Id.* at 94–95.

13. 24 F. Cas. 792 (C.C.D. Va. 1859) (No. 14, 445).

14. *Id.* at 795.

15. *Id.* at 807.

16. *Id.* at 810.

17. 14 Md. 135 (1859).

18. *Id.* at 149.

19. *See*, Brackett, *supra* at 126; *compare*, Cobb, *supra* at 263–265, stating that slaves were not ordinarily included within the scope of criminal statutes.

20. *See, generally*, 2 John Henry Wigmore, *Evidence* § 575–580 (James Chadbourn, ed., Boston, 1979); *see, also*, McCormick, *supra* at § 65.

21. *See*, Wigmore, *supra* at § 576–577.

22. 48 N.C. (3 Jones) 348 (1856).

23. *Id.* at 348–351.

24. *Id.* at 351.

25. *Id.*

26. *Id.* at 352, *citing, State v. Kimbrough*, 13 N.C. 370 (2 Dev.) 431 (1830).

27. *Id.* at 352–353.

28. *Id.* at 353–354, *distinguishing*, *State v. Charity*, 13 N.C. 465, 465–467, 2 Dev. 543, 543–546 (1830) (Ruffin, J.).

29. *See, Austin v. State*, 14 Ark. 555 (1854); *Spence v. State*, 17 Ala. 192 (1850); *State v. Marshall*, 8 Ala. 802 (1845); *Isham v. State*, 7 Miss. (6 How.) 35 (1841); *Elijah v. State*, 20 Tenn. (1 Hum.) 99 (1839); *cf.*, *State v. Aaron*, 4 N.J.L. 269 (Sup. Ct. 1818) (allowing master to testify after passage of the gradual emancipation law). For the Georgia statute, *see*, Cobb, *supra* at 272 n. 2.

30. *Isham v. State*, *supra* at 41–42.

31. Cobb, *supra* at 272.

32. *Id.*

33. *See, State v. Charity*, *supra*, 13 N.C. at 468–471, 2 Dev. at 547–550 (Henderson, C.J.).

34. *See*, Flanigan, *supra* at 134–135.

35. 33 Miss. 347 (1857).

36. *Id.* at 352.

37. *See*, Flanigan, *supra* at 129–131.

38. *Id.* at 131.

39. *Id.* at 132.
40. 32 Miss. 382 (1856).
41. *Id.* at 387.
42. 50 N.C. 232, 5 Jones 233 (1858).
43. *Id.* at 235; 5 Jones at 233.
44. *Id.* [Emphasis omitted].
45. *Id.*
46. *Id.* at 234, 5 Jones at 236.
47. 47 Va. 888, 6 Gratt. 712 (1849); 49 Va. 317, 7 Gratt. 613 (1850).
48. 38 Tenn. (1 Head) 190 (1858).
49. 35 S.C.L. 54, 4 Strob. 103 (1849); 35 S.C.L. 74, 4 Strob 142 (1849).
50. *See, e.g.,* Flanigan, *supra* at 107–109; "Fairness," *supra* at 79–81.
51. *See, generally,* Milton Green, *Basic Civil Procedure* 111–112 (New York, 2d ed., 1979).
52. *State v. Lavinia,* 25 Ga. 311 (1858); *Ex parte Brown,* 18 S.C.L. 151, 2 Bail. 323 (1831).
53. *See,* Flanigan, *supra* at 110–111.
54. 12 N.C. 95, 1 Dev. 142 (1826).
55. *Id.* at 97, 1 Dev. at 144–145.
56. *See,* "Fairness," *supra* at 84.
57. Flanigan, *supra* at 116–120.
58. *Id.* at 119–120.
59. *Id.* at 120.
60. *Id.*
61. *See, Faretta v. California,* 422 U.S. 806, 95 S. Ct. 2525, 45 L. Ed. 2d 562 (1975).
62. Flanigan, *supra* at 122.
63. Cobb, *supra* at 232–233.
64. *Id.* at 233.
65. *See,* Flanigan, *supra* at 121.
66. *See,* Howington, *supra* at 152, *quoting,* Law of Tennessee, 1858, ch. 86.
67. *See,* Howington, *supra* at 152, *quoting,* Charles B. Dew, "Black Ironworkers and the Slave Insurrection Panic of 1856," 41 *Journal of Southern History* 836, 337 (1975).
68. *See,* Howington, *supra* at 151.
69. *See,* Flanigan, *supra* at 142, *quoting, Alabama Code* Part 4, Title 1, Ch. 2, Art. X Sec. 3321–3324.
70. *See, generally, e.g.,* Stampp, *supra* at 132–140, 190–191.
71. *See,* Watson, *supra* at 134.
72. *Id.* at 138.
73. "Fairness," *supra* at 78–79.
74. Edward L. Ayers, *Vengeance & Justice: Crime and Punishment in the 19th-Century American South* 135 (New York, 1984).

CHAPTER 10

# The Recognition of Slave Humanity to Settle the Rights of Whites That Were Embodied in Slaves

IN COUNTLESS cases the Southern courts treated slaves like ordinary—but valued—articles of commerce. Judge A. Leon Higginbotham sums up the abolitionist view of the law: "Generally neither the courts nor the legislatures seemed to have been any more sensitive about commercial transactions involving slaves than they were about sales of corn, lumber, horses, or dogs."[1] Until recent years, however, this commercial law has received scant attention.[2] This is unfortunate because the business law of slavery is an essential factor in the development of a comprehensive jurisprudential theory of the law of slavery. In addition, this law must be compared with the antebellum law of the free states before we can arrive at a complete picture of the development of "American" non-criminal law, as well as the transformations that occurred in that law in the nineteenth century.[3]

This chapter leaves the latter point for another day and focuses on the former: How is the treatment of slaves as property relevant to the theory of slave law advanced by the abolitionists? Indeed, this "business law" is very relevant, it shows how readily the courts and legislatures recognized that slaves were property—not people. The pervasiveness of this notion is shown first by the specific performance doctrine that developed in the antebellum South. That doctrine further illustrates the irrelevance of slave rights to a theory of slave law. This is because judges equated slave humanity with the absence of any right in the slave; the slave's humanity mattered only in establishing the relative rights of whites to possess slave property.

## *Specific Delivery of Slave "Humanity"*

It is by now axiomatic that slaves were treated as ordinary articles of commerce in the antebellum South. The buying and selling of slaves was indeed the most dehumanizing blow to slave "rights" and "personhood." This point is well argued by George Stroud:

> . . . [I]t must not be forgotten that the slave is a human being, and, although his degraded condition may have blunted or perhaps destroyed the nicer sensibilities of our nature, yet is he susceptible of many of the feelings which attach those of the same species to each other, and even to insensate objects. *As man*, he must be alive to the ties of consanguinity and affinity. *As man*, he must know what friendship is. *As man*, it is scarcely possible he should not feel an attachment even *to place*. And *as man*, the indulgence of these feelings cannot fail to contribute largely to his happiness. To be torn from such endearments, without the hope of a restoration, and yet live, must inflict a pange agonizing beyond description. The terror which his master's presence inspires renders those of his own condition more dear.[4]

The other abolitionist writers catalogued, with appropriate shock, the existence of slave sales and other transactions, as well as the debasement explicit and implicit in the sale and delivery of human flesh and blood.[5]

Nevertheless, while it dehumanized the slave, the law of slave commerce recognized slave "humanity" in the specific performance cases. The notion of slave "humanity" is revealed to be entirely perverted by these cases, however. The slave's humanity merely made him a valuable and unique chattel. The humanity recognized in these cases enhanced the slave's position in the hierarchy of chattels, but confirmed that the slave's legal standing was entirely as an object of the rights of others and not the possessor of rights. Despite his humanity, and indeed because of it, the slave was subject to sale and specific performance.

As noted earlier, the nineteenth century law defined slaves to be personal property. By then, the common law rule had been established that Courts of Equity would order specific performance of contracts for the sale of real estate and thus would order a reluctant seller to convey the specific lands to the buyer.[6] But the buyers of personal property were generally not able to obtain an order requiring delivery of a personal chattel purchased. A buyer of personalty could obtain specific performance only by proving the goods were unique, or that other special equities existed. This is still the rule; buyers of personal property are presumed to be limited to monetary damages, while real estate purchasers have a presumed right to specific performance.[7] A leading treatise explains this rule:

> In applying this doctrine the courts of equity have established the further rule that in general the legal remedy of damages is inadequate in all agreements for the sale or letting of land, or of any estate therein; and therefore in such class of contracts the jurisdiction is always exercised, and a specific performance granted, unless prevented by other and independent equitable considerations which directly affect the remedial right of the complaining party.[8]

There are, however, few reported cases that find equitable considerations sufficient to deny a real estate buyer specific performance.[9] The history of this presumption is explained in a recent case:

> The principle underlying the specific performance remedy is equity's jurisdiction to grant relief where the damage remedy at law is inadequate. The text writers generally agree that at the time this branch of equity jurisdiction was evolving in England, the presumed uniqueness of land as well as its importance to the social order of that era led to the conclusion that damages at law could never be adequate to compensate for the breach of a contract to transfer an interest in land. Hence specific performance became a fixed remedy in this class of transactions.[10]

The rule for personal property was to the contrary because of the different perceptions as to the importance of chattels in the social order.

As to personalty, Professor Corbin writes that, "The ordinary subjects of trade and commerce are prima facie not subjects for specific performance; and yet in a particular case any one of them may be shown to be so related to other matters that damages are inadequate." The buyer has the burden of showing this inadequacy, unlike his counterpart who purchases real estate. Corbin does, however, refer to slaves as being among the types of personal property that "are prima facie subjects for specific performance, although in any particular case the defendant may be able to upset the presumption." Other examples listed are "ships, patent rights, family pictures, [and] copyrights."[11] Indeed, although slaves were personal property, the majority of Southern courts presumed that a slave owner or buyer had a right to specific performance: "Special delivery of slave property became the general rule, with exceptions where the interest of the petitioner in the slave was solely the slave's cash value."[12]

Apparently, slave owners were not satisfied with the usual common law remedies provided to buyers of chattels: they sought and obtained special treatment for slaves. An example is the 1856 Virginia case of *Summers v. Bean*.[13] The plaintiff, Bean, was the son-in-law of the defendant, Mrs. Summers, a widow.[14] Mrs. Summers agreed "to secure to Bean the services of Caroline, a negro girl about twelve years of age, and McKendry, a black boy . . . which two slaves . . . Bean was to have during the life of Mrs. Summers."[15] Bean alleged that Mrs. Summers should be ordered to specifically perform the agreement and turn the slaves over to him.

The Court agreed with Bean and ordered specific performance of the contract.[16] Judge Richard Moncure wrote for the court and recognized the common law rule that specific performance would routinely lie for real, but not personal property.[17] The distinction, Moncure noted, was that money damages did not provide the buyer of real estate with an adequate remedy, but that in most sales of personalty money damages were adequate.[18]

Moncure held that, as a matter of law, money damages did not afford a slave buyer adequate relief:

> Slaves are not only property but rational beings; and are generally acquired with reference to their moral and intellectual qualities. Therefore damages at law, which are measured by the ordinary market value of the subject, will not generally afford adquate compensation for the breach of contract for the sale of slaves. There is at least as much reason for enforcing the specific execution of a contract for the sale of slaves, as of a contract for the sale of real estate.[19]

Thus, the Court "laid down as a general rule" the proposition that a Court of Equity can specifically enforce a contract of sale for slaves "though it be neither alleged in the bill nor proved that they have any peculiar value."[20]

The Court writes that this deviation from the common law general rule was adopted elsewhere in the South.[21] It was so ruled in South Carolina, North Carolina, Mississippi, Tennessee, and Arkansas.[22] In Georgia, Kentucky, and Alabama decisions and *dicta* required the plaintiff to plead and prove the slave's uniqueness or peculiar value, in accord with the general rule. Thus, the plaintiff would have to show that the slaves were especially skilled or were family slaves.[23] In *Summers*, Judge Moncure notes that the Virginia decisions were divided before 1856, but he aligned his state with the majority rule in the Southern states.[24]

Moncure also finds that many of the cases in which owners sought specific performance were not slave sales cases. Masters often strove to enjoin an allegedly wrongful execution sale.[25] As Tony Freyer shows, masters also were involved in many transactions intended to defraud creditors.[26] Slave owners would sell a slave to a preferred creditor or neighbor, below the market rate, on an oral promise to reconvey when the purchase price could be repaid.[27] Terrence Kiely states that these transactions led to petitions in equity for specific delivery of the slaves.[28]

In *Summers*, Judge Moncure wrote that a stronger case for equity existed in an ordinary sale. He found that an owner—unlike a contract purchaser—might have remedies at law, such as trover or detinue, which could lead to the recovery of a wrongfully detained slave. On the other hand, Moncure stated that a master seeking recovery of slaves, "may have formed an attachment to the slaves from long connection with them," but this was not a requirement for equitable intervention according to the majority rule.[29]

Kiely cites cases that indicate exceptions to the slave specific performance presumption. One of interest is a sale to a slave trader, who would resell the slave as merchandise.[30] Another would arise if a mortgagee sought possession of a mortgaged slave.[31] Consequently, Kiely correctly concludes that the majority rule affording specific delivery of slaves was one example of how the Southern courts molded "the pliable system of the common law to fit the needs of a slave and cotton economy, thus serving as protectors of the interests of the slaveholding community."[32] The rule allowing specific performance of slaves was also an example of judicial concern for slaveholder interests in slaves that were bought, sold, mortgaged, and devised. The courts were not as protective of mere traders and money lenders when their interests clashed with planters.

I have stated elsewhere that the antebellum law of slave sales was more protective of the slave buyer than the antebellum law of the North. I draw upon warranty cases and statutes, as well as the specific performance cases. All of these legal materials indicate "consumer protection" of the interests of slave sellers and traders. Of course, our law today does more to protect the consumer than did Northern antebellum law.[33] The slave sales law was not a direct ancestor of modern law, but several interesting questions are suggested by this analogy.

Regarding specific performance, it is now recognized that our courts have become more willing to grant buyers specific delivery of chattels.[34] We are in a time of heightened consumer protection that parallels the pro-buyer stance taken by the Southern courts in the antebellum years when slaves were sold. With increasing concern for the buyer's interest comes a great likelihood that specific performance will be awarded in the sale of chattels.

The Southern courts did in some way recognize slave humanity when they presumed slaves to be as unique to the buyer as land. But this recognition of slave personhood shows that the slave's "moral personality" was relevant only in regard to the battle between the slave's competing rulers—the buyer and seller. The slave's humanity was thus proved to be entirely irrelevant, as it created no rights in the slaves.

Professor Tushnet's analysis suggests another reading of the specific performance cases. He wrote that the courts "did not resolve the question of specific performance by simple analogy to land."[35] Although he acknowledges that there are references to real estate in the slave specific performance cases, such as in the *Summers* case, Tushnet concludes, "But these references meant only that for the *same* reasons that land was unique, so were slaves."[36]

Nevertheless, two pages later, Tushnet states that the courts indeed failed to invoke a real property analogy. Instead, he argues that the courts "relied directly upon the totalistic relations between masters and slaves, which generated ties of sentiment and affection that justified special legal treatment of those relations."[37] This is what Tushnet calls "sentiment" or recognition of slave "humanity." Did the courts support specific performance of land, then, in recognition of the "humanity" of land and the "totalistic relations" between man and soil? I think not. A buyer of a slave who never received delivery would not have developed any relations with his slave before delivery. Thus, the "ties of sentiment and affection" were a legal fiction, if they were in any way relevant, under the majority rule. That rule epitomized the slave's lack of right—his personhood merely increased his economic value. The slave's legal status was as a valuable commodity, and nothing more. This point is illustrated by countless cases in the commercial law of slavery.

## *Recognition of Slave Humanity in Fixing Civil Liability When Slaves Were Injured or Killed*

In Chapters 5 and 6 we examined criminal and civil liability of whites who physically abused slaves. The focus here is on cases of negligence or carelessness that resulted in damage to slave property. These cases show how slave "humanity" was merely an interest that was equated in the calculation of liability between the person who caused the injury and the owner who was injured. Again, the notion of humanity was so perverted that it came to mean the absence of right.

The case of *Harrison v. Berkeley*[38] is typical. The plaintiff owner sued a defendant who sold liquor to a slave on December 24, 1845. That night, or during the early morning that followed, the slave died of exposure. The sale of liquor to slaves was made illegal by statute, but the statute provided no remedy to the plaintiff; thus, the action was one of negligence.

The issue was whether the sale was the proximate cause of the damage to the owner, or whether the slave, as humanity, was an intervening agent whose own actions were the legal cause of the death. At trial, Justice D.L. Wardlaw submitted that issue to the jury, and the defendant appealed. The defense was based upon the "humanity" of the slave, which, as a matter of law, was the proximate cause of the slave's death—according to the defendant.

Justice Wardlaw, writing for the Appeals Court, affirmed. He rejected the defendant's contentions as follows:

> [W]here the mischievous purpose of the slave is manifest, or should be foreseen by ordinary prudence, the injurious act embraces the will of the slave, as one of its ingredients;—the wrong consists, in part, in ministering to the purpose, and natural consequences of that purpose, (although the purpose may have been carried to an extent not anticipated, or the consequences may have been altogether undesigned and unusual,) are the legal consequences of the injurious act.[39]

Therefore, Wardlaw left it to the jury to decide "whether the drinking and intoxication of Bob, were the natural and probable consequences of selling liquor to him"[40]

Consequently, the slave's humanity was relevant in fixing the defendant's liability. The courts did not close their eyes to the slave's personhood. But the slave's human characteristics were relevant only in fairly establishing the allocation of risks among the slave's white oppressors.

Time and again, similar issues arose in cases in which slaves were hired out and were injured, or when slaves were damaged while entrusted with common carriers. These cases involved economic issues, the allocation of unforeseen damage to slave property. Similarly, when slaves died or escaped during the term of hire, the courts had to take the slave's humanity into account, but they did so only to arrive at a "fair" allocation of the economic loss.

Mark Tushnet begins his study of slave law with one such case.[41] In *Gorman v. Campbell*,[42] a plaintiff slave owner sued a steamboat captain and hirer for the value of a hired slave who died while in the defendant's employ. The slave was a steamboat hand who fell into a river and drowned while working in the water attempting to cut a log and thereby free the boat from obstruction. The trial judge instructed the jury that the defendant would be liable if he ordered or permitted the slave to work in the water. The Court stated that the captain would be free of liability if the slave worked in the water of his own free will.

Justice Joseph Lumpkin reversed, holding that the hirer was negligent in allowing, or failing to prevent, the slave from working in the water. That dangerous employment was in violation of custom and the contract of hire, according to Lumpkin. In any case, Lumpkin opined that the hirer had the duty to carefully supervise the slave. The slave's human volition did not provide a defense; the hirer was obligated to "use coercion even to chains, if necessary, for the protection of the property from peril[.]"[43] Thus, oppression was the hirer's duty; if he was too lax and afforded the slave too much freedom he faced civil liability.

The opinion goes on, however, to contain an "appeal to humanity," according to Tushnet. Indeed, Lumpkin writes that his holding is required by "humanity to the slave, as well as a proper regard for the interest of the owner[.]" He found the need to impose a high duty of care on hirers because of the inferior nature of blacks. "Their improvidence demands it. They are incapable of self-preservation, either in danger or in disease." Consequently, Lumpkin fashioned "a direct appeal to the pocket of the delinquent party."[44]

Tushnet finds this appeal to humanity to be of great importance. He acknowledges that this is a peculiar form of humanity; it would lead the hirer to put the slave in chains. Tushnet does not dismiss the invocation of humanity as "high irony" because he says the opinion could have omitted "humanity" and could have referred only to the "interest" of the master. He writes:

> If the owner's economic interest were all that had to be considered, the opinion would have focused, not on the captain's misbehavior, but on the expectations of [the plaintiff] in entering into the contract of hire. It might have argued . . . that [the plaintiff] was not entitled to recover because the contract price included or should have included a risk premium that took account of the fact that the slave might exercise his volition in dangerous ways. Or it might have justified the result the court reached by pointing to the expectation that [the slave] would be used only as a boathand, and that the hirer's liability flowed . . . from the deviation from the expected use.[45]

Consequently, Tushnet concludes that, "Justice Lumpkin's opinion, then, if not the court's result, can be understood only if we take the dual invocation of humanity and interest seriously."[46]

It is correct that we take the words Lumpkin used seriously. But we must do so only in light of the result and the relevant interests. The issue was the battle between the hirer's economic interest and that of the owner. In fact, Lumpkin had to balance the owner's economic interest against that of the hirer. To allocate the loss, he looked at the behavior of the defendant and the economic investment of the owner in light of the "humanity" of the slave; therefore, Lumpkin considered the slave's human characteristics in defining the scope of the hirer's duty. We must take the reference to humanity "seriously," but when we do so in light of the holding of the Court, we again see the invocation of humanity only as a means to allocate the competing interests of the slave's oppressors—no right is afforded to the slave.

Furthermore, Lumpkin's holding can be reconciled with his pro-master and anti-hirer views expressed in other cases of this type. For example, he held the hirer for a term liable to the master for rents if the slave died during the term of hire.[47] In so ruling Lumpkin wrote:

> Humanity to this dependent and subordinate class of our population requires, that we should remove from the hirer or temporary owner, all temptation to neglect them in sickness, or to expose them to situations of unusual peril and jeopardy... Let us not increase their danger, by making it the interest of the hirer to get rid of his contract, when it proves to be unprofitable. Every safeguard, consistent with the stability of the institution of slavery, should be thrown around the lives of these people.[48]

Of course, the invocation of humanity occurred in an allocation of risks among masters and hirers.

Lumpkin also refused to apply the fellow servant rule to cases in which slaves were hired out and were injured by the negligence of the hirer's employees—the slave's fellow servants.[49] Lumpkin rejected the rule as to slaves stating, "But interest to the owner, and humanity to the slave, forbid its application to any other than *free white agents.*"[50] He adds:

> The *restriction of this rule is indispensible to the welfare of the slave.* In almost every occupation, requiring combined effort, the employer necessarily intrusts it to a variety of agents. Many of those are destitute of principle, and bankrupt in fortune. Once let it be promulgated that [as to] negroes hired to the numerous navigation, railroad, mining and manufacturing companies which dot the whole country, and are rapidly increasing... that for any injury done to this species of property, ... that the *employer* is not liable ... I hesitate not to affirm, that the life of no *hired* slave would be safe. As it is, the guards thrown around this class of our population are sufficiently few and feeble. We are altogether disinclined to lessen their number or weaken their force.[51]

Thus, Lumpkin again equated the slave's humanity with his unique value to the owner.

Both of these stands taken by Lumpkin were somewhat

controversial in the South. David Langum writes of how Lumpkin's views on the former case were "overruled" by legislation in Georgia.[52] And Paul Finkelman shows how Lumpkin was with the Southern majority with the latter opinion,[53] with the significant expectation of Ruffin in *Ponton v. Wilmington Railroad Co.*[54]

Accordingly, when the holding of *Gorman v. Campbell* is read in context, it is clear how the invocation of humanity had become "high irony." It was significant to allocate the loss between the "real" people, but afforded no direct claim of right on the slave. To the contrary, the slave's legal nothingness is confirmed by this case.

Tushnet does not see this because he focuses upon the use of specific language in judicial opinions, rather than the significance of the pattern of similar or different results the courts reached in certain types of cases. Thus, he forgets that lawyers and judges in the slave South argued about and decided the flesh-and-blood cases before them, and that the "important" cases had an effect upon the competing interests that brought these cases to the judiciary for resolution. Tushnet also fails to factor into his interpretation the idea that different judges, in different areas and times, might perceive these competing interests in different ways, thus providing a means to reconcile the contradictions of slave law by reference to the social, political, and economic factors that influenced judicial perceptions of interest.

This level of analysis can, for example, be applied to the differences in opinion of Judges Ruffin and Lumpkin in the cases cited above. Ruffin sat on the North Carolina bench, while Lumpkin held court in Georgia. By the antebellum era, slavery in these two states was not precisely the same institution, and the judge's perceptions of the interests of the various participants in their cases may have also differed. Therefore, in Georgia, with its larger cotton plantations, Lumpkin resolved the conflict between hirer and master in favor of the planter and declined to apply the fellow servant rule to deny the master damages when slaves were killed. But Ruffin, in the more industrialized North Carolina, reached a result more favorable to hirers, many of whom were by then the railroads and industries, in his state.[55]

## *Slave Theft and the Confirmation of Dehumanization*

The courts and legislatures further confirmed the slave's dehumanized status with the law of slave stealing. This offense is considered here as part of the business law of slavery because the lawmakers were so obviously concerned with protecting the master's interest in the slave, and prohibiting the business of slave theft. It is also worth seeing how the slave's humanity was of very minor importance to the courts and legislatures.

The law of slave theft in South Carolina provides an example, and is aptly analyzed by Judge John Belton O'Neall. He writes that the slave code of 1740 declared that slaves were "chattels personal." He adds, "The first consequence legally resulting from this provision would have been without any Act of the Legislature that the stealing of a slave, should be a larceny (grand or petit), at common law."[56] Nevertheless, a 1754 act was passed making the theft of a slave a felony, punishable by death with the benefit of clergy.

The preamble to that act recited the fact that slaves, as chattels, "are in every respect as much the property of their owners, as any other goods and chattels are[.]" The preface notes further that

> ... no punishment can be inflicted, by the laws now in force, upon persons inveigling, stealing and carrying away any such slaves from their lawful owners or employers, that is adequate to so great and growing an evil[.]

Thus, the lawmakers perceived the need for new legislation to prevent "great injustice and damage[.]"

Therefore, the 1754 act punished any person

> ... who shall inveigle, steal and carry away any negro or other slave ..., or shall hire, aid or council any person ... to inveigle, steal or carry away as aforesaid any such slave, so as the owner or employer of such slave ... shall be deprived of the use and benefit of such slave[.][57]

O'Neall stated that the legislation acknowledged

> that for inveigling, stealing, and carrying away, there was no adequate punishment not that there was no punishment. When, by the Act of 1740, 7 Stat., 397, slaves were declared to the chattels personal, stealing them became like any other larceny of goods; this most usually would be grand larceny and the then punishment, imprisonment and branding. This punishment was supposed to be inadequate, and owing to the facility of committing the offence, the Act of 1754 increased the punishment to death.[58]

The legislators found that the stealing of slaves was a more serious crime than even grand larceny; thus, more severe penalties were enacted.

The Act also has a substantive content. The common law crime of larceny is made of two key elements—taking and carrying away of the property by the thief.[59] To these, the Act adds the inveigling offense. Judge O'Neall explains that the Act was

> intended to make the stealing of a negro, no matter how effected, death to the principal and the accessory. To inveigle, as is said by Judge Nott in . . . [State v. Miles], is to seduce, entice and decoy . . . What is that but stealing a negro? The only difference between such stealing and that of a bolt of linen is, a slave is a human being capable of assent, and hence, that therefore, inveigling is a means by which the larceny is affected.[60]

Thus, Judge O'Neall recognized that the slave's humanity required more protection than a bolt of linen because the slave could be enticed away from his owner as well as taken away physically.

The slavemasters feared slave theft. Therefore, in South Carolina, slave theft was made a capital offense seventy years before willful murder of a slave achieved that status. Obviously, the slave thief did not embody the public interest in slave control that the slave killer potentially represented. Indeed, the slave owner's fears of slave theft were not without foundation. John A. Murrell reportedly headed a 450-person slave stealing ring that operated throughout the Mississippi Valley. The gang conspired with slaves. It even stole slaves and resold slaves repeatedly to the same master. In 1835, Murrell was convicted in Tennessee of slave stealing and was sentenced to a ten-year jail term.[61]

It is significant that the early South Carolina statutes made slave stealing a capital offense. For another example, the Tennessee statutes of 1799 established slave killing, slave stealing, and horse theft as capital offenses. All three crimes were obviously seen to be offenses of equal importance.[62] H.M. Henry explained the interests involved in slave theft:

> Slave-stealing was dangerous in that it threatened the entire stability of the whole system and was subversive of the interests of society. The slave-stealer was the anarchist of Southern serfdom. Suppose it had been allowed to become a common offense: property in slaves would have been insecure; other property would have been endangered by the lawlessness of the depredators; lives of the whites would not have been secure, for it would have encouraged and made possible insurrection and general disorder which was the nightmare of the Southern white; the slave thief would have been in position, with the assistance of his captives, to carry out his plans of the highwayman with organized method.[63]

Capital punishment was thus perceived as a necessary deterrent because of the high value placed upon slave property.

As a part of the reform of the criminal law in the nineteenth century, however, the penalties for slave stealing were generally reduced to fines and imprisonment.[64] Nevertheless, slave stealing was still considered to be a dangerous crime. The statutes thus provided that the crime of slave stealing could be committed by slaves or free persons.[65] Theft generally was held to exist if the defendant sought to expropriate the slave for his own use—as prohibited by the common law of larceny. In addition, the statutes made it a crime for the defendant to steal a slave with the intent to carry the slave to a free state—an offense that was held not to constitute common law larency.[66]

Southern statutes also prohibited the harboring or concealing of slaves belonging to another. The penalties for harboring were generally less severe than stealing. Nevertheless, the intentional aiding of a runaway or stolen slave was a serious crime in the South.[67] Henry explained this offense as follows:

> Closely akin to the stealing of slaves was the "harboring" of slaves. The presumption in harboring seems to have been that it was an effort to deprive the master temporarily of the services of his slave. Then harboring was somewhat like assisting him to runaway or becoming an accessory before the fact of slave stealing.[68]

Thus, the statutes strove to protect slave property from theft. Antebellum court decisions also expressed concerns about slave stealing.

The judicial concern for the master's interest is revealed by the 1812 South Carolina case of *Robinson v. Culp*.[69] The plaintiff was a slave owner who sued the defendant in an action on the case, alleging theft of the plaintiff's slave by the defendant. The trial judge instructed the jury that the offense of slave stealing was a felony by statute; therefore, the civil action must follow a felony prosecution.

On appeal, the majority disagreed. The opinion by Judge Abraham Nott recognized the maser's interest in his slave property and upheld the owner's election to first seek a civil remedy. It is worth noting that Judge O'Neall applied this holding and reasoning in an 1833 case of cow killing.[70] Obviously, there was little perceived difference in law between slaves and cows, at least in Judge O'Neall's reasoning as it was applied in these cases.

The master's right to use self-help to recover stolen slaves was limited by the 1845 case of *State v. Curtis*.[71] the opinion by Chief Justice Catron disapproved of the master's right to breach the peace and recover his slaves. Slave stealing was a serious offense; the court could not, therefore, condone the alleged owner's acts of "breaking the house, and committing a violent outrage on the defendant Marshall's house and family[.]"[72] Masters had a right to be secure in the possession of their slaves. This right was vigorously enforced by the Southern lawmakers. By doing so, however, the slave's property status was further emphasized.

It is significant and symbolic that the Southern lawmakers did not analogize slave abductions with kidnapping. That crime is generally defined in American law as the unlawful taking and carrying away of a human being by force and against his will. At common law, the crime was a misdemeanor.[73] The legislators made slave stealing a felony, but did so by adapting property crimes, such as larceny, not the common law crime of kidnapping, which required that the victim be a person whose will was violated. Slaves could have no such will.

The law would have had to amend kidnapping for cases involving slaves to require that the abduction be against the master's will, not the will of the slave. Obviously, a slave could not be a willing victim for an escape to freedom or to a new master. Nevertheless, the lawmakers did not view slave stealing as a crime against the slave's person; instead, slave theft was seen as a property crime when it was perceived through the lens of slave relations. In contrast, the New Jersey kidnapping statute of 1796 included the stealing of a person—whether bond or free—within the crime of kidnapping of a person. In the South, however, the crime of slave stealing was viewed as a more serious property crime, and it had attached to it more severe penalties than kidnapping.[74]

The Southern lawmakers did not equate slave stealing with the crime of abduction, either. That ancient English statutory felony was the forcible capture of an heiress for profit through her property that would be acquired by marriage. That offense was concerned with protecting the rights of the heirs of the abducted woman. Although abduction reflected the woman's second-class status as a person, she still was viewed as a person. The abduction had to be against her will.[75] Slaves were not persons, and the law did not recognize their will. Thus, slave theft was viewed explicitly as a property crime.

## *Conclusion*

The business law of slavery obviously is entitled to take its rightful place next to the antebellum law of the North. This brief sketch shows how this neglected area of law confirms the slave as a legal nullity, except as a pawn in the battle between his oppressors. We must be careful not to have our own conceptions warped so that we fail to see this fundamental truth about the master and slave relationship as it was reflected in law, and as that legal reality was reflected back on society.

Indeed, the eloquent words of William Chambers, a visiting Scotsman, highlight this social and legal reality. After witnessing a typical slave auction that was held in Richmond, Virginia, in 1853, Chambers described his feelings:

> I had never until now seen human beings sold; the thing was quite new. Two men are standing on an elevated bench, one white and the other black. The white man is auctioning the black man. What a contrast in look and relative position! The white is a most respectable-looking person; so far as dress is concerned, he might pass for a clergyman or church-warden . . . Beside him is a man with black skin, and clothed in rough garments. His looks are downcast and submissive. He is being sold, just like a horse at Tattersall's, or a picture at Christie and Manson's—I must be under some illusion. That dark object, whom I have been always taught to consider a man, is not a man. True, he may be called a man in advertisements, and by the mouth of auctioneers. *But it is only a figure of speech*—a term of convenience. He is a man in one sense, and not in another. He is a kind of man—stands upright on two legs, has hands to work, wears clothes, can cook his food (a point not reached by monkeys), has the command of speech, and, in a way, can think and act like a rational creature—can even be taught to read. But nature has thought fit to give him a black skin, and that tells very badly against him. Perhaps, also, there is something wrong with his craniological development. Being, at all events, so much of a man—genus *homo*—is it quite fair to master him, and sell him, exactly as suits your convenience—you being, from a variety of fortunate circumstances, his superior? All this passed through my mind as I sat on the front form in the saleroom of Messrs _____, while one of the members of that well-known firm was engaged in pursuing, by the laws of Virginia, his legitimate calling.[76]

Chambers thus understood the futility of thinking of slaves as people, except as a figure of speech. Legally and socially, it was considered normal and necessary that slaves were bought and sold, much like horses and art objects.

Slave theft, moreover, reveals how the notion of "humanity" was skewed in the South, as it was applied to slaves. The courts could not admit that slaves were humans who could be kidnapped. Instead, the law held that bondsmen were chattels whose "humanity" posed a unique problem for the law of theft. The perverted notion of slave "humanity" is also evident in the law that developed concerning the separation of slave families.

# NOTES

1. *See*, Higginbotham, *supra* at 11-12.
2. Recent studies include, Judith Schafer, "'Guaranteed Against the Vices and Maladies Prescribed by Law': Consumer Protection, the Law of Slave Sales, and the Louisiana Supreme Court, 1809–1862," 31 *American Journal of Legal History* 306 (1987); Paul Finkelman, "Slaves as Fellow Servants: Ideology, Law & Industrialization," 31 *American Journal of Legal History* 269 (1987) (hereinafter cited as "Slaves as Fellow Servants"); Andrew Fede, "Legal Protection for Slave Buyers in the U.S. South: A Caveat Concerning *Caveat Emptor*," 31 *American Journal of Legal History* 322 (1987); Thomas D. Morris, "Society is Not Marked by Punctuality in the Payment of Debts: The Chattel Mortgage of Slaves," in *Ambivalent Legacy: A Legal History of the South* 147–170 (Jackson, 1984) (hereinafter cited as "Morris"); David J. Langum, "The Role of Intellect and Fortuity in Legal Change: An Incident from the Law of Slavery," 28 *American Journal of Legal History* 1 (1984); Thomas D. Morris, "'As if the Injury was Effected by the Natural Elements of Air or Fire': Slave Wrongs and the Liability of Masters," 16 *Legal & Society Review* 567 (1982); Kiely, *supra* at 876–894; John E. Stealey, "The Responsibilities and Liabilities of the Bailee of Slave Labor in Virginia," 12 *American Journal of Legal History* 336 (1968); *see, also*, Tushnet, *supra* at 158–159.
3. *Compare*, Hall, *supra* at 119–122, 134–136, comparing aspects of Southern and Northern commercial law, *with*, Horwitz, *supra*, which generally omits Southern law.
4. Stroud, *supra* at 33 [footnote omitted] [emphasis in original].
5. *See*, Documentary History, *supra* at 137–172; Goodell, *supra* at 44–62; Stowe, *supra* at 257–305; Stroud, *supra* at 33–88. *See, also*, Wheeler, *supra* at 107–151 (compiling pre-1838 cases).
6. *See, generally, e.g.*, 5A Arthur Corbin, *Corbin on Contracts* § 1143 (St. Paul, 1964).
7. *See, e.g., Pruitt v. Graziano*, 215 N.J. Super. 330, 521 A. 2d 1313 (App. Div. 1987).
8. 1 John N. Pomeroy, *A Treatise of Equity Jurisprudence* § 221(b) at 381 (Spencer Symons, ed., Rochester, 5th ed. 1941) [footnote and emphasis omitted].
9. *See, e.g., Blake v. Flatley*, 44 N.J. Eq. 228 (E. & A. 1888) (specific performance denied because of the low purchase price).
10. *Centex Homes v. Boag*, 128 N.J. Super. 385, 389, 320 A. 2d 194, 196 (Ch. Div. 1974). [Citations omitted].
11. *See*, Corbin, *supra* § 1146 at p. 153–154. For a recent discussion of specific performance, *see*, Anthony Kronman, "Specific Performance," 45 *University of Chicago Law Review* 351 (1978).
12. *See*, Kiely, *supra* at 888; *compare*, Tushnet, *supra* at 158–169.
13. 54 Va. 162, 13 Gratt. 404 (1856).
14. *Id.*, 54 Va. at 170, 13 Gratt. at 404–405.
15. *Id.*, 13 Gratt. at 405–406.
16. The court cited an alternative ground for the holding. This was based upon the inability to calculate damages for the widowhood of Mrs. Summers.

The court found that reference to "tables of longevity" would provide a result that was too uncertain. See, *Id.*, 54 Va. at 174–175, 13 Gratt. 418–419. This was another reason why the plaintiff's remedy at law was inadequate. But the court wrote at much greater length about the other ground discussed *infra*.

17. *Id.*, 54 Va. at 172, 13 Gratt. at 410–412.
18. *Id.*
19. *Id.*, 54 Va. at 172, 13 Gratt. at 412–413.
20. *Id.*, 54 Va. at 174, 13 Gratt. at 418.
21. *See, Id.*, 54 Va. at 173–174, 13 Gratt. at 413–418.
22. *See,* for South Carolina, *e.g., Young v. Burton,* 16 S.C. Eq. 109, 1 McMul. 255 (1841); North Carolina, *e.g., Williams v. Howard,* 7 N.C. 59, 3 Mur. 74 (1819); Mississippi, *e.g., Murphy v. Clark,* 9 Miss. 81, 1 S. & M. 221 (1843); Tennessee, *e.g., Loftin v. Epsy,* 12 Tenn. (4 Yerg.) 84 (1833); Arkansas, *Sanders v. Sanders,* 20 Ark. 610 (1859); Missouri, *Beaupied v. Jennings,* 28 Mo. 254 (1859); *see, generally,* Kiely, *supra* at 886–894 for a discussion of the development of this rule.
23. *See, e.g., Baker v. Rowan,* 2 S. & P. 361, 369–372 (Ala. 1830); *Caldwell v. Myers,* 3 Ky. (Hardin) 560 (1808); *Mallery v. Dudley,* 4 Ga. 52, 65–67 (1848). The Kentucky courts adhered to the English rule. The *Baker* decision was a holding in favor of equitable relief; thus, its "rule" is *dictum. Mallery* presents the most interesting case. Professor Kiely notes that that decision may have been influenced by a statute that allowed slave owners a right to summary recovery of slaves wrongfully taken. *See,* Kiely, *supra* at 894 n. 166. Indeed, in the *Mallery* decision Joseph Lumpkin notes this. *See, Mallery v. Dudley, supra* at 67. Moreover, Lumpkin states he favors a requirement that a party seeking specific performance "prove peculiar circumstances," because "in a majority of the suits instituted for the recovery of slaves, humanity to both races requires that there should not be a *specific delivery.*" *Id.* at 66. Lumpkin was referring to cases in which a mortgagor, years after default, seeks to redeem slaves. *Id.* This issue is discussed in Morris, *supra* note 2.
24. *See, Summers v. Bean, supra,* 54 Va. at 173–174, 13 Gratt. at 414–418; *see, also,* Tushnet, *supra* at 158–169 for a discussion of these cases.
25. *See, Summers v. Bean, supra* at 174, 13 Gratt. at 418.
26. *See,* Freyer, "Law and the Antebellum Southern Economy: An Interpretation," in *Ambivalent Legacy, supra* at 56–58.
27. *See,* Kiely, *supra* at 884–885.
28. *See, Id.* Thomas D. Morris writes about the ways slave owners used the courts of equity to enforce chattel mortgages in slaves, the owner being the debtor. Morris concludes that the Southern courts generally favored slave owners by finding transactions to be mortgages, rather than conditional sales that would result in a forfeiture of the owners equity in the slave. Thus, the mortgagor could redeem his chattel by paying off the debt. But by the late antebellum years, the courts and legislatures put time limitations on the redemption rights. *See,* Morris, *supra,* note 2.
29. *See, Summers v. Bean, supra* at 174, 13 Gratt. at 418.
30. *See,* Kiely, *supra* at 890.
31. *See, Id.*

32. *See, Id.* at 894.
33. *See,* Fede—1987, *supra; see, also,* Schafer, *supra* for Louisiana and Watson, *supra* at 48–53.
34. *See,* Peter Linzer, "On the Amorality of Contract Remedies—Efficiency, Equity and the Second Restatement," 81 *Columbia Law Review* 111, 126–139 (1981).
35. *See,* Tushnet, *supra* at 166.
36. *See, Id.* at 167 [emphasis supplied].
37. *Id.* at 169.
38. 32 S.C.L. 223, 1 Strob. 525 (1847).
39. *Id.* at 234, 1 Strob. at 550.
40. *Id.*
41. *See,* Tushnet, *supra* at 3–6.
42. 14 Ga. 137 (1853).
43. *Id.* at 143.
44. *Id.*
45. *See,* Tushnet, *supra* at 5.
46. *See, Id.*
47. *See, Lennard v. Boynton,* 11 Ga. 109 (1852).
48. *Id.* at 113.
49. *See, Scudder v. Woodbridge,* 1 Ga. 195 (1846).
50. *Id.* at 198 [emphasis in original].
51. *Id.* at 199 [emphasis in original].
52. *See,* Langum, *supra passim.*
53. *See,* "Slaves as Fellow Servants," *supra* at 289–291.
54. 51 N.C. (6 Jones) 245 (1848).
55. The last two paragraphs are adapted from Fede-1984, *supra* at 310. *See, generally,* Robert S. Starobin, *Industrial Slavery in the Old South* 128–137 (New York, 1970) on industrial slavery.
56. *See,* O'Neall, *supra* at 17.
57. *See,* The 1754 Act is *quoted in, State v. McCoy,* 29 S.C.L. 295, 297, 2 Speers 711, 715–716 (1844).
58. *Id.* at 297, 2 Speers at 716.
59. *See, generally,* LaFave, *supra* at 631–633.
60. *State v. McCoy, supra,* 29 S.C.L. at 297, 2 Speers at 716–717, *citing, State v. Miles,* 11 S.C.L. 1, 2 Nott & McC. 1 (1819).
61. *See, Negro in Tennessee, supra,* at 45, Henry, *supra* at 109.
62. *See, Negro in Tennessee, supra* at 44, Note, "Justice on the Tennessee Frontier: The Williamson County Circuit Court 1810–1820," 32 *Vanderbilt Law Review* 413, 440 (1979).
63. *See,* Henry, *supra* at 108.
64. *See,* Henry, *supra* at 108–114. For the statutes in various states, *see, e.g.,* for Tennessee, *State v. Curtis,* 24 Tenn. (5 Hum.) 601, 603 (1845) (*quoting in,* 1835 act); *Marshall v. Penington,* 16 Tenn. (8 Yer.) 424, 429 (1835) (*quoting* a 1799 act); for Maryland, *see,* Goodell, *supra* at 233, Brackett, *supra* at 79–81; for Virginia, *Commonwealth v. Peas,* 31 Va. 1080, 4 Leigh 692, 43 Va. 503, 2 Gratt. 629 (1834); for Alabama, *Mooney v. State,* 8 Ala. 328, 331 (1845) and Sellers, *supra* at 276; for Texas, Campbell, *supra* at 101; for North

Carolina, *Young v. McDaniel*, 50 N.C. 111, 5 Jones 103 (1857) (under 1856 Code Ch. 34 § 81) and *Dark v. Marsh*, 4 N.C. 214, 2 Car. L. Rep. 249 (1815) (under act of 1791); for Mississippi, *Slavery in Mississippi, supra* at 105–106, 160.

65. *See*, Goodell, *supra* at 232; O'Neall, *supra* at 30; *State v. Whyte*, 11 S.C.L. 71, 2 Nott & McC. 174 (1819).

66. *See, State v. Hawkins*, 8 Port. 461 (Ala. 1838).

67. *See*, Wheeler, *supra* at 442–443 n.* for citations to various statutes; *see, also*, for Alabama, *McElhaney v. State*, 24 Ala. 71 (1854); for Georgia, *Cook v. State*, 26 Ga. 593 (1858); for Texas, Campbell, *supra* at 101–102 and *Scott v. State*, 26 Tex. 116 (1861); for South Carolina, Henry, *supra* at 114.

68. *See, Id.*

69. 6 S.C.L. 68, 1 Tread. 231 (1812).

70. *See, Cannon v. Burris*, 19 S.C.L. 149, 150, 1 Hill 372, 373 (1833).

71. 24 Tenn. (5 Hum.) 601 (1845).

72. *Id.* at 431–432.

73. *See, generally, Black's Law Dictionary* 781 (5th ed. 1979), 51 *C.J.S.* "Kidnapping" § 1(a) (1967). The common law definition required that the victim be taken out of the country, and in the United States, removal from the state was sufficient. *See, Id., State v. Gibbs*, 79 N.J. Super. 315, 323–324, 191 A. 2d 495, 499 (App. Div. 1963).

74. *See, Id.* at 323, 191 A. 2d at 499. The New Jersey statute provided for a $1,000 fine and/or 5 years' imprisonment.

75. *See, e.g., State v. Johnson*, 67 N.J. Super. 414, 419–420, 170 A. 2d 830, 833–834 (App. Div. 1961).

76. *Documentary History, supra* at 150, *quoting*, William Chambers, *Things As They Are in America* (Philadelphia, 1854) [emphasis added].

## CHAPTER 11

# The Impotence of Slave Humanity as an Impediment to the Separation of Slave Families

**THE SEPARATION** of slave families was possibly the most inhumane aspect of chattel slavery. Slaves were denied the right to material possessions, education, satisfying and self-motivated labor, self-improvement, and social mobility. All they had were their family ties and their religious beliefs. Nevertheless, they could be wrenched from their families when it suited their master's whim. Except in a few limited instances, the slave family was subject to the inhumanity of instant destruction.

Historian Frederic Bancroft explained the fragility of the slave family:

> Virtually everybody preferred to be humane, according to Southern standards, when it was not financially disadvantageous or inconvenient to be so. Persons whose interests led them to be otherwise naturally wished to conceal the fact or tried to place the blame elsewhere, for there was no respectability without at least the appearance of being humane. But slavery maintained as a profitable and convenient institution was essentially ruthless in general and inhumane in some of its main features.
>
> Neither marriage nor fatherhood among slaves was legally recognized because recognition would have gravely interfered with property rights; and the legal prohibitions against dividing families were very slight. Whatever recognition family relations received was, with few exceptions, voluntary.[1]

Indeed, the "few exceptions" to the general rule illustrate two points of great importance. First, the lawmakers did permit masters and others great discretion in separating slave families; and, second, by doing so, the law closed its eyes to the obvious inhumanity of allowing *any* separation at all.

John Anthony Scott discussed the importance of slave family life:

> If the family was . . . important for white Americans, how much more crucial a role ought it to have played in the lives of black Americans! Black people had been torn forcibly from Africa, and their tribal and family organizations had been shattered or left behind. In facing the harsh American world they would need—much more than whites—the protection of whatever new family ties they could create.

Scott also observed that:

> the family, after all, is a form of social organization. It gives its members protection; it endows them with the power to struggle; it knits them with a bond of blood; and it endows them, when necessary, with a passion for revenge.[2]

Thus, the emotional pain caused by the division of slave families must be kept in focus when the legal limitations are assessed for their "humanity." Before we can evaluate the law of family separation, however, we must review the historical background on the frequency of slave sales and the ways that families could be divided. Only then can the legal materials be evaluated for their "humanity."

## *The Frequency of the Division of Slave Families and the Ways Division Took Place*

Historians have long debated the issue of the frequency of the separation of slave family members in the antebellum South. Indeed, there is evidence that many slave owners were reluctant to separate slave families; nevertheless, all serious students of slavery admit that slave families, in some number, were the subject of division.[3] The difficult questions are: How often did slaves face the indignity of family separation, and how much separation was "humane"? According to Herbert Gutman and Richard Sutch, an antebellum slave with a thirty-five-year life expectancy had a 49.3 percent to 70.8 percent risk of sale in his or her lifetime. Marriages, with an average twenty-four-year duration, had a 29 percent chance of a breakup because of the sale of a slave.[4] The separation of children from the family was even more likely to happen.

This is because children over the age of twelve were considered "single" slaves for the purposes of sale. Thus, the separation of a child that young from his parents and siblings was perceived to be the norm in the South. Michael Tadman estimates that, in the Upper South, the percentage of antebellum children separated from their parents was "almost one in two." Fogel and Engerman estimate that 9.3 percent of the slaves sold in the New Orleans' slave market were children under the age of twelve.[5] Thus, the market limited only the sale of very young children away from their mothers. Bancroft observed that, "As a rule, the dividing line between children that were worth more with their mothers and those who were worth more without them was at about eight years of age."[6] Obviously, the concern was that a young child separated from its mother might die. This simple fact of animal husbandry flows from the long period of dependency that young children have upon their parents. In addition, the lack of work that an infant could do for its owner was apparently considered by the market that fixed the slave prices.

The market, of course, was merely the reflection of the attitudes of slave buyers and sellers. In realty, the division of slave family members did take place with some frequency when slaves who were husband and wife were separated, when children were sold from their parents, and when aunts, uncles, cousins, and grandparents were severed from their kin. This separation happened in several ways. First, and most obvious, was the sale by the master of any slave kin, if the master owned the entire slave family.

Slave masters had the legal right to buy and sell slaves, and they exercised this privilege in direct transactions between themselves.[7] Moreover, the business of slave trading was an important Southern industry that included African trade and domestic intrastate and interstate transactions. Domestic slave trade became more significant in the antebellum South after the legal African trade was closed in 1808 and while soil exhaustion in the Old South and the cotton boom in the Deep South created the relative oversupply of slave labor in the former states and undersupply in the developing Southwest. Consequently, between 1790 and 1860 large numbers of slaves were involuntary migrants from the Old South to the cotton producing states, and interstate slave trading contributed to the southward flow of slave chattels.[8]

The ubiquitous slave trader was an important actor in a large number of interstate and intrastate transactions, including both private sales and public auctions.[9] Bancroft argued that slave owners thought that the slave trading class included unscrupulous individuals as well as men who built up profitable and respectable businesses that were, at least in part, devoted to interstate slave trade. Accordingly, slave owners had ambivalent attitudes toward slave traders. Some traders were despised because of their sharp practices and were the "scapegoats" of the system, while others achieved a degree of respectability.[10]

Nevertheless, Kenneth Stampp observed that:

> The majority of slaveholders agreed that only the most calamitous circumstances could justify dealings with professional traders. In fact, it was hard to find a master who would admit that he sold slaves as a deliberate "speculation"—a business transaction whose object was a profit—rather than an unhappy last resort.[11]

Thus, Stampp contended that most masters sold slaves only if they had an excess number, if they needed to divide an estate, or if slaves were used to secure a loan the master could not pay.[12] Michael Tadman challenges this interpretation. He concludes that "speculative sales and family separations" were "central both to the realities of the Old South and to the myth-making in which its white citizens so lavishly indulged."[13] Moreover, Norrece Jones shows that slave owners sold slaves to rid themselves of "recalcitrant and incorrigible bondsmen," and used the potential for sale as a threat to keep slaves in line.[14] Consequently, sales between masters and transactions involving traders were not unheard of, and these transactions were potential sources for the division of families.

The second example of family division took place because slave families were often dispersed among numerous owners in a local area. In such a case, slaves could maintain some contact with their relatives. Even these ties could be broken if a master moved with his slaves to another state, and thus severed the familial ties of his slaves. This, no doubt, happened often in the great antebellum migration of owners and slaves from the Upper South to the Deep South.[15]

A third case of separation arose when the will of an owner specifically devised various slaves to different heirs. Separation could also take place when slaves were part of the residuary of an estate, which had to be divided or sold.[16]

A fourth instance of the division of slave families occurred in credit transactions. When slaves were mortgaged by the owner, families could be separated when slaves were taken in satisfaction of the mortgage.[17]

The fifth example took place when slaves were the subject of execution by a judgment creditor of an owner. Slave families could be torn apart if the master failed to pay his debts or was insolvent.[18]

## The Role of the Law

The obvious inquiry is whether, in these five instances of potential family division, the law preserved the slave family or lent its legitimacy to the division of families. On the whole, the courts and legislatures legitimated the master's right to divide families. Despite occasional references to concern for slave humanity, this area of law shows how the range of possible legal limitations was narrowed by the perceived dictates of slave society.[19]

This is most clear from the almost unlimited power that masters had to sell their slaves during the owner's lifetime. Louisiana was the only state that regulated *inter vivos* sales. An 1829 provision prohibited the sale of children separately from their mothers when the children had not "attained the full age of ten years."[20] No common law state limited the master's right to sell off slave children. Obviously, there was logic for the ten-year limitation based upon the market value of children and the principles of animal husbandry. Harriet Beecher Stowe also questioned how this law could have been enforced in light of the fact that slaves had no right to sue an offender in court, no could they testify.[21] It is significant to note that, in effect, this statute legitimized all sales of slaves who were ten years old or older.

Therefore, even in Louisiana, wives could be sold from husbands, and young teenagers could be ripped from their mother's care. As Gutman and Sutch point out, "Any child, including an unmarried teenager, sold from his parents counts as evidence of the breakup of a *slave family*."[22] These authors quote Frederick Douglass to show how the sales of slaves over the age of ten from their families were inhumane and were distinguishable from the decisions of white teenagers to leave home and set out on a new life. Douglass explained the slave's trauma as follows:

> The people of the north, and free people generally, I think, have less attachment to the places where they are born and brought up, than have the slaves. Their freedom to go and come, to be here and there, as they list, prevents any extravagant attachment to any one particular place, in their case. On the other hand, the slave is a fixture; he has no choice, no goal, no destination; but is pegged down to a single spot, and must take root here, or nowhere. The idea of removal elsewhere, comes, generally, in the shape of a threat, and in punishment of crime. It is, therefore, attended with fear and dread. A slave seldom thinks of bettering his condition by being sold, and hence he looks upon separation from his native place, with none of the enthusiasm which animates the bosoms of young freemen, when they contemplate a life in the far west, or in some distant country where they intend to rise to wealth and distinction. Nor can those from whom they separate, give them up with that cheerfulness with which friends and relations yield each other up, when they feel that it is for the good of the departing one that he is removed from his native place. Then, too, there is correspondence, and there is, at least, the hope of reunion, because reunion is possible. But, with the slave, all these mitigating circumstances are wanting. There is no

improvement in his condition probable,—no correspondence possible,—no reunion attainable. His going out into the world, is like a living man going into the tomb, who, with open eyes, sees himself buried out of sight and hearing of wife, children and friends of kindred tie.[23]

*A fortiori*, the spectre of separation must have been many times more terrifying in the states that did not bar sales of children under ten.

Some masters did refrain from separating young children from their mothers. The point is that the law did not require this humanity. In fact, numerous cases upheld the owner's right to sell his slaves. In a Kentucky case, two masters owned the two mothers of young children separately from the children. This separation came about because Kentucky law condoned all slave sales. The owners agreed, however, to swap the children so that the youngsters could be with their mothers. This humane gesture was aborted when one slave child died. The Kentucky Supreme Court held that the living child had to be turned over to its rightful owner and taken away from its mother. This was because the switch was only a bailment that terminated upon the election of the master who had possession of the slave that died.[24] Such were the limits of the humanity embodied in the law. Indeed, Frederic Bancroft recites numerous examples of sales of young children as single slaves. The law saw no inhumanity in this.[25]

Nor did the law in Louisiana or elsewhere declare that the separation of husband and wife was inhumane. No statute or case sought to regulate or limit the master's whim to break up a slave marriage. The attitude of the lawmakers is hard to ascertain in the absence of legal enactments. The words of Thomas Cobb provide insight, however. Cobb called for limitations on the separation of families "by the officers of the law, in cases of sales made by the authority of the Courts, such as the Sheriffs' and administrators' sales."[26] Nevertheless, Cobb did not question the masters' *inter vivos* right to divide families, and wrote in favor of this right:

> [T]o fasten upon a master of a female slave, a vicious, corrupting negro, sowing discord, and dissatisfaction among all his slaves; or else a thief, or a cut-throat, and to provide no relief against such a nuisance, would be to make the holding of slaves a curse to the master.[27]

Indeed, it was of no relevance to Cobb that slavery was a curse on the slave. Moreover, the master did not need a good faith reason to wish to be rid of a slave. Economics or mere whim could be the legitimate reasons that motivated a sale of a husband from a wife in all of the Southern states.

Masters were also free to divide their slaves as they chose by will. Therefore, after the master's death, slave families could be split up without any limit if the master's specific bequests called for separation.[28]

The courts had no effect on these family divisions unless they were called upon to interpret ambiguous will provisions concerning the children of slaves. One typical fact pattern arose when a master bequeathed a female slave and her increase to a named heir. An issue that arose was whether children born after the execution of the will but before the death of the testator, went with their mother or were a part of the residuary of the master's estate. The courts in Virginia held that after born children were included in the specific devise. In an 1809 case, the three judge High Court of Chancery so decided. There were three opinions. The opinion of Judge Spencer Roane does state that the will's ambiguity should be resolved in favor of "humanity," to "prevent the separation of children from their mother."[29] The other two members of the court—St. George Tucker and William Fleming—agreed with this result but without reference to "humanity." Instead, they looked to evidence of the master's intent.[30]

Another relevant case is *Gayle v. Cunningham*,[31] an 1824 decision of the South Carolina Equity Court of Appeals. The issue was whether a child born after a will was executed was included in a bequest of the mother, when the bequest did not explicitly mention the slave's increase. Chancellor De Saussure held that the child should pass with the mother, in an opinion joined by Chancellors Waites and Thompson. De Saussure held that a contrary result "would separate even sucking infants; for in most cases of legacies, the children would be young." He concluded that "humanity and policy combine to recommend the principle upon which I decree, of partus sequitur ventrem." Thus, he applied the civil law rule that the child's status followed the mother.

It is worth noting, however, how the Chancellor viewed the relevant interests. He wrote that the separation of young children from their mothers

> would be revolting; we cannot therefore be called upon in a doubtful case, to decide in such a way. Sound policy, as well as humanity, requires that everything should be done to reconcile these unhappy beings to their lot, by keeping mothers and children together. By cherishing their domestic ties, you have an additional and powerful hold on their feelings and security for their good conduct. As a question of property, it is unimportant how the rule is settled, for it will operate alike on all. Since then, our statute of 1740 established the general principle that the issue of female slaves shall follow the condition of the mother; that principle should govern every case where, as in the present, there is nothing to constitute a lawful or reasonable exception.[32]

Thus, pragmatic concerns for slave control were combined with the notion of humanity.

Nevertheless, Chancellor Theodore Gaillard dissented. He wrote that an "inquiry into the civil law on this subject" was unnecessary. He found that the testator could have amended the will to refer to the after-born child and did not; therefore, the court should not so hold. Gaillard noted that "the inhumanity of separation, may so hold. Gaillard noted that "the inhumanity of separation, may make us wish that the law were otherwise; but what the law is and what it ought to be, are very different considerations[.]" He opined that the law of South Carolina, unlike the *Code Noir*, did not prohibit the separation of families. He concluded that children could pass with their mother only if they were accessories, and reasoned:

> According to Domat, an accessory of a thing bequeathed, which not being a part of the thing itself, has, nevertheless, a connection with it, will pass with the thing. The shoes of a horse will pass with the horse, and the frame of a picture with the picture; it is in relation to their use that accessories are connected with principal things bequeathed. In this respect, children are not connected with the mother.[33]

Chancellor William D. James wrote an opinion agreeing with Gaillard.[34]

In the 1832 decision in *Tidyman v. Rose*,[35] the Court of Appeals went out of its way to overrule *Gayle v. Cunningham*. The opinion of Judge Harper had the concurrence of Judges Johnson and O'Neall. Harper noted first that the rule in *Gayle* caused dissatisfaction in the public and the legal profession. He called the rule of that case "a departure from the most firmly settled principles," and he concluded that the *Gayle* decision "constitute[s] an anomaly in our system[.]"[36]

Harper's reasoning is as follows:

> The true principle is a very simple and obvious one. Nothing passes under a bequest but what is included under the description of the subject of the bequest. We are not to conjecture a man to have given what he has not expressed his intention to give.[37]

Harper stated that the *Gayle* holding might apply if the child was "an infant, to whom the care of the mother may be still necessary[.]"[38] In the *Tidyman* case, the children were of full age; nevertheless, Harper's opinion sweeps with a broad brush:

> Weight has properly been attributed to what is said by Sir Samuel Romilly, in the case of Norris vs. Harrison, 2 Mad. R. 481: "Suppose a female slave is bequeathed, and she has afterwards a son, who grows up to man's estate, and then testator dies, does the bequest

of the mother pass the son? or if a mare be bequeathed, which afterwards has a foal that grows up to a horse, and then testator dies, does the gift of the mare pass also the horse? Surely not." The expressions of Sir Samuel Romilly, are clear with respect to the son grown to manhood, or the colt grown to a horse; and there may be room to conjecture from his words, that a different rule would obtain, if they were still in infancy of immaturity. This is no more, however, than vague conjecture. The cases of Haynesworth vs. Cox, and Gayle vs. Cunningham, however, make no distinction of this sort, and it might be inferred from them, that though the children were grown up, or had families of their own, all must still pass under the bequest of the female ancestor. And indeed, by what authority could we make a distinction, and lay down any rule on the subject. Shall we say, that when the son has arrived at full manhood, he shall no longer pass as accessory to the mother? or at the age of puberty, when the parent's superintendence may be less necessary? or at the age of weaning, when the mother's care may be supposed no longer indispensable? In this uncertainty, we have only to resort to the rule of our own law, that nothing shall pass, which was not intended to be given. Considerations of humanity might be of weight in a doubtful case, but apart from the decisions in question, I cannot regard this as a doubtful case. It is little that legal decisions can and I do not fear that a single infant will be left to perish by being prematurely separated from its mother, in consequence of our present determination.[38]

Consequently, the court would rely on the owners of slaves to wait until infants could be safely separated from their mothers; this was all that humanity required, and it was the same rule that applied to horses.

Harper continued:

> The maxim "partus sequitur ventrem," applies to the condition of these persons as slaves or free. It is a rule of property also, so far as to indicate, that the owner of the mother, and not of the father, shall be entitled to the children; but it can have no application to a disposition made by the owner, both of the parents and the children.

> The principal case of Norris vs. Harrison may serve to illustrate the rule, that the time of the testament is to be regarded in determining what passes under the bequest. In that case, the testator bequeathed £11,000 Bank Stock. After the making of the will, the Bank, under the authority of an Act of Parliament, in respect of profits accumulated, declared an additional capital, by which the Stock was increased to £13,760, and it was held, that the additional £2,750, did not pass under the bequest.[39]

The analogy between slaves and stock was also found to be persuasive. This approach was upheld in numerous cases thereafter.[40]

In a related legal issue, the courts generally held that in the case of a life estate or an estate for a term, the increase of a female slave born during that estate went to the remainderman, not the "temporary owner."[41] The courts of Maryland dissented from this rule.[42] But it was elsewhere held that children should not be separated from their mothers at the end of the term of the estate in question. The policy behind this rule was considered by Chancellor De Saussure in the 1816 case of *Milledge v. Lamar*.[43]

De Saussure stated the issue thus:

> The question to be examined is, who is entitled to the issue of female slaves, where there is no positive disposition made; the tenant for life, or any other particular estate, (the usufructuarius,) or the remainder man or reversioner, (the proprietarius.)?[44]

He then quoted Blackstone and other authorities for the rule that the usufructuarius was only "the temporary right of using a thing, without having the ultimate property or full dominion of the substance[.]"[45] He also noted that the civil law distinguished the offspring of slaves, who went to the remainderman, with the increase of farm animals, which were held by the temporary owner.[46]

The court examined the policy behind this rule and stated that "one cannot prevent the considerations of humanity from migling in the judgment." He considered the two arguments that were made, stating that it was alleged on the "one hand,"

> that if the right of property in the issue be not given to the usufructuary, he would not be led by the strong temptation of interest, to take care of the helpless infants, who would rather be burthensome and expensive to him for many years, besides the loss of service of the mother during her pregnancy, and some time after;—whence it is inferred that humanity would be promoted by bestowing the right of property on the usufructuary.

> On the other hand it is alleged, that if the absolute right of property be decided to be in the usufructuary, and that the issue of the female shalt not go over to the remainder man, or ultimate proprietor, there will be a cruel and painful separation of the children, even those at the breast, from their parents.

The court reconciled these arguments as follows:

> There is weight in both views of the case; but there is more I think in the latter. The separation would be a great and certain evil. The

> want of care in the usufructuary, if deprived of the absolute right of property in the issue, might occur in a few cases; but we may trust in general to the humanity of the possessors, and more to the attention of the mothers themselves. On this ground then, I think the consideration of humanity is in favor of the adoption of the civil law rule. To this it may be added, that the remainder man, who is ultimately the main object of the bounty of the testator or donor, would, if the intermediate estate should be protracted, considerably, as is frequently the case, receive only an infirm and broken set of laborers, if the usufructuary were to keep the issue.[47]

Consequently, policy prevailed in the name of humanity.

The slave was a capital asset. Her value came from the work she performed. Unlike most income-producing assets, however, the slave could reproduce herself. Thus, the majority rule allowed the life tenant, or temporary owner, the right to the slave's labor. The remainderman received the slave's increase, however, so that he could, in the future, also profit from slave labor. This rule made economic sense, despite the reference to humanity made by the Chancellor.

It must be recalled that these cases did not limit the master's right to devise children separately from their parents. The only issue was how the ambiguous statements of the master's intent would be interpreted. Even if the expressed concern for slave humanity in these cases is real, the limits of this notion of humanity must be obvious. The devisee or remainderman who obtained the mother and her increase had the power to immediately sell the offspring without any limit in all the Southern states, except Louisiana, and in that state he need only wait until the child reached the age of ten, or fabricate the child's birth date if the need for cash was so pressing.

Estate sales and sales pursuant to an execution or attachment by a creditor of a master also provided the potential for the division of slave families. In Georgia, the legislature did not regulate execution sales but forbade administrators, executors, or other fiduciaries from separating children not above the age of eight from their mothers. Nor could husbands or wives be sold separately, in those instances, if the "marriage" was recognized by the master and the husband and wife were owned by the same master.[48] The Alabama slave code also contained a limitation similar to the Georgia statute:

> § 2057. In all sales of slaves under any decree, or order of the chancery or probate court, or under any deed of trust, or power of sale in a mortgage, the slaves must be offered, and, if practicable, sold in families; unless affidavit be made, as required in the preceding section, and delivered to the officer, or other person, having the charge or management of such sale.

The preceding section stated:

> § 2056. No execution can be levied on a child, or children, under the age of ten years, without including the mother; or upon the mother, without including the child, or children, as aforesaid, if living, and belonging to the defendant in execution; and the mother and child, or children, must be sold together, unless the parties in interest, or one of them, make affidavit and delivers the same to the officer, that he believes his interest will be materially prejudiced, by selling the slaves together, when they may be sold separately; but no levy or sale shall be made, by which a child under five years of age shall be separated from its mother.[49]

Bancroft analyzed that statutory scheme as such:

> At first blush, the Alabama law seems to have had some substantial humanity in it. It forbade levying any execution on a child under ten years of age without including the mother, if living, (and *vice versa*); and they must be sold together *unless* a party in interest made affidavit that his interest would be materially prejudiced. In this case they might be sold separately, unless the child was under five years of age. And "in all sales of slaves under any decree, or order of the chancery or probate court, or under any deed of trust, or power of sale in a mortgage, the slaves must be offered, and, if practicable, sold in families [i.e., the mother and her young offspring]; unless" some party in interest made affidavit that selling them together would be to his material disadvantage. Thus not humanity but expectation of profit or loss was the criterion.[50]

Indeed, humanity took a back seat to economics. Bancroft also discussed a Mississippi statute:

> Mississippi provided, as part of its law to exempt from seizure under execution or attachment certain kinds of property supposed to be required for the owner's welfare, that if a debtor should elect to retain a female slave, then she and also her children while under six years of age should be exempt. This latter provision, much like the exemption of a growing crop, was evidently to prevent a sacrifice of the debtor-master's interest—not to give special protection to the slaves.[51]

In fact, the Mississippi statute allowed slaves to be part of a "homestead" exemption that protected the debtor-masters rights against creditors.[52]

As Bancroft wrote, "Not one of these provisions . . . in any way referred to or hampered the *owner of unencumbered* slave property: he might sell or pawn or mortgage or give [his slaves] away according to profit or whim, regardless of age or kinship."[53] In the other states, moreover, there was no statutory limit regarding the separation of slaves in court, estate, or other involuntary sales. The courts were also divided as to whether they should limit or control these sales and estate divisions. In the 1801 Virginia case of *Fitzhugh v. Foote*,[54] the court held that the equal division of an estate pursuant to a will did not require the separation of infants and their mothers, if money adjustments could equalize the values. The court states, "an equal division of slaves, in number or value, is not always possible and sometimes improper, when it cannot be exactly done without separating infant children from their mothers, which humanity forbids, and will not be countenanced by a Court of Equity."[55] The courts were reluctant to extend the notion of humanity any further, however. Only young children were kept with their mothers in such sales.[56]

The courts did not favor large sales in masses of slaves, as such a sale might decrease the overall value. This view was lucidly explained by Thomas Ruffin in an 1830 case.[57] Ruffin referred to the sale of four boys who were directed to be sold under a will. The boys were brothers, and at the time of the sale they ranged in age from eight to four. They were purchased in one lot for $1,025.[58]

Judge Ruffin commented on this sale:

> The Court does not favor sales by executors in large masses . . . Sometimes, indeed, as much, or more, can be had, when the property is disposed of in one, than more parcels, as in the instance of a *family* of slaves, when children are *all* of tender years.

Ruffin cautioned, however, that a fiduciary who makes a sale in gross "does it at his peril, and must answer for the true value" if an inadequate price is obtained.

Ruffin acknowledged that it "would certainly have been harsh to separate these four boys, and sever ties which bind even slaves together." Nevertheless, Ruffin stated that this "must be done, if the executor discovers that the interest of the estate required it; for he is not to indulge his charities at the expense of others."[59] Thus, Ruffin's analysis is similar to the Alabama statute cited above. The interests of the heirs and creditors of an owner always gave way to the charity "owed" to the slaves.

This approach is also evident in the law of slave mortgages. Thomas D. Morris cites the case of *Lee v. Fellowes & Co.*,[60] in his study of slave mortgage law. In that 1849 opinion:

> The court rules that sales of mortgaged [slave] property under execution could not be sold in gross . . . A sale in gross (i.e., of all the slaves together) could, of course, preserve the family and personal relations of those involved. In the view of the court, however, "a sale

in gross would be often detrimental to the best interests of the debtor and creditor. . . ."⁶¹

Therefore, the court ordered that the sale in gross be set aside so that the slaves could be sold individually.

Consequently, when mortgaged slaves were sold, the potential for family division was great. Morris cites the *Lee* case as an example of "the blunted morality created by a social system resting upon slavery." He also states that, in mortgage law, "case after case refers to a thirteen-year-old girl, a ten-year-old boy, or other minors."⁶² Indeed, this law could be viewed as humane only through the filter of a "blunted morality."

This peculiar morality is further illustrated by the rule that was applied to the mortgage of a female slave who gave birth to offspring during the term of the mortgage. According to the general rule, the child of the mortgaged slave was included in the lien of the mortgage. Therefore, the status of the children followed the mother, under the doctrine of *partus sequitur ventrem*.⁶³ In a Maryland case, the court actually stated that this rule of law was humane:

> [W]e are happy to find that in this instance, the law of the land, and the law of nature, so far from being at variance, are in perfect harmony; and that whilst on the one hand, full and ample justice will be administered to the honest creditor, the claims and feelings of nature will not be violated on the other.⁶⁴

The notion of humanity had been so perverted that the use of people as pawns in credit transactions was not seen as *a priori* inhumane and unnatural.

It is also important to note that this rule of "nature" was recognized as being consistent with the claims of an honest creditor. In fact, the same rule was applied to mortgages given on farm animals. A mortgage on stock was held to apply to the increase of the stock if the debtor owned the mother.⁶⁵ Thus, the rule that applied to livestock also applied to slaves. In both instances, the law was designed to protect the creditor's expectations; it was not, in either case, a rule of humanity. Moreover, the idea of humanity was used here, and elsewhere, to mask the inherent inhumanity in the very idea of laws that treated slaves like farm animals and other chattels.

## The Failure of Reform

A few Southerners saw through the rhetoric of the fictional humanity of this law. In fact, some called for laws recognizing slave families and marriages. These efforts were largely unsuccessful.[66]

One proposal was made by John B. O'Neall. He noted that slaves were "treated as other personal chattels, so far as related to questions of property, or liability to the payment of debts." His proposal was as follows:

> In consequence of this slight character which they bear in legal estimation, as compared with real estate, (which has itself, in our State, become of too easy disposition,) slaves are subjected to continual change—they are sold and given by their masters without writing; they are sold by administrators and executors, and by the sheriff, (and may even be sold by constables.) These public sales by administrators, executors or the sheriff, may be for payment of debts or partition—they (slaves) are often sold under the order of the Ordinary, without any inquiry, whether it be necessary for payment of debts or division. This continual change of the relations of master and slave, with the consequent rending of family ties among them, has induced me to think, that if by law, they were annexed the freeholds of their owners, and when sold for partition among distributees, tenants in common, joint tenants and coparceners, they should be sold with wholesome change of the law. Some provision, too, might be made, which would prevent, in a great degree, sales for debts. A debtor's lands and slaves, instead of being sold, might be sequestered until, like *vivum vadium* they would pay all of his debts in execution, by the annual profits. If this should be impossible on account of the amount of the indebtedness, then either court, law or equity, might be empowered to order the sale of the plantation and slaves together or separately; the slaves to be sold in families.[67]

Thus, O'Neall called for stability in slave families; slaves would become a "fixture" on the plantation, and would be bought and sold with the land in gross.

This reform proposal was not entirely novel. Stroud pointed out that the *Code Noir* prohibited the selling of a husband without his wife and children without their parents.[68] Stroud also quoted Stephen for the idea that, in the "Old World" slaves could not be seized and sold separately from the soil they cultivated. This was because

> Plantation slaves, not only in the Spanish and Portuguese, but in the French colonies also, are *real estate*, and attached to the soil they cultivate, partaking therewith all the restraints upon voluntary alienation to which the possessor of the land is there liable; and they cannot be seized or sold by creditors for satisfaction of the debts of the owner.[69]

These reforms were rejected as being unnecessarily humane in the antebellum South.

As Eugene Genovese observed:

> [P]roposals concerning protection of family life evoked more praise than censure across the South, but most of all they evoked silence. The slaveholders understood that such reforms threatened the economic viability of capital and labor markets. No other issue so clearly exposed the hybrid nature of the regime; so clearly pitted economic interest against paternalism and defined the limits beyond which the one could not reinforce the other.[70]

Indeed, the rejection of reform revealed how the dictates of the economic interests of the slave owners robbed the Southerner's notion of humanity of its normal meaning.

Stanley Elkins considered this process in his analysis of the slave family and marriage relations. He stated that the law "destroyed" the "most ancient and intimate of institutional arrangements, marriage and the family[.]" Thus, Elkins wrote that "the law never showed any inclination to rehabilitate [the family]." Elkins also stated:

> Here was the area in which considerations of humanity might be expected most widely to prevail, and, indeed, there is every reason to suppose that on an informal daily basis they did: the contempt in which respectable society held the slave trader, who separated mother from child and husband from wife, is proverbial in Southern lore.[71]

Nevertheless, Elkins noted that this proverbial contempt for the slave trader was not translated into significant limitations on the master's power to separate families.

Elkins explained this failing as follows:

> On the face of things, it ought to have been simple enough to translate this strong social sentiment into the appropriate legal enactments, which might systematically have guaranteed the inviolability of the family and the sanctity of the marriage bond, such as governed Christian polity everywhere. Yet the very nature of the plantation economy and the way in which the basic arrangements of Southern life radiated from it, made it inconceivable that the law should tolerate any ambiguity, should the painful clash between humanity and property interest ever occur. Any restrictions on the separate sale of slaves would have been reflected immediately in the market; their price would have dropped considerably. Thus the law could permit no aspect of the slave's conjugal state to have an independent legal existence outside the power of the man who owned him[.][72]

Michael Tadman argues that the master's distaste for the trader, speculation, and the separation of families was a part of the "myth-making" of the South. He concludes that racism and the image of the hated trader were combined in the minds of the white Southerners to justify the separation of families and their speculation in slave flesh.[73] Elkins and Tadman correctly suggest that the plantation economy created social conditions that compelled masters and lawmakers to mask and reify the oppression of slavery. Their definition of humanity was therefore limited by these dictates of economics and perceptions of the possible. Thus, the reformer's words fell on deaf ears.

## *Conclusion*

No matter how many slaves were actually divided from their kin, *all* slaves had to live with the fear of the "potential for forced separation[.]"[74] This inhumanity was perceived by some masters. There were owners who did show respect for the families of their slaves.[75] But there is also evidence that some pro-slavery theorists denied the slave's ability to forge familial ties. The black's racial inferiority, according to Harper, included his "want of domestic affections, and insensibility to the ties of kindred."[76] Thomas Dew argued that there were "hundreds of slaves" who would desert their families "to follow a kind master—so strong is the tie of master and slave."[77] George Sawyer also observed that "the 'options of parental and kindred attachment' did not 'grow in the negro's bosom.'"[78]

Whether these insensitive views were held by the minority or the majority of slave owners, the law sided with the pro-slavery view. It denied the inhumanity of slave family division and did so in the name of humanity.

## NOTES

1. Bancroft, *supra* at 197.
2. Scott, *supra* at 93. *See, also, e.g.*, on slave family ties, Oaks-1990, *supra* at 148–151; Herbert G. Gutman, *The Black Family in Slavery and Freedom, 1750–1925* (New York, 1976). For a discussion of the literature on the slave family, *see*, Fogel, *supra* at 162–168.

3. *See, e.g.*, Michael Tadman, *Speculators and Slaves: Master Traders & Slaves in the Old South* 133–178, 211 (Madison, 1989); Fogel & Engerman, *supra* at 47–58; Genovese, *supra* at 451–458; Stampp, *supra*, 229–230.

4. Herbert Gutman and Richard Sutch, "The Slave Family: Protected Agent of Capitalist Masters or Victim of the Slave Trade," in *Reckoning with Slavery*, *supra* at 110–111, 127; *see, also*, on marriage breakups, Tadman, *supra* at 170–171; Fogel, *supra* at 152; Gutman, *supra* at 144–155; *see, generally, e.g.*, Peter Kolchin, *Unfree Labor: American Slavery and Russian Serfdom* 114–120 (Cambridge, 1987); John W. Blassingame, *The Slave Community: Plantation Life in the Antebellum South* 89–92 (New York, 1972).

5. *See*, Tadman, *supra* at 172; Fogel & Engerman, *supra* at 49–52; *see, also*, Gutman, *supra* at 129–138; Gutman and Sutch, *supra* at 129–130; Bancroft, *supra* at 199–214.

6. *Id.* at 197; *see, also*, Gutman and Sutch, *supra* at 158–160.

7. *See*, Stampp, *supra* at 237. The following three paragraphs are adapted from Fede—1987, *supra* at 329–330.

8. *See*, Tadman, *supra* at 3–108; Bancroft, *supra* at 1–18, 382–406. For a general discussion of slave trading, *see*, Patterson, *supra* at 146–166.

9. *See*, Phillips, *supra* at 155–159; William Calderhead, "The Role of the Professional Slave Trader in a Slave Economy: Austin Woolfolk, A Case Study," 23 *Civil War History* 195 (1977); T.D. Clark, "The Slave Trade Between Kentucky and the Cotton Kingdom," 21 *Mississippi Valley Historical Review* 331 (1934); *see, also*, Patterson, *supra* at 365.

10. *See*, Bancroft, *supra* at 365–381. Bancroft notes the social status and wealth of the most successful traders. *See, Id.* at 186–191, 234; *See, also*, Tadman, *supra* at 179–-210.

11. Stampp, *supra* at 240.

12. *See, Id.* at 241; *see, also*, Fogel & Engerman, *supra* at 55.

13. *See*, Tadman, *supra* at 211.

14. Norrece T. Jones, Jr., *Born a Child of Freedom, Yet a Slave: Mechanisms of Control and Strategies of Resistance in Antebellum South Carolina* 38, 41–43 (Hanover, 1990).

15. *See*, Gutman & Sutch, *supra* at 94–105; *see, also*, Goodell, *supra* at 44–62; Stroud, *supra* at 33–34. Historians disagree as to the extent that this migration of slaves was caused by sales, rather than masters moving west with their slaves. *Compare*, Fogel & Engerman, *supra* 48–55; William Calderhead, "How Extensive Was the Boarder State Slave Trade? A New Look," 18 *Civil War History* 42 (1972); *with*, Tadman, *supra* at 11–46, and 237–247; Gutman & Sutch, *supra* at 99–110. A related issue is whether masters were systematic slave breeders. *Compare*, Tadman, *supra* at 121–129; Fogel & Engerman, *supra* at 78–86, with, Herbert Gutman and Richard Sutch, "Victorians All? The Sexual Mores and Conduct of Slaves and Their Masters," in *Reckoning with Slavery*, *supra* at 154–161; Richard Sutch, "The Breeding of Slaves for Sale and the Westward Expansion of Slavery, 1850–1860," in *Race and Slavery in the Western Hemisphere: Quantitative Studies* 173–210 (Stanley Engerman and Eugene Genovese, eds., Princeton, 1975); Stampp, *supra* at 245–251.

16. *See,* Goodell, *supra* at 68–76; Stroud, *supra* at 33–34.
17. *See,* Stroud, *supra* at 33–34; Morris, *supra* at 151–164.
18. *See,* Goodell, *supra* at 63–68; Stroud, *supra* at 34–36; Wheeler, *supra* at 41–42, n*.
19. *See, e.g.,* Stampp, *supra* at 199–201.
20. *See,* Tadman, *supra* at 142, n. 14; Stowe, *supra* at 125; *see, also,* Bancroft, *supra* at 197–198.
21. *See,* Stowe, *supra* at 175–176.
22. Gutman & Sutch, *supra* at 132.
23. *Id.* at 132–133, *quoting,* Frederick Douglas, *My Bondage and My Freedom* 176–177 (New York, 1855). [Emphasis omitted].
24. *See, Willis v. Willis' Administrators,* 36 Ky. (6 Dana) 48 (1837).
25. *See,* Bancroft, *supra* at 208–214; *see, also,* Tadman, *supra* at 171–172; Gutman & Sutch, *supra* at 129–132.
26. Cobb, *supra* at 246.
27. *Id.*
28. *See, e.g., Bank's Ad'm v. Marksberry,* 13 Ky. (3 Litt.) 275, 280 (1823).
29. *See, Reno's Executors v. Davis,* 14 Va. 889, 892, 4 Hen & M. 283, 291 (1809).
30. *See, Id.* at 290–293, 4 Hen & M. at 891–892; *see, also, Puller's Executors v. Puller,* 24 Va. 482, 3 Rand. 83 (1824) (Judges Brooke and Cabell held devise of slave woman and increase included children alive at the time the will was written; Coalter, J., dissented).
31. 5 S.C. Eq. 54, Harp. Eq. 124 (1824).
32. *See, Id.* at 56, Harp. Eq. at 129.
33. *See, Id.,* Harp. Eq. at 130–131.
34. *Id.* at 56–57, Harp. Eq. at 131–132.
35. 9 S.C. Eq. 118, Rich. Cas. 294 (1832).
36. *Id.* at 120, Rich. Cas. at 297.
37. *Id.*
38. *See, Id.* at 121, Rich. Cas. at 300.
39. *Id.,* Rich. Cas. at 300–301.
40. *See, e.g., Boyd v. Satterwhite,* 33 S.C. Eq. 99, 12 Rich. Eq. 487 (1866) (devise of slave and increase does not include children born before will); *Donald v. Dendy,* 27 S.C.L. 52, 2 McMul. 123 (1841) (same); *Donald v. McCord,* 14 S.C. Eq. 140, Rice Eq. 330 (1839) (same); *Seibels v. Whatley,* 11 S.C. Eq. 299, 2 Hill Eq. 605 (1837) (same); *Murphy v. Riggs,* 8 Ky. (1 A.K. Marsh.) 532 (1819).
41. *See, Id.* at 533–534; *see, also, e.g., Erwin v. Kilpatrick,* 10 N.C. (2 Hawk.) 456 (1825); *Milledge v. Lamar,* 4 S.C. Eq. 247, 4 Des. 617 (1816); *Ellis v. Shell,* 4 S.C. Eq. 245, 4 Des. 611 (1815); *Glasgow v. Flowers,* 2 N.C. 304, 1 Hayw. 233 (1795); *Timms v. Patter,* 1 N.C. (Mart.) 8 (178-).
42. *See, e.g., Stanford v. Amoss,* 1 H & J. 526 (Md. 1804).
43. 4 S.C. Eq. 247, 4 Des. 617 (1816).
44. *Id.* at 256, 4 Des. at 640.
45. *Id.*
46. *See, Id.,* 4 Des. at 640–641.

47. *Id.* at 256–257, 4 Des. at 641–642. The Court of Appeals in Equity affirmed this decision in 1817. *See, Id.*, 4 S.C. Eq. 258, 4 Des. 645.
48. *See,* Bancroft, *supra* at 198–199.
49. *See, Documentary History, supra* at 189.
50. Bancroft, *supra* at 198 [footnote omitted].
51. *Id.* [footnote omitted].
52. Homestead exemption laws allow the head of a household to designate certain property as a "homestead" that is free from execution for general debts. *See, Black's Law Dictionary* 661 (5th ed. 1979).
53. Bancroft, *supra* at 199.
54. 7 Va. 427, 3 Call 13 (1801).
55. *Id.* at 428, 2 Call at 17.
56. *See, e.g., Lawrence v. Speed,* 5 Ky. (2 Bibb.) 401 (1811) (execution sale, child 2 or 3 sold with mother to further humanity).
57. *Cannon v. Jenkings,* 16 N.C. (1 Dev. Eq.) 422 (1830).
58. *Id.* at 422–426.
59. *Id.* at 426.
60. 49 Ky. (10 B. Mon.) 117 (1849).
61. *See,* Morris, *supra* at 163.
62. *See, Id.*
63. *See, Id.* at 161, *citing Boner v. Mahle,* 3 La. Ann. 600 (1848); *Evans v. Merriken,* 8 G. & J. 39 (Md. 1836); *Hughes v. Graves,* 11 Ky. (1 Litt.) 317 (1822); *see, also, Fowler v. Merrill,* 52 U.S. (11 How.) 375, 396, 13 L. Ed. 736, 744 (1850).
64. *Evans v. Merriken, supra,* 8 G. & J. at 49–50.
65. *See, e.g., Cumberland Bank v. Barker,* 57 N.J. Eq. 569, 41 A. 704 (Ch. 1898) (referring to parallel between animals and slaves and relying on *Fowler v. Merrill, supra*), 14 *C.J.S.* "Chattel Mortgages," § 121 (1939), 11 *C.J.* "Chattel Mortgages" §§ 171–172 (1917), *Annot.*, "Chattel Mortgage on Livestock as Including Increase," 39 *A.L.R.* 153 (1925).
66. *See,* Genovese, *supra* at 52–53, 69.
67. *See,* O'Neall, *supra* at 18; *see, also,* Morris, *supra* at 149 stating that under the *vadium vivum,* "the creditor took possession of the property and used its profits to pay off the debt." The *vadium mortuum,* or mortgage, allowed the creditor to take possession of the property on default.
68. Stroud, *supra* at 34.
69. *Id.* at 35.
70. Genovese, *supra* at 53.
71. Elkins, *supra* at 53.
72. *Id.* at 53–54.
73. *See,* Tadman, *supra* at 211–221.
74. Genovese, *supra* at 457.
75. *See,* Gutman, *supra* at 284–290; Genovese, *supra* at 452–455; Stampp, *supra* at 229–231.
76. Harper, in *The Pro-Slavery Argument, supra* at 56.
77. Thomas R. Dew, "Professor Dew on Slavery," in *The Pro-Slavery Argument, supra* at 457, note*.
78. *See,* Gutman, *supra* at 292; *see, also,* Tadman, *supra* at 212–216.

# Chapter 12

# Conclusion: The Reification of Humanity

**In the** United States South, slaves were chattels who were the objects of right, but could not be the bearers of any legal rights. Because of the nature of the master-and-slave relation, however, slaves had to be recognized as people when the criminal law imposed upon them extra-human duties. This mixture of legal concepts epitomized the "despotism" of slavery.[1]

Furthermore, the oppression of slavery so warped the legal minds of the antebellum South that phrases such as slave "humanity" and slave "rights" came to express—in legal terms—the slave's economic value, and to define the relative rights and duties of the slave's white oppressors. Slave law was merely an expression of the conflicting interests of whites that were embodied in slaves. Thus, the notions of slave rights and humanity became reifications.

Reification is the substitution of an abstract and positive word or idea in the place of the complex reality of oppressive personal relations.[2] The work of Robert Gordon provides a helpful analysis:

> "Law" is just one among many . . . systems of meaning people construct in order to deal with one of the most threatening aspects of social existence: the danger posed by other people, whose cooperation is indispensable to us . . ., but who may kill us or enslave us.[3]

Slave owners already had enslaved their bondsmen; their obvious concern was to preserve their dominant position over their slaves as well as poor whites, whose cooperation was indispensable. These lower classes could, of course, combine and rebel.

Because of these perceived threats, Gordon states that legal "belief structures," along with economic and political ones, are constructed by the elites to rationalize "their dominant power positions[.]" These belief systems "define rights" in ways that reinforce "existing hierarchies of wealth and privilege." This the master class did with the pro-slavery ideology and the law of slavery. The ideology of the

South, through racism, denied the slave's humanity. Similarly, the law defined slaves as chattels to cut them off from all claims to the ordinary rights enjoyed by humanity. These were the "belief structures" that the Southern elites constructed to rationalize their dominant position.

Gordon states, more importantly, that these systems of belief make "the social world as it is come to seem natural and inevitable." This occurs when people "externalize" beliefs by attributing "to them existence and control over and above human choice; and, moreover [people] believe that these structures must be the way they are."[4] Thus, Gordon concludes that reification

> is a way people have of manufacturing necessity: they build structures, then act as if (and genuinely come to believe) that the structures they have built are determined by history, human nature, [and] economic law.[5]

Accordingly, Southerners believed that the law of slavery was determined by history, human nature, and economic law. With this belief, they rationalized the inhumanity of slavery. They thought they were merely acting out the perceived dictates of the reality that they had, nevertheless, created.

The definition of slaves as property was the key to the belief system of the law of slavery. It rendered all references to slave "right" and "humanity" into rationalizations that masked the total oppression of slavery. For example, in *Jones v. Carper*,[6] an 1857 Tennessee case, the Supreme Court rejected the idea that a master could be denied his right to sue the perpetrator of a battery against his slave. The opinion states that the deprivation of this privilege would "ignore the plainest principles of reason and of right," and "would be justly esteemed a reproach to humanity in any condition of civil society above the level of barbarism."[7] According to Michael Flanigan, this language "demonstrated how slavery could warp the values of the slaveholders. Civil suits to recompense masters for the value of the labor or lives of their slaves did not reduce but instead encouraged 'barbarism.'"[8] Indeed, the "barbarism" of slavery was reified because the court's references to humanity and right helped to obscure the oppression of the fundamentals of the master and slave relation.

Moreover, Southerners thought that the law of slavery had to be as it was. Thus, they believed the law allowing the division of slave families was as humane as it could be and as it ought to be. The elite's eyes were closed to the possibility that a humane law would—at the very least—protect the slave family from division and sale. Slave masters and the lawmakers comforted themselves with the idea

## Conclusion: The Reification of Humanity

that they had no choice but to allow the separation of families in almost all instances. Therefore, the reformer's suggestions fell on deaf ears.

Accordingly, references in law to slave right and humanity did mask the real purposes of slave law. Justice Wardlaw demystified the notions of slave humanity and right when he wrote that the law, to the slave, was "only a compact between his rulers."[9] This was also the case even when the law regulated the slave master's right to kill, abuse, starve, sell, and emancipate his slaves. Alan Watson writes that the main object of Roman slave law was the need "to maximize the benefits of slavery for the owner."[10] The master's right to free and to abuse slaves required regulation, however, to promote the public welfare. As to slave abuse, Watson states, "violence and punishment may seem to give the master greater satisfaction. But an unfettered freedom for masters to act cruelly to their slaves is bad for the members of the free society, not just morally but also economically, since resentment among slaves may lead to repercussions."[11] This analysis is also true for the U.S. South.

Watson notes further that this view was known to the Roman jurists. He quotes Gaius as follows, "For it is to the advantage of the state that no one use his property badly."[12] Similarly, interests other than humanitarianism motivated the lawmakers in the United States South. This is why concern for slave rights and humanity is an interest that is left out of the list of relevant interests implicated by slave law, as set forth in Chapter Two.

The concept of slave rights or slave humanity is not ignored in this analysis. Rather, invocations of these terms are seen as camouflage that served to disguise the real interests implicated in slave law, as well as the inherent inhumanity of slavery. The law regarding white liability for slave abuse provides an initial example.

In the nineteenth century, the criminal liability of white slave abusers increased. Here, Southern lawmakers often wrote of protecting slave rights, but they did not afford slaves the full protection of the common law; whites were always granted some rights to physically abuse slaves with impunity in the interest of slave control. The lawmakers thus used the terminology of the common law of crimes to create crimes against slave property to protect the master class interest in slaves and to regulate the rights of white strangers to damage slaves. Moreover, these crimes also represented a legal expression of the master class hostility toward poor whites and overseers.

Therefore, the lawmakers struck a different balance of the relevant interests over time in reference to the scope of violence whites could legally inflict on slaves. Nevertheless, they never afforded slaves with the status of "persons"; they merely used the common law terminology to create new crimes against property and in support of the power and authority of the master class. Slaves were never equated with free white people when issues of personal safety were raised. The reified language in the cases allowed masters and lawmakers to obscure the oppressive nature of this legitimation of violence.

The courts also expanded the trial rights of slaves in the nineteenth century. In the colonial era, the slave codes denied bondsmen accused of crimes the protection of the common law procedural rights although masters were afforded the right to compensation when slaves were punished for criminal conduct. The heightened procedural protections in slave trials were put in place as the number of capital offenses that slaves faced grew, and as slave property values rose, in real terms. Accordingly, it is logical to conclude that slave masters and lawmakers came to believe that the state owed slave owners greater procedural safeguards before they were deprived of rights in such valuable property.

Nevertheless, the cases and statutes concerning slave trials cannot be reconciled based upon concern for slave rights because slaves were not afforded all of the common law's rights. Even in the nineteenth century, the substantive and procedural criminal law discriminated against slaves. If slaves were considered to be real people, the lawmakers could have applied the established criminal law to slaves without deviation. This was not done, however, because slaves were viewed as being unworthy of the equal protection of the law.[13]

Simply put, then, slave law was "created by the South," and was fundamentally inhumane when it is compared to the common law that it supplanted.[14] Even the antebellum slave law legitimized the violence and inhumanity that was inherent in slavery. This law appears inhumane not only when it is compared with an ideal of justice, or even modern law, but also when it is compared with the common law that it replaced. Indeed, notions of slave rights and humanity became reified, so that they helped hide these simple truths. Nevertheless, Justice Taney, Judges Wardlaw and Ruffin, and the abolitionists saw through the fiction of slave rights. They recognized the pervasive reality of the "despotism" that lawyers, judges, and legislators legitimized in the name of law, justice, right, and humanity.[15]

# NOTES

1. *See*, Stowe, *supra* at 233.
2. *See, generally*, Louis B. Schwartz, "With Gun and Camera Through Darkest CLS-Land," 36 *Stanford Law Review* 413, 442 (1984) for a non-C.L.S. analysis. *See, e.g.*, Peter Gabel, "Reification to Legal Reasoning," in 3 *Research in Law and Sociology* 25–51 (Stephen Spitzer, ed., Greenwich, Ct., 1980) and Kelman, *supra* at 269–275 for C.L.S. discussions.
3. Robert W. Gordon, "New Developments in Legal Theory," in *The Politics of Law: A Progressive Critique* 288 (David Kairys, ed., New York, 1982).
4. *Id.*
5. *Id.* at 289.
6. 36 Tenn. (4 Sneed) 279 (1857).
7. *See, Id.* at 285, *quoted in*, Flanigan, *supra* at 171.
8. *Id.*
9. *Ex parte Boyleston*, 33 S.C.L. 20, 21, 2 Strob. 41, 43 (1847).
10. *See*, Watson, *supra* at 1.
11. *Id.* at 2. Watson attributes the origin of this observation to Plato. *Id.*
12. *Id.* at 120.
13. Some may call this a harsh indictment of slave law and the lawmakers. As noted in Chapter 1, there are other possible interpretations. In fact, Mark Tushnet as employed the Critical Legal Studies analysis to arrive at a very different interpretation. *See*, Fede-1984, *supra* at 303–311 for a discussion of Tushnet's views and a critique.
14. *See*, John Anthony Scott, "Book Review," *Challenge* 65, 66–67 (May–June 1975) [emphasis omitted]. Scott adds;

> To argue that slaves fled from this cruel system of law into the waiting arms of paternalistic "protectors" is to fly in the face of historical facts. The "protectors" after all, were the very ones who had set the law up, who supported it, and who continued to benefit from its operation.

*Id.*

15. *See*, Richard Hildreth, *Despotism in America; An Inquiry into the Nature, Results and Legal Basis of the Slave-Holding System in the United States* 169-177 (New York, 1970, reprint ed.) (1854) for an analysis of these issues.

# Selected Bibliography of Secondary Sources

## Books

Ayres, Edward L. *Vengeance and Justice: Crime and Punishment in the 19th Century American South.* New York, 1984.

Blassingame, John W. *The Slave Community: Plantation Life in the Antebellum South.* New York, 1972.

Brackett, Jeffrey R. *The Negro in Maryland. A Study of the Institution of Slavery.* 1889. Reprint: New York, 1969.

Breen, T.H., and Stephen Innes. *"Myne Owne Ground." Race and Freedom in Virginia's Eastern Shore 1640–1676.* New York, 1980.

Bruce, Dickson D., Jr. *Violence and Culture in the Antebellum South.* Austin, Texas, 1979.

Campbell, Randolph B. *The Peculiar Institution in Texas 1821–1865.* Baton Rouge, 1989.

Catterall, Helen T. *Judical Cases Concerning American Slavery and the Negro.* 1926. Reprint: New York, 1968.

Cobb, Thomas R.R. *An Inquiry Into the Law of Negro Slavery in the United States of America.* 1858. Reprint: New York, 1968.

Cover, Robert. *Justice Accused: Antislavery and the Judicial Process.* New Haven, 1975.

Davis, David Brion. *The Problem of Slavery in the Age of Revolution 1770–1823.* Ithaca, 1975.

———. *The Problem of Slavery in Western Culture.* Ithaca, 1966.

Eaton, Clement. *The History of the Old South: The Emergence of a Reluctant Nation.* 3rd ed. New York, 1975.

Elkins, Stanley M. *Slavery: A Problem in American Institutional Life.* 3rd ed. Chicago, 1976.

Finkelman, Paul. *The Law of Freedom and Bondage: A Casebook.* New York, 1986.

———. *An Imperfect Union: Slavery, Federalism, and Comity.* Chapel Hill, 1981.

Finley, M.I. *Ancient Slavery and Modern Ideology.* New York, 1980.

Fitzhugh, George. *Cannibals All! or Slaves Without Masters.* 1857. Reprint: Cambridge, 1960.

Flanigan, Daniel. *The Criminal Law of Slavery and Freedom 1800–1868.* New York, 1987.
Fogel, Robert W. *Without Consent or Contract: The Rise and Fall of American Slavery.* New York, 1989.
Fogel, Robert W., and Stanley L. Engerman. *Time on the Cross: The Economics of American Negro Slavery.* Boston, 1974.
Fox-Genovese, Elizabeth, and Eugene Genovese. *Fruits of Merchant Capital: Slavery and Bourgeois Property in the Rise and Expansion of Capitalism.* New York, 1983.
Franklin, John H. *The Militant South 1800–1861.* Cambridge, 1956.
Friedman, Lawrence M. *A History of American Law.* 2nd ed. New York, 1985.
Genovese, Eugene D. *Roll, Jordan, Roll: The World the Slaves Made.* New York, 1974.
———. *The World the Slaveholders Made: Two Essays in Interpretation.* New York, 1969.
———. *The Political Economy of Slavery: Studies in the Economy and Society of the Slave South.* New York, 1961.
Goodell, William. *The American Slave Code.* 1853. Reprint: New York, 1968.
Gray, Lewis C. *History of Agriculture in the Southern United States to 1860.* 1932. Reprint: Washington, D.C., 1958.
Gutman, Herbert G. *The Black Family in Slavery and Freedom, 1750–1925.* New York, 1976.
———. *Slavery and the Numbers Game: A Critique of "Time on the Cross."* Urbana, 1975.
Hall, Kermit, ed. *American Legal History: Cases and Materials.* New York, 1991.
———. *The Magic Mirror: Law in American History.* New York, 1989.
Hening, William W., ed. *Statutes at Large of Virginia.* Richmond, Va., 1809–1823.
Henry, Howell Meadoes. *The Police Control of the Slave in South Carolina.* 1914. Reprint: New York, 1968.
Higginbotham, A. Leon. *In the Matter of Color: Race and the American Legal Process: The Colonial Period.* New York, 1978.
Hildreth, Richard. *Despotism in America: An Inquiry Into the Slave-Holding System in the United States.* 1854. Reprint: New York, 1970.
Hindus, Michael S. *Prison and Plantation: Crime, Justice, and Authority in Massachusetts and South Carolina, 1767–1878.* Chapel Hill, 1980.
Hoffer, Peter, ed. *American Legal Records: Criminal Proceedings in Colonial Virginia.* Athens, Ga., 1984.
Horwitz, Morton. *The Transformation of American Law, 1780–1860.* Cambridge, 1977.
Howington, Arthur. *What Sayeth the Law: The Treatment of Slaves and Free Blacks in the State and Local Courts of Tennessee.* New York, 1986.
Hurd, John C. *The Law of Freedom and Bondage in the United States.* 1862. Reprint: New York, 1968.
Hurst, J. Willard. *The Growth of American Law: The Law Makers.* Boston, 1950.

Jones, Norrece T., Jr. *Born of Freedom, Yet a Slave: Mechanisms of Control and Strategies of Resistance in Antebellum South Carolina.* Hanover, N.H., 1990.
Jordan, Winthrop. *White Over Black: American Attitudes Toward the Negro, 1550–1812.* Chapel Hill, 1968.
Klein, Herbert S. *Slavery in the Americas: A Comparative Study of Virginia and Cuba.* New York, 1946.
Kolchin, Peter. *Unfree Labor: American Slavery and Russian Serfdom* Cambridge, 1987.
La Fave, Wayne, and Austin W. Scott, Jr. *Handbook on Criminal Law.* St. Paul, 1972.
Lewis, Ronald L. *Coal, Iron and Slaves: Industrial Slavery in Maryland and Virginia, 1715–1865.* Westport, Ct., 1979.
Llewellyn, Karl N. *The Bramble Bush: On Our Law and Its Study.* New York, 1930.
Meier, A., and E. Rudwick. *From Plantation to Ghetto.* 3rd ed. New York, 1976.
Morgan, Edmund S. *American Slavery American Freedom: The Ordeal of Colonial Virginia.* New York, 1975.
Morrison, Samuel E. *The Oxford History of the American People.* New York, 1972.
Nash, Roderick R. *The Rights of Nature: A History of Environmental Ethics* Madison, Wisc., 1989.
Oakes, James. *Slavery and Freedom: An Interpretation of the Old South.* New York, 1990.
———. *The Ruling Race: A History of American Slaveholders.* New York, 1982.
O'Neall, John B. *The Negro Law of South Carolina.* Columbia, S.C., 1848.
Patterson, Caleb. *The Negro in Tennessee, 1790–1865.* 1922. Reprint: New York, 1968.
Patterson, Orlando. *Slavery and Social Death: A Comparative Study.* Cambridge, 1982.
Phillips, U.B. *American Negro Slavery.* 1918. Reprint: Baton Rouge, 1966.
———. *The Slave Economy of the Old South: Selected Essays in Economic and Social History*, edited by E. Genovese. Baton Rouge, 1968.
Prosser, William L. *Handbook of the Law of Torts.* 4th ed. St. Paul, 1971.
Rose, Willie Lee. *Slavery and Freedom.* New York, 1982.
———. *A Documentary History of Slavery in North America.* New York, 1976.
Rosengarten, Theodore. *Tombee: Portrait of a Cotton Planter.* New York, 1986.
Scarborough, William C. *The Overseer: Plantation Management in the Old South.* Baton Rouge, 1966.
Schwarz, Philip J. *Twice Condemned: Slaves and the Criminal Law of Virginia, 1705–1865.* Baton Rouge, 1988.
Scott, John A. *Hard Trials on My Way: Slavery and the Struggle Against It, 1800–1860.* New York, 1974.
Sellers, James. *Slavery in Alabama.* 2d ed., University, Alabama, 1964.
Sobel, Mechel. *The World They Made Together: Black and White Values in Eighteenth Century Virginia.* Princeton, 1987.

Spindel, Donna J. *Crime and Society in North Carolina, 1663–1776*. Baton Rouge, 1989.
Stampp, Kenneth M. *The Peculiar Institution: Slavery in the Antebellum South*. New York, 1956.
Starobin, Robert S. *Industrial Slavery in the Old South*. New York, 1970.
Stowe, Harriet Beecher. *The Key to Uncle Tom's Cabin*. 1853. Reprint: New York, 1968.
Stroud, George M. *A Sketch of the Laws Relating to Slavery*. 1853. Reprint: New York, 1968.
Syndor, Charles. *The Development of Southern Sectionalism 1819–1848*. Baton Rouge, 1966.
———. *Slavery in Mississippi*. 1933. Reprint: Gloucester, Mass., 1965.
Tadman, Michael. *Speculators and Slaves: Master Traders and Slaves in the Old South*. Madison, Wisc., 1989.
Tannenbaum, Frank. *Slave and Citizen*. New York, 1946.
Tushnet, Mark, V. *The American Law of Slavery 1810–1860: Considerations of Humanity and Interest*. Princeton, 1981.
United States Bureau of Census, *Historical Statistics of the United States: Colonial Times to 1970*. Washington, D.C., 1975.
———. *Negro Population in the United States 1790–1915*. 1918. Reprint: New York, 1968.
Wade, Richard C. *Slavery in the Cities: The South 1820–1860*. New York, 1964.
Watson, Alan. *Slave Law in the Americas*. Athens, Ga., 1989.
———. *Roman Slave Law*. Baltimore, 1987.
Wheeler, Jacob D. *A Practical Treatise on the Law of Slavery*. 1937. Reprint: New York, 1968.
Wiecek, William W. *The Sources of Antislavery Constitutionalism in America, 1760–1848*. Ithaca, 1977.
Wood, Peter. *Black Majority: Negroes in Colonial South Carolina from 1670 Through the Stono Rebellion*. New York, 1974.
Wooster, Ralph A. *Politicians, Planters, and Plain Folk: Courthouse and Statehouse in the Upper South, 1850–1860*. Knoxville, Tenn. 1975.
Wyatt-Brown, Bertram. *Southern Honor: Ethics and Behavior in the Old South*. New York, 1982.

## Articles

Alpert, Jonathan L. "The Origin of Slavery in the United States—the Maryland Precedent." *American Journal of Legal History* 14 (1970): 189–221.
Brady, Patrick S. "Slavery, Race and the Criminal Law in Antebellum North Carolina: A Reconsideration of the Thomas Ruffin Court." *North Carolina Central Law Journal* 10 (1979): 248–260.
Fede, Andrew. "Legal Protection for Slave Buyers in the U.S. South: A Caveat Concerning *Caveat Emptor*." *The American Journal of Legal History* 31 (October 1987): 322–358.

———. "Legitimized Violent Slave Abuse in the American South, 1619–1865: A Case Study of Law and Social Change in Six Southern States." *The American Journal of Legal History* 29 (April 1985): 93–150.

———. "Toward a Solution of the Slave Law Dilemma: A Critique of Tushnet's 'The American Law of Slavery.'" *Law and History Review* 2 (Fall 1984): 301–20.

Finkelman, Paul. "Slaves as Fellow Servants: Ideology, Laws, and Industrialization." *The American Journal of Legal History* 31 (October 1987): 269–305.

Flanigan, D. "Criminal Procedure in Slave Trials in the Antebellum South." *Journal of Southern History* 40 (1974): 536–64.

Gordon, Robert. "New Developments in Legal Theory." In *The Politics of Law: A Progressive Critique*, edited by David Kairys, 281–293. New York, 1982.

———. "J. Willard Hurst and the Common Law Tradition in American Historiography." *Law and Society Review* 10 (1975): 9–21.

Grindle, David J. "Manumission: The Weak Link in Georgia's Law of Slavery." *Mercer Law Review* 41 (1991): 701–712.

Hay, Douglas. "Property, Authority and the Criminal Law." In *Albion's Fatal Tree: Crime and Society in Eighteenth-Century England*, edited by Douglas Hay et al., 25–63. New York, 1975.

Higginbotham, A. Leon. "Racism and the Early American Legal Process, 1619–1896." *Annals of the American Academy of Political Science* 407 (1973): 1–17.

———. "Relevance of Slavery: Race and the American Legal Process." *Notre Dame Law Review* 54 (1978): 171–80.

Higginbotham, A. Leon, and Barbara Kopytoff. "Property First, Humanity Second: The Recognition of the Slave's Human Nature in Virginia Civil Law." *Ohio State Law Review* 50 (1989): 511–540.

Higginbotham, Don, and William S. Price, Jr. "Was It Murder for a White Man to Kill a Slave? Chief Justice Martin Howard Condemns the Peculiar Institution in North Carolina." *William and Mary Quarterly* 36 (1979): 593–601.

Hindus, M.S. "Black Justice Under White Law: Criminal Prosecutions of Blacks in Antebellum South Carolina." *Journal of American History* 63 (1976): 575–99.

———. "The Contours of Crime and Justice in Massachusetts and South Carolina, 1767–1878." *American Journal of Legal History* 21 (1977): 212–37.

Howington, Arthur F. "Not in the Condition of a Horse or an Ox: Ford v. Ford, the Law of Testamentary Manumission and the Tennessee Courts' Recognition of Slave Humanity." *Tennessee Historical Quarterly* 34 (Fall 1975): 249–63.

Kiely, T.F. "Hollow Words: An Experiment in Legal Historical Method as Applied to the Institution of Slavery." *DePaul Law Review* 25 (1976): 342–94.

Langum, David, J. "The Role of Intellect and Fortuity in Legal Change: An Incident from the Law of Slavery." *The American Journal of Legal History* 28 (1984): 1–16.

Moore, Wilbert E. "Slave Law and the Social Structure." *Journal of Negro History* 26 (April 1941): 171–202.

Morris, Thomas D. "'As If the Injury was Effected by the Natural Elements of Air or Fire': Slave Wrongs and the Liability of Masters." *Law and Society Review* 16 (1981–82): 569–99.

———. "'Society is Not Marked by Punctuality in the Payment of Debts': The Chattel Mortgages of Slaves." In *Ambivalent Legacy: A Legal History of the South*, edited by David J. Bodenhamer and James W. Ely, Jr., 147–70. Jackson, Miss., 1984.

Nash, A.E. Kier. "A More Equitable Past? Southern Supreme Courts and the Protection of the Antebellum Negro." *North Carolina Law Review* 48 (February 1970): 197–242.

———. "Fairness and Formalism in the Trials of Blacks in the State Supreme Courts of the Old South." *Virginia Law Review* 56 (February 1970): 64–100.

———. "Negro Rights, Unionism, and Greatness on the South Carolina Court of Appeals: The Extraordinary Chief Justice John Belton O'Neall." *South Carolina Law Review* 21 (Spring 1969): 141–90.

———. "Reason of Slavery: Understanding the Judicial Role in the Peculiar Institution." *Vanderbilt Law Review* 32 (January 1979): 7–223.

———. "The Texas Supreme Court and Trial Rights of Blacks, 1845–1860." *The Journal of American History* 58 (December 1971): 622–42.

Reid, J.P. "Lessons of Lumpkin: A Review of Recent Literature on Law, Comity, and the Impending Crisis." *William and Mary Law Review* 23 (1982): 571–624.

Schafer, Judith K. "Guaranteed Against the Vices and Maladies Prescribed by Law: Consumer Protection, the Law of Slave States, and the Supreme Court in Antebellum Louisiana." *The American Journal of Legal History* 31 (October 1987): 306–322.

Schwarz, Philip J. "Forging the Shackles: The Development of Virginia's Criminal Code for Slaves." In *Ambivalent Legacy: A Legal History of the South*, edited by David J. Bodenhamer and James W. Ely, Jr., 125–46. Jackson, Miss., 1984.

———. "Gabriel's Challenge: Slaves and Crime in Late Eighteenth-Century Virginia." *The Virginia Magazine of History and Biography* 90 (July 1982): 283–309.

Scott, John A. "Segregation: A Fundamental Aspect of Southern Race Relations, 1800–1860." *Journal of the Early Republic* 4 (Winter 1984): 421–41.

———. "Book Review." *Challenge* (May–June 1975): 65–71.

Sio, Arnold. "Interpretations of Slavery: The Slave Status in the Americas." *Comparative Studies in Society and History* 7 (1964–1965): 289–308.

Sirmans, M.E. "The Legal Status of the Slave in South Carolina, 1670–1740." *Journal of Southern History* 28 (1962): 462–73.

Smiddy, Linda O. "Judicial Nullification of State Statutes Restricting the Emancipation of Slaves: A Southern Court's Call for Reform." *South Carolina Law Review* 42 (1991) 589–655.

Stealey, John E. "The Responsibilities and Liabilities of the Bailee of Slave Labor in Virginia." *American Journal of Legal History* 12 (October 1968): 336–53.

Stephenson, M.W. and D.G. Stephenson. "'To Protect and Defend': Joseph Henry Lumpkin, the Supreme Court of Georgia, and Slavery." *Emory Law Journal* 25 (1976): 579–608.

Tushnet, Mark. "Approaches to the Study of the Law of Slavery." *Civil War History* 25 (December 1979): 329–38.

———. "The American Law of Slavery, 1819–1860: A Study in the Persistence of Legal Autonomy." *Law and Society Review* 10 (Fall 1975): 119–84.

Watson, Alan D. "North Carolina Slave Court, 1715–1785." *North Carolina Historical Review* 60 (January 1983): 24–36.

Wiecek, W.M. "Slavery and Abolition Before the United States Supreme Court, 1820–1860." *Journal of American History* 65 (1978): 34–59.

———. "*Somerset*: Lord Mansfield and the Legitimacy of Slavery in the Anglo-American World." *University of Chicago Law Review* 42 (1974): 86–146.

———. "The Statutory Law of Slavery and Race in the Thirteen Mainland Colonies of British America." *William and Mary Quarterly*, 3d ser., 34 (1977): 258–80.

# Index

Abatement of public nuisance, 162
Abolitionists' analysis of slave law,
  generally, 3–4, 85–86, 134,
  201–202
Abuse of slaves, legitimized:
  by masters and hirers, 105–115;
  by overseers and patrols, 115–
  118;
  by strangers, 100–105
Alabama slave law:
  defining slaves as personal
  property, 36; homicide of
  slaves, 75, 81, 83, 85;
  manumission, limits, 137; non-
  fatal abuse of slaves, 105,
  111, 112–113, 115; patrol
  laws, 117; procedures, slave
  prosecutions, 183, 189, 193;
  required masters to feed and
  clothe slaves, 132, 134;
  separation of families, 231–
  232, 233; slave criminal law,
  175; slave rebellion, 195–196;
  specific performance, 204
Alpert, Jonathan, 30
Animals:
  cruelty to, 24, 102, 113;
  mortgages of, 234; ownership
  of offspring, 146
Arkansas slave law:
  contracts between master and
  slave, 138; manumission,
  limits, 136, 173; non–fatal
  slave abuse, 101, procedures,
  slave prosecutions, 183, 189;
  slave criminal law, 165, 168,
  specific performance, 204
Ayres, Edward, 197

Bancroft, Frederic, 221, 223, 226,
  232
Baptism of slaves, 33
Barbados, 30
Bay, Elihu, 117
Blacks, whether always slaves in
  the United States, 30–31
Blackstone, William, 230
Brady, Patrick, 169
Brockenbrough, William, 108–110

Campbell, Randolph, 112
Cassius, Gaius, 196, 243
Catron, John, 147, 213
Catterall, Helen, 147, 149
Chambers, William, 215
Chaplin, Thomas, 83
Clarke, J.G., 3, 75
Class conflicts, whites, 47–50, 72–
  77
Cobb, Thomas R.R., 7, 140, 149,
  174, 176, 189, 226
*Code noir*, 228, 235
Collier, Henry W., 60
Colonial law of slavery, 29–41
Comity, 150–152
Common law:
  accommodation of slavery, 11–
  12, 29–41; assault and
  battery, 102–121; civil remedy
  lost services, 101; confessions,
  admissibility, 190; crimes
  *contra bonos mores*, 107;
  generally, 11; murder,
  preemption of, 62;
  presumption of freedom, 37–
  38; 141–142; public nuisance,
  131; required felony

prosecution before civil action, 71, 75–76; slaves denied marital privilege, 195; slave law supplanted, 244
Conviction ratios:
  slave murder, 86–87; non-fatal slave abuse, 120
Corbin, Arthur, 203
Cotton:
  and growth of plantations, 47; prices of, 50
Criminal law:
  capital offenses of slaves, 166; discrimination against slaves in mitigation and extenuation of crimes of slaves, 167–176; discrimination against slaves in substantive law, 163–166; double jeopardy, in slave trials, 193; indictments, in slave trials, 193; legitimized violence against slaves, 31–33, 61–121; purposes of, generally, 162; purposes of, when slaves are prosecuted, 159–163; slave master juries in slave trials, 193; slave's right to counsel, 193–194
*Cy pres*, 142, 144

Dade, William, 107–111
Dale's laws, 30
Dargan, G.W., 145
Davis, David B., 29
DeBow, J.D., 39
Delaware slave law:
  manumission, limits, 136
Dew, Charles B., 195
Dew, Thomas, R., 54, 237
Deodands, 163
*Deo dandum*, 162–163
De Saussure, Chancellor, 227, 230
Dicta, in slave law opinions, 24, 61, 75, 111, 146
Double jeopardy, in slave trials, 193
Douglass, Frederick, 225

Elkins, Stanley, 8, 236, 237
Engerman, Stanley, 223

Families, slave:
  frequency of division of, 222–224, separation of, generally, 220–237
Fellow servant rule, 209–210
Fifth Amendment, 184–185
Finkelman, Paul, 150, 210
Finley, Moses I., 20, 89
Fitzhugh, George, 54
Flanigan, Michael, 166, 190, 192, 193, 194, 195, 242
Fleming, William, 227
Florida slave law,
  manumission, limits, 137
Fogel, Robert, 223
Forfeiture, 162–163, 193
Formalism, legal, 143, 193
Fornication, 33
Freyer, Tony, 204
Frost, Edward, 133
Fugitive slaves, 143

Gaillard, Theodore, 228
Gaston, William 169–171
Genovese, Eugene, 7, 8, 20, 52, 236
Georgia slave law:
  fellow servant rule, 209–210; hirer's liability for rent if slave dies, 209; homicide of slaves, antebellum law, 67; homicide of slaves, colonial statutes, 62–63; homicide prosecution not required before civil suit by master if slave killed, 75–76; manumission, limits, 54–55, 137, 138, 141, 142, 143, 144; nonfatal abuse of slaves, 100; procedures in prosecutions against slaves, 39, 183, 189, 195; required master to feed and clothe slave, 132; separation of families, 231;

## Index

slave criminal law, 173–176; specific performance, 204
Gibbons, Lymon, 175
Goldberg, Arthur, 163
Goodell, William, 4, 7, 8, 100, 106, 112, 133, 169, 176
Gordon, Robert, 23, 241–242
Green, Nathan, 146, 171
Gutman, Herbert, 222, 225

Handlin, Oscar and Mary, 29
Handy, Alexander, 151, 190
Harper, William, 54, 76, 228, 229, 237
Harris, William, 78–79
Hay, Douglas, 67–68
Henderson, Leonard, 190
Henry, H.M., 76–77, 81, 86, 212, 213
Higginbotham, A. Leon, 6, 11, 30, 31, 201
Hindus, Michael, 8, 86, 120, 182
Hirers:
civil liability for injury to slaves, 207–208; liable for rents if slave hired dies, 209; right to abuse slaves, 105, 115; right to kill slaves, 84–85
Hoffer, Peter, 39
Hohfeld, W.H., 19, 21
Holmes, George Frederick, 54
Holmes, Oliver W., 73
Homestead exemption, slaves as, 232
Homicide:
mitigation of murder when whites killed slaves, 72–74; of slaves by whites, in antebellum law, 66–89; of slaves by whites, in colonial law, 31–32, 62–66, of whites by slaves, 168–176
Howard, John, 5, 184–185
Howard, Martin, 63
Howington, Arthur, 8, 83, 137, 138, 140, 141, 142, 146, 166, 168, 172, 182, 195
Hughes, Henry, 54

Hurd, John Codman, 18

Illinois, criminal law, free blacks, 167
Indictments of slaves, 193
*In rem* proceedings, 159, 162, 192

James, William D., 228
Johnstone, Job, 151
Jones, Norrece T., 224
Jordan, Winthrop, 29, 30
Kennedy, Duncan, 143
Kentucky slave law:
homicide of slaves, 73; manumission, limits, 136, 173; non-fatal abuse of slaves, 105; separation of families, 226; specific performance, 204
Kidnapping, 214
Kiely, Terrence, 205
Konig, David, 30
Kopytoff, Barbara, 11

Langum, David, 210
Latin American slave law, 8
Law:
as an instrument of social change, 22–25; autonomy of, 23, 24; legitimization of slave relations, 11, 17, 18–19; legitimization of violence by whites against slaves, 31–33, 61–89, 99–121; purposes of slave law, 3; real interests implicated by slave law, 22–25; regulation of the master's power over slaves, 11, 19–22
Llewellyn, Karl, 23
Louisiana, slave law:
criminal procedure, 182; sale of children, 225, 226, 231
Lumpkin, Joseph, 54–55, 143, 145, 173, 208–210

Mansfield, Lord, 29
Manumission:
cases were not libertarian, 139–140; implied, doctrine of, 147–

150; limitations on master's right, 135–153; low rate of in U.S. South, 135; of children born after will calling for parent's manumission, 146–147; reasons for hostility to, 137; restriction, generally, 29, 51, 54–55; viewed as threat to slave system, 135, 137–138, 143
Martin, J.H., 20–21
Marxist analysis of slave law, 8–9
Maryland slave law:
colonial codes, development, 30; homicide of slaves, 82; increase of slaves, 230; manumission, limits, 136, 137, 139, 142, 147–149, 150; presumption of slavery, 37; procedures in slave prosecutions, 183, 186–187; required master to feed and clothe slaves, 132; slave criminal law, 165
Masters:
as victims of slave violence, 168; civil actions against slave killers, 69–72; duty to feed and clothe slaves, 131–134; limits on right to kill and free slaves related, 83–84; not liable for slave crimes, 161–162; on juries in slave trials, 193; political power of master class, 51–54; real party in interest in slave crime cases, 159; right to abuse slaves, 105–115; right to breach peace to recover slaves, 213–214; right to compensation if slave abused by strangers, 100–101; right to free slaves limited, 135–153; right to kill slaves, 77–85; right to punish slaves for crimes, 39–40; right to sell slaves, 221–237, right to testify in slave trials, 187–192; social class conflicts with overseers and poor whites, 48–50, 72–77, 87–89, 103–105, 116–117; stratification within master class, 47, 49–50, 84; use of slave to kill others, 192
Mayhem of slaves, 102, 108, 114–115
Missouri slave law:
manumission, limits, 136, 139, 150; non–fatal slave abuse, 113
Mississippi slave law:
homicide of slaves, 73–76, 77–80; manumission, limits, 137, 150–151; master's civil action against slave killers, 71–72; nonfatal abuse of slaves, 116; procedures in slave prosecutions, 183, 189, 190, 191; separation of families, 232; slave criminal law, 164, 166; slaves as people and property, 3–4; specific performance, 204
Mitigation of murder in cases of slave homicide, 72–74, homicide by slaves, 167–176
Moncure, Richard, 204
Morgan, Edmund S., 29, 30, 31
Morris, Thomas D., 36 , 233 , 234
Mortgages, of slaves, 233, 235
Murrell, John A., 212

Nash, A.E. Kier, 6, 8, 9, 139, 140, 141, 142, 182, 193, 196
Nash, Frederic, 172
Negligence, causing injury to slaves, 206–210
New Jersey, slave law:
kidnapping, 214; manumission, 147, 150
New Orleans, slave market, 223
New York, slave law:
manumission, 150
Nisbet , Eugenius A., 75
North Carolina slave law:
homicide of slaves, antebellum law, 66–67, 72–73, 81, 82, 84;

# Index

homicide of slaves, colonial law, 63–64, 87; manumission, limits, 173, 148–150; non–fatal abuse of slaves, 100, 103–105, 106, 109–113; patrol laws, 117; procedures in prosecutions against slaves, 39, 183, 187–189, 191; required master to feed and clothe slaves, 132; separation of families, 233; slave criminal law, 167, 168–173, 193; slave's inability to own property, 20–21; specific performance, 204

Nott, Abraham, 213
Noxal actions, 163

Oakes, James, 19, 82, 224
O'Neall, John Belton, 5, 7, 102, 139, 144, 149, 151, 152, 165, 166, 211–213, 228, 235
Outlaws, slaves, 64
Overseers:
income levels, 49; right to kill slaves, 85; social class conflicts with planters, 48–49

Pass laws, 164
*Partus sequitur ventrem*, 234
Patrol laws, 32, 116, 118
Patterson, Orlando, 7, 17, 18, 33, 37, 135, 137, 139, 161
Pearson, Richmond, 10, 21, 172, 187, 189, 191–192
*Peculium*, 21, 138
Peters, John, Lewis, and Mary, 113
Phillips, U.B., 7, 8, 9, 49, 50, 51
Plantation slavery, patterns of development, 46–48
Poor whites:
social conflicts with master class and slaves, 48–49, 72–77, 87–89, 103–105, 116–117
Positive good, slavery as, 54–55
Pro-slavery interpretation of slave law, 7, 9
Public nuisance, slaves as, 131, 162

*Quasi*-freedom, 143–144, 145

Racism, 37–38, 242
Rebellions, slaves, statutes, 195–196
Reform, failure of, 235, 237, 242–243
Reification, 11, 55, 237, 241–244
*Res judicata*, 193
Rights:
definition of, 18–20; fallacy of notion of slave rights, 1, 10, 18–22, 40–41, 87–89, 194, 241–244
Roane, Spencer, 227
Ruffin, Thomas, 21, 81, 109–111, 172, 189, 210, 233, 244

Sandiford, James H., 82
Sawyer, George, 237
Schwarz, Philip, 72, 175
Scott, John A., 29, 221–222
Sellers, James, 81, 83
*Senatus consultum silaninum*, 196
Sio, Arnold, 8
Slavery:
and racism, 37–38; and white class conflicts, 48–50; business law of, 201–215; development of plantation slavery, 46–48; essential elements of, 17–18; law of sales regarding, 205; oppression of, epitomized, 39–40; positive good ideology, 54–55; reform of, failure, 235–237, 242–243
Slaves
as capital asset, 231; as homestead exemption, 232; choice of master or of freedom, 144–145; crimes of, 4–5, 163–176; confessions of crimes, 190–192; damages for wrongful detention in slavery, 142; denied marital privilege, 195; fallacy of notion of rights of, 1, 10, 19–22, 40–41; families, separation of, 221–237; fraternizing with poor

whites, 76–77, 103–105;
inability to inherit property,
148, 150–152; inability to
initiate prosecutions, 85–86;
inability to testify in court,
86, 194–195; insolence, 4–5,
165–166; legal duties, 10–11;
marriages, broken, 222;
mortgages in, 233–234, 235;
negligent injury of, 206–210;
no right to enforce contracts,
138–139; no right to
manumission, 138–139, 140,
142, 153; offspring as slaves,
33; population growth, 31, 35,
46; prices of, 50–51;
procedures in prosecutions of,
33, 39–40, 181–197; right to
counsel in criminal cases,
193–194; runaways, 32–33, 76;
sales of, legitimized, 221–237;
self-defense against whites,
167–176; specific performance
regarding, 202–206; theft by,
132; theft of, 210–214
South Carolina slave law:
ambiguous wills, separation of
families, 227–231; colonial
laws requiring maiming of
slaves, 114–115; defining
slaves as personal property,
36; homicide of slaves,
antebellum law, 68–70, 76–77,
81–82, 83, 86–87; homicide of
slaves, colonial statutes, 62,
65; insolence of slaves, 4–5,
165–166; manumission, limits,
137, 144–145, 148–149, 151–
152; negligent injury to
slaves, 206–207; non-fatal
abuse of, 100, 101, 102; patrol
laws, 117–118; procedures in
prosecutions against slaves,
39; procedures in slave trials,
182; required master to feed
and clothe slaves, 132, 133–
134; slave criminal law, 164;
specific performance, 204;
theft of slaves, 68–79
Specific performance:
of real estate, 202; of slave
contracts, 202–206; related to
law in North, 205
Spindel, Donna, 87
Stampp, Kenneth, 6, 8, 120, 223,
224
Starnes, Ebenezer, 173
Steen, Thomas, 112
Stephenson, Mason W. and D.
Grier, Jr., 54, 173
Stowe, Harriet Beecher, 3, 9, 17,
82, 83, 225
Stroud, George, 86, 134, 135, 136,
137, 163, 164, 166, 169, 202,
235
Sutch, Richard, 222, 225
Sydnor, Charles, 52

Tadman, Michael, 222, 224, 237
Taney, Roger, 5–6, 184–186, 244
Tannenbaum, Frank, 7, 8
Taylor, John, L., 72–73, 103–104,
148, 193
Tennessee slave law:
battery, of slave, damages, 242;
homicide of slaves, antebellum
law, 67, 68, 73–75, 83;
homicide of slaves, colonial
law, 66; manumission, limits,
137, 138, 141–142; master
required to feed and clothe,
134; master's right to
damages, slave battery, 242;
non-fatal slave abuse, 115;
procedures, slave prosecutions,
189, 192; slave criminal law,
166, 167, 168, 171; slave
rebellions, 195; specific
performance, 213–214; theft of
slaves, 67, 212
Texas slave law:
homicide of slaves, 73–75;
manumission, 137; non-fatal
slave abuse, 111–112
Theft of slaves, 210–214
Thompson, Chancellor, 227

*Index* 261

Traders, of slaves, 35–36, 205, 233
Tuck, William, 186
Tucker, St. George, 38, 227
Turner, Nat, 137
Turley, William, 168
Tushnet, Mark, 7, 8, 138, 141, 142, 143, 206, 207–210

Villenage, 29, 75–76, 148
Virginia, growth of population in colonial era, 31, 35
Virginia slave law:
 colonial codes, 30–37; colonial laws requiring maiming of slaves, 114; defining slaves as property, 35–36; development, 30–37; homicide of slaves, antebellum law, 66, 72, 80, 83; homicide of slaves, colonial law, 31–33, 65; manumission, limits, 137, 142; non-fatal abuse of slaves, 100, 102, 106–109, presumption of slavery, 37–38; procedures in prosecutions of slaves, 33, 39–40, 182, 184–186, 192; separation of families, 227, 233; slave criminal law, 166, 174–175; specific performance, 204–205

Waites, Chancellor, 227
Wardlaw, D.L., 4, 133, 151, 207, 243, 244
Watson, Alan, 243
Weber, Max, 17, 19
Wheeler, Jacob, 135–136, 140
Wheeler, Royall T., 75
Whipping of slaves, frequency, 89, 99–100, 120–131
Wiecek, William, 30, 34, 40, 41
Wills, interpretation of:
 ambiguous provisions, separation of families, 227–229; children born after will calling for parent's manumission, 146–147; *cy pres*, 142, 144; free/send wills, 143; send/free wills, 142–143; *quasi*-freedom, 143–144, 145
Wooster, Ralph A., 52
Wyatt-Brown, Bertram, 51, 82, 84
Wythe, George, 37, 38

*Corrigenda*

p. x line 35: "in the pre Civil War South." should read "in the pre-Civil War South."
p. xiii line 12: "78 Yale L.J. 198" should read "78 *Yale L.J.* 198"
p. 13 n. 1: "1 Walker 88" should read "1 Walker 83"
p. 19 n. 35: "W.H. Hohfeld" should read "W.N. Hohfeld"
p. 37 line 5: "Pattersons's" should read "Patterson's"
p. 51 line 5: "salve" should read "slave"
p. 64 line 39: "murder the creating" should read "murder and creating"
p. 66 line 19: "influence" should read "influenced"
p. 68 line 14: "writes slave killers" should read "white slave killers"
p. 73 line 14: "this" should read "his"
p. 76 line 25: "tortured the slave the death." should read "tortured the slave to death."
p. 82 line 27: "have" should read "gave"
p. 82 line 36: omit "a" at the end of the line
p. 83 line 2: "Chapin" should read "Chaplin"
p. 88 in table, under "Masters/Hirers: Slave Boom," line 9: "exculpation or 'moderate' correction'" should read "exculpation if 'rebellion' or 'moderate correction'"
p. 93 n. 70: "These same result were" should read "These same results were"
p. 94 n. 82 line 1: "*Robbins* was indicated" should read "*Robbins* was indicted"
p. 94 n. 82 line 3: "had failed to fee a horse." should read "had failed to feed a horse."
p. 97 n. 103: "relationship was also evidence by" should read "relationship was also evidenced by"
p. 107 line 9: "maliciously,'" should read "'maliciously,'"
p. 108 line 27: "right or property" should read "'right of property"
p. 113 line 29: "defendant" should read "defendants"
p. 126 n. 80, line 3: "of slave humanity.'" should read "of slave 'humanity.'"
p. 133 line 26: at the end of the line change the comma to a semicolon
p. 136 line 1: "When it considered" should read "When it is considered"
p. 140 line 24: "did the master's intend" should read "did the master intend"
p. 142 line 18: "manumission case, while" should read "manumission cases, while"
p. 145 line 9: "enforced two deed that" should read "enforced two deeds that"
p. 146 line 25: "that" should read "but"
p. 154 n. 18, line 2: "The Care and Feeding of Slave" should read "The Care and Feeding of Slaves"
p. 155 n. 25, line 12: at the end of the line change the semicolon to a comma
p. 155 n. 28, line 2: add a semicolon after "(1846)"
p. 157 n. 66: "(846)" should read "(1846)"
p. 164 line 32: "status and perceived as" should read "status and was perceived as"
p. 165 line 9: "slave with a 1847 decision" should read "slave with an 1847 decision"
p. 171 line 25: "equal standard" should read "equal standards"
p. 172 line 32: "not excuse a batter" should read "not excuse a battery"
p. 173 line 10: "form immoderate" should read "from immoderate"
p. 187 line 35: "'he is our master-'" should read "'he is your master-'"
p. 188 line 45: "to five testimony in" should read "to give testimony in"
p. 191 line 5: "not the slave's owner." should read "not the slave's owners."
p. 194 line 6: ". . . slaves appointed appeared to have" should read ". . . slaves appeared to have"
p. 211 line 31: "declared to the chattels" should read "declared to be chattels"
p. 213 line 31: "recognized the maser's" should read "recognized the master's"
p. 213 line 38: "the opinion by Chief" should read "The opinion by Chief"
p. 218 n. 64: "*in,* 1835 act);" should read "an 1835 act);"
p. 225 line 15: "no could they testify." should read "nor could they testify."
p. 228 lines 7 & 8: omit "may so hold. Galliard noted that 'the inhumanity of separation,"

p. 229 line 22: "decisions can and I do not" should read "decisions can do to enforce humanity; this must depend on public opinion and I do not"
p. 232 line 37: "the debtor-masters rights" should read "the debtor-master's rights"
p. 233 line 34: "always gave way to" should read "always superseded"
p. 242 line 24: "*Jones v. Carper*" should read "*James v. Carper*"
p. 242 line 30: "Michael Flanigan " should read "Daniel Flanigan"
p. 245 n. 6:     should read "36 Tenn. (4 Sneed) 397 (1857)."
p. 245 n. 7:     should read "*See, Id., quoted in*, Flanigan, *supra* at 171."
p. 245 n. 13 line 3: "Tushnet as employed" should read "Tushnet employed"
p. 249 line 46: "Sobel, Mechel" should read "Sobel, Mechal"
p. 256 column 2, line 29: "Hohfeld, W.H." should read "Hohfeld, W.N."
p. 257 column 1, line 12: "Flanigan, Michael" should read "Flanigan, Daniel"